LANDSCAPE APPRECIATION
Theories since the Cultural Turn

David Jacques

PACKARD PUBLISHING LIMITED

CHICHESTER

LANDSCAPE APPRECIATION
Theories since the Cultural Turn

© David Lawson Jacques

First published in 2019 by Packard Publishing Limited, 14 Guilden Road, Chichester, West Sussex, PO19 7LA, UK.

All rights reserved. No part of this publication may be reproduced, stored in a retrieval system, transmitted in any form, or by any means, electronic, mechanical, photocopying, recording or otherwise, without the written permission of the Publisher, or a licence permitting limited copying by the Copyright Licensing Agency, or its national equivalents throughout the world. This book may not be lent, resold, hired out or otherwise disposed of by way of trade in any form other than that in which it was originally published without the prior permission of the Publisher.

ISBN: 978 1 85341 128 1 (paperback)

A CIP Record can be obtained from the British Library.

Cover photo: View from the summit of Monte Aizkorri (1,528m) in the Basque country, Spain. To the left of the shelter – out of picture – is a chapel dedicated to Christ, referring to the miraculous properties ascribed to a crucifix inside – an example of the spirituality that can accompany outstanding landscapes.

Title page: Moraine Lake, Banff National Park, Canada.

Edited and prepared for press by Michael Packard.

Design and layout by Hilite Design, Marchwood, Southampton, Hampshire.

Printed and bound in the UK by KnowledgePoint Ltd., Winnersh Triangle, Winnersh, Wokingham, Berkshire.

CONTENTS

Foreword: A wilderness of prospects

PART A: THE UNFATHOMABLE WORKINGS
OF THE UNIVERSE   1

1. **Art into landscape**   3
   The problems with functionalism   3
   Landscape among the fine arts   8
   Ideas into form   13
   The laws of the universe   18
   Unconscious expression   22
   Notes and references   30

2. **Landscape beauty**   33
   The English countryside   33
   The selection of the British National Parks   38
   The search for objectivity   42
   Formal qualities   46
   Notes and references   49

3. **Natural instincts**   51
   Environmental determinism   52
   Unity with nature   53
   People and the land   56
   The imperative of climate and soil   60
   The ethics of the land   65
   New landscapes   68
   Self-ordering complexity   74
   Stewarding the biosphere   76
   Prospect, refuge and hazard symbolism   79
   Notes and references   85

PART B: THEORISING IN THE LATE
TWENTIETH CENTURY   88

4. **The post-modern condition**   89
   Shattered dreams   90
   Uncertainty and practical knowledge   96
   Complexity and chaos   97
   Cognition   100
   Consciousness and creativity   102
   An aesthetic experience   107
   The use of history   108
   The sociology of criticism   115
   Notes and references   119

5. **Facts, value and ideology**   123
   Reading the landscape   124
   Knowledge gives value   130
   The rise of cultural landscapes   134
   Morality and action   137
   The logic of ecocentrism   142
       Deep ecology and ecosophy   142
       Direct realism   144
       What if the logic is flawed?   148
   The metaphysics of nature   152
   Notes and references   156

6. **Landscape preferences**   161
   An unconscious recognition of beauty   161
   An hereditary feel for beauty?   165
   Form revealing idea?   169
   How preferences arise   172
   Place and pleasure   174
       Action/place   175
       Place and identity   176
       Landscape and emotion   180
       Everyday satisfactions   182

Landscape assessment methods	184	PART C: REFLECTIONS	267
Landscape beauty	184	Notes and references	270
Landscape character	186		
Notes and references	191	**9. Philosophical movements**	**271**
		Metanarratives	271
7. Memory maketh humanity	**195**	Cosmology	274
Restoration tragedies	196	Phenomenology	275
Conservation and interpretation	203	Notes and references	279
Change and ephemerality	208		
Conservation guidelines for landscape	212	**10. Environmental aesthetics**	**280**
Florence Charter 1981	213	Ronald Hepburn	281
The desire for accuracy	216	Cognitive versus non-cognitive perception	282
US Guidelines for the Treatment of Cultural Landscapes 1996	218	Disinterestedness and engagement	284
		Relevance and preparation	288
Architectural principles in gardens	219	Objective versus subjective	289
The integrated approach	222	Notes and references	293
The cultural landscapes approach	223		
The World Heritage Criteria	224	**11. Satisfactions**	**295**
La Petite Pierre 1992	225	Sensual pleasure	295
Czerniejewo Guidelines 1994	232	Formalism	296
Burra Charter 1999	233	Beauty	299
Unifying the criteria	234	The sublime	301
Notes and references	237	Designed landscapes	306
		The meaning of gardens	313
8. Post-modern designs	**241**	Assessing aesthetic value	316
Contextualism	243	Notes and references	321
Philosophy becomes design	248		
Designer ecology	251	**Bibliography**	**324**
Land art	259	**Abbreviated captions to illustrations**	**335**
New work in historic contexts	263	**Credits**	**340**
Notes and references	265	**Index**	**341**

FOREWORD: A WILDERNESS OF PROSPECTS

A puzzle and a frustration to me ever since being a student in the early 1970s was that those engaged in the landscape professions treated the theoretical basis of their work with such superficiality. I had joined them because garden history showed that landscape design had addressed some of the questions judged to be important by thinkers in the eighteenth century, and the focus of my own interest, then and now, has been the history and philosophy of landscape.

I have now explored garden and landscape history for fifty years, and gained much stimulation from it as a demonstration of how ideas connect with places. Here the ethics and aesthetics of landscape care and treatment since the Second World War have been examined. My observations have been drawn partly from involvement in landscape reclamation, landscape assessment, landscape planning, garden conservation, garden restoration and cultural landscapes, and partly from observation of the work of other professions such as architecture, art, history, philosophy and psychology. The emphasis has been upon the analysis, issues and appreciation of the wider landscape and new design. Some areas are not explored in any detail: I have strayed only so far across the broad plains of design theory, and into the muddy swamp of environmental ethics, as needed to indicate the context.

At the same time, digging down uncovered a more-or-less coherent (though never fully articulated) post-war modernist landscape philosophy which is here woven together from many diverse threads. A particular theme was the attempt to catch imagined greater truths. Brenda Colvin and Sylvia Crowe thought that way, and they drew on precedents from the sculptors Henry Moore and Barbara Hepworth. It is with a sense of regret that it is necessary to dismiss much of their theory. People such as Geoffrey Jellicoe, Ian McHarg and Jay Appleton, all of whom I consulted about their ideas, are heroic figures who provided a generation with original and characteristic landscape theory.

While that generation had a distinctive mindset, it was quite different from my own. They were modernists of a sort, but the characteristic feature was, on the whole, a belief in the unfathomable workings of the universe, and the aim was to comprehend them as best as possible. One key indicator was the supposed nature of truth. The search for the ultimate answer may be a galactic hitchhiker's joke to me, but not so to the earlier generation. A desire to believe absolutely led them to faith in metaphysical dogma beyond the boundaries of logical and scientific inquiry. My contemporaries, though, relied on judgement to decide on the reasonableness, credibility or probability of a proposition being true. They would hold a conviction only for as long as it was intellectually useful. This approach gave 'practical' knowledge; in other words it gave the opportunity to think and act in a common-sense way in everyday life.

In retrospect the 1970s marked an indistinct watershed when the rust-spots became visible in the shiny bodywork of architectural modernism. Environmentalism was rising fast through the ranks of political priorities, while landscape design found itself being relegated to merely one of the possible forms of solution to environmental problems. A significant number of those trained during the 1970s did not share their elders' assumptions or pre-occupations, and I gained immeasurably from contemporaries, many outside the landscape professions. It was even possible that a theory stating the fundamentals on the inner self pondering experience and values in Part B of this book could have been assembled about 1980. The shift of general attitude had already taken place by then, and only became more clarified and focused over time.

The world about was ever more complex, with more events and information, but fewer certainties. Post-war social and physical planners favoured simple and bold propositions, yet complexity could be welcomed. A diversity of viewpoints made for an interesting world, so that categorisation of actions into absolute right or absolute wrong was difficult to sustain. That did not mean that ethics were redundant: far from it. The intelligent person grasps the interconnections between events to acquire a keener sense of responsible action.

These days it is de rigueur to give a nod towards ethical imperatives stemming from the ability of humans to act beyond the Earth's recuperative powers, and even to tinker with the processes of nature itself. However, if we wish to concern ourselves with the condition of the Earth we must first address the condition of the human psyche. We must devise practical ethics, and practical aesthetics, that allow us to proceed in tackling the problems before us. We need to emphasise management rather than the creative urge, a spirit of safety rather than exploitation.

This book has been focused not so much on theories in landscape architecture, a now-flourishing genre heavily dominated, as one might expect, by professors of landscape architecture, but on the wider context of the individual in his world, more particularly perception, ethics and aesthetics. Tracing ideas through history does not follow a necessarily straight path because unravelling them can only be as one looks forwards, backwards and to the side.

It is time to pin down the meaning of 'landscape' as it is employed in this book. There are, as everyone knows, as many definitions as there are writers. There are many possible ways to define landscape depending on the phenomenon under consideration and the direction from which it is seen. Nevertheless, there is a very common thread that it is not just land: it is the land *as perceived*. This is a useful inclusion in the European Landscape Convention, recited here:

> 'Landscape' means an area, as perceived by people, whose character is the result of the action and interaction of natural and/or human factors.

The 'action and interaction' phrase sounds good to many theorists of ecology, phenomenologists and aestheticians of engagement, though the overall formulation is for 'a landscape' seen merely as an area of land, rather than the wider cultural understanding of 'landscape'. A definition that is about the qualities of areas, that deals with the broader concept and one which takes those perceptions forward into action, for example by the landscape profession, would be more to the point, so this is 'landscape' as understood here:

> The physical world, as perceived by people, and which is the object of study, representation, design and care to satisfy their aesthetic, ethical and/or other wants.

In 1987 I was given the stimulus to consider some of the above themes when asked to give a lecture on modern landscape, to be treated historically, at a Garden History Society meeting at the Commonwealth Institute in London. In the same year Jane Crawley, who later set up Barn Elms Publishing, was considering a reader on modern landscape theory. The motivation was to explore a valid theory for that time. My ideas needed testing, though, and I took care to visit many places in Britain and North America where it seemed that new ideas were being explored. One memorable early visit was with Peter Goodchild to Geoffrey Dutton's garden near the Bridge of Cally, Perthshire, in 1988. The books by the modernist landscape theorists were re-read. These historical figures were, most of them, still practising, so I went to see them.

During 1988 my enthusiasm became earnest intent, but then slowed to a crawl because of my workload at English Heritage deriving from the great storms of 1987 and 1990. The book that Jane wanted was not forthcoming, and would anyway have been made redundant by

Marc Treib's *Modern Landscape Architecture: A Critical Review* (1993), although mine on Christopher Tunnard was an eventual outcome. From the early 1990s, though, this present book spluttered into existence. The theme, then and now, is the replacement of one body of theory by another. Progress was halted by a PhD thesis, and publication was delayed. It was then reworked in 1999.

It is now another two decades since that point, which has given the opportunity to take a long view of the subject. On picking up my task once more, it seemed that the story of the change from one mindset to another was completed, more or less, by the 1999 rewrite. I came to see that text as the record of an intellectual journey at the time, a large part of which had been the realisation that webs of ideas had existed in landscape theory, though inadequately recognised. With due modesty, I hope, my earlier analysis had held up satisfactorily, and after review only minor changes to the content have been necessary. The sources that were known and which impressed then are retained. But, taking a long view also made it imperative to review recent philosophical directions, including 'environmental aesthetics', and to address the wider subject of 'satisfactions'. Hence, while the first two parts of the book set out the theory in place in the 1970s and how it came to be replaced by a new mindset, the last part – 'Reflections' – evaluates the more recent offerings in landscape aesthetics, and concludes by proposing approaches for today's practitioners.

This book has surveyed the landscape of ideas that shaped, and then re-formed the fundamentals of landscape appreciation and ethical treatment for half a century. Landscapes, after all, are only what we choose to perceive, and succeeding generations have a habit of seeing and feeling differently. Despite much scholarship, no dramatic upheavals in outlook have occurred, and the present may appear to us to be a relatively placid stretch in terms of theory. Yet there are probably undercurrents that we hardly notice now, but which will come to the surface as streams of thought as significant as those of the late twentieth century. That seems to be how landscape theory moves onwards.

Sugnall, Stafford

2019

PART A

THE UNFATHOMABLE WORKINGS OF THE UNIVERSE

The post-war generation of landscape practitioners sought a new theory, but found they needed something more nourishing than 'functionalism'. Their first hope was inspiration through fine art and architectural theory, though landscape also had its own concerns, for the connections and involvement in the wider physical world brought obligations for ethical approaches to the treatment of landscape. A variety of metaphysical dogmas concerning the workings of the Earth and of the human mind were explored in the search for more fundamental principles.

A brief overview of the three chapters below will explain this in a little more detail. Chapter 1 describes how theories derived principally from architecture were supplemented by new approaches by landscape architects in the 1950s and 1960s. One was to insist more vigorously that landscape architecture should be accepted among the fine arts. Some designers realised that more than that was needed, and forms appropriate to the century were sought by calling upon the power of the 'zeitgeist', the spirit of the age. Beauty was investigated as a quality of the object automatically perceived using concepts from 'neo-Platonism' or ideas on 'significant form'. Finally, designs that were significant to the human psyche were tried, based on Carl Jung's ideas on the unknowable collective unconscious.

Chapter 2 tackles the attempts to define beauty (visual quality) in landscape. One approach, more apposite to the working countryside, relied upon an automatic aesthetic response supposed by functionalist theory. The alternative, more relevant to the National Parks, was the sublime response to mountains. Practitioners, when called upon to make more objective assessments, reckoned that Platonic ideas and 'significant form' could be theoretical bases for methods that allowed the calculation and prediction of 'visual quality' by analysis of a scene's components.

Chapter 3 charts how the precepts of human ecology were imported into landscape practice. Overwhelmingly, this implied assumptions and presumptions on evolution, some of which make for difficult reading in an age repelled by eugenics and racism. There were fresh outcomes as well, principally respecting the ethics of stewardship, and a new theory of the aesthetic appreciation of landscape driven by long-obscured hunting instincts. However, human ecology is not just a science; for many, maybe most, it was intertwined with the metaphysics of 'holism', and increasingly overlaid with moral imperatives.

The common theme must by now be obvious. A modern age may discount any or all of these hypotheses and metaphysical approaches, but it is possible to conclude that there was a mood, a mindset, a zeitgeist even, that was shared by the several theorists of the time.

Lights of the Forest.

CHAPTER 1

ART INTO LANDSCAPE

Some Modern Movement buildings were very stylish in their own way, but in the field of landscape architecture it was difficult to design in a modernist way if all you stood for was that you did not like Arts and Crafts. A few attempts at grass terracing, often with pools and mobiles, were too formal and failed to look convincing. The asymmetric stripped-down functionalism of the Belgian landscape architect Jean Canneel-Claes was tried pre-war a few times by Christopher Tunnard, but looked a bit too functional and undecorative (fig. 1.1).[1]

In reality, even the most radical British and American architects subscribed to modernism for little better reason than that it was the ascendant international style, and not because it presented a source of theoretical insight. For the most part Oliver Hill and Raymond McGrath gratefully accepted already mature landscapes, and inserted their new country houses with minimal accompaniment. Lebanon cedars or pines looked marvellous against or behind the plain white walls of the houses, and grass swept up to the patio doors (fig. 1.2).

After the Second World War new towns, schools, housing estates and hospitals all needed landscape design, and a new era began for the professional landscape architect in Britain engaged in public works.[2] Architects, planners and landscape architects were faced with the actual business of turning an ideology into concrete form.

The problems with functionalism

'Modernism' in landscape manifested itself in different ways at different times. Here the attention is on the post-war generation of the landscape profession, mostly in Britain. The theorists discussed below tended to work with little reference to the others, so that there was no self-conscious movement. If one believes in the zeitgeist, though, it may be seen at work, for the ideas came to fruition and collectively formed a dogma that served the profession. The decade when it reached more-or-less full development was the 1960s, though actually timing is a bit fuzzy, for pre-war thoughts were carried over to the post-war period, and there is continuity with some of the theories still being developed in the 1970s.

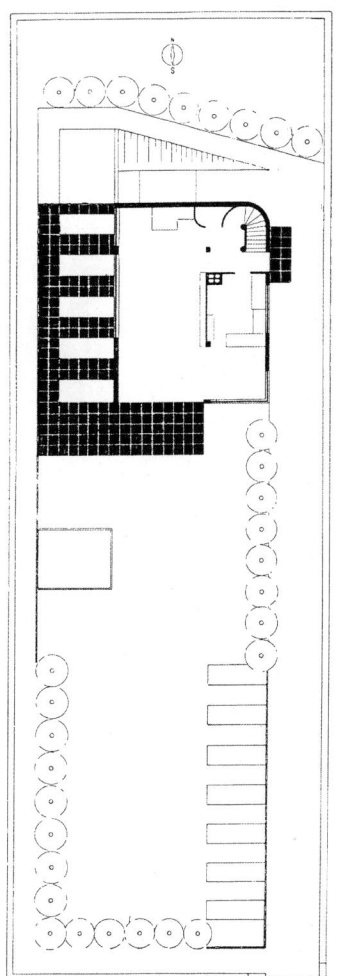

Figure 1.1 *Jean Canneel-Claes's ultra-functionalist design for his own house and garden in Belgium which he supplied to Christopher Tunnard for Tunnard 1938, drawing on p.64.*

Figure 1.2 *The contrast between mature trees and architecture so much desired by Modernist architects; here is Holthanger at Wentworth, designed by Oliver Hill. In George Taylor,* The Modern Garden *(1936), photo on p.15.*

Starting pre-Second World War, then, the architectural historian Nikolaus Pevsner proposed what it would take to put the modern movement in its rightful place as 'the genuine and legitimate style of our century'. The architect would have to be committed to the new machine age: 'the architect, to represent this century of ours, must be colder, cold to keep in command of mechanised production, cold to design for the satisfaction of anonymous clients'. He absolutely proscribed 'the craving of architects for individual expression, the craving of the public for the surprising, and fantastic, and for an escape out of reality into a fairy world'.

The idea of an architectural design was supposed to express itself in qualities such as rhythm, proportion, elegance, clarity, dignity, simplicity, crispness, honesty, delicacy, and purity of form. Walter Gropius was a hero, the living embodiment of the ability of the greatest architects to turn buildings into art through mastery of material and form. He had showed that 'genius will find its way'. Pevsner added:

> It is the creative energy of this world in which we live and work and which we want to master, a world of science and technology, of speed and danger, of hard struggles and no personal security, that is glorified in Gropius's architecture, and as long as this is the world and these are its ambitions and problems, the style of Gropius and the other pioneers will be valid.[3]

Pevsner's stand for functionalism in the 1930s had seemed brave and noble at the time. The public was supposed to derive aesthetic satisfaction from cold, disinterested, observation. The closest Pevsner came to being emotional was saying that we must have a 'romantic faith in speed and the roar of machines'. Such a conception of art may have been intellectual and chimed with functionalism, but it was not uplifting. Pevsner was dedicated and with no discernible sense of humour: in truth, how could he have expected the ideas he stood for to take root in England?

The principal theoretical work on landscape modernism in the English language was Christopher Tunnard's inspirational book, *Gardens in the Modern Landscape* (1938). Advocating functionalism, and borrowing ideas from Continental designers, he had nevertheless abdicated from defining the forms of the modern movement's landscape too closely. He had written about the plastic form of sculpture, the patterns of the painter and asymmetry in layout, but these are all theoretical ideas, not a vocabulary of motifs. In 1949, in the USA, Garrett Eckbo lamented that 'we have not yet stabilized a social pattern long enough to produce a lasting cultural expression'.[4] Peter Shepheard, an English landscape architect, was still remarking in 1953 that examples of true modern-movement gardens 'are hard to find'.[5]

One Arts and Crafts landscape architect in Canada could thus taunt his modernist rivals:

> We need only to glance at the modernist's pitiful attempts out of doors to know that he is stuck. In most cases he has thrown up his hands and done nothing. The few examples where any serious effort has been made are of such severity, or of such grotesqueness, as to have little resemblance to anything we should recognise as a garden.[6]

The problems with functionalism

Figure 1.3 *The Kelmarsh Hall fan rose garden: one of the garden areas developed by Nancy Lancaster after she moved back to Kelmarsh in 1948.*

It was not surprising that, in the absence of anything demonstrably better, the prewar traditions were carried forward by Russell Page, Lanning Roper, and several others who cared little for modernist dogma (fig 1.3).

This realisation could have taken the modernist theoretician one of three ways, all of them recognising that the sort of functionalism espoused by Pevsner had been a blind alley. One was to admit that ornament was indeed one of the pleasures of gardens of all ages, and to rebuild bridges to traditional practice unashamedly. Second, the artistically inclined could press on exploring the correspondences between sculpture, painting and garden art in the hope of discovering the authentic style of the twentieth century. Geoffrey Jellicoe, for example, said in 1954: 'we are now tending to turn art into landscape by approaching the subject not merely from the point of view of utility'.[7] 'Association', neo-Platonism, 'expressionism', and 'space theory' were amongst the ideas for turning art into landscape. Third, the human ecologists said that any attempt to contrive a style for the age was doomed anyway, because the influences of climate, soil, cultural traditions, etc., inexorably determine the national character of gardens (see Chapter 2).[8]

6 *Art into landscape*

Tunnard, after ten years and having converted to town planning, came to realise that he had been simplistic and over-optimistic, and opted for the first of these ways. His new foreword in the 1948 edition of *Gardens in the Modern Landscape* frankly stated that 'The author's attitude toward modern art, architecture and landscape architecture has changed somewhat'.[9] For a start, 'the author's original rather cursory estimate of the nineteenth century has undergone considerable revision'. Indeed he told one professor from North Carolina that 'in England at any rate, by far the best work was done over a hundred years ago'.

His reappraisal, however, was more fundamental than just his embrace of history. The best ideas, he then thought, are inherited, experimented with and improved upon: 'creative art has a firmer foundation when based on the accumulation of acquired knowledge rather than on intuitiveness alone'. Tunnard thus thought he could put modernism back on course through experimentation and adaptation. The modern-movement designer needed 'to keep trying his hand at all sorts of solutions' to avoid getting stale. 'A style for our own times may not be anything like what we imagined a few years ago: perhaps it should, in fact, be more like what was current a hundred years ago – meshing of several styles or idioms with entirely dissimilar physical results'. This was an astonishing observation indicating his radically altered views from ten years beforehand.

Tunnard of course was still only suggesting an approach: not the form that a new style would take. However, implicit in his thinking was that the human needs fulfilled by landscape design were far less changeable than those served by architecture, and that while functionalism may have been an appropriate response in architecture, it had not been so in gardens. Brenda Colvin said it for him anyway, in responding to his 1938 edition:

> It may be true, as Christopher Tunnard claims, that no new style in garden design equivalent to modern architecture has yet appeared ... But architecture is dealing with completely new materials as well as new needs, whereas the natural materials of landscape (land and vegetation) and the basic human needs which landscape fulfils are ageless.[10]

Joseph Hudnut, dean of the Harvard Architectural School and Tunnard's mentor in America, shared with him a distaste for abstract forms. His piece on 'The Modern Garden' was added as a postscript to the 1948 edition of *Gardens in the Modern Landscape*. Hudnut had found 'that very provocative principle which is called functionalism' to be insufficient as an ethic, pointing out that gardens, like houses, have in all ages expressed 'inward promptings', not merely needs, techniques and materials. Hudnut wrote that he disliked garden design that reflected no more than new materials and technique:

> I find somewhat boring those tubular metal seats 'designed for mass construction' ... and all those accessories in paving, furniture, and lighting intended as unmistakeable assertions of modernity.

Peter Shepheard also put his finger on the problem when he pointed out that the garden was by nature decorative, non-functional and lacking in the sort of technical revolution that had made the modern-movement house possible.[11] Functionalism might then have served as an ethic in architecture, or in the planning of agricultural and forested landscapes, but Colvin, Hudnut and Shepheard were reminding readers that gardens were an extra room for outdoor living, and space for personal expression. One would have no more thought of leaving a garden undecorated than one would one's living room.

Landscape among the fine arts

The accepted mode of appreciation of 'high art' at this time was that it should be enjoyed through a frame in a disinterested way, in contradistinction to matters of everyday life that were judged by their practical effect on the observer. A painting had no use, but was art, whilst a lump of coal was the reverse. A trained art critic would have been able to differentiate art from everyday things and to assess it independently from sentiment and self-interest, in the same way that, say, a surgeon or soldier viewed their work. This line of reasoning was sanctioned by Immanuel Kant's *Critique of Judgement* (1790).

Another theory prevalent at the time was the metaphysical doctrine of the zeitgeist supposedly acting as the unseen force translating political, economic and social forces into the artistic productions of the day (fig 1.4).[12] Painting, architecture and landscape design had been seen as the physical manifestations of the mood of the time; and these were thought to have had the power to speak back, imbuing the observer with a spiritual understanding of their significance.

There were some, according to that view, who were blessed with an original genius for unconsciously translating the zeitgeist into design. The reasons for this were mysterious: a designer was thought to just 'have it' or not. Such a person would be accorded special respect, and written about in revered tones. Of course every designer would like to have been in that class. Hence one eminent American landscape architect, James Rose, professed not to understand his own method, or at least to be unable to describe it. 'It happens,' he says, 'which he considers a complete and satisfactory explanation ...'[13] The same designer 'mistrusts the "influence game" '; by which was meant that, like most of his contemporaries, he detested the thought of being pigeonholed in stylistic terms, because that would have denied him the status of an original genius.

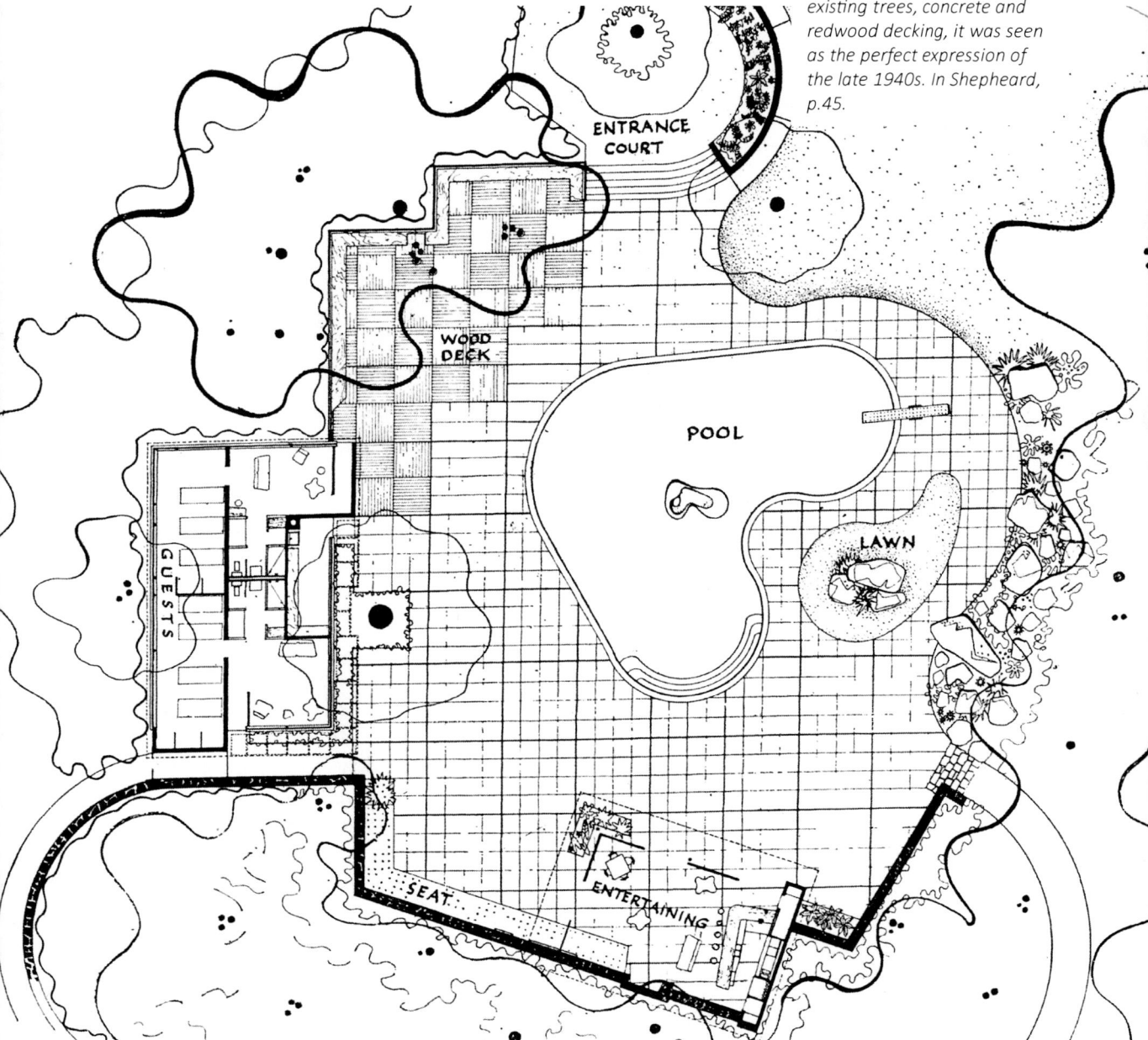

Figure 1.4 *The swimming pool and surrounds at the Donnell residence at Sonoma by Thomas Church and Lawrence Halprin. Designed in interesting shapes, in a way that fitted the function, climate and hillside situation, and with appropriate use of existing trees, concrete and redwood decking, it was seen as the perfect expression of the late 1940s. In Shepheard, p.45.*

Landscape among the fine arts

Figure 1.5 *Bosquet at Schönbrunn Palace, Vienna; formal design like this was considered to be 'living architecture'.*

It was tempting for landscape architects to adopt the ethos of other arts which had already embraced modernism, principally painting and sculpture. For example, when Geoffrey Jellicoe delivered his address, 'Consider your forebears', to the Institute of Landscape Architects in 1954, he subtitled it 'or Art into Landscape', with apologies to John Betjeman and Sir Kenneth Clark. The latter, not to be confused with Frank Clark, was an art historian who had written *Landscape into Art* (1949), an examination of various themes in landscape painting. Jellicoe's purpose was 'to stimulate a study of painting, and to see whether it is possible for the landscape architect to reach the heights the painters do, not only on the drawing board but in the field'. This indicated his life-long mission to establish landscape design among the fine arts. In view of the close connections between the sister arts of poetry, painting and landscape design in the eighteenth century, their revival must have seemed a perfectly reasonable aim.

Jellicoe considered that arts could be classified into high and low forms. In this he was responding not just to eighteenth century ideas about the sisterhood, but to the ethos of international art history in his own time.

Figure 1.6 *'Still life' (1945) by Ben Nicholson shows his interplay of geometry and subject matter that appealed to planners and garden designers; his sculptures were likewise carefully composed.*

One of his acquaintances via the International Federation of Landscape Architects (IFLA) was the Belgian, René Pechère, who was likewise conscious of the historical dimension of gardens, and shared the same urge to establish them among the high arts.[14] He regarded gardens as 'living architecture', and was always dubious about the English landscape garden on the basis that true arts impose the will of Man upon Nature, which the landscape garden affects not to (fig. 1.5). French and Belgian legislation distinguishes *monuments* from the lesser *sites*, and it was one of Pechère's proudest achievements to have gardens accepted as monuments by the International Council on Monuments and Sites (ICOMOS) in 1982.

What made 'high art'? Jellicoe's contention was that in both painting and landscape, the purpose of the artist was to 'penetrate through to the idea', by which he meant that organising force that composed the parts into a whole. From Poussin to Cézanne 'one can feel a relationship between landscape and form, and sense the organisation of an otherwise disordered scene ... everything is brought into one comprehensive whole'. A parallel in modern landscape was a rural housing scheme by some architects who had 'interpreted feeling, colour, form and shape and fitted their groups of dwellings into the landscape so that without them the scenery would seem incomplete'.

Landscape among the fine arts

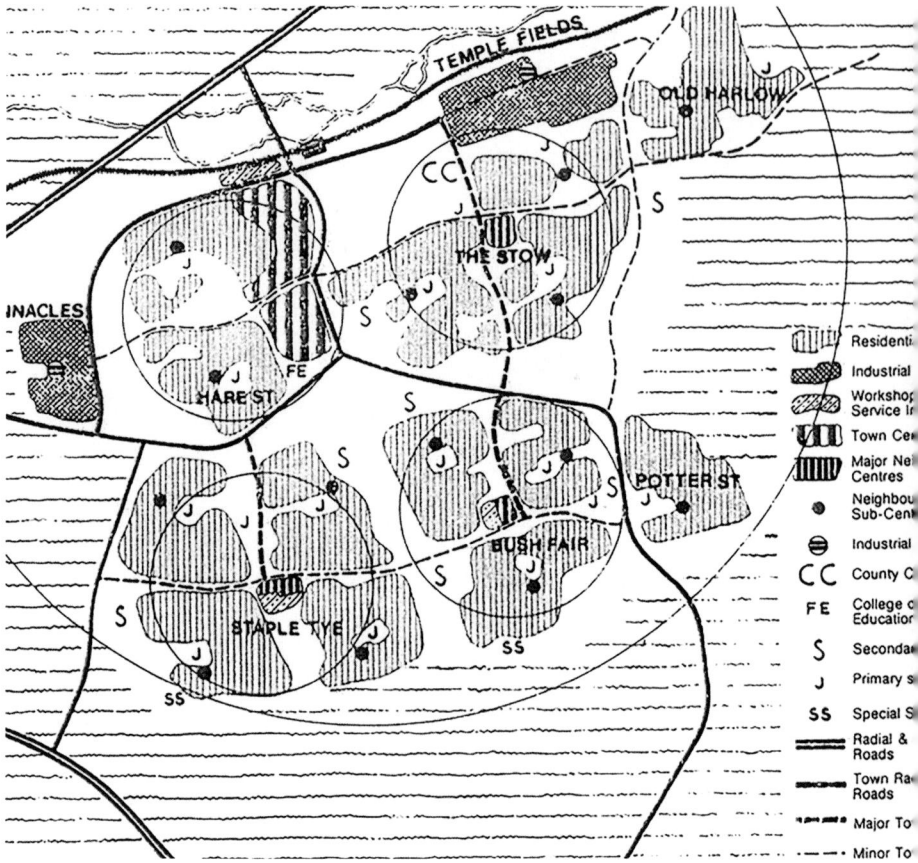

Figure 1.7 *The Master Plan for Harlow New Town devised by Frederick Gibberd in 1947 and in which Geoffrey Jellicoe saw parallels with the work of Ben Nicholson.*

The Victorians had lost their way, according to Jellicoe. The gardens at Crystal Palace, 'instead of being a study of form ... had coloured flowers en masse'. As for William Robinson, he was a genius as far as inspiring everybody to a back-to-nature idea of gardening, but he was not an artist: 'I miss the sense of the heroic'. However, the painter Paul Nash showed modern landscape architects how to reintroduce noble ideas. Also, the severe but exquisite compositions by Ben Nicholson (fig. 1.6) were an inspiration for their:

> ... geometric pattern and interlocking with this is the natural scenery. Compare that with the original plan of Harlow and you will see the geometry of the neighbourhood unit, and floating through and around it is the biological theme of the landscape.[15]

The master plan for Harlow had been formulated by his Highgate neighbour, Frederick Gibberd (fig. 1.7). The other 'modern' whom Jellicoe mentioned was Henry Moore, who 'will burst upon you suddenly as being really terrific'.

12 *Art into landscape*

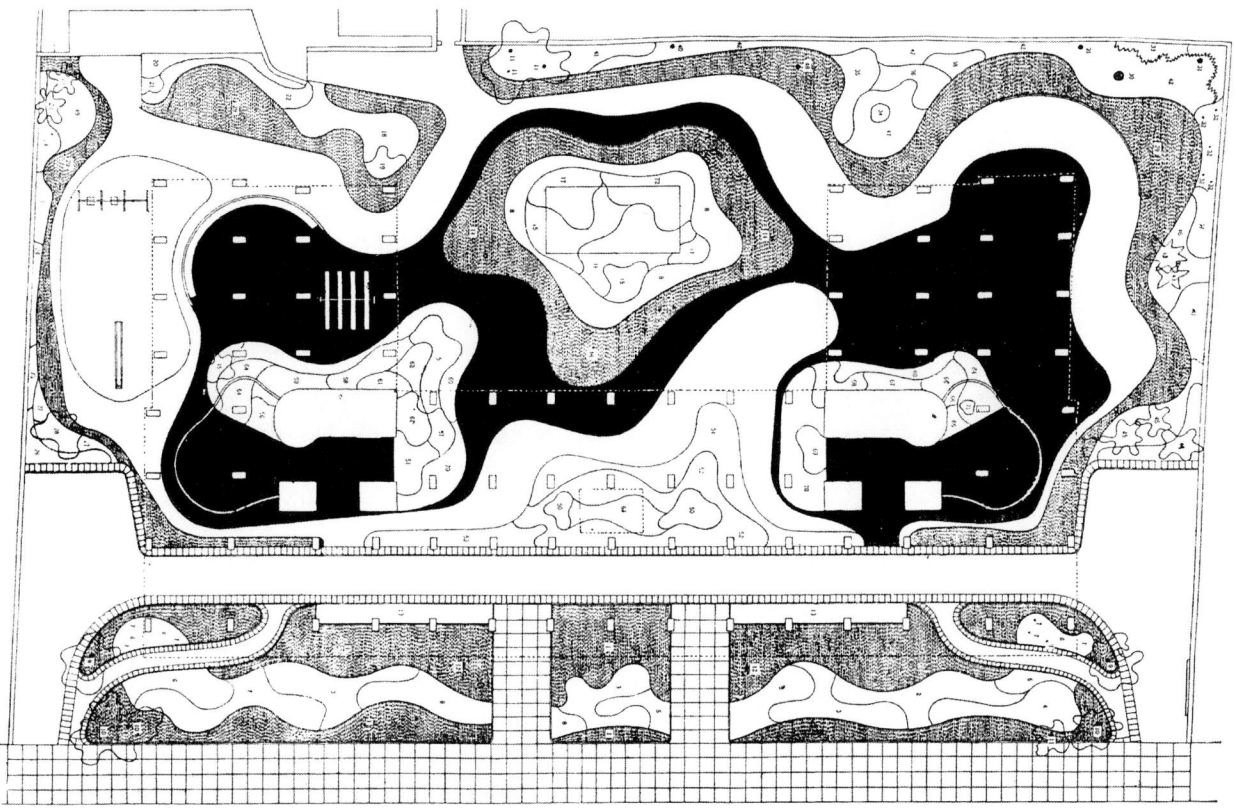

Figure 1.8 *Plan of a garden under and around a house in São Paulo by Burle Marx, admired for its stylishness by many late modernist landscape architects. In Shepheard 1953, fig. 32.*

Ideas into form

The more the lack of convincing modern style became apparent, the more anxiously the loyal modernist landscape architect searched. When the lust to strip away useless ornament had been slaked, and abstract shapes had been tried, the designer experienced merely an inspirational void. The creative urge yearned for there to be something more to respond to, something that could provoke creative responses. No wonder that the exuberant and stylish gardens of Roberto Burle Marx from Brazil and Thomas Church from California were to be seized upon by modernists, irrespective of their dubious appropriateness in more northerly climes (fig. 1.8).

The more thoughtful realised that if modernism was to gain credibility in landscape design, forms had to be found that themselves had meaning stemming from the twentieth century itself. This was just as true in landscape as in architecture.[17] In 1949 Garrett Eckbo, tired of the myriad of traditional national styles to be seen in contemporary gardens, was urgently asking this question:

> What principles of organization must we establish to wade through this eclectic hash and determine a clear, clean, and beautiful way of solving our own problems on their own terms with the materials we have at hand? [18]

Eckbo introduced some de Stijl-like and cubist-inspired geometry into his designs, worked within the spirit of the patio-door-and-swimming-pool house-planning of the Los Angeles of the time, and developed a graphic style very different from his Beaux-Arts contemporaries. His designs were right in California at that time, but whether they could have led to an international modern style for gardens is open to question.

Meanwhile Frank Clark had been searching for the key to how forms appropriate to their time are generated. He, like many others, shared Pevsner's art-historical view that the mark of the best designers was that they expressed the zeitgeist, the spirit of their own age, through their work. This concept supposedly promoted creativity. Until the eighteenth century the whole idea of creativity would have been beyond comprehension. If someone discovered something, or achieved something, that was the work of the divine, acting through that person. In Greek culture the Muses were seen as passing on inspiration from the Gods. The Romans invoked the concept of an external creative 'genius', linked to the sacred or the divine. In Judaism and early Christianity creation was the sole province of God; humans were not considered to have the ability to create something new – just to be the conduit of God's revelation. Hence it was believed that Jehovah communicated knowledge through communication with angels. The very word 'creativity' was an early twentieth-century invention.

Nevertheless the concept of the zeitgeist had a good pedigree in artistic circles. It was a working assumption of German art historians from the early nineteenth century. Britain and America received many of them when they fled the fatherland in the 1930s. Hence, from the early 1930s, most of the English-language theorists of the modern movement soon adopted the doctrine of zeitgeist. Hudnut's view of creativity, for example, was that 'men, from the beginning of recorded history ... have striven to reshape ... in accordance with a spiritual need, ... in accordance with [their] inward promptings ... They looked into the heart of their time and made it visible'.[19]

Architectural historians had pointed out that Gothic cathedrals, with their soaring columns, appear to reflect the desire for a soaring spirit, that the Baroque indicates a different temper of society, and so on. When it came to gardens, Italian ones were said to display in their planning a Renaissance rationality, the vast layouts of André le

Nôtre were supposed to indicate political absolutism, the irregularity of the English landscape garden was supposed to indicate freedom, the Picturesque romanticism, and the modern movement efficiency.

Frank Clark favoured the logic inherent in the zeitgeist's hypothesis, which was that forms should be understood merely as the physical manifestation of ideas, and it was the ideas that were in reality beautiful and that mattered. For example, he argued that it was the spirit, and not the precise detail, of Lord Burlington's gardens at Chiswick House (fig. 1.9) that mattered in their restoration: 'What, I should imagine to be more important, is scale and an understanding of the original designer's intentions ...'[20]

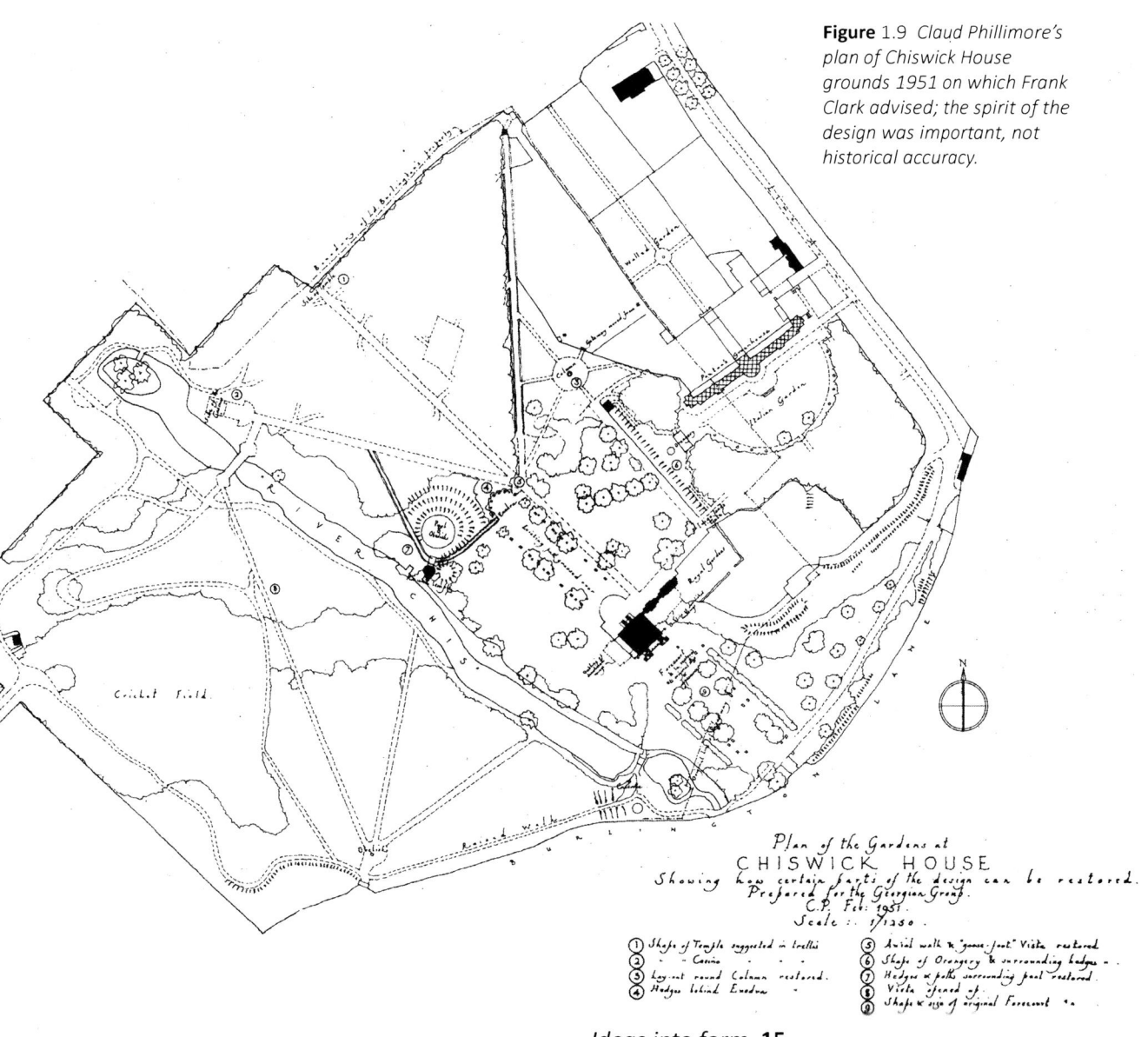

Figure 1.9 *Claud Phillimore's plan of Chiswick House grounds 1951 on which Frank Clark advised; the spirit of the design was important, not historical accuracy.*

Figure 1.10 *The landscape garden recycled - an illustration by Gordon Cullen of a house and garden for relaxation in the Surrey commuter belt: in Tunnard 1938, drawing on p.72.*

It was an age that looked to history for its lessons, though not necessarily its forms. Christopher Tunnard had tried before the war, being inspired by the aesthetic of the landscape garden (fig. 1.10), and now Frank Clark was to ransack history again. He differed slightly from the art historians who saw the operation of the zeitgeist as unconscious, because he viewed the association of forms with ideas at least in part as a conscious act. 'It is one of the characteristics of the best art that it is highly charged with either association or symbolism which has current meaning,' he suggested. He was, in effect, resurrecting the Principle of Association, originally formulated in the 1790s by Archibald Alison, of which he was fully aware:

> According to the aesthetic theory of the age, it was the association of ideas set up by an object, and not the object itself which produced the beautiful or sublime effect. The imagination was stimulated to conceive a connected train of thought in unison with that which was first suggested by the particular form, and so these forms could also be called beautiful for having been the parent of such a train.[21]

Clark hoped that knowledge of garden history would reveal the process whereby forms became associated with ideas, and thus help in his twentieth-century quest for a new aesthetic. This was to be the object of a book, to be called *'Landscapes on Earth'* in the early years of the Second World War. This was abortive, but being in the Civil Defence, he had been able to spend much time on historical research in the library of the British Museum when off duty. He showed his work to architectural historians. For once a garden historian, though comparatively unlearned, was ahead of his architectural counterparts. Rudolf Wittkower published Clark in *The Journal of the Warburg and Courtauld Institutes* in 1943, and Pevsner, who had become editor of *Architectural Review (AR)*, published Clark's article on 'Lord Burlington's Bijou, or Sharawadgi at Chiswick' in 1944.

Clark's historical researches were summarised in *The English Landscape Garden* (1948). Of course the role of conscious association was brought out. He emphasised the eighteenth-century sensibility to the charms of nature and the state of mind that turned England into Elysium. He had come to see that 'their landscape was, it seems, a dream landscape'. Surprisingly, in view of his collaboration with Tunnard in denouncing Romanticism ten years before, Clark now gloried in the landscape garden being 'a truly romantic conception'.[22]

Persisting with the search for appropriate modern forms, Clark wrote an article on 'the Sense of Beauty' in 1957. It was an examination of how beauty, as conceived in painting, was rationalised by the theorists and then translated into real landscape. Clark posed the question to which he was still inconclusively searching for an answer thus:

> There seem to be two rather distinct kinds of things from which we draw aesthetic pleasure, from machines and from natural objects. We like, I think, the clean pure forms of modern aircraft, the formal qualities of some contemporary architecture, the relationships of line and colour in certain schools of abstract painting, the tonal experiments of certain contemporary composers. We also are moved by natural objects, the accidental but the almost inevitable fitness of the texture and colour found in weathered stone, of the strange alertness of fallen tree trunks, of the timelessness of old trees and the beauty of form in all plant life.
>
> These differing tastes have found expression on the one hand in the garden designs of Burle Marx and on the other in the social landscapes of Scandinavian designers. Does the future of landscape design lie in the abstractions of science or in the poetry of nature or in a compromise between the two or perhaps in neither?[23]

Neither he nor anyone else had a convincing answer, it transpired.

The laws of the universe

Wittkower and Pevsner had simultaneously been turning their attention to English Palladianism and the landscape garden. Though each had something slightly different to infer from their researches, both were exploring the thought that there are fundamental, universal and natural laws of order and harmony that transcend the ordinary rules of taste.

Pevsner would have liked to shake out whimsy from design, which he had found in Victorian and Beaux-Arts formality. He became struck by the fact that the principles of the picturesque and the modern movement both sought to obtain aesthetic interest from asymmetrical planning.[24] He wrote on the picturesque in *AR*,[25] and braved considerable hostility from architects to whom old-fashioned picturesqueness smacked of the Garden City aesthetic that the modern movement had been trying to leave behind. What many did not recall, though, was that the qualities of the picturesque, as originally expounded by Uvedale Price well before the Victorian era – variety, intricacy, irregularity, contrast, surprise, irritation and accident – were the antithesis of formality. Pevsner had spotted that these qualities were also the visual qualities of the best modern design.

Frank Clark understood the implications, and the last paragraph of his *English Landscape Garden* (1948) proclaimed that 'the English had invented a new environment ... The irregular informal landscape ... was the enemy of the monumental, of geometry, of regularity and the formal'. Tunnard agreed too, speculating that 'Sharawadgi' – the picturesque beauty of the irregular – about which he, Clark and Pevsner had been writing, 'might well have a present-day application'.[26]

Many years later Wittkower explained the links he saw between nature, classicism and the landscape garden, resulting in conclusions similar to Pevsner's. He explained that:

> ... enlightenment ideas centred around the concept of the simplicity and uniformity in Nature, and as a corollary of this one agreed that the laws in Nature are eternally valid and universally intelligible ... Burlington's classicism was simple, reasonable and universally intelligible.[27]

For him the landscape garden was an attempt to conjure up an ideal nature, which, though romantic in spirit, also concerned the fundamentals of nature. Hence both Burlington's Palladianism, and the English landscape garden, were devices to express the laws of nature. So, 'neoclassicism and socalled romanticism vis-à-vis nature were two sides of the same medal'.

Wittkower went on to explain the laws of aesthetic satisfaction which he traced back to the eternal order of the universe. This emerged from his interpretation of the symbolic meaning of the geometry of Renaissance churches. In his *Architectural Principles in the Age of Humanism* (1949), he implied that the tradition of classical design had provided spaces that were inherently beautiful. He reminded his readers of the connection between mathematics and music, and between beauty and geometry, that the ancient Greek philosophers such as Pythagoras and Plato had seen:

> Renaissance artists ... were convinced of the mathematical and harmonic structure of the universe and all creation. If the laws of harmonic numbers pervade everything from the celestial spheres to the most humble life on earth, then our very souls must conform to this harmony ... An inborn sense makes us aware of harmony ... All Platonic thinkers agree that beauty can only be perceived by virtue of a correspondence between the structure of the soul and the harmony in the object.[28]

The adherents of such neo-Platonism not surprisingly emphasised the harmoniousness of form. Wittkower himself discussed geometrical forms like spheres, crosses and cubes, and showed how the Renaissance builders used them to invest buildings with proportion and architectural 'harmony'. This was not of merely historical interest to practising architects and civic planners. Supporters of Burlington's Palladianism might not have been surprising among the inspectors of the Office of Works restoring Chiswick House and its gardens, but when it made converts from functionalism like William Arthur Eden it had evidently found new force and purpose.[29] An article in *AR* in 1955 explained the unexpected success of Wittkower's seemingly esoteric work. Its message that:

> ... function and form were significantly linked by the objective laws governing the Cosmos (as Alberti and Palladio understood them) suddenly offered a way out of the doldrums of routine functionalist abdication, and neo-Palladianism became the order of the day.[30]

Clive Bell, an art critic, had many years before argued for the inherent beauty of certain forms produced by painters and sculptors. He dismissed the view of art as representing people or landscape, and was an early supporter of abstract art. He proposed that certain lines, colours and forms, and their combinations, together with 'rhythm' and 'movement' (altogether creating 'significant form', a doctrine often referred to as just 'formalism'), aroused emotional aesthetic appreciation according to 'unknown and mysterious laws'.[31] Bell afterwards thought that the explanation might have been that 'significant form' touched some

Figure 1.11 *Scene in Barbara Hepworth's garden in St Ives, displaying exercises in pure sculptural form; she thought that artists could thereby express the laws of the cosmos.*

spiritual 'ultimate reality'. Before long, sculptors were discussing pure form, and talking in terms of the universals it expressed (fig. 1.11). Barbara Hepworth later explained that:

20 *Art into landscape*

Figure 1.12 *'New shapes are evolving which relate not to the human scale, but to cosmic forces, the sea, the clouds, and the mountains':* an artist's impression of Dounreay nuclear power station in Scotland from the 1950s. Crowe, Landscape of Power, *fig. 11.*

… art … reflects the laws and the evolution of the universe —both in the power and rhythm of growth and structure as well as the infinitude of ideas which reveal themselves when one is in accord with the cosmos and the personality is then free to develop.[32]

Correlations between neo-Platonism, significant form and the 'unconscious' were being explored in the 1940s as aspects of the idea of universal laws, as were their implications for the 'creative instinct'.[33] Sylvia Crowe, who approached the matter as a human ecologist, picked up this train of thought and firmly believed in fundamental natural laws that transcended human experience and understanding. She felt that one of the happy achievements of her *Garden Design* (1958) was to demonstrate the congruence of Neo-Platonic and ecological laws.[34] These 'mysterious' laws were revealed when the human mind found itself in tune with them, for example when appreciating the mathematical harmonies of colour, form and music. 'Since the dawn of civilisation men have found their deepest satisfaction in discovering and expressing their own relationship to these laws.'

The laws of the universe **21**

She saw a special role for the artist in exploring this 'relationship between our minds and the universe', comprehending these laws, and then translating them through the artist's medium into the physical world (fig. 1.12). She herself felt that they pointed to the importance of proportion, rhythm, balance, harmony and composition: 'To make a garden ... entails the same understanding of the laws of harmony and composition that go to the making of any work of art'. No surprise, then, that after examining the great garden traditions of the world, she should write that 'underlying all the greatest gardens are certain principles of composition which remain unchanged because they are rooted in the natural laws of the universe'.

Crowe explained how modern designs were 'in tune with the eternal struggle of the artist to relate the physical world to the conceptions of men's minds'.[35] In Europe 'the classic proportions and spatial relationship' of the architect were fleshed out with the free, organic, forms of the landscape architect. Then sculpture or other structures were reintroduced to reassert the human influence. In American examples 'the organic pattern is organised back into formal shapes' reminiscent of abstract painting (fig. 1.13).

Having obeyed the universal rules, 'the really great gardens have an air of inevitability'. The more immediate causes of aesthetic satisfaction were not explained, but she seems to have assumed that the unconscious would have been at work. Crowe characterised this satisfaction mainly as contentment, 'peace' or 'serenity': 'even without knowing why, we are aware of the immense peace of certain gardens'. Some others 'give a sense of exhilaration'.

Unconscious expression

The role of the unconscious assumed great importance to many others besides Crowe. This was the age of Sigmund Freud and Carl Jung, who seemed to be explaining that there are, indeed, underlying processes of the mind, more important and more fundamental than conscious thought. These were appropriated by those who sought explanations of creativity and the perception of beauty.

In the first half of the twentieth century certain psychiatrists thought that they had discovered that each person has an unconscious mind, a doppelgänger personality, derived from biological impulse but driven underground by experiences of socialisation as an infant. Although obscured by the veneer of civilisation from the conscious mind, the unconscious was supposed to be just as real and as vital, and wider

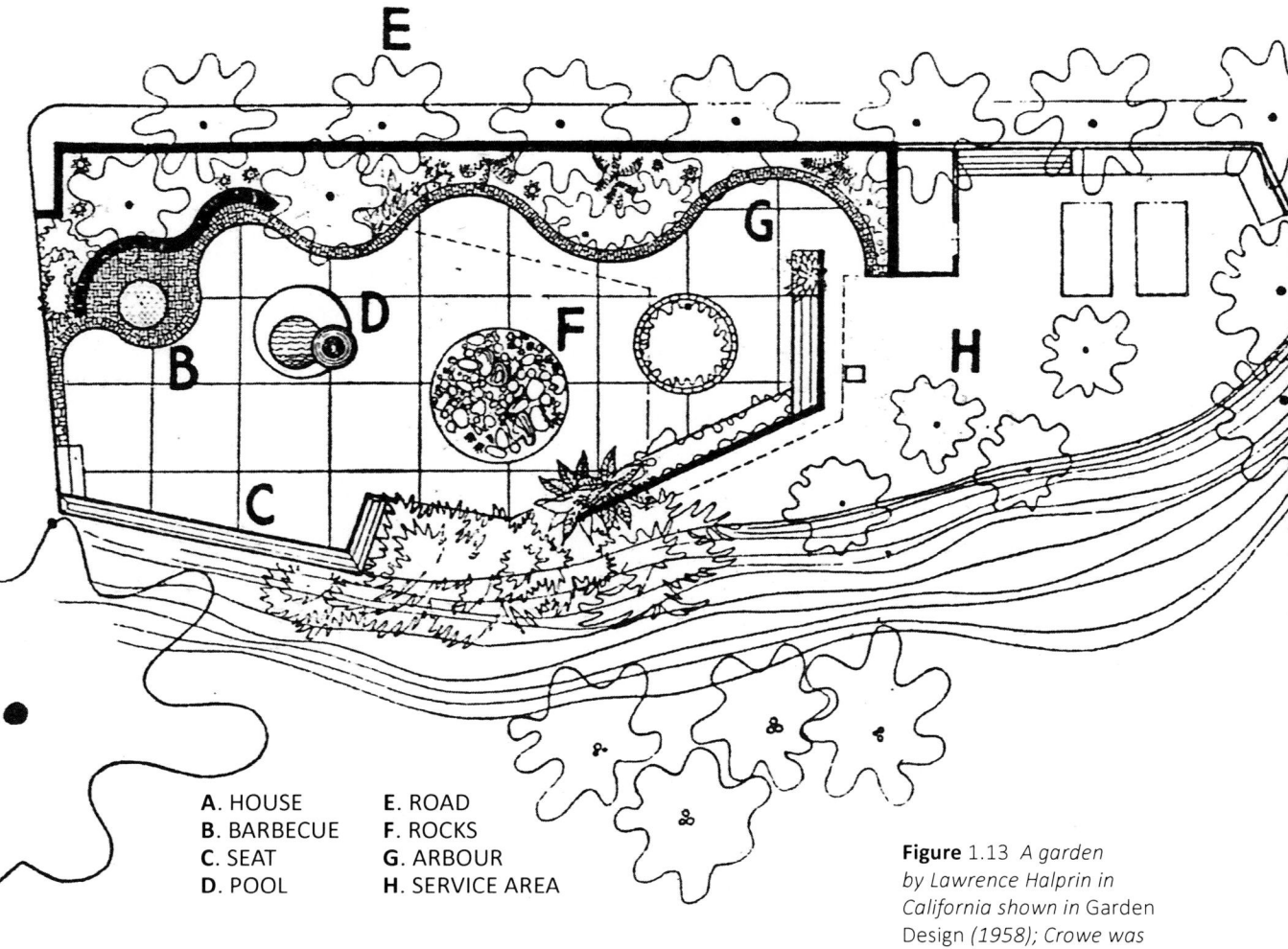

Figure 1.13 *A garden by Lawrence Halprin in California shown in* Garden Design *(1958); Crowe was impressed by the way such designs were informal, and yet 'organised back into formalised shapes' reminiscent of abstract painting. In Crowe 1958, Fig. 12*

A. HOUSE
B. BARBECUE
C. SEAT
D. POOL
E. ROAD
F. ROCKS
G. ARBOUR
H. SERVICE AREA

and richer in potential. The sophisticated, civilised, approach to life was said to be a grand delusion, serving only to remove us from our true selves.

Jung made a series of assertions that he defied others to dispute. He said that the unconscious controls the conscious for the satisfaction of inner drives, and expresses itself indirectly through hysteria, certain types of pain, abnormal behaviour, and dreams. On the subject of dreams:

> The two fundamental points in dealing with dreams are these: first, the dream should be treated as a fact, about which one must make no previous assumption except that it somehow makes sense; and second, the dream is a specific expression of the unconscious.[36]

Unconscious expression **23**

If, however, anyone had the temerity to disagree with the Jungian interpretation, they were told that 'consciousness naturally resists anything unconscious and unknown', and that they were suffering from a condition called 'misoneism', a deep and superstitious fear of novelty!

He thought that symbols were the language of the unconscious: 'the unconscious aspect of any event is revealed to us in dreams, where it appears not as a rational thought but as a symbolic image'. These images were adopted and used according to each individual's experiences. It was only once the meanings of a person's symbols, and the identification of those that are archetypal, were discerned, that dreams could be reduced to certain basic patterns revealing the unconscious. Hence the extreme complexity of the psychoanalytic process would defeat any attempt at a general language of symbolism of the Jungian kind.

On the other hand, Jung claimed that aspects of the unconscious were inherited and common to all, affecting human behaviour in general, though not transparent in the case of any individual. Using an explanation of instinctive reactions to landscape that was strikingly similar to that of the human ecologists, he maintained that there was 'a general unconsciousness that is the undeniable common inheritance of all mankind'.

The role of artists was to free their minds and rediscover the power of the unconscious for the benefit of ordinary mortals, allowing their insights to be translated into symbolic form. This seemed to tie in with the presumed special ability of the artist to bypass everyday experience and feel the force of mysterious universal natural laws, or, if you preferred, somehow to express the spirit of the age. Furthermore, the surrealist painting movement in Spain was showing this new awareness in operation.

The sculptor, Henry Moore, had come to know primitive art in his twenties, and was much affected by the way that it brought out inner feelings with great immediacy. This, then, was his duty as an artist: to affect the emotions directly, not via an intellectual understanding of some academic set-piece. He became convinced that vitality of expression was more important than classical beauty (fig. 1.14). He explored free association between *objets trouvés* and real objects, and allied himself with the surrealists.

Meanwhile, Paul Nash had become familiar with Jung's writings and saw that much art consisted of replacing a representational likeness with a rendering of psychological reality. The artist's work was thus 'parallel to

Figure 1.14 *'Two-Piece Reclining Figure: Points' by Henry Moore, 1969, in the Alten Pinakothek in Munich; surreal objects were his means to express emotions and meaning.*

Figure 1.15 *An example of the work of Paul Nash, 'Landscape of the Megaliths' (c.1937), at a time when he was fascinated by psychological reality and the symbolism of nature.*

Unconscious expression **25**

the experiments of the great analysts' (fig. 1.15). By the late 1930s Moore too was seeing his own work in this light: 'There are universal shapes to which everybody is subconsciously conditioned and to which they can respond if their conscious control does not shut them off.'[37]

Jens Jensen from Chicago was an early example of a landscape designer voicing such thoughts:

> Deep down in the primitive there lies the secret of the significance of life and of the infinite. It is a hidden, creative force visible only to those who seek and are attune[d] with the Master's great creation.[38]

Kenneth Clark's comments that expressionism 'may be the only possible means by which the individual human soul can assert its consciousness', and that 'the human spirit ... will always succeed in giving itself a visible shape', was conventional but profound wisdom when committed to paper in 1949. Clark's further point that 'all art is to some degree symbolic and recognition depends on certain long-accepted formulae'[39] nicely represented Jellicoe's line of thinking from the mid-1950s.

Geoffrey Jellicoe already believed in the spirit of the age, in the conformity of ideas and form, and in an underlying unity in the universe. When he read about the unconscious mind in Jung's *Memories, Dreams, Reflections* (1963) he thought he had found a scientific basis for them. Particularly gratifying was Jung's belief in an underlying congruence between the structure of the mind and the structure of the universe — what the ancients called the 'sympathy of all things' — allowing the unconscious to inform the conscious of universal truths. Jung had also claimed that artists, philosophers and even scientists owed some of their best ideas to inspirations that appear suddenly from the unconscious after intense conscious thought. 'The ability to reach a rich vein of such material ... is one of the hallmarks of what is commonly called genius.'[40]

These truths from the unconscious would not be expressed as clear precise thoughts, but through a language of symbols of which the conscious mind would be largely unaware. The most accessible source of such messages was dreams, thought Jung, and they were consequently given great prominence in his psychoanalytical theory. He and his followers had also given examples of painters — Paul Klee, Piet Mondrian, Paul Nash, *et al.* — who had gained inspiration from the unconscious, and whose work could be analysed for their symbolic content. To Jellicoe the question was that if painters can draw upon the well of the unconscious, why not landscape architects?

This gave him fresh inspiration to seek out how the forms of landscape could impart meaning to the unconscious. He reasoned that if there was a common unconscious, accessible to all, then symbolism would be meaningful to everyone's unconscious. The answer, he felt, was to bypass the conscious intellect, and address the unconscious in its own language of symbolism. This, then, could be the basis of an expressive landscape art that could be both powerful and universally meaningful.

If the designer could liberate his own 'individual subconscious, whose tremendous creative powers lie restless and unused under a mountain of intellect', he could have a powerful influence on the visitor.[41] Jellicoe liked incorporating symbols in his designs that the unconscious would fathom, and rather enjoyed the idea of playing with the unconscious without the visitor realising. There were different types of symbols; some could induce terror or delight, while others could represent the unification of all things. In the latter case, the unconscious could be brought into contact with the cosmos, as in some Eastern mysticism. Nothing should be made too obvious: 'once the intellect gets going you are sunk'. His advice was that the visitor should simply walk round a design, taking it in without thinking about what he was seeing, and 'three or four days later the significance of what you have seen will hit you'.[42]

The first occasion upon which Jellicoe put these thoughts fully into practice was the Kennedy Memorial at Runnymede in 1964. The site was modest in extent and topography. Jellicoe sought some way to lift the prosaic to the momentous and tragic idea of the assassination. He hit upon making an analogy to John Bunyan's *Pilgrim's Progress*. The 60,000 granite setts of the approach path which were laid in an uphill stream symbolised a multitude of pilgrims, the huge block of Portland stone with the inscription was a catafalque borne on the shoulders of the multitude, and the American scarlet oak behind the stone symbolised the spilt blood. Two seats of contemplation set at some distance to one side of the inscribed stone signified the idea of the thrones of a great ruler and his consort [43](fig. 1.16).

Jellicoe doggedly pursued this line after Runnymede. His most extraordinary opportunity to explore these ideas came very late, in 1983, when the Moody Foundation started to involve him in the development of the Moody Gardens at Galveston, Texas. The Director of Horticulture explained the theme adopted, that is, historic design through the ages:

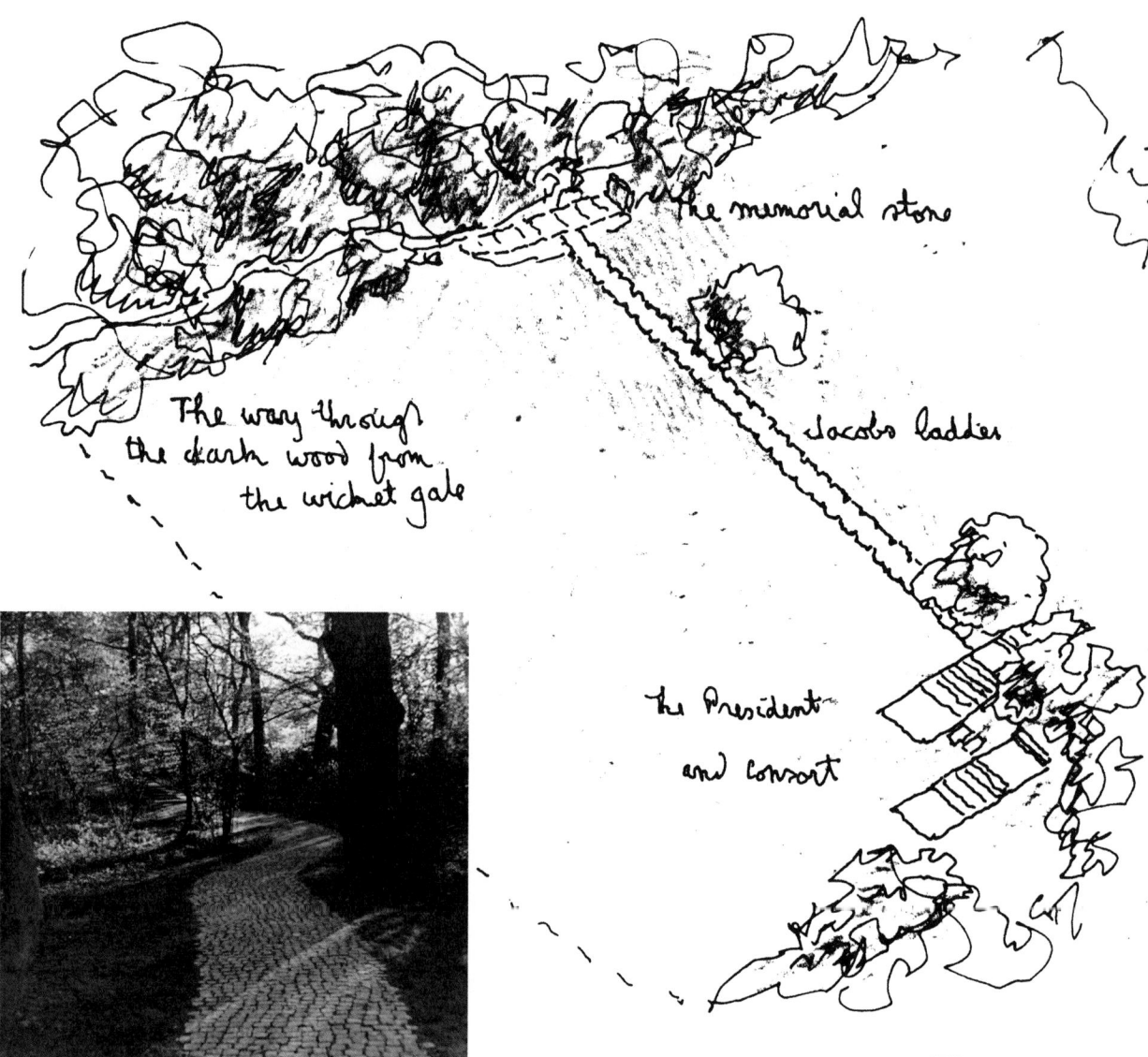

Figure 1.16 *The Kennedy Memorial of 1964 at Runnymede, Surrey; a sketch of how the seats of the President and consort were in the light, and connected to the shades around the memorial stone itself reached through a dark wood. The crowd of granite setts represented 'pilgrims'.*

The basis of the garden is the concept that the individual is but a very minute part of the entire cosmos. The visitor will be exposed to a landscape that will hopefully generate feelings from within that will play upon the subconscious.[44]

Towards the end of her life Jellicoe's contemporary, Brenda Colvin,[45] wrote and privately published a little book, called *Wonder in a World* (1977). She described herself as an agnostic, not a total disbeliever, as far as Christianity was concerned, and was anxiously searching for something greater than the self.

She did believe in some intelligence and design controlling all matter and imbuing it with the spirit which makes life:

> ... this Universe, this four-dimensional creation, must be designed for a purpose beyond human comprehension, by an intelligence unlimited by those dimensions except within the framework set for this creation.

She had had 'personal experience of the means of contact or communication between the individual mind and the universal unconscious', though only in quickly-fading flashes. As this last remark suggests, she was inclined to believe in Jung's notion of a 'Collective Unconscious', and an 'inherited subconscious memory' as a form of afterlife.

Colvin wrote at a time when many feared that the human race would extinguish itself through nuclear warfare or uncontrolled pollution. 'Humanity,' she thought, 'is incapable of full knowledge, though capable of glimpses of a Purpose ... for existence.' She was thus convinced that 'there is a Purpose and that humanity has a task'.[46] These late thoughts by Jellicoe and Colvin encapsulate that generation's doubts about organised religion and yet its yearning to believe in a force, however indistinctly knowable, that controlled all things.

Figure 1.17 *Paul Cézanne,'The Mont-Sainte-Victoire' (1904-6). Kenneth Clark used it as an illustration in his* Art into Landscape *(1949) commenting that it was one of a series of paintings of this mountain which was 'like a ritual act of worship in which he could achieve perfect self-realisation'.*

Unconscious expression **29**

NOTES AND REFERENCES

1 David Jacques & Jan Woudstra, *Landscape Modernism Renounced: The Career of Christopher Tunnard (1910-1979)* (London, 2009).

2 Geoffrey Collens, 'The Profession', in Sheila Harvey & Stephen Rettig (eds), *Fifty Years of Landscape Design* (Reigate, 1985), pp. 153-66.

3 Nikolaus Pevsner, *Pioneers of the Modern Movement* (London, 1936), pp. 38, 214 & 216-7.

4 Garrett Eckbo, *Landscape for Living* (New York, 1950), p. 3.

5 Peter Shepheard, *Modern Gardens* (London, 1953), p. 13.

6 Howard Dunington-Grubb, 'Modernismus Arrives in the Garden – To Stay?' *Landscape Architecture*, 32 (1942), 57-64.

7 Geoffrey Jellicoe, 'Consider Your Forbears', *The Journal of the Institute of Landscape Architects* (November 1954), 4.

8 Brenda Colvin, *Land and Landscape* (London, 1948), pp. 48 & 110, and Maria Terese Parpagliolo, 'The Lost Gardens of Pompeii', *Landscape and Garden* (Winter 1934), 24-7.

9 Christopher Tunnard, *Gardens in the Modern Landscape*, 2nd edn. (London, 1948), p. 5.

10 Colvin, op. cit., p. 62.

11 Shepheard, op. cit., pp. 13-14.

12 David Watkin, *Morality and Architecture* (Oxford, 1977), p. 80 *et seq.*, discusses the zeitgeist, especially as manifested in Pevsner's writings.

13 Marc Snow, *Modern American Gardens – Designed by James Rose* (New York, 1967), pp. 9 & 77.

14 At the ICOMOS conference at Oxford in September 1987 Pechère issued a 'Memorandum on the origins of IFLA, and the International Committee of Gardens and Historic Sites of ICOMOS-IFLA', in which he recalled meeting Jellicoe at the ILA international conference in London and Cambridge in 1948.

15 Jellicoe, op. cit., 4, 8 & 11.

16   Eliel Saarinen, *Search for Form: a Fundamental Approach to Art* (New York, 1948), p. v.

17   James C. Rose, 'Articulate Form in Landscape Design', *Pencil Points* (February 1939), 100.

18   Eckbo, op. cit., p. 10.

19   Joseph Hudnut, 'The Modern Garden', in Tunnard, op. cit., p. 175.

20   H.F. Clark, 'The Restoration and Reclamation of Gardens', *Garden History Society Occasional Paper No. 1* (1969), p. 6.

21   H.F. Clark, 'Eighteenth Century Elysiums: the Role of "Association" in the Landscape Movement', *Journal of the Warbug and Courtauld Institutes*, VI (1943), 166 & 177.

22   H.F. Clark, *The English Landscape Garden* (1948), pp. 15 & 19.

23   H.F. Clark. 'The Sense of Beauty in the 18th, 19th and 20th Centuries', *Journal of the Institute of Landscape Architects* (March 1957), 2 & 18.

24   Nikolaus Pevsner, 'Conclusions', in *The Picturesque Garden and its Influence outside the British Isles*, Dumbarton Oaks Proceedings of Colloquium II (Washington DC, 1974), p. 119.

25   Nikolaus Pevsner, 'The Genesis of the Picturesque', *Architectural Review*, 96 (1944), 139-46.

26   Tunnard, op. cit., p. 7.

27   Rudolf Wittkower, 'English Neo-Palladianism, the Landscape Garden, China and the Enlightenment', *L'Arte* (1969), 177–90.

28   Rudolf Wittkower, *Architectural Principles in the Age of Humanism* (London, 1949), p. 24.

29   From 1936-7 William Arthur Eden was appointed Lecturer and Studio Instructor at the School of Architecture at Liverpool, and was appointed Honorary Lecturer in Rural Planning in the Department of Civic Design for the session 1937-8. When Professor Holford resigned from the latter department in 1947 Eden was asked to be Acting Head. However, he took up the position as Head of the Leeds School of Architecture in 1948. In common with Pevsner and his allies, Eden was becoming increasingly interested in Palladian architecture. This was against the trend in the schools, and in 1952 he took on the much more suitable position as Head of Historic Buildings at the London County Council, and at the Greater London

Council from 1964. He was, for example, chiefly responsible for the restoration of Marble Hill House, the Palladian villa by the Thames in Twickenham, and he built up his department as a formidable force for conservation based on sound historical research. In 1970 he retired with an OBE.

30   Reyner Banham, quoted in David Watkin, *The Rise of Architectural History* (London, 1980), p. 154.

31   Clive Bell, *Art* (London, 1914), p. 11.

32   Barbara Hepworth, *A Pictorial Autobiography*, rev. ed. (London, 1978), p. 24.

33   Saarinen, op. cit., pp. 109-20.

34   Interview with Dame Sylvia Crowe, 2 March 1989.

35   Sylvia Crowe, *Garden Design* (London, 1958), pp. 12 & 75.

36   Carl Jung, *Man and His Symbols* (London, 1964), pp. 23 & 31-3.

37   Susan Compton, *Henry Moore* (London, 1988), pp. 30-1.

38   Jens Jensen, *Siftings* (Chicago, 1939), p. 9.

39   Kenneth Clark, *Landscape into Art* (London, 1949), pp. 2, 111 & 143.

40   Jung, op. cit., p. 38.

41   Geoffrey Jellicoe, 'Journey into the Future', in *Landscape 89: The Environmental Review* (Reigate, 1989), p. 12.

42   This quote is from Jellicoe's talk at the Architectural Association on 2 February 1989.

43   Sir Geoffrey Jellicoe, *The Guelph Lectures on Landscape Design* (Guelph, Ontario, 1983), pp. 86-99.

44   Sir Geoffrey & Susan Jellicoe, *The Landscape of Civilisation* (London, 1989), p. 14.

45   Brenda Colvin, CBE (1897-1981) had been trained at the Swanley Horticultural College in 1920, and was a garden designer before the Second World War. She took a keen interest in ecology, including the writings of Sir George Stapledon and Arthur Tansley. A series of lectures at the Planning School of University College London, led her to compose *Land and Landscape* (London, 1948; 2nd ed. 1970).

46   Brenda Colvin, *Wonder in a World* (Burford, 1977), pp. 2, 36-7.

CHAPTER 2

LANDSCAPE BEAUTY

The English countryside was historically much appreciated for its beauty and the opportunities for walking holidays. In the early twentieth century strong lobbies arose to protect these qualities. However, it was also a working landscape and thus the object of some early functionalist thinking.

One of the progressive movements of the late nineteenth century in the United States had been the establishment of National Parks, which were large areas of wilderness of such natural beauty that they should be spared the attentions of housing developers, and 'devoted forever to popular resort and recreation'. National Parks in England and Wales were designated several decades later, based on 'natural beauty' though being far from natural. If there was to be public policy to protect areas of great landscape beauty, a rationale that could encapsulate the perception of society as a whole was desirable. For much of the late twentieth century, methods of assessing the aesthetic value of the countryside were tried in the endeavour to find an 'objective', even scientific, way to achieve this.

The English countryside

Dudley Stamp, Professor of Geography at the London School of Economics and organiser of the *Land Utilisation Survey of Britain 1930-4*, and Thomas Sharp, who had many years' experience of producing town plans, were prominent in the campaign to limit urban sprawl.

Sharp's prognosis was that people had to reawaken their pride in the creation of towns (fig. 2.1). New towns and cities should be designed to be frankly urban, with proper streets, squares and high densities at the centre. He attacked the garden-city suburb's 'romanticism' (fig. 2.2). Despite purporting to be rural in spirit, such places were to him unnecessary urban sprawl, a 'popular edition of Bournemouth'.[1] This was disturbing to the many planners who had spent their careers attempting to reduce housing density from ten units per acre to six.[2]

His polemical *Town and Countryside* (1932), followed by *English Panorama* (1936), praised the 'composed', 'intimate', charm of the English countryside: it displayed 'a deep accord between man and Nature ... It has a lived-in character ... It is a humanised landscape. It is the landscape of a high civilisation'.

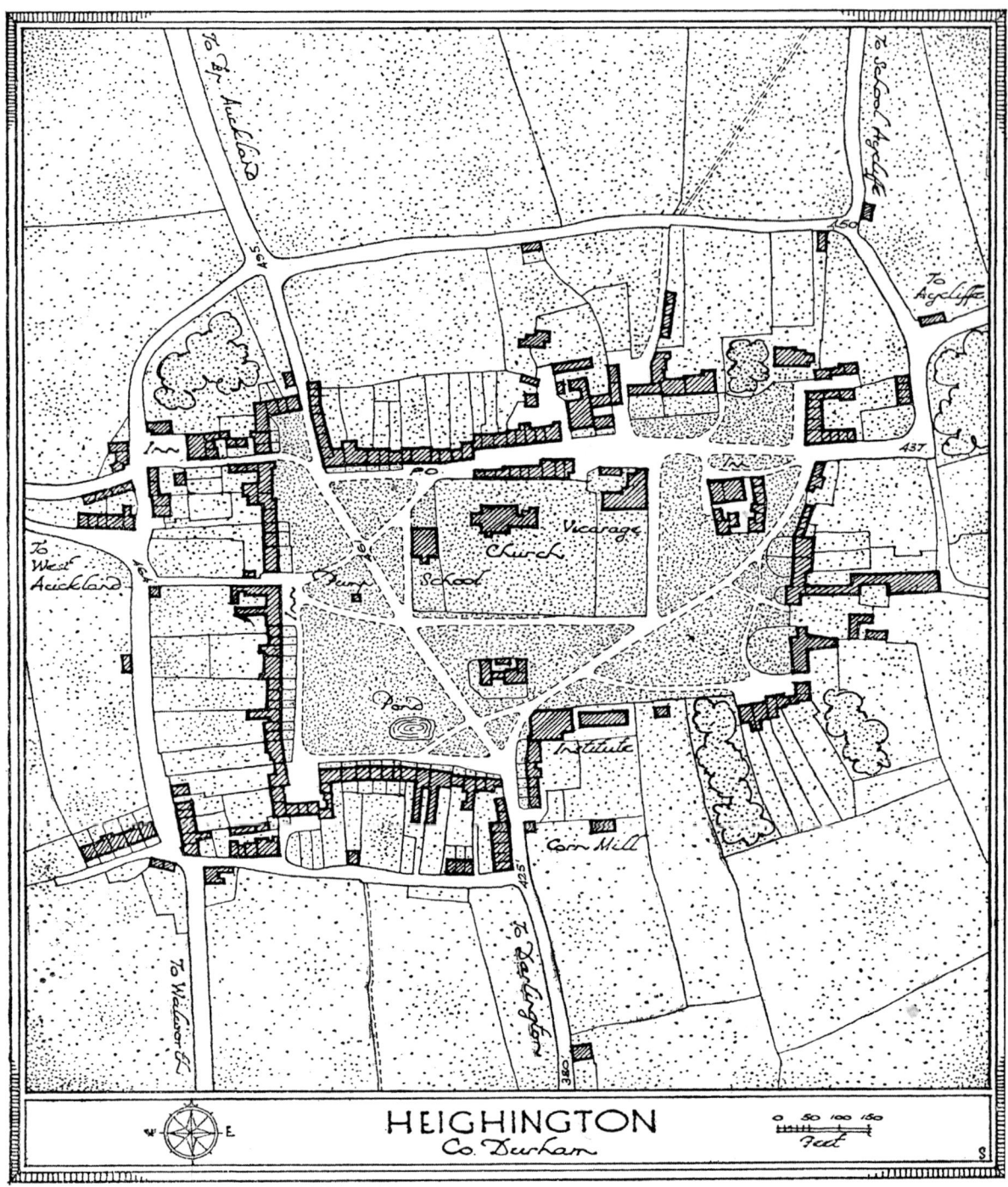

Figure 2.1 *The rural tradition of planning on rational principles: Heighington was one of Thomas Sharp's examples in Sharp 1932, Fig. 5.*

Figure 2.2 *The Garden City aesthetic: Port Sunlight by T. Raffles Davison, 1916; 1930s thinkers rejected it as 'romanticism'. In Sharp, 1936, p.85.*

Stamp and Sharp argued that if town and country were designed for the purposes intended, a clear distinction between them would be to the aesthetic benefit of both. Stamp argued that suburbs were far from a rational outcome of their function, and consequently they were both inefficient and ugly.[3] This functionalist argument was seen also in connection with garden design. Christopher Tunnard, for example, was to argue that beauty was not something to be aimed at directly, but would be a by-product, the mind's unconscious aesthetic response to a perception of harmony between idea and form. Functional success would have automatically looked right to the eye.

The magazine *Architectural Review* (*AR*) was highly instrumental in making the new ideas accessible to British readers. William Arthur Eden, an architect running the Civic Design course at the University of Liverpool, adopted Sharp's version of the landscape's history and its humanisation when he wrote a series on 'The English Tradition in the Countryside' for *AR* in 1935. The term 'tradition' was carefully defined, though, in order to discover 'a guiding principle' behind the evolution of the countryside. Eden thought it meant the tradition of continual improvement for human purposes:

The English countryside 35

D. **1700. Enclosure**

- The fields no longer held in common.
- Private owners enclose them with fences.
- Extension of farming.
- The forest has been cut down for house building, ship building, and fuel.
- Few trees over forty years old.
- Avenues planted at the Manor.

E. **1800. The Age of Planting**

- The big landowner builds a country seat.
- The hill becomes a park.
- The road becomes a drive.
- The river becomes an ornamental lake.
- The manor garden has been landscaped.
- By tree planting the landscape has been laid out as a garden.

F. **1900. The Humanized Landscape.**

- First appearance of the "typical" English countryside.
- The trees have grown up.
- The vision of the eighteenth century is realized.
- The humanized landscape.

Figure 2.3 *Some of the drawings by Robert Austin included with W.A. Eden's articles in the* Architectural Review *illustrating the way the landscape has evolved to meet human requirements. Ref:* Architectural Review, *Vol. 77 (1935), p. 91.*

Ours is, in fact, a humanized landscape. To the great end of humanizing the landscape all the improvement schemes of the eighteenth century were directed. Every small squire of the period was simply trying to make his immediate countryside the open-air part of his home. "Nature" ... was not his god. Rather was he the "Creator and Ordinator of things" who was anxious to reduce to a human order whatever of the original chaos was still existing in his day.

This was the point in the argument when Eden reintroduced the tradition of improvement and humanisation. We must remember that 'what was an adequate home for the landowner and village community of the eighteenth century can no longer be regarded as suitable for the needs of today'. Nowadays, 'We must in some manner substitute the community for the individual landowner, but we can still regard the landscape as the open-air part of man's home' (fig. 2.3). The necessity of concerted action to fulfil his vision led Eden to believe that 'the State … must have a proper control over the use of the land'.[4]

So the countryside was timeless, beautiful and with great recreational potential, while also being functional and deserving of modernisation. Before and after the Second World War, several theorists sought a reconciliation between these seemingly conflicting positions, and crafted new theories about what constituted beauty. The laws of the

Figure 2.4 *Cathedral Rocks, Yosemite Valley, by Albert Bierstadt, c. 1872; this landscape was withheld from development to preserve its scenic beauty.*

The English countryside **37**

Figure 2.5 *The British national park: areas protected from further development for their scenic quality; Keswick and Derwentwater, Lake District, print by the Detroit Publishing Company, 1905.*

universe, human evolutionary traits and the unconscious were invoked, and, more significantly in the long term, new ideas on the ethics of the care of the land were formulated.

The selection of the British National Parks

Until the late twentieth century conservation of the wider landscape was very largely landscape preservation, in other words 'freezing' it in the hope that such action would prevent change. This was seen in the United States when a large unclaimed area around Yosemite in California was withheld from division and sale by the Government (fig. 2.4). That was the germ of the US National Park Service. In the private arena concerned citizens might club together to purchase land of public interest, say, as a beauty spot which they would then keep or re-sell with restrictive covenants or easements, thus denying developers the opportunity of despoiling landmarks for private gain. That idea crossed over to England where the National Trust set about acquiring large swathes of the Lake District by purchase or gift (fig. 2.5).

Figure 2.6 *English Country village admired for its picturesque beauty: Water Street, Castle Combe, Wiltshire.*

When it was proposed to establish several National Parks in the United Kingdom, it was realised they could not be created on the North American model. All their land was already owned, and it would have taken many decades of patient land-acquisition to place them into trust or government ownership. Besides, they were farmed, and that was an important reason for their appearance. These matters were debated from the 1920s. The UK Government's National Park Committee of 1931 affirmed them as of national importance,[5] with the result that several were established by Act of Parliament after the Second World War.

Views on what made beauty in the countryside varied. The traditional, non-functionalist, perspective attributed it to the layout of fields, lanes and villages with their varying hills and ancient trees, a testament to the history of the once rural nation, and picturesque in its fine grain, little scenes and surprises (fig. 2.6). The report of the 1931 Committee expressed admiration for this centuries-old humanised countryside thus:

> The happiest moments and recollections of millions are bound up with her quiet places. If the grandeur of the natural features of other countries is lacking, there is to be found instead an intimate charm, and an association of the land and its monuments with the life history of the race, which is justly regarded as an invaluable national heritage.

Selection of the British National Parks

Figure 2.7 *When human intervention was least evident, the beauty of nature could be fully expressed; John Ruskin's drawing of the Aiguille de Blaitière, in the Mont Blanc massif, in 1856.*

The aesthetic aspect of mountainous areas was rather different in evoking awe and admiration. Underlying most such aesthetic opinion was John Ruskin's that 'there may be proved to be indeed an increase of the absolute beauty of all scenery in exact proportion to its mountainous character'.[6] This painterly appreciation drew attention to the shades and shadows of rocky terrain and how these effects generally heightened with altitude, as wildness increased and the footprint of mankind decreased (fig. 2.7).

Part of the evidence to the 1931 Committee related to the definition of beauty, and one of the more influential participants, the National Trust, was keen to express its ideas on wild areas.[7] Its witnesses admired the United States and Canadian National Parks, for which the stimulus had been the protection of the pristine natural world (fig. 2.8). Since it was important that the ordinary person should be enabled to experience nature, wider access to the countryside was a major plank in the argument. The Trust accordingly defined its concept of British National Parks thus:

> ... something large enough for the nation to enjoy and important enough to justify the intervention of the State. It must have enough of the untouched in it, whether of forest, mountain, moor or water, to

Figure 2.8 *The wonders of nature: Banff National Park, Canada.*

give the sense of nature as she is in herself, of wild nature unworked by man, undisfigured and unadorned ... it must serve as a place of public recreation in the widest sense: it must be valuable for its fauna and flora and must be used for their preservation: and above all it must be a place of noble or beautiful scenery.[8]

Wild scenery and wild animals were here bundled together in the concept of the 'natural'. Areas protected for flora and fauna became 'nature reserves', whilst rugged scenery with marginal agriculture was said to have 'natural beauty'.

Therein lay the point of difference from what could be achieved in Britain, though. In such intensely developed and cultivated countries, it was more sensible to think of the wilder areas being intermixed with 'farms and parks and gardens bringing their contribution of history and personality, variety and beauty, to contrast with that uncultivated portion set apart for public access'. Furthermore, 'wild' landscapes were the least capable of coping with extensive access, and botanists and ecologists pointed out this inherent conflict.[9] Brenda Colvin was to warn that 'we too readily assume that the highest landscape beauty results from complete and utter "wildness" from the absence, that is, of any human use whatsoever'.[10]

Selection of the British National Parks **41**

Figure 2.9 *John Dower's recommendations for the English and Welsh national parks, at a time when an expert's personal preferences were respected, in Dower, Map 1.*

Areas suggested for the first 10 National Parks in England and Wales.

National Parks came into focus in the post-war years as part of the vision for a new Britain, largely because of the desirability of the countryside to provide for recreational use. An expert, John Dower, who in each case sought out 'an extensive area of beautiful and relatively wild country', prepared suggestions for boundaries (fig. 2.9). When the Hobhouse Committee considered the National Park boundaries in 1947, it affirmed that 'the essential requirements of a National Park are that it should have great natural beauty, a high value for open-air recreation and substantial continuous extent'.[11] It did not define the phrase 'natural beauty', or how it was gauged. It seemed enough that ten wise men were content with the assessments of Dower and his colleagues.

The search for objectivity

There had been very little discussion of methods of assessment of aesthetic value in the designation of the North American or British

42 Landscape beauty

National Parks, nor the German nature areas. This changed in the late 1960s after Governments in both the United States and the United Kingdom became impressed by the claims of 'rational comprehensive' regional planning (fig. 2.10) to be able to produce computer models of how factors interacted in the dynamics of land-use change. By manipulating the various inputs, it was thought, government could control land use in order to achieve political goals. Planning authorities were thereby induced to assess all high-value landscapes quantifiably as potential constraints within models of land use and transportation, a much more complex task than just delineating National Parks.

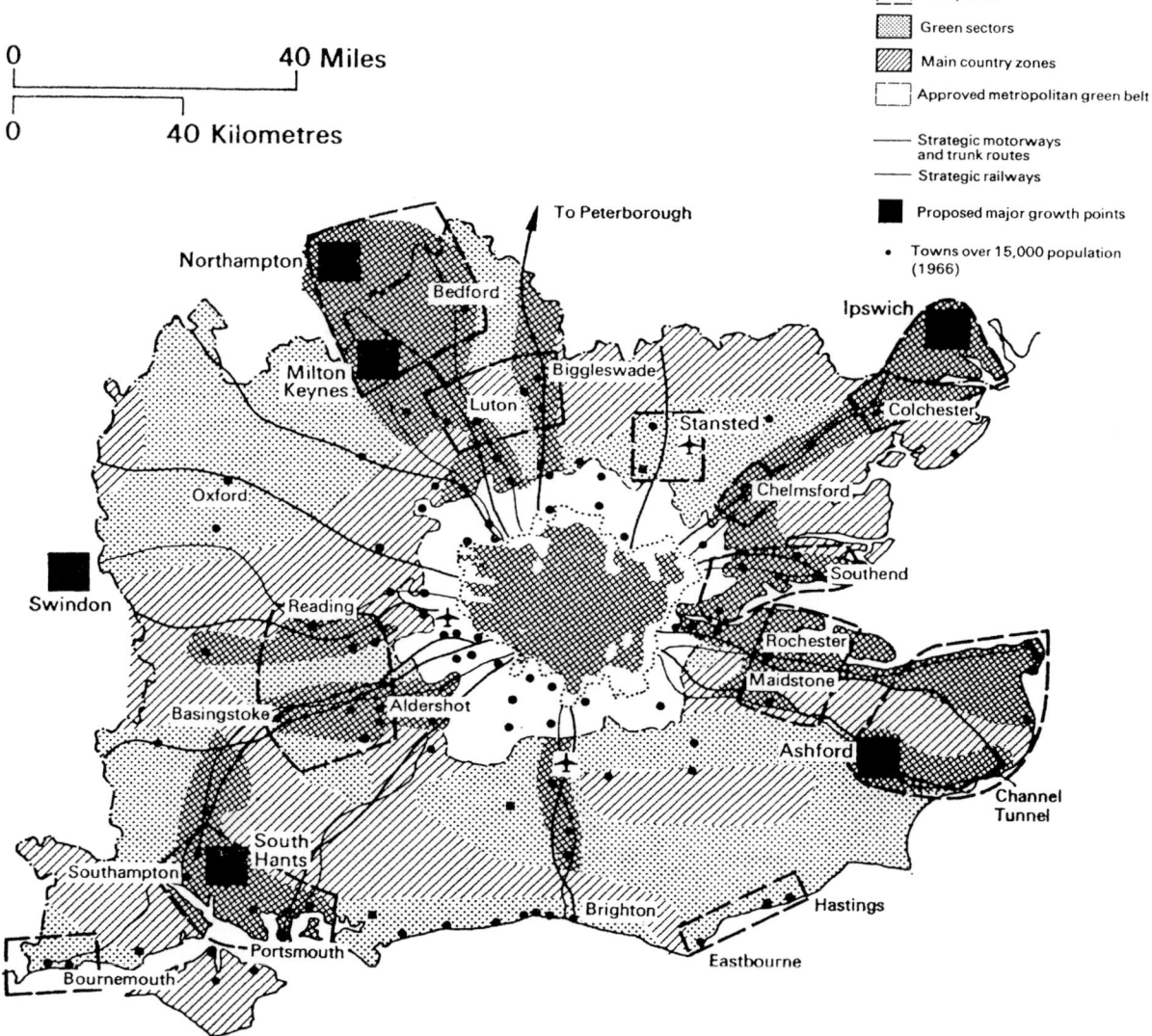

Figure 2.10 *Diagram from* A Strategy for the South East *(1967) by the British Economic Planning Council, proposing sectors for growth and growth points based on land use and transportation models. In Glasson, fig. 10.4.*

Search for objectivity **43**

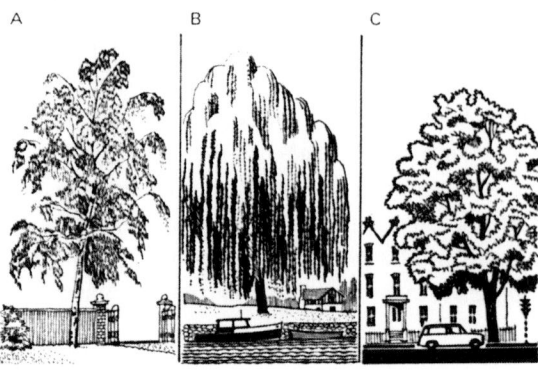

Examples of the use of this method of valuation.

A. A medium sized birch tree in a fairly secluded garden in a well-wooded residential area.
1. Size — medium — scores 2 points
2. Useful life expectancy — 40-100 years — „ 3 „
3. Importance in landscape — little — „ 1 „
4. Presence of other trees — many — „ 1 „
5. Relation to setting — very suitable — „ 3 „
6. Form — fair — „ 2 „
7. Special factors — none — „ 1 „

Total score = 2 x 3 x 1 x 1 x 3 x 2 x 1 = 36 (say £36).

B. A weeping willow between a village pub and a river.
1. Size — large — scores 3 points
2. Useful life expectancy — 20-40 — „ 2 „
3. Importance in landscape — some — „ 2 „
4. Presence of other trees — some — „ 2 „
5. Relation to setting — especially suitable — „ 4 „
6. Form — good — „ 3 „
7. Special factors — none — „ 1 „

Total score = 3 x 2 x 2 x 2 x 4 x 3 x 1 = 288 (say £288)

C. A healthy plane tree about 50 years old in a prominent position in the centre of a small town.
1. Size — large — scores 3 points
2. Useful life expectancy — 40-100 — „ 3 „
3. Importance in landscape — considerable — „ 3 „
4. Presence of other trees — none — „ 4 „
5. Relation to setting — very suitable — „ 3 „
6. Form — good — „ 3 „
7. Special factors — none — „ 1 „

Total score = 3 x 3 x 3 x 4 x 3 x 3 x 1 = 972 (say £972)

Note: The values given are for 1974 and should be raised to to allow for inflation since then.

Figure 2.11 *Pressure to derive numerical methods of landscape assessment: the Tree Council's method for valuing trees from 1974. Helliwell, p. 5.*

There was thus a strong onus on researchers to devise numerical methods of assessment of landscape beauty, so that this factor could be plotted on maps, just like rainfall, population density, or social deprivation (fig. 2.11). David Linton, a geomorphologist[12] who regarded scenery as a natural resource, exemplified the attitude of some physical geographers. His view in 1968 was that 'forest resources may be described as so many million board-feet in trees of a certain girth in this territory and so many million in that ... Ideally we should like to make a comparable statement about scenery'.[13]

Linton attempted to suppress subjectivity entirely by devising a means of assessment that was independent of the human observer. He wanted a desk-study method and objectively ascertained factors. He sought 'an analysis of those features of the landscape that contribute most fundamentally to its quality', and thought that there are 'two really basic elements ... one is the form of the ground ... the other is the mantle of forests and moorlands, farms and factories... by which the hard rock body of the landscape is clothed'. He devised scores for landform (0 for lowland and 8 for mountains) and land use (-5 for industrialised landscapes and +6 for wild landscapes). Combining scores derived a composite resource-rating.

Linton's formulation was generally thought to be too coarse and detached from reality, making it unworkable. Most experts wanted a method that measured 'visual quality' in the field, and, as in the assessment of fine art, accepted as a matter of common sense that the only available instrument of measurement was the human being.

The methods found rested on the idea that beauty was an absolute quality in the landscape and that suitably prepared assessors might be able to detect this quality, giving judgements that were effectively objective. The argument ran thus: Wittkower, neo-Platonists and many modernists combined in the thought that beauty was a by-product of the immutable cosmic laws by which the universe operated to create form; everyone was subject to the same cosmic laws; thus beauty in an object was an objective matter, one that was perceived instantaneously without the intercession of the intellect. This was the twentieth-century way of re-stating picturesqueness without using the dreaded word itself. Modern artistic criticism had emphasised form over content, just as picturesque theory once had, and if the landscape of nature could be seen in a formalist way there was the possibility of 'landscape evaluation' being put on a modern footing.

Awkwardly for these suppositions, human responses were observed to be variable, the product of personal preferences. Garrett Eckbo theorised that subjectivity arose from 'empathic relationships established in viewing landscape and receiving a pleasurable sensation', implying that any individual's assessments would be coloured by background, training and mood.[14] Such significant and unavoidable deviations from the norm were problematic for the mathematical methods of 'landscape evaluation'. Researchers thus had to devise a method that used human perceptions, yet could rationalise their variability to produce standard, or objective, values for the quality of beauty.

Formal qualities

Among the earliest of the new generation of 'landscape-evaluation' studies was that of East Sussex by K.D. Fines from 1963 to 1967.[15] Taking a formalist approach, he wanted to isolate 'response to visual beauty in the purest sense of the harmony of form, colour and texture'. He acknowledged three potential sources of impurity. First, there were the non-visual senses, particularly sound. Second, there were 'psychological' factors, by which he meant the emotions of sentiment, fear, curiosity, surprise and veneration that landscapes could induce. Third, there were the sequential experiences derived from season, atmosphere and the movement of the observer. In order to reduce these sources of possible bias in his own assessments, he devised a world-wide scale of values from 0 to 32, asked groups to score photographs by using it, and attempted to calibrate his own assessments thereby.

Further studies expanded upon Fines's faith that beauty was to be explained by the formal qualities of the landscape. These were listed in one report of 1976 as:

1. the inherent formal qualities (shape, proportion, colour, etc.) of individual objects ...
2. the relationship between these individual objects (i.e. their spacing, scale, composition, number, etc.) ...
3. the relationship between these individual objects, or groups of objects, and a setting.[16]

If it could be supposed that the sensation of beauty, in its pure form, was a Platonic response to such 'formal qualities of individual objects', the way was open to analysing 'visual quality' in terms of the components in the view and their relationships. Further, it could be assumed that individual subjectivities would be ironed out when aggregated, and so normal, correct, or objective, assessments could be derived, making the method open to mathematical analysis. No researcher could provide concrete evidence that perception worked like this, but a procedure had been devised that met the condition that the only available instrument of measurement was the human being. On both sides of the Atlantic, this and similar rationales that promised a more rigorous statistical treatment were accepted.

Because the untrained person might suffer from too many distractions, though, and be unable to free up the mind to get in tune with the universe, the best hope of ascertaining beauty reliably would be

Figure 2.12 *Suitably sensitised professionals pondering paradise: a humorous drawing in an occasional paper. University College London, Department of Geography, Occasional Paper 25 (1975).*

to use detached yet sensitised experts like the researchers themselves (fig. 2.12).[17] Naturally, as a deputy planning officer for East Sussex, Fines had considered himself to be an adequately qualified assessor.

In the mathematically more ambitious studies views, sometimes in the form of photographs, were dissected in terms of their components, the views were scored, and the mathematical technique of multiple regression analysis would identify the supposed contributions by those components to the score. The beauty of views yet unseen could thus, in theory, be predicted.[18] Researchers became very ingenious at demonstrating that their formulae and weightings for the components yielded high correlations with assessments of beauty by suitably sensitised professionals.

Meanwhile an environmental scientist who had previously studied glare from lights used the same approach in calculating visual intrusion.[19] He was concerned with such situations as sitting by a window, observing a heavy lorry passing by on the road outside. He thought that its intrusion

Formal qualities 47

Figure 2.13 *Component analysis: the analogy to painting by numbers; the scene happens to be Castle Combe (see fig.2.6). In* Transactions of the Institute of British Geographers, *66 (Nov. 1975), p.119.*

would depend upon its prominence in the field of vision (expressed in terms of the 'solid angle' subtended), and how intrinsically intrusive it was (expressed by an 'Hedonic Index'). A whole view could be scored by analysis of all its components, good and bad, and the effect of changes to that view could be calculated (fig. 2.13). This had many similarities with the component analysis of the landscape architects, not least of which was the apparent objectivity.

48 *Landscape beauty*

NOTES AND REFERENCES

1. Thomas Sharp, *English Panorama* (London, 1936), p. 88.

2. Peter Youngman who worked under Thomas Adams remembered this well.

3. Simon Rycroft, 'Mapping, Modernity and the New Landscape', in Michael Spens (ed), *Landscape Transformed* (London, 1996), pp. 30-7.

4. William Arthur Eden, 'The English Tradition in the Countryside', *Architectural Review*, 77 (1935), 87-94, 142-52 & 193-202.

5. Christopher Addison, *Report of the Addison Committee* (London, 1933), pp. 7-8.

6. John Ruskin, *Modern Painters*, IV (London, 1856), p. 355.

7. The National Trust for Places of Historic Interest or Natural Beauty was founded in 1895 in order to acquire such land and hold it for the public's enjoyment. It had been assembling picturesque landscape, notably in the Lake District, since that date. The Trust had a very similar and slightly older sister in Massachusetts: the Trustees of Public Reservations, founded in 1891.

8. Addison, op. cit., p. 54.

9. The British Correlating Committee for the Protection of Nature, quoted in Addison, p. 67: 'Two distinct meanings may be attached to the idea of National Parks: first, to provide opportunities for the members of the community to enjoy a holiday in the open air and in pleasant surroundings and to study wild life; and secondly, to preserve, unaltered as far as possible, the animals and plants of the district. Except in very large Parks ... these two aspects of the idea cannot well be reconciled'.

10. Brenda Colvin, *Land and Landscape* (London, 1948), p. 150.

11. *Report of the National Parks Committee* (The Hobhouse Report) (London, 1947), p. 9.

12. Linton had worked for many years on glaciation in Scotland and Scandinavia, and combined a scientist's appreciation with that of the aesthete. He became President of the Institute of British Geographers in 1963, when Professor of Geography at the University of Birmingham. In his presidential address, 'The Forms of Glaciation', he mentioned his excitement at the grandeur of the sculpted forms of glaciated landscapes and their infinite variety.

13 David L. Linton, 'The Assessment of Scenery as a Natural Resource', *Scottish Geographical Magazine*, 84 (December 1968), No.3, 220-38.

14 Garrett Eckbo, *The Landscape We See* (New York, 1969), quoted by Robinson *et al.*, *Landscape Evaluation* (Manchester, 1976), p. 41.

15 K.D. Fines, 'Landscape Evaluation: a Research Project in East Sussex', *Regional Studies*, 2 (1968), 41-55.

16 D.G Robinson, I.C. Laurie, J.F. Wager & A.L. Traill, *Landscape Evaluation*. Report for the Countryside Commission. (Manchester, 1976). pp. 46-7.

17 The American philosopher, Monroe C. Beardsley, should be mentioned. In his *Aesthetics* (1958), he argued that differing aesthetic values between objects stemmed from their differing capacities to yield aesthetic pleasure. These capacities originated in the object itself, and existed irrespective of whether the object was observed or not. However, observers' own abilities to realise the capacity varied too, producing apparent variabilities between objects. Broadly, though, skilled observers would acknowledge objects of high capacity as such.

18 Early examples were Elwood L. Shafer, John F. Hamilton & Elizabeth A. Schmidt, 'Natural Landscape Preferences: A Predictive Model', *Journal of Leisure Research*, 1 : 1 (Winter 1969), 1-19; *Coventry-Solihull-Warwickshire: A Strategy for the Sub-Region* (1971), pp. 134-7: and Robinson *et al*, op. cit., (1976).

19 R.G. Hopkinson, 'The Quantitative Assessment of Visual Intrusion', *Journal of the Royal Town Planning Institute* (1971), 445-9.

$$\overline{V}_j = \alpha_0 + \sum_{i=1}^{q} \beta_i F_{ij} + \sum_{h=1}^{m} \gamma_h Z_{hj} + u_j$$

where

$\overline{V}_j$ = the mean quality score for the jth survey unit.

α_0 = the regression constant.

β_i = the regression weight associated with the ith factor in the jth survey unit.

F_{ij} = the value of the ith of q factors in the jth survey unit.

γ_h = the regression weight associated with the hth external variable in the jth survey unit.

Z_{hj} = the value of the hth of m external variables in the jth survey unit.

u_j = the random disturbance term.

Figure 2.14 *An equation for predicting visual quality-scores of places unseen from regression analysis of the factors and scores of those unseen places. University of Manchester,* Landscape Evaluation *(1976), p. 170.*

CHAPTER 3

NATURAL INSTINCTS

The law of natural selection was thought by many to support the premise that the physical environment of topography, climate and biology has shaped the course of human evolution in both bodily and psychological terms. More certainly it would have affected the development of human societies.

The presumed timescale for these changes had implications in several ways. If it was in the medium term, one might have a rationale for various perceptions about racial characteristics. Some argued, for example, that evolution had led to those inhabiting lush tropical latitudes to being predisposed to a relaxed care-free lifestyle, while those living in harsh northern climates had developed, perforce, a strong work ethic over time and were thus industrious by nature.[1]

Such ideas accepted that genetic changes happened slowly over millennia, but there was also an hypothesis (inaccurately referred to as 'Lamarckism') that physiological changes acquired during the life of a person or animal could be passed on to descendants. So, famously, limbs used more often become stronger and larger, while unused ones waste away, and this was thought to be inheritable.

Both these lines of thought fell out of favour for good reasons (being bad science and politically unacceptable). However, it was still thought that human interactions with, and responses to, the processes of ecology might have a genetic basis, so that humans were added to the many ingredients of ecosystems. When it came to the influence of topography and climate on certain human behaviours, such as agricultural practices and garden design, these were accepted as cultural practices, rather than evolutionary outcomes.

The subject of 'human ecology' actually had several origins. Herbert Spencer, the sociologist who coined the phrase 'survival of the fittest', suggested that the evolution of society was analogous to the concept of biological evolution, and ecological concepts, such as competition, mutualism and succession, were used as metaphors for the behaviour of social groups. Human ecology was thus important in the early days of sociology and to the understanding of cities and the town-planning concepts of Patrick Geddes and Lewis Mumford.

Meanwhile plant ecologists saw human ecology in terms of their analysis of the relations between the environment and plants and animals being extended to that with human beings. Important works on ecology began to be published from around 1900, and the schema of many species combining into communities adapted to particular habitats led soon after to that of holism and the interrelatedness of all things.

Environmental determinism

In the early twentieth century 'environmental determinism', the assumption that the history of peoples and societies are determined by the environment in which they develop, was one of the dominant theories. The first person to use the term 'human ecology' had defined it as 'the study of the surroundings of human beings in the effects they produce on the lives of men', which is virtually indistinguishable from the concept of environmental determinism.[2] One advocate, Ellen Churchill Semple, expressed the rationale thus:

> Man is a product of the earth's surface. This means not merely that he is a child of the earth, dust of her dust; but that the earth has mothered him, fed him, set him tasks, surface directed his thoughts, confronted him with difficulties that have strengthened his body and sharpened his wits, given him his problems of navigation or irrigation, and at the same time whispered hints for their solution. She has entered into his bone and tissue, into his mind and soul ...

> ... the watching of the grazing herd gives him leisure for contemplation, and the wide-ranging life a big horizon, his ideas take on a certain gigantic simplicity ... Chewing over and over the cud of his simple belief as the one food of his unfed mind, his faith becomes fanaticism; his big spacial ideas, born of that ceaseless regular wandering, outgrow the land that bred them and bear their legitimate fruit in wide imperial conquests.

> Man can no more be scientifically studied apart from the ground which he tills, or the lands over which he travels, or the seas over which he trades, than polar bear or desert cactus can be understood apart from its habitat.

> In every problem of history there are two main factors, variously stated as heredity and environment, man and his geographic conditions, the internal forces of race and the external forces of habitat.[3]

The bulk of her book, then, was about the distribution of the races and their cultural development. One of her concluding observations was:

The white race, identified primarily with Europe, that choice and diversified continent, ... the rapid expansion in recent centuries of the most advanced peoples of this race has made them the apostles of civilization to the whole world.[4]

There were problems with environmental determinism. It taught that there were forces larger than the human's puny attempts to evade them, and this could lead either to fatalism or to the inevitable destiny of a people. This in turn led on to racialist beliefs, eugenics (the improvement of races) and regrettable political developments. It made religion and other forms of faith largely redundant in explaining the meaning of life.

Unity with nature

'Holism' was a term proposed by General Jan Smuts in 1926 (fig. 3,1).[5] It was the idea that biological, social, economic and other systems and their properties should be viewed as wholes, not just as collections of their parts. It was in some ways a spiritual epiphany concerning the ordering of the universe.

Although he was best known as a general, politician and statesman, Smuts's private passion was botany and ecology.[6] In this he was fellow traveller with the Scots-born botanist, John William Bews, the Principal of the Natal University College. Smuts provided an introduction to Professor Bews's book, *Human Ecology* (1935) in which he commended him for having shown how the tropical flora of Africa had continuously adjusted itself to the new conditions of climate, latitude, soil, and rainfall as it migrated southwards over millions of years.

This was also an occasion for Smuts to re-state his conception of holism:

> The world is not a chaos, a chance selection of items and fragments. It is a closely interwoven system of patterns. What we in our human way call plan and design is present everywhere ... certain dominant features in it — rhythm, regularity, inter-connexion, and linkings up, an interplay of active relationships which is creative of structures, forms, patterns. Such is reality — a vast Pattern of patterns. And to trace these patterns or wholes is to discover the lineaments of beauty in all its forms, whether we call them beauty or truth or good. They are all, but holistic harmonies in the nature of things. Nothing exists for itself alone ...[7]

Figure 3.1 *Jan Christiaan Smuts, the person who coined the term 'holism', in 1919.*

Bews emphasised that 'environment-function-organism' was one inseparable whole, and described human ecology as 'the all important, all embracing, question of how and why man is as he is, and behaves as he does. It unifies all the human sciences and enables each one to find its proper place in a generalized study of man'. As a disciple of holism, he regarded it as a 'philosophy of life'.

Bews wrote much about the understanding of heredity in plants, and was cautiously ready to apply the principles to animal species and human races. He speculated on the evolution, diversification and achievement of human societies through the lens of human ecology, in other words entering the fields of anthropology and sociology. He considered that

Figure 3.2 *John Dewey, a towering figure in North American philosophy in the early twentieth century, and whose writings on art and appreciation continued to have a strong influence in the late twentieth century.*

the human's 'functional relationship to his environment is not merely physiological but psychological as well', and that it was 'possible to examine many departments of man's intellectual activities, e.g. his literature, art, music, &c., from this new standpoint'.[8]

Smuts and Bews were among the more persuasive advocates of human ecology as an all-embracing viewpoint. Over time their almost religious perspective of the world and the place of plants, animals and humans within it became immensely influential within the ecological movement. One early adherent who was to carry the message to the realms of landscape architecture and planning was Brenda Colvin, who quoted Bews:

> ... life apart from environment does not exist, and cannot be conceived. Life consists essentially of a process of interchange between the life-substance or protoplasm and the environment. At the same time the term environment apart from life is, of course, meaningless.[9]

In 1934 Smuts had arranged a conference in South Africa to which the American philosopher John Dewey was invited (fig. 3.2). The latter's *Experience and Nature* (1925) had laid the foundations for a theory of experience based on the then-current scientific understanding of the sensory interactions between humans and their environment. He was a leading figure in the philosophical school of 'American Naturalism' and he signed the 'Humanist Manifesto' of 1933 which, inter alia, proclaimed that: 'man is a part of nature and he has emerged as the result of a continuous process'.[10]

In *Art as Experience* (1934) Dewey, though no ecologist, at first sight appears to subscribe to its holism: 'life goes on in an environment; not merely in it but because of it, through interaction with it'. However, differences emerge because, while the holists thought that aesthetic perception was instantaneous, without cognition (i.e. the mental processes of understanding through thought), Dewey believed that it came about through that 'continuous process':

> An instantaneous experience is an impossibility, biologically and psychologically. An experience is a product, one might almost say by-product, of continuous and cumulative interaction of an organic self with the world. There is no other foundation upon which esthetic theory and criticism can build.[11]

Nevertheless both strains of thought emphasised how the human acted in unity with the environment, and needed to be at one with it, harmoniously in balance. For most of the later ecological theorists that was the significance of Dewey's writings.

People and the land

Perhaps all peoples have been prone to at least a mild identification of land and people in their popular culture, so landscape easily became an icon of nationalistic values. At the extreme, some believed in a mystical bond between the land and its people, the mingling of blood and soil. Belonging to the land bestowed fundamental values, inner strength and national virility, contrasting with the artificial and sophisticated lifestyle of the city. The converse was true too: the land belonged to its people.

The Group of Seven artists had a declared aim to sharpen the Canadian national identity (fig. 3.3). The group became aware of the symbolism

Figure 3.3 *The Group of Seven strove to clarify Canadian identity through their painting: this is 'Autumn Hillside' by Franklin Carmichael, 1920.*

of 'The North' in Scandinavian art through an exhibition in Buffalo, New York, in 1913.[12] This suggested a theme that they could develop in order to cut 'straight through the muddle of imported notions: the clear, replenishing, Virgin north that must resound in the greater, freer depths of the soul'. It was suggested that those, like Italians and Africans, who were bred in southern climates, would be unsuited in northern ones.

These beliefs in national character being determined by environment, and the superiority of the north, were shared by Jens Jensen, himself born a Dane:

> The world is divided into many little worlds, each of which exerts a certain influence on those living within it. This influence is found in the character of the people and expressed in their economic and spiritual life ... The influence of the Mediterranean, where the Latin races live, has created a distinct character quite different from that of the Germanic races ... Environmental differences of the hot south have almost destroyed the strong and hardy characteristics of these northern people; whereas, the New Englander has maintained his Scotch characteristics. The farther south a northern people migrate, the more degenerating are the influences of environment ...[13]

People and the land

The British plant breeder and agrarian philosopher, Sir Reginald George Stapledon, argued for closer linkage between people and the land in *The Land Now and To-morrow* (1935). He was convinced that 'deep in the inner recesses of man's subconscious mind lies the indelible impression of the land', and, rather as Carl Jung would have thought, the unconscious, employed properly, 'could be galvanised into a mighty power'. Among his concerns was that the nation had become degenerate, and he put this down to so many living in towns. Britain had become 'a nation that has lost touch with nature and with the land'. So 'ought we to be careful to return to nature itself for our further nourishment and inspiration'.

Stapledon went further: he had some tips from breeding: 'the country stock in large measure is a pure stock' and 'every breeder knows that a foundation of pure stocks constitutes an essential reservoir upon which to draw in the improvement and development of a race'.[14] Hence 'our diminished country stock is a much-to-be-treasured asset to the nation, of immense value genetically'. He proposed that as much of the population as possible should be shifted from town to country.

He accepted, though, that most of the population had to remain in towns. Fortunately, 'there is no doubt that the love of nature is latent in every human being' and 'this urge to mingle with the universe and with life as a whole ... is latent in every urban dweller'. The important lesson for the townsman was that 'evolve as he may, he can never hope to be in a state of perfect equilibrium with his environment unless that environment satisfies his organism as a whole'. This would never be achieved 'if he persists in creating for himself environmental conditions which are not in harmony with the inexorable dictates of his genetical makeup'. Hence:

> ... the problem of today is how to create environmental conditions for every one of us that will cater not only for the sophisticated sides of our natures, but also ... for the animal, vegetable and primitive sides of our natures – the sides which ... still contribute most to our makeup in its totality.[15]

Stapledon was among those in England who felt that the spiritual and physical refreshment provided by the countryside was a national need, a necessary antidote to the miserable amenities of industrial cities. Man was excessively urbanised and needed contact with the land.[16]

Such thoughts were not so far from those in Scandinavia and Germany, which had been indulging in nature-worship (fig. 3.4). In 1906 the Prussian Minister of Education had set up an authority for the protection of natural amenities and places of interest, while in

Figure 3.4 *The preservation of scenery and objects of nature early became government policy in Sweden: this is Hällingsåfallet nature reserve in Jämtland.*

1907 experts advising the Swedish Government had thought that 'the preservation of scenery and all objects of nature should be a subject of lectures and addresses'. Two years after that the Swedes had passed legislation to safeguard objects of natural interest. In 1935 the German Reich passed a law for protecting the natural beauties of the country, with the stirring preamble that 'today as formerly Nature in Wood and Field is the object of the desire, the joy, and the recreation of the German people'.[17]

Back in Britain, Professor Cyril Joad argued the case for a rounded education of body, mind and spirit:

> One of the objects of education is to enable us to develop our latent potentialities, to extend our capacities to the full, to become all that we have it in us to be. In this full development of personality the culture of the body as well as the mind must play its part, and to the culture of the body familiarity with nature in walking and riding, in swimming and climbing, is an essential contribution. Confined in towns we need the country ...[18]

Behind his claims for the value of the countryside was his conception of how humanity stood in relation to nature. He believed that she and her laws were the only real permanence; humans had been shaped by her, and should understand her dictates. He wrote that from Plato's Republic one might 'learn how the soul of man is wax to take the impression of its environment'.

This hypothesis tallied with the then traditional social-scientific view of the mind at the time: that of an immensely powerful general-purpose intelligence, initially handicapped by empty memory-banks and virtually no fixed patterns of thought. This 'blank slate' or 'empty vessel' state of the mind was supposed to give it tremendous flexibility in the long term, but at the cost of an extended period of learning and development.[19] The mind, unquestioning and awaiting stimulus from its environment, developed as it absorbed facts and culture from the world around. So:

> Let a boy grow to manhood among the beautiful sights, harmonious sounds, and just institutions, and his soul will give forth beauty, harmony, and justice. Let him grow up in the midst of brutality and violence, among squalid sights and ugly sounds, and he will be unjust and violent in his dealings, his soul will give forth ugliness, and he will not know how to come to terms with gentleness and beauty.[20]

Such sentiments became woven into visions of Britain after the Second World War.[21]

The imperative of climate and soil

In many countries there were landscape designers and planners who valued the distinctiveness of national and local scenery deriving from landform, climate, soil and use (fig. 3.5). Jensen carried northern European notions across the Atlantic to America where he was employed in the Chicago park system. In old age he recorded his thoughts in *Siftings* (1939), in which he strongly advocated design and plant choice springing from the regional landscape. He wrote:

> Life is made rich and the world beautiful by each section developing its own beauty ... the only source from which the art of landscaping can come is our native landscape. It cannot be imported from foreign shores and be our own.[22]

Brenda Colvin too thought it was more apposite for local conditions, rather than mere artistic fashion, to determine the style of garden design. Hence she was curious to see the still rigidly formal French garden when attending the First International Congress of Garden Architects in Paris in 1937, adding: 'The findings of the Conference itself seemed to show a great similarity of ideal among the various countries, but how remarkably different, in practice, is the approach to the ideal.'[23]

Granite. *Chalk.*

Figure 3.5 *Distinctiveness of local scenery deriving from landform, climate, soil and use; Colvin drew a landscape in granite country (A), and one in chalk country (B), illustrating the influence of geology on landscape. In Colvin 1948, Fig. 3.*

It was 'the climatic and other conditions which tend to cause these differences', she explained (fig. 3.6), a point that was expanded in 1948: 'Climatic influences act mainly through the varying needs of different types of people for light, shade and shelter.' Hence in Persia shade and water were valued, and the style consisted of fountains, canals, walks under trees and open pavilions. In Italy, the brilliant clear atmosphere made for strong contrasts of light and shade, and 'the patterns they form becomes a principal theme of the design'. In England sunlight was precious, and the 'dripping moisture from damp foliage is an unwelcome sound'. On the other hand England had fine turf, while 'because of a comparatively mild climate, the need for shelter planting has not limited the size of the open spaces'. For these reasons:

> ... one of the outstanding characteristics of most of the more famous English gardens is a feeling of spaciousness ... This is particularly true of the eighteenth-century landscape garden and all its progeny: it is no exaggeration to say that that style could only have arisen in our climate, or rather that in any other climate the causes which produced it would have led to something of a very different character.

In landscape design 'any conscious effort to create a "new style" will be sterile'; appropriate solutions would evolve anyway 'if the designer is to be truly responsive to the indications of individual sites and the uses to which the sites are to be put'. 'The "style" matters only in so far as it promotes full interaction between function and environment, and that organic unity and balance of the whole from which beauty itself arises.'[24]

The imperative of climate and soil

Figure 3.6 *An archetypal garden in Italy, drawn by Cecil Stewart, showing the consequences of climate upon design; the garden is small because the heat is oppressive and exercise is kept to a minimum, but it is full of contrasts such as light and shade, vertical foreground and horizontal distance, etc. In Colvin 1948, Fig. 8.*

Colvin advised caution on the use of exotic plants, noting that 'in some situations exotic groups or plants not adapted to their context may strike a very inharmonious note. The cypress and almond group … a Persian scene … could never have that intimate and essential fitness which is felt when native plants form a pleasing group' in the English landscape. She advised 'restraint', which 'brings its own reward in the resulting sense of unity and of harmony: that "oneness" with nature itself, giving simplicity which is calm, enduring and full of deep repose'.[25] Such thoughts echoed Jensen's.[26] 'Every plant has its fitness and must be placed in its proper surroundings so as to bring out its full beauty.'

Sylvia Crowe developed this ecological approach into fuller guidelines for design ten years later in *Garden Design* (1958). A long historical analysis maintained the imperative of climate and soil. Hispano-Arabic gardens 'bear the unmistakeable hallmark of a genuine creation arising from a unique conjunction of place, climate and philosophy', and the English Landscape Garden was 'as

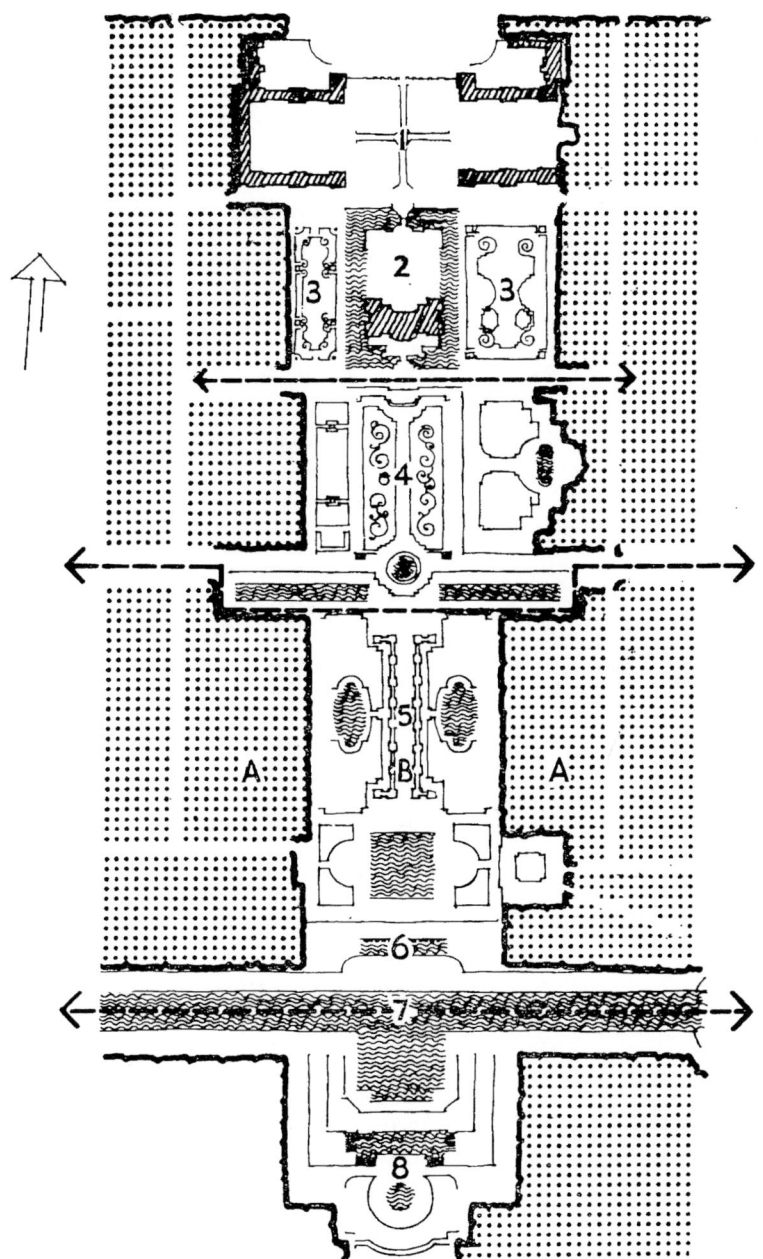

Figure 3.7 *Sylvia Crowe's analysis of Vaux-le-Vicomte; she felt that the combination of French weather, and the political and intellectual climate of the French Court at the time, led to nature being controlled absolutely. Key: A. Dark enclosing mass of woodland. B. Open central space. 1. Avant Cour. 2. Cour d'honneur. 3. Parterre. 4. First terrace. 5. Second terrace. 6. Cascades. 7. Great Canal. 8. Grotto. 9. View to hill and Farnese Bull. Crowe, Garden Design 1958, Fig. 5.*

inevitable to her land, climate and spirit, as the gardens of Le Nôtre had been to those of France' (fig. 3.7). Even the Italian garden was 'a natural result of the combination of a hot sunny climate, which favours the pattern of deep clefts cut in surrounding shade, and of a steep terrain that led to the development of terraces'.[27]

The imperative of climate and soil **63**

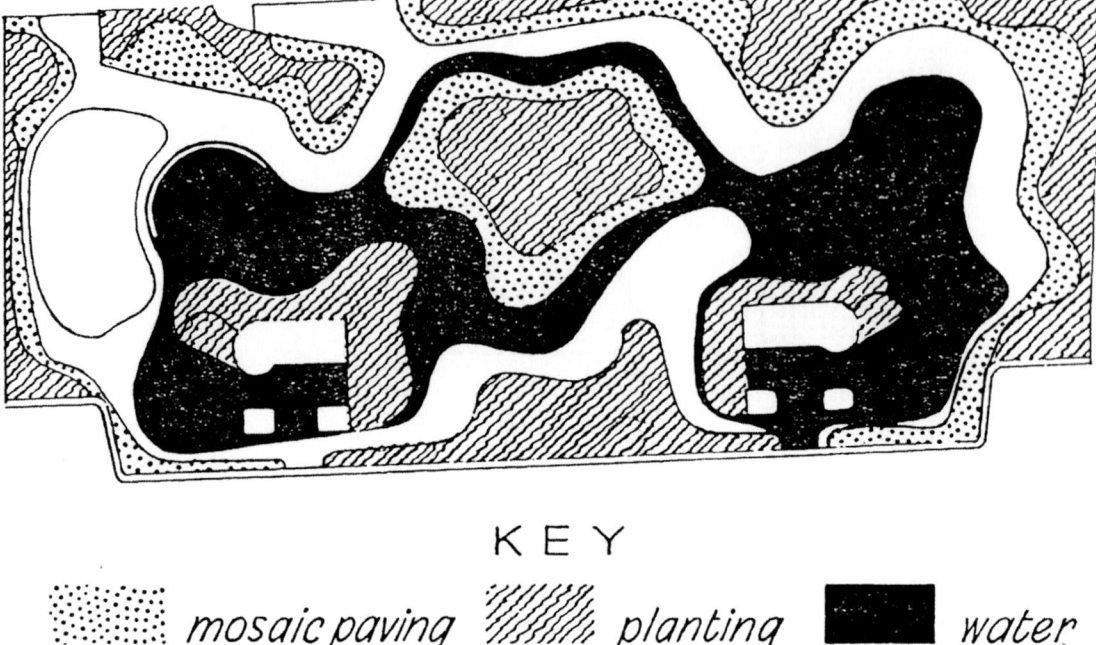

Figure 3.8 Crowe's rendering of Burle Marx's garden in São Paulo; she pointed out the abstract shapes of modern painting, and linked such exuberant design to the distinctive land and climate of Brazil. In Crowe Garden Design 1958, Fig. 13.

Garden Design drew in other current ideas from Pevsner and Jellicoe, such as proportion, order and the sisterhood of the arts. Crowe's historical analysis picked out 'certain principles [which] remain constant however much their application may change'. The most important of these was 'unity' of intention and expression, in other words consistent style. Unity might have been imposed by climate or soil, or could be created by attention to the dominance of the house, axes, flowing landform, congruity in planting, congruity of form, or themes such as water and colour.

It was perhaps in Brazil that the modern garden had recently crystallised into the most definite style. 'Here it is evident that, although it is the offspring of history, a new expression has evolved from the fusing of the old traditions with the spirit of the age in a distinctive land and climate.' Roberto Burle Marx's abstract forms in massed colour and texture are 'in keeping with the size and brilliance of the Brazilian scene' (fig. 3.8). Crowe warned that 'the danger of their influence lies in imitations':

> Blind copying of another garden never succeeds because gardens are made in response to a unique set of circumstances: the stress and aspiration of an age, set against the climate and the landscape of the country.[28]

64 *Natural instincts*

The ethics of the land

If the land or the countryside was so essential to the human being, the obvious deduction was that it was in the human's interests to care for it. Stapledon made the case that 'farming ... is a mode of life ... with its own very definite ethical standards'. Acquaintances of his would carry out land improvement, such as the clearance of bracken, even when knowing that by the rules of economics it was not worthwhile:

> There is more to the land and farming than the extraneous advantages to be gained from a substantial balance at the bank. The land itself in its kindly responsiveness to patient and careful nursing holds rewards and treasures that cannot be purchased with gold ...[29]

Happiness, he assured his readers, was granted to the rural worker 'who in his very marrow feels he owes a duty to the land'.

The concept of nature-conservation value was relatively recent, and that of ecological value was even more so. During the early twentieth century a variety of analogies, such as the 'organism', had been tried in attempts to explain plant and animal communities. The British botanist and ecologist, Arthur George Tansley, saw the philosophical errors in developing what was only a useful metaphor into a supposition that communities actually were organisms, and blamed holistic thinking. He therefore proposed the term 'ecosystem', contracted from 'ecological system', in 1935 in order to concentrate the mind on scientifically-justifiable ecological theory. At that time it was influenced by systems theory, which explains why 'equilibrium' was so valued.[30]

Ironically, though, holistic ideas were so very attractive to the philosophically incautious that Tansley's word became the by-word for the holistic concepts that he had energetically warned against. This was chiefly because of its use by two holists, in Eugene and Howard Odum, in their textbook, *The Fundamentals of Ecology* (1953). In it they argued for management of ecosystems: 'The principle of the ecosystem is the basic and most important principle underlying conservation.'[31] The supposedly scientific basis for policies on nature conservation have seldom been questioned since.

Ecological value did not, in itself, give a working principle for human ecologists, but for them the ideal interaction between humans and their environment would be one of harmonious balance. Bews had believed that 'for a healthy life the environmental interactions with the organism must run smoothly'. Living in 'harmony' resulted in happiness and beauty, but 'maladjustment' brought unhappiness and ugliness.[32] Dewey, though concerned with aesthetics rather than ethics, wrote that; 'the live being recurrently loses and re-establishes equilibrium with his surroundings. The moment of passage from disturbance into harmony is that of intensest life.'[33]

In Connecticut, Aldo Leopold, proposed a 'land ethic' with, as might be expected from an employee of the US Forest Service, a forest-resource bias. His test of the health of the land concerned the whole living community from plants through animals and birds to humans. He wrote in *The Sand County Almanac* (1949) that land was not a 'commodity belonging to man, but a community to which we belong'. His 'land ethic' thus:

> ... changes the role of Homo sapiens from conqueror of the land-community to plain member and citizen of it. It implies respect for his fellow-members, and also respect for the community as such.

Hence 'a thing is right when it tends to preserve the integrity, stability and beauty of the biotic community'.[34]

Colvin too was committed to an ethical view of 'equilibrium' between humans and their environment. This meant that, if humans exploit the land, they also should have a sense of responsibility towards it. Colvin's phrase to express the idea was 'biological balance', the state of grace when humans have settled into a stable working relationship with the land. As a human ecologist she believed in the 'mystical sense of life's unity with Nature' which, she was convinced, had inspired the gardens of the Far East.

Technical progress, when mishandled, could create an imbalance that could create sterile conditions for humans. Perhaps with the Villa Savoye in Poissy in mind (fig. 3.9), she even criticised Le Corbusier's designs – a brave thing to do in those days – for being:

> ... a very mechanical affair, making no provision for man-as-part-of-nature, but only for man-as-master-of-his-fate. Such a conception is incomplete and immature ... It is not enough to select pre-existing sites and dump something completely alien into them – the building and its surroundings must fit together, must be part of a whole.[35]

The creation of slums and distressed areas was even more of an outrage against nature – the result of allowing false values to over-rule natural laws on a large scale – and the landscape it brought was 'a measure of its social and ecological results'. The corollary was that 'if the social structure of the human community is out of gear, the biological balance, and with it the landscape, does suffer in time'.

Working from the same ecological standpoint as her ethics, Colvin argued that the perception of beauty is the visual confirmation of biological balance:

Figure 3.9 *Villa Savoye, Poissy, by Le Corbusier; Brenda Colvin criticised this for symbolising the 'man-as-master-of-his-fate' mentality, rather than 'man-as-part-of-nature'.*

... landscape is an expression of the underlying relationship of land and life: its beauty has therefore a deep potential significance over and above the pleasure the eye may take in that which is seen.[36]

One could be quite sure that:

... when landscape beauty is destroyed ... we may feel sure that other evil results are in the offing. It is a warning appealing directly to our senses and instincts, often before it becomes evident to the intellect, that all is not well – a sign of 'imbalance'.

She argued that mankind depended on 'biological balance' and so needed beauty for 'inborn', 'instinctive' or 'psychological' reasons. Spiritual well-being depended on it: 'the full development of intellectual or spiritual life, no less than mere existence, requires contact with nature and natural beauty.' Hence she quoted on her title page a passage from G.M. Trevelyan's *History of England* that 'without vision the people perish, and without the sight of the beauty of nature the spiritual power of the British people will be atrophied'.

The most important implication for the landscape architect was that:

... correct biological balance in the widest sense, comprising the whole life-cycle, through soil, plants, animals and man, must be applied to the whole land if it is to remain beautiful ... The most satisfying examples of

The ethics of the land **67**

Figure 3.10 *Colvin said that the blurring of town and country produced a 'complete debasement of landscape', and cited Peacehaven, in Sussex, where part of the South Downs had been sold off randomly, lot by lot, as shown in this aerial photograph of about 1928.*

modern architecture are those that do not ignore human dependence on natural beauty, but which provide for as close and constant a relationship as possible between natural and man-made forms. Some of the Swedish buildings of recent years show a strong sense of such a unity.[37]

Colvin divided the existing landscape into 'three main types – "wild", agricultural and urban – and each type could be subdivided'. Geographically, these main types were not in neat zones, but made an interlacing pattern. Nevertheless 'we like the character of each to be strongly marked'. The character of the British landscape derived from the 'highly evolved maturity' of its agricultural use.[38] 'The general blurring of outline and loss of individuality that result when a town spreads indeterminately over open country ... amounts to complete debasement of landscape' (fig. 3.10). If the main types were to remain distinct and undiluted, 'there is need for very broad-scale planning, embracing the whole country'.

New landscapes

A highly mechanised agricultural revolution was taking place in the Britain of the 1960s and 1970s, leading to the loss of many areas of the older English countryside of small fields, copses and winding lanes. The Countryside Commission was convinced that it should adopt the more optimistic view that beauties would result from the redesigned landscape, and launched its 'New Agricultural Landscapes' initiative.[39] Sweeps of corn were envisaged on the good agricultural land, with woodland on the steep and less productive slope behind, the overall form of the landscape responding to the inherent qualities of soil and topography (fig. 3.11). Such a landscape, with formal qualities representing rational land use, would automatically be beautiful.

These thoughts derived from Colvin, Crowe and Nan Fairbrother. To Colvin, a land ethic was not inimical to its exploitation – far from it – and though she did not think of herself as a 'functionalist', her views on countryside planning were mostly compatible with, for example, Eden's.

Figure 3.11 *Fitness for purpose in a new agricultural landscape with natural vegetation on the marginal land; the wooded chalk scarp is now the Sundon Hills Country Park in Bedfordshire. In Fairbrother, p.334.*

Her remark that 'certain pylons in certain positions, when viewed objectively and judged by the eye alone, are beautiful', showed the influence of the functionalists upon her aesthetic sensibilities. 'Good use of the land is found to be essential to fine landscape,' she claimed, and conversely 'when ugliness is examined and analysed it turns out to be the result, in the main, of waste space and waste material'.[40]

In her book, *Land and Landscape* (1948), she rehearsed the point that the countryside had evolved according to the needs of each age. She noted that:

> ... landscape is always changing, and at certain stages it undergoes periods of rapid and drastic change. Several such major changes have affected it in the past and another may be about to change it in the near future, and it is as well for all those who are interested in landscape ... to face the fact and understand the causes at work.

The pace of changes to be brought about by a mechanised drive for self-sufficiency in agriculture would be greater than in the unconscious evolution of the past, and could either be disastrous to the landscape, or it could create new beauties.

Thus 'we have reached a stage where the control and conscious design of the landscape has become definitely a human responsibility'. Good control and design would create a fitness for purpose. Just as the first conscious attempts at landscape design were to combine uses such as tilting, archery and bowling harmoniously, so in modern landscapes 'it is this integration of various uses or types of use which elicits landscape-planning'. Differences of use, climate and soil would then automatically create distinctive and attractive new landscapes.[41]

Colvin's friend, Sylvia Crowe, expanded on functionalism applied to landscape planning in her book, *Tomorrow's Landscape* (1956). Here were to be found remarks such as 'we must recreate the landscape', 'man must hasten the evolution of the landscape', 'a new beauty from man's industrial needs',[42] and 'beauty must be created through the fulfilment of the consciously felt needs'. Crowe was thus more extreme in her faith in the working landscape: 'If there were no other consideration than the highest standard of silviculture and agriculture, this in itself would produce a pleasant landscape.' One loose end in this theory of beauty was how to explain why the most generally admired scenery is mountainous. This was the least useful landscape to humans, and where beauty clearly could not have derived from use. Crowe's response was the 'antidote theory', rather as Stapledon stated it, that the town-dweller's liking for mountains is a natural reaction to an over-organised style of urban living.[43]

The British general election of 1964 brought in a government sympathetic to bold and innovative planning. With great increases in population and economic prosperity forecast, the time seemed right for massive reorganisation after the post-war anticlimax. The New Towns programme picked up with huge new cities being designated, Milton Keynes being the most famous. The Planning Advisory Group, set up in 1964, accepted ideas originating in America on an 'aims'-orientated approach to planning by contrast to the old-fashioned 'problems approach'. The aspirations of society thereby became the overriding consideration, and planning was the vehicle through which to achieve them. In the Town and Country Planning Act of 1968 a new system of development planning was initiated through which aims were to be translated into strategic objectives set out in Structure Plans prepared by County Councils, and then into site-specific policies of Local Plans prepared by the District Councils.

Nan Fairbrother responded with her ideas for a functional landscape. Her much-acclaimed *New Lives, New Landscapes* (1970) was Colvin's and Crowe's message crafted intelligently and wittily by a skilled wordsmith. Fairbrother's purpose was to show that 'the new landscapes for our new lives must now be consciously achieved by positive and clear-sighted adaptation of the habitat to our new industrial condition'.[44] She set out to fire up planners with a vision of reshaping of the landscape, and to shed their hitherto mainly restrictive attitudes.

Fairbrother could quote the White Paper which preceded the new Act in her book: 'What matters is whether the physical environment as a whole is being properly shaped to meet evolving social and economic needs.' This mention of 'evolving needs' was fortuitous. 'The old farming landscape evolved,' she noted. 'The rural countryside developed by a long process of trial and error to suit the slowly-developing business of agriculture.' Like Colvin, Fairbrother was at pains to explain that the forms of the landscape derive from a rational combination of the function and the materials of landscape: 'The beauty of the old landscape is due to three things – the beauty of the raw materials of land and plants; the effects of our mercurial climate; and our particular British gift for compromise, which adapted rather than subdued the natural habitat.' The result is that, 'To many of us in Britain our countryside is the most beautiful landscape in the world'.[45]

Fairbrother for the most part bravely affected an unsentimental attitude to the old, as shown by several comments: 'the true tragedy is not that the old must go but that the new should be bad'; 'though preservation is an understandable attitude it is seldom a workable

Figure 3.12 *Nan Fairbrother thought that a grain silo was as 'at home in the landscape as the church it resembles', seeing form rather than meaning; she would have likened the Charnes estate yard in Staffordshire to a chapel.*

policy'; 'the rising flood cannot be controlled by resistance'; and 'a negative policy of not disturbing the old cannot therefore for long succeed'. Intervention by planners was required to re-establish harmoniousness by a conscious act of will: 'We must disturb it to survive – on a vast scale and everywhere.' Indeed, 'The whole structure of our landscape now needs reshaping from first principles, for the fossilised setting of an agricultural society cannot be made to accommodate our new land-uses by muddled and piecemeal adaptation of the obsolete, however beautiful.'[46] (fig. 3.12)

The best vehicle for this intervention, thought Fairbrother, was creative land-use planning (fig. 3.13). Hence 'the proposals in this book have been an attempt to translate accepted land-use policy into appropriate landscape by simple general principles.' She was flattering to planners, and put her proposals in terms they could understand. On the theme that regional variety should be an objective, for example, she proposed 'three maps – of man-made environments, of natural habitat, and of potential vegetation'. Combining them would show that the appropriate landscape for each region was unique.[47]

Being bravely unsentimental was not the whole answer, though. The problem for such a stance was the enormous destructive power of technology noted by Leopold, Colvin and indeed by Fairbrother

72 *Natural instincts*

Figure 3.13 *The urban edge problem solved rationally and creatively: 'Green-urban farming successfully insulated from new housing by a main road and belts of trees' on Easterly Road, Leeds In Fairbrother p. 222.*

herself: 'we are energetically interfering with Nature's arrangements all over the world.' While 'It is possible that given enough time good industrial landscape would also evolve of itself to suit our new land-uses ... there is no longer enough time'. 'Our landscapes no longer evolve but are crudely manufactured by destruction of the old.'[48]

Fairbrother thereby allowed doubts about unrestrained functionalism to creep into her argument, and was open to the idea of it being modified by environmental ethics. She was clearly impressed by Julian Huxley's axiom that 'proper land-use planning is applied human ecology'.[49] To Fairbrother this new science seemed to offer a scientific route to the most important of questions – the human's proper relationship to nature: 'even though present knowledge of human ecology is primitive and sketchy, in theory at least we are now moving towards this all-embracing concept of the relationship between man and habitat.' Huxley's case for the controlled evolution of the environment also carried the germ of the new ethics of habitat: 'if we are to survive as a species it can only be by replacing nature's controls by our own, not only birth control but control of our use of the whole environment.'[50]

New landscapes **73**

Self-ordering complexity

In a somewhat metaphysical work, called *The Fitness of the Environment* (1913), an American biochemist, Lawrence Joseph Henderson, had the idea that 'the whole evolutionary process, both cosmic and organic, is one, and the biologist may now rightly regard the universe in its very essence as biocentric'.[51] He even suggested that the non-organic processes taking place in the atmosphere and the seas qualified the Earth itself to be, in a sense, 'organic'. To him, the Darwinian theory of the evolution of animals and humans to fit the environment was only half the story; he felt that the environment was itself the fittest of all possible worlds in which evolution could take place. This was argued in terms of the Earth's fortuitous chemical balance and the ideal conditions for the processes of life such as photochemical fixation of nitrogen and photosynthesis. In other words, no other environment could possibly possess the same number of characteristics fitted for life, and thus displayed 'fitness' for evolution, just as much as the products of evolution showed a 'fitness' to the environment (fig. 3.14).[52]

Henderson was cited by Bews and again by Ian McHarg, a Scottish landscape planner turned American professor, who observed that:

> ... when we see the atmosphere and hydrosphere as evolutionary, exhibiting the characteristics of organisms, responsive, having self-regulating mechanisms, our conception of the biosphere must expand to include not only the film of living creatures on the earth, but the atmosphere above the extensive oceans as well.

McHarg bandied the term 'negentropy', the opposite of entropy, which is the state of energy exhausted. 'In contrast, idealised negentropy would exhibit high order, complexity, diversity, uniqueness, and ability to perform work.' This offered him 'a means of both diagnosis and prescription'. We could 'conclude on the state of any system on an evolutionary scale and, moreover, could decide whether it was evolving or retrogressing'. The ethical implications were obvious: 'We have formulated a rudimentary value system, and we are further on the path to the formulation of a workman's code, the view of the good steward.'[53]

An appreciation of the Earth as a complex system was similarly provided by the 'Gaia hypothesis'. This was promulgated in the 1960s by James Lovelock, a British chemist who was at the time working for NASA on the possibility of life on Mars. He called it after Gaia as she was the goddess who was among the first to spring from Chaos, and who became the personification of the Earth.[54] The hypothesis was that the Earth

Figure 3.14 *Evolution from a primitive state to an advanced one: hostile environments like the summits of mountains and the oceanic depths do not advance beyond primitive and simple organisms; elsewhere there is greater complexity and diversity. In McHarg, p.122.*

had developed to be a complex, self-regulating, self-repairing organism capable of keeping its life-giving physical and biological processes in balance. Gaia's work provided the environment that protected and nurtured the human race. No longer was nature a machine, contrasted to man, but self-transforming and creative with the human race a high-level consequence.

Yet self-centred and imprudent people who would ignore or thwart Gaia were seen everywhere. Lovelock thought that the environmentally aware must seek to redress the balance: 'to see the Earth as a living organism makes tangible the concept of stewardship and focuses our hearts and minds on what should be our prime concern; the care and protection of the Earth itself and especially of the forests of the humid tropics.' Whilst Lovelock intended his allegory as a means to express a strictly scientific phenomenon, it inevitably became lodged among some environmentalists' metaphysical baggage. Jonathan Porritt wrote that: 'The heroic element of Jim Lovelock's Gaia hypothesis lies precisely in its potential for bringing together science and religion ... couldn't the Green movement be a small part of Gaia's response to the destructiveness of the human species?'[55]

Self-ordering complexity

Stewarding the biosphere

In 1969, McHarg summed up his philosophy honed by years of discussion with colleagues and students at the University of Pennsylvania. Perhaps the factor that made his book, *Design with Nature*, so popular with a generation of students was that its author was no lone writer appealing to a tiny professional sub-group. Instead the book grew out of the popular environmental concerns of the 1960s, and was immediately perceived to be in tune with ideas of return-to-nature, flower power, small is beautiful and so forth, that were so popular on American university campuses at the time.

McHarg's view of the rivers, oceans, forests and animal life of the world was as 'co-tenants of the phenomenal universe, participating in that timeless yearning that is evolution, vivid expression of time past, essential partners in survival and with us now involved in the creation of the future'. His aim was 'a working method by which the least of us can ensure that the product of his works is not more despoilation', and for man to do this, and act responsibly, 'we require only a deference born of understanding to fulfil man's promise ... He must become the steward of the biosphere. To do this he must design with nature'.

His book contained much standard landscape-planning practice, though expressed with stylish, but eventually irritating, verbosity. Where McHarg made actual advances on Colvin's exposition of human ecology was in tackling the question of how, in practice, ecological criteria could be inserted into the decision-making processes of land-use planning. Furthermore he had several student projects and real-life case studies by his planning practice with which to illustrate his points.

Some land-use decisions did not primarily hang on cost (fig. 3.15). By understanding the processes of nature herself, one could, for example, have selected the optimal location for housing development within a coastal dune-system which did not involve trampling down dune grasses, lowering groundwater, interrupting littoral drift or destroying the richest wildlife areas. McHarg stressed the benefits of respecting nature by relating the story of catastrophic damage from storms along the New Jersey coastline in 1962. The losses were greatly compounded by greedy speculators having interrupted the processes by which dunes build themselves up.

He argued that actions should be assessed in the light of their impact on the totality of 'the biophysical world', and that 'natural processes can be construed as values in such a way as to permit a rational response to a social value system'. Incidentally, the concept of ecology as a process

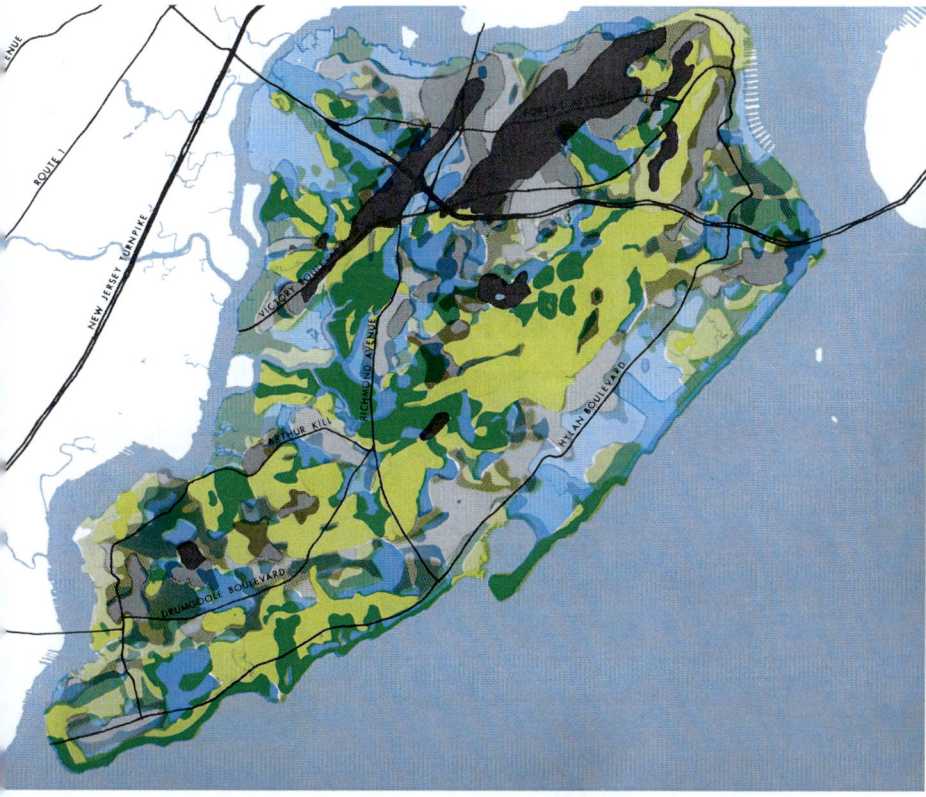

Figure 3.15 *Better landuse planning through understandng natural and social systems; conservation and recreation potentials on Staten Island; colours indicate suitability for various land uses. In McHarg, p.114.*

was one he returned to frequently. It was as if he visualised humanity hitching a ride on the self-renewing cycles of nature, and that unless it understood this in devising its own processes it could foul up the very cycles to which it should be attuned.

Like Leopold, McHarg was scathing about the approach to land-use allocation by land speculators, highway planners and economists. These 'merchant's minions' were lambasted for their limited conception of economics. The cost-benefit analyses of McHarg's day looked like financial balance sheets, but to him any sensible cost-benefit analysis should include the financially unquantifiable and intangible. He was outraged by the developers':

> ... most barefaced effrontery that we accommodate our value system to theirs. Neither love nor compassion, health nor beauty, dignity nor freedom, grace nor delight are important unless they can be priced. If there are non-price benefits and costs they are relegated to inconsequence.

This was a point well taken in the 1980s, but when he argued it in the 1960s he faced a largely uncomprehending planning community.

Stewarding the biosphere

Other ways of inserting environmental criteria into the planning process were sought. Hence his interest in 'sieve maps', which would help define lines of least resistance to, say, a new highway (fig. 3.16). These maps would depend on the ranking of such factors as wildlife, scenic quality, historic buildings and recreational value. Of course there was no way of giving an objective weight to each of these factors, but the hope was that some areas could be found which had no significant value of any sort, thus giving the 'minimum social cost alignment'.[56] It is perhaps no coincidence that the quasi-science of 'landscape evaluation' (see Chapter 2) was emerging at this date as a response to the desire for objective criteria for use in land-use planning.

Figure 3.16 *Sieve-map layers: several constraints being overlain to give the path of minimum damage. See McHarg, pp.38-39.*

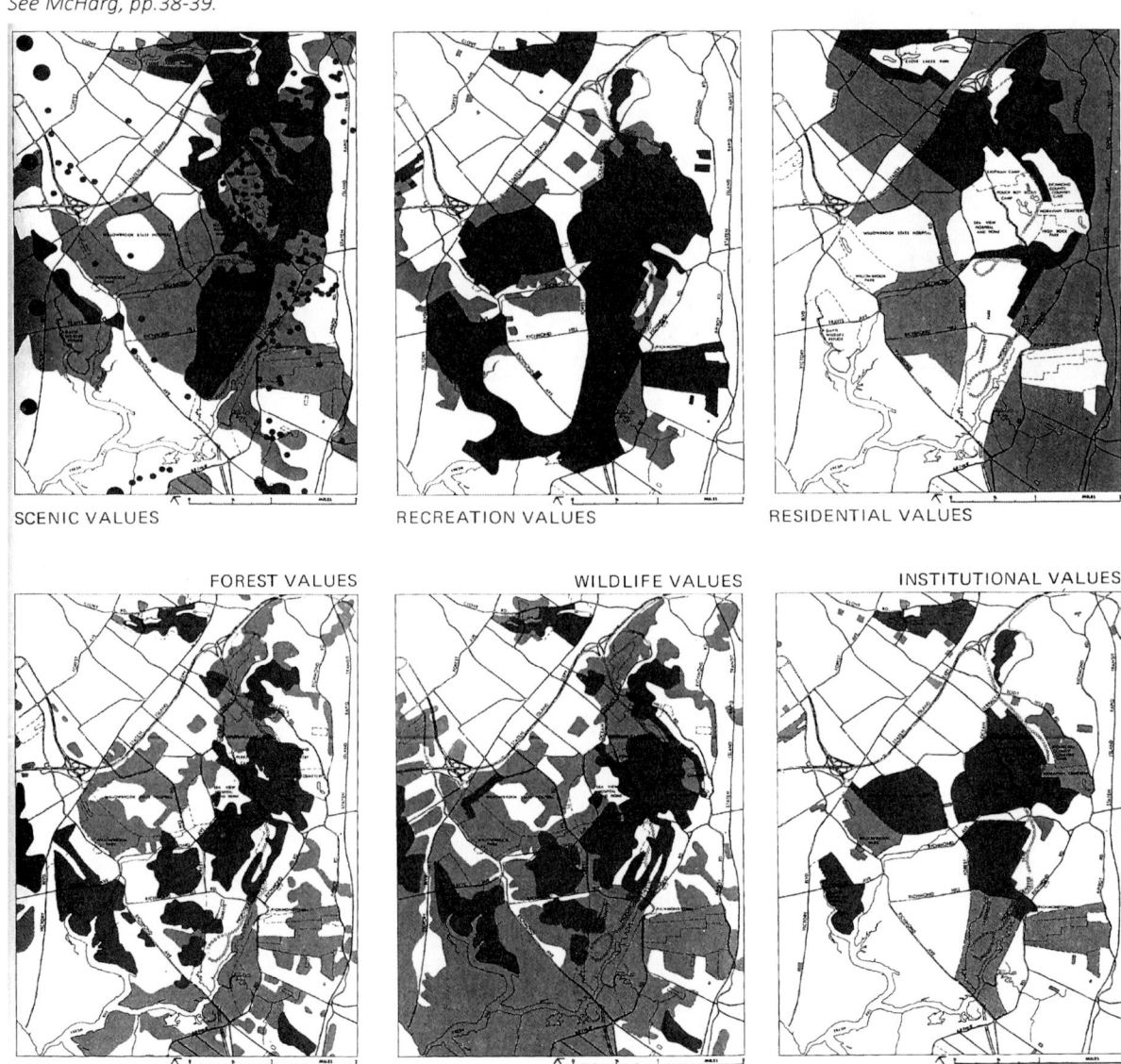

78 *Natural instincts*

Prospect, refuge and hazard symbolism

The idea that aesthetic sensibilities were inheritable rather than acquired might be seen as plausible in the light of Jung's collective unconscious and the conception of human ecology held by Stapledon, Colvin and Leopold. Rachel and Stephen Kaplan, during the infancy of 'environmental psychology' in America, undertook many studies for the US Forest Service, and found themselves seeking up-to-date answers to the old question: 'What kind of environments do people prefer?' They hypothesised that humans seek to make sense of, and be involved in, their landscapes, and had pre-programmed, evolved methods of processing information which promoted survival. After all, poor preferences for landscapes could prove terminal. Landscape preferences derived from satisfactory perceptions of their biological advantages:

> ... preference – even aesthetics for that matter – is closely tied to basic concerns ... preferred environments will in general be ones in which human abilities are more likely to be effective and needs are more likely to be met.

Some tentative thoughts on the qualities promoting preferred environments identified diversity, coherence, mystery and legibility.[57]

About the same time, Jay Appleton, a British geographer with a passion for aesthetics, and looking for predecessors, found two of particular note. One was Brenda Colvin, whose 1970 edition of *Land and Landscape* he described as 'an admirable introduction to the approach of the modern landscape architect'. She, it will be remembered, thought that beauty derives from the unconscious recognition of harmony between humans and nature. 'I doubt,' wrote Appleton, 'whether there is a single page in the book which does not furnish some example of landscape design consistent with the theories which are here considered in this book.'[58]

The other much-quoted predecessor was John Dewey who Appleton thought supported the view that the human-being had inherited genetically-programmed responses fundamental to human nature. Actually, the central plank of Dewey's theories on art set out in *Art as Experience* (1934) was the role of experience, which he saw as the cumulative process of interacting with the world, in making personal aesthetic judgements (see Chapters 4 and 7), rather than any insights into evolutionary history. Nevertheless, there were several passages of interest to Appleton. He reminded his readers of this one:

> Having the same vital needs, man derives the means by which he breathes, moves, looks and listens, the very brain with which he co-ordinates his senses and his movements, from his animal forebears. The organs with which he maintains himself in being are not of himself alone, but by the grace of struggles and achievements of a long line of animal ancestry.[59]

Appleton commented that: 'Dewey, from a post-Darwinian viewpoint, was able to see a far more fundamental relationship between man and his surroundings.' He then expressed regret that Dewey did not develop the point into a theory of landscape preferences:

> ... we are still waiting for someone to work out in detail the connection between 'experience' as understood in Dewey's aesthetics and 'landscape' as understood by geographers, painters, landscape architects and the man with the rucksack.

Nevertheless, 'at this point in the twentieth century Dewey's philosophy commends itself as the most promising starting point for any further enquiry into the aesthetics of landscape', thought Appleton.[60] He drew attention to various passages in Dewey that implied that patterns of behaviour are inherited from our forebears, for example:

> ... there are stirred into activity resonances of dispositions acquired in primitive relationships of the living being to its surroundings, and irrecoverable in distinct or intellectual consciousness.[61]

Much space was devoted to the behaviour of animals that serve their needs, and in showing that humans are not so different. Appleton then asked:

> Is it reasonable to believe that we have inherited all these inborn desires but that, for some reason, the spontaneous awareness of the perceived environment, which is such a conspicuous feature of all the higher animals, has 'dropped out'?

His answer was of course 'no', in which case what had become of these inborn desires? And how could awareness of the environment become an aesthetic activity? Appleton supported the idea that pleasures arise when the environment seems to be conducive to meeting biological needs.

'The point at which we always seem to run up against a brick wall,' lamented Appleton, 'is in understanding more precisely how the actual ingredients of landscape operate on the aesthetic sense.' Rather than look for a logical explanation he summoned up the powers of the unconscious and its language of symbolism:

> What matters is not the actual potential ... but its apparent potential as apprehended immediately rather than considered rationally. In a sense we see the objects which comprise our environment as symbols suggesting by association properties which are not necessarily inherent in the objects themselves.

This led to the proposition that landscape components act symbolically in suggesting the favourability of a particular place, 'whether they really are favourable or not'. This he called his 'habitat theory'.

Appleton still needed to explain how the gratification of biological needs led to a sense of beauty. His view that the mechanisms must be unconscious once again provided scope for a speculative way forward. Humans, through having developed knowledge, reasoning, and the power of association, and being no longer at the mercy of their environment, had lost their spontaneous awareness of a landscape's value for survival. However, 'the mechanisms do not immediately die out in the species but continue to be transmitted from one generation to another'.[62] 'The removal of urgent necessity does not put an end to the machinery which evolved to cope with it; rather it frees that machinery to achieve different objectives which themselves are constantly changing with the aspirations and caprices of society.' He gave a parallel of how release from self-preservation sublimates the gratification of biological needs into an aesthetic experience: 'The partners who practice contraception do not say that ... there is no point in attempting sexual intercourse. They say rather that contraception enables them to gratify their inborn inclinations in isolation from any ulterior functional process.'[63]

The basic activities that a human or animal would find important to survival of course include ingestive behaviour, that is, eating and drinking; seeking shelter; sexual behaviour; and investigatory or exploratory behaviour. All could theoretically give clues to how to develop the 'habitat theory', and indeed Appleton did mention some outrageous theories about how certain landscape features might symbolise sexual organs. However, none of these activities individually gave a good enough explanation of aesthetic behaviour. A passage by the animal behaviourist, Konrad Lorenz, about human behaviour in a forest – 'we do what all wild animals ... do: we reconnoitre, seeking, before we leave cover, to gain from it the advantage which it can offer alike to hunter and hunted, namely to see without being seen' – suggested to Appleton the significance of hunting, and its corollary, escape behaviour (fig. 3.17). This thought was to provide Appleton with the inspiration for a 'prospect-refuge theory', which postulates that:

Prospect, refuge and hazard symbolism

Figure 3.17 *Man the hunter; the stage of human evolution when Appleton thought that a 'prospect-refuge' appreciation of the landscape developed: illustration by Bernard Long c.1980.*

… because the ability to see without being seen is an intermediate step in the satisfaction of many (biological) needs, the capacity of an environment to ensure the achievement of this becomes a more immediate source of aesthetic satisfaction.[64]

A substantial proportion of *The Experience of Landscape* was devoted to the language of prospect-refuge symbolism (fig. 3.18). Prospect symbolism sought to explain the place of panoramas and peepholes, and would be modified by the type of vantage point (fig. 3.19). Refuge symbolism was found in hides, shelters, caves, trees and long grass. However, prospect and refuge symbolism favours savannah, totally unlike the mountainous scenery with lakes that Appleton knew is actually most prized aesthetically. A modification was required; perhaps dangers experienced during hunting could be expressed symbolically too? In which case, 'prospect and refuge symbolism also demand a hazard symbolism to make them work'.[65] 'Hazard' symbolism included suggestions of risk from animals, precipices, the weather, and other potential dangers: also impediments and deficiencies of various sorts.

Figure 3.18 *The apotheosis of prospect symbolism in painting, according to Jay Appleton; 'Mount Lefroy' (1930) by Lawren Harris, one of the Group of Seven, used on the cover of* The Symbolism of Habitat *(1990).*

Appleton had some general precepts to offer on the question of taste in gardens. Garden style should be investigated in terms of underlying symbolism, not outward forms. The development of fashionable taste could be expected when people had had different experiences and inclinations to respond in different ways. Hence, 'taste is an acquired preference for particular methods of satisfying inborn desires'. The avenues of André le Nôtre and the parks of Capability Brown, for example, though outwardly very different, were merely two local idioms to express prospect symbolism (fig. 3.20).[66] In contemporary landscape design, 'we should again find distinctive idioms rather than new principles'. As with Colvin and Crowe, then, with their principles from climate and soil, Appleton believed in a biological imperative that should set the parameters for fluctuating yet merely fashionable design.

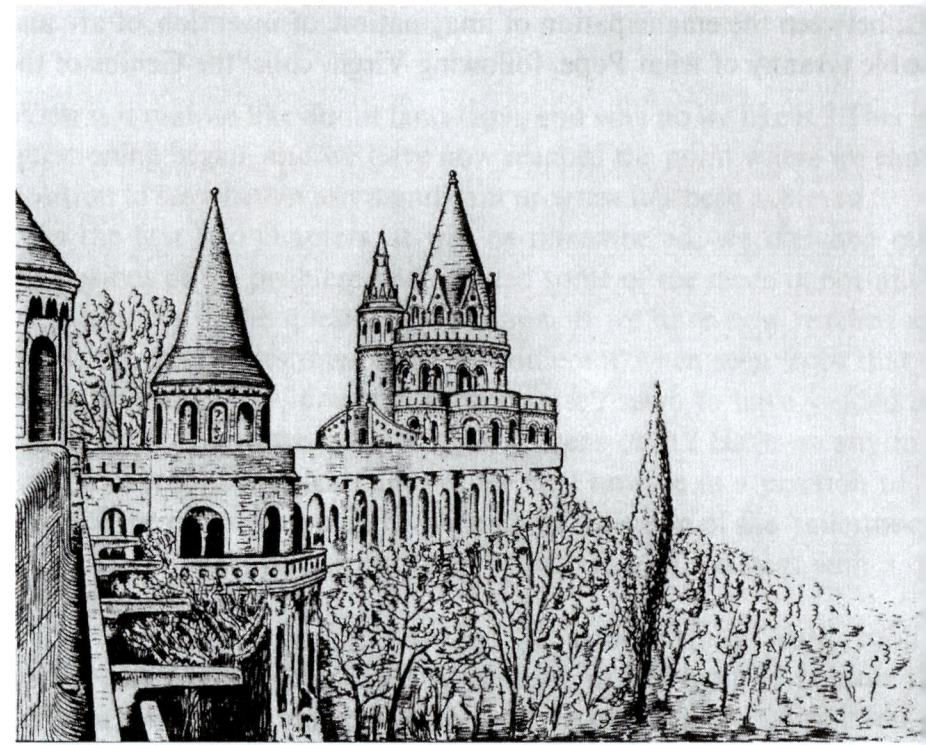

Figure 3.19 *Dual symbolism of prospect and refuge: the 'Fisherman's terrace' at Buda Castle, Budapest, drawing by Keith Scurr from a photograph by Jay Appleton, in* The Experience of Landscape, *fig. 49.*

Figure 3.20 *Paintings like 'River landscape with Apollo and the Cumaean Sibyl' (c.1665) by Salvator Rosa were thought to be steeped in prospect-refuge symbolism by Jay Appleton who reproduced it in* The Experience of Landscape (1975), *fig. 32.*

NOTES AND REFERENCES

1   This way of thinking has been called 'environmental determinism', and was highly regarded a century ago, and seen in the writings of Cyril Joad, Brenda Colvin and Sylvia Crowe, but fell out of grace because of its misuse in the interpretation of racial differences.

2   Ellen H. Richards, *Sanitation in Daily Life* (Boston, 1907), p. v.

3   Ellen Churchill Semple, *Influences on Geographic Environment* (New York, 1911), p. 1.

4   Ibid., p. 174.

5   Jan Christiaan Smuts, *Holism and Evolution* (London, 1926). An earlier version of oneness was the 'Monism' promulgated by Ernst Haekel, the scientist who had coined the term oekologie in the 1860s.

6   Smuts was Prime Minster of South Africa twice, and prominent in the founding of both the League of Nations and the United Nations after two world wars, during both of which he served as a general (later field marshal) in the British forces. The troubled politics and racial divisions in which he was embroiled back in South Africa unfortunately often occlude assessments of his intellectual achievements.

7   John William Bews, *Human Ecology* (Oxford, 1935), p. x.

8   Ibid., pp. 14, 16, 50 & 52.

9   Brenda Colvin, *Land and Landscape* (London, 1948), p. 1, quoting from Bews, op. cit., p. 1.

10 The American Humanist Association, *A Humanist Manifesto* (Salt Lake City, 1933).

11 John Dewey, *Art as Experience* (New York, 1934), pp. 12 & 229.

12 Brian S. Osborne, 'The Iconography of Nationhood in Canadian Art', in Denis Cosgrove & Stephen Daniels (eds), *The Iconography of Landscape: Essays on the Symbolic Representation, Design and Use of Past Environments* (Cambridge, 1988), p. 169.

13 Jens Jensen, *Siftings* (Chicago, 1939; new ed., Baltimore, 160), pp. 24-6.

14 Reginald George Stapledon, *The Land Now and To-morrow* (London, 1935), pp. 3, 231 & 315.

15 Ibid., pp. 2 & 6.

16 R.G. Stapledon, 'Economics and the National Park', in Clough Williams-Ellis (ed), *Britain and the Beast* (London, 1937), pp. 113-121.

17 Lord Howard of Penrith, 'Lessons from Other Countries', in Williams-Ellis, op. cit., pp. 279-297; p. 284.

18 Cyril Edwin Mitchinson Joad, 'The People's Claim', in Williams-Ellis, op. cit., pp. 64-85; pp. 64-5.

19 David L. Uzzell, 'People, Nature and Landscape: an Environmental Psychological Perspective' (a report to the Landscape Research Group) (1989), pp. 5-6, reviewed the 'empty vessel' hypothesis, including its connection to architectural determinism.

20 Joad, op. cit., p. 71.

21 Report of the Committee on *Land Utilisation in Rural Areas* (The Scott Report) (London, 1942).

22 Jensen, op. cit., pp. 42 & 63.

23 Brenda Colvin, 'Some Differences in French and English Garden Design', *Landscape and Garden* (Autumn 1937), 142.

24 Colvin (1948) op. cit., pp. 61-2, 111, 113-4 & 255.

25 Ibid., pp. 143 & 146.

26 Jensen, op. cit., p. 41.

27 Sylvia Crowe, *Garden Design* (London, 1958), pp. 24, 32 & 50.

28 Ibid., pp. 12 & 97.

29 Stapledon (1935), op. cit., p. 127.

30 Arthur G. Tansley, 'The Use and Abuse of Vegetational Concepts and Terms', *Ecology* 16 (1935), 284-307.

31 Eugene & Howard Odum, *The Principles of Ecology* (Philadelphia, 1953), p. 317.

32 Bews, op. cit., pp. 284, 289 & 300.

33 Dewey, op. cit., p. 16.

34 Aldo Leopold, *A Sand County Almanac* (New York, 1949), pp. 204 & 224.

35 Colvin (1948), op. cit., p. 61.

36 Ibid., pp. 1, 3 & 5.

37 Ibid., pp. 2 & 61.

38 Ibid., pp. 147 & 173.

39 Countryside Commission, *New Agricultural Landscapes*, CCP 76 (Cheltenham, 1974).

40 Colvin (1948), op. cit., pp. 6, 57, 82 & 148.
41 Ibid., pp. 5 & 81.
42 Sylvia Crowe, *Tomorrow's Landscape* (London, 1956), p. 12.
43 Ibid., pp. 54 & 167.
44 Ibid., p. 6.
45 Nan Fairbrother, *New Lives; New Landscapes* (London, 1970), pp. 5-8, 175.
46 Ibid., pp. 5, 7-8, 163 & 174.
47 Ibid., pp. 348 & 383.
48 Ibid, pp. 3 & 7.
49 Sir Julian Huxley, 'The Future of Man - Evolutionary Aspects', in Gordon Wolstenholme (ed), *Man and his Future* (London, 1963), p. 10.
50 Fairbrother, op. cit., p. 3.
51 Laurence J. Henderson, *The Fitness of the Environment* (New York, 1913), p. v.
52 Ibid., p. 312.
53 Ian McHarg, *Design with Nature* (Garden City NY, 1969), pp. 51 & 53.
54 James Lovelock & Sidney Epton, 'The Quest for Gaia', *New Scientist*, 65 (6 February 1975), 304.
55 *The Independent Magazine* (10 December 1988).
56 McHarg, op. cit., pp. 5, 25 & 31.
57 Stephen Kaplan & Rachel Kaplan (eds), *Humanscape: Environments for People* (North Scituate MA, 1978), pp. 53 & 147-9.
58 Jay Appleton, *The Experience of Landscape* (Chichester, 1975), p. 227.
59 Dewey, op. cit., p. 12.
60 Appleton, op. cit., pp. 50 & 58.
61 Dewey, op. cit., p. 29.
62 Appleton, op. cit., pp. 67-71.
63 Ibid., pp. 169-170.
64 Ibid., pp. 69 & 73.
65 Ibid., p. 96.
66 Ibid., pp. 226 & 237..

PART B

RE-THEORISING IN THE LATE TWENTIETH CENTURY

The foreword to this book has suggested that a significant discontinuity opened up in landscape theory in the 1970s. Part A has described the approaches up to that decade and has identified that they did share enough to be considered a unified body of thought. The task of Part B is to identify the approaches of the last quarter of the century, to see whether and how they superseded the older ones, and enquire whether they had any coherence.

The following five chapters thus chart how new realities and paradigms in the period known as 'post-modern', led to a critique of modernism and several trains of thought in initially-unrelated areas of enquiry. It is always problematic to use the inherently slippery term 'post-modernism', but especially in relation to landscape when it had so few connections to architectural post-modernism, and so this term is used sparingly.

This part commences in Chapter 4 with that new world view, concentrating upon those aspects that came to be particularly relevant to the ethics and aesthetics of landscape. Chapter 5 examines the adjustments made necessary as formerly-valued concepts had to be jettisoned in the light of the new world view, and how landscape theory was reconstructed, principally on the basis of values. It continues with a brief examination of 'ecocentrism' which was a radically different outlook developing alongside.

Chapter 6 examines more closely the question of landscape preferences, accepted as subjective and often value-driven, and starts by deconstructing the old theories that asserted that objectivity was possible. It describes how beliefs in 'objective' landscape beauty were abandoned as a new outlook on the land as the repository and evidence of past and present values emerged in the 1990s. Chapter 7 expands upon the rise of conservation philosophy, particularly for gardens, and how this led to widespread adjustment of national and international charters and guidelines. Then some interesting approaches to design inspired by the new thought are described in Chapter 8.

In summary, this part of the book demonstrates that a new set of landscape theories took shape based on a world view that no longer focused on matters outside one's self, but on the experiences and values of the inner self, and made itself manifest in landscape planning, landscape design and conservation.

CHAPTER 4

THE POST-MODERN CONDITION

It was not so certain that the modern movement would gain a foothold in the English-speaking world; the innate conservatism of the British and American establishments could have ensured that it was no more than the waking dream of the intellectual. It took the unreality of war and then reconstruction to make it seem real to the official professions of architecture and landscape architecture, certainly so far as public works and landscape were concerned.

Yet, whenever rich men and women have chosen their own gardens in Britain, the modern movement never threatened the tradition to which Gertrude Jekyll, Percy Cane and Russell Page (none of whom was in the Institute of Landscape Architects) belonged (fig. 4.1).[1] Likewise, the 'colonial' style, coupled with the image of the English landscape garden, has proved to be the dominating taste in leafier American suburbs, 'an inherent part of a society's permanent aesthetic value system', and resistant to the blandishments of modernism.[2]

The motives of the modern movement's promoters were not altogether trusted. Their belief, that through machines doing the work, humanity could enter a new era of leisure, in which the benefits of good

Figure 4.1 *The Culpepper garden at Leeds Castle, replanted by Russell Page in the 1980s, clearly rejecting the fashionable motifs of the modern movement, as did most of his work till near the end of his career.*

design could be made available to all, thus enriching both body and soul, was noble enough. Also the time seemed propitious: new materials and new technology made the dream seem almost within grasp. Yet the political and economic changes that would also be needed seemed too drastic. The modernist scenario embraced the enforced centralisation of resources, and equity in their distribution. The implications were politically offensive to many citizens, and confirmed the worst suspicions of the anti-intellectual conservative. Besides, by this time it was clear that the modernist project was not delivering on its promises.

The 'post-modern' thinking of the 1980s and 1990s reflected these doubts, but it was more than just a reactionary return to pre-modern norms: it derived from an altered mindset, one that no longer gave credence to the beliefs and assumptions of the modernists. In the field of architecture designs referred back to the classical tradition, but chiefly in order to start again in finding a basis for a new convention. In psychology, mysterious notions of the unconscious were sidelined by the new thinking on consciousness. In aesthetics, grand over-arching theories were dismantled and thinkers started 'from the ground up' by considering the point of view of the individual.

Shattered dreams

Most artists and professional designers of the modern movement had operated on the basis of two classes of knowledge. First, there were the greater mysteries which were not susceptible to rational analysis, and which had to be accepted as part of an individual's system of belief. These included concepts of God, the workings of the universe, the gift of genius, the existence of the unconscious and the cause of beauty. Second, there were lesser mysteries: all those susceptible to intellectual analysis. Once the greater truths had been properly grasped, it was assumed, the truth about the lesser mysteries should fall quite readily into place.

Other mental habits had included 'dualism' (or 'polarities', or 'binary oppositions') and 'historicism'. The former had differentiated instinct versus intelligence, inheritance versus environment, culture versus nature, mind versus body, art versus craft, and conscious versus unconscious. They were even said to have characterised the English approach to art.[3] Historicism supported a belief in inexorable social evolution to an enhanced state of civilisation. A mentality of progress ruled, onwards and upwards. Society would not only be uplifted in the process, but also become simpler, as inequalities would be erased, social classes broken down, and political consensus achieved. Hence modernist planners saw their role as controlling physical and economic development in order to ease the inevitable. They had not concerned themselves unduly with the fine-grained workings of society, and most planners and architects had proceeded on the comfortable assumption that the planning of new communities was principally a matter of space allocation and layout.

The reality of the late twentieth century turned out somewhat differently. The human race had not entered a glorious new phase in its evolution; it was still the same old species, more enlightened, healthier and richer in some places, but still struggling to register on God's scale of perfection.

In hindsight, these expectations of progress along a predicted course had been only a figment of wishful thinking. Few of the idealistic aims and assumptions to which planners worked from the 1940s to the 1960s came to fruition. The state of technology, birth rates, music and future leaders were not amongst the readily programmed aspects of society (fig. 4.2). It was salutary to recall the assumptions that the planners held even as late as the 1960s about life in the 1990s, and to how wildly in error many were. Projections of economic and population-growth figures turned out to be markedly excessive. Heavy industry was still going to be the mainstay of the economy: who had predicted accurately the catastrophic collapse of coal, iron and shipbuilding, the huge service sector, and the impact of electronics and information technology generally?

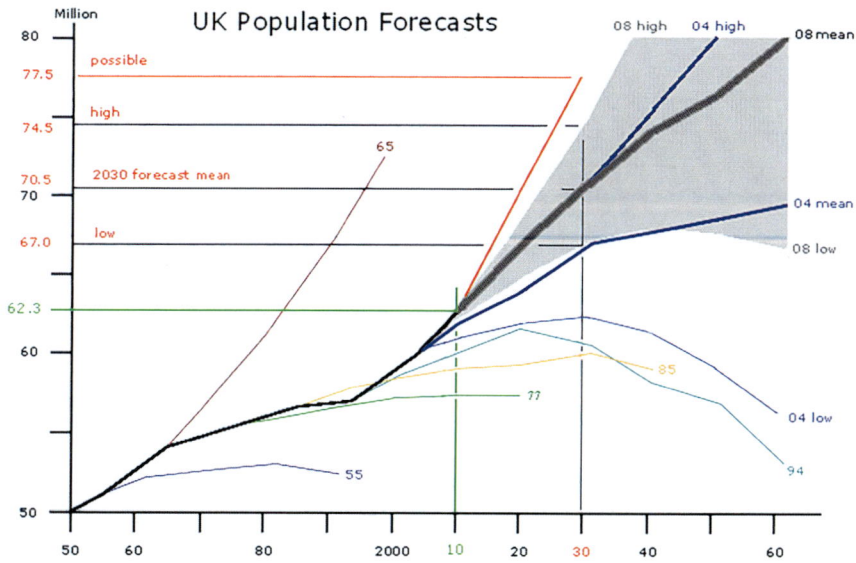

Figure 4.2 *A graph of projected population in Britain in 1955, 1965, 1977, 1985, etc.: foreseeing birth rates has never been an exact science, and those used shortly after 1965 were grossly in error.*

Shattered dreams

Figure 4.3 *The A40 Westway near to the White City in London; rational planning in the late 1960s that met with enormous public resistance and which hastened the introduction of public participation in the planning process.*

Meanwhile the consensus that had been hoped for never materialised. Instead, society remained stubbornly fragmented, resisting attempts to apply consistent standards throughout. Of course, society had proved itself not to be as orderly and controllable as had been hoped, and from the 1970s 'pluralism' – the diversity of social, cultural and political attitudes – increasingly had to be acknowledged.

Hand-in-hand with the belief in consensus had been faith in the detached expert. Utopians characteristically glory in taking bold decisions of which others repent because of unexpected side-effects. Some big mistakes were made in the 1960s, for example with urban-highway networks (fig. 4.3). Radicalised objectors to official schemes found the prescription of the expert propping up the values of modernist orthodoxy. It was remarkable how public participation was demanded after the heyday of rational comprehensive planning in the late 1960s. Maybe, as remembrance of the ideological origins of official policy faded, the experts had not even realised that there was a political basis to their judgements. Hence those who were supposed to be the avant-garde of a unified society had come to be regarded as the enemy by factions within.

The reaction against designers sometimes became extreme when they were seen as the agents of an unfeeling bureaucracy.[4] To take one minor example, Louis le Roy, posing as a man of the people, became well known during the 'silent revolution' in The Netherlands, that is in the period in the late 1960s and early 1970s when, in common with other countries, there was a reassertion of the rights of the individual and minorities in a democratic society.[5] 'Architects and planners lacked the necessary vision and had lost touch with the people for whom they planned and the land they managed,' he opined. Once people were freed from the inhibitions of a plan and its dubious aesthetic values, people could create their own park – a 'People's Park' – he thought. Le Roy had managed to polarise the situation, and was accused of rabble-rousing and anarchy by park officials who actually had good technical reasons for opposing his schemes. His supporters claimed the opposition was because he was too successful as

Figure 4.4 *The traditional use of public parks being acknowledged by restorations, for example that at Rowntree Park, York, from 1999; modernists were puzzled as to why the money was not spent on meeting 'modern needs'.*

Shattered dreams 93

Figure 4.5 *Design as one tool of environmental policy; converting disused mineral lines in Stoke-on-Trent into attractive and useful walkways and cycleways. Drawing by Richard Westmacott of Land Use Consultants in 1972.*

an advocate of people's feelings. In retrospect, the whole episode was most useful as a reminder that, if designers do not consider public wishes more overtly, they risk unnecessary conflict.

Citizens' leisure interests had not changed as anticipated either. The machine age had been going to free people to reach a new plane of existence where leisure permitted self-expression and enlightenment. It had been thought that increased leisure time would mean more of those pursuits thought to be healthy to the body, such as swimming, walking and active sports. This would necessitate, for example, the redesign of parks for lidos, football and other field games, country parks, and virtually unlimited access to the countryside.

The more exotic forms of recreation actually changed unpredictably; the 1930s dreamer would not have predicted the lions and tigers at Woburn Abbey in the late 1950s, and the dreamer then would not have foreseen eco-tourism in the Antarctic in the 1990s. Meanwhile the ordinary needs of the citizen had stayed much the same. Gardening remained the most important out-of-doors recreation in Britain, and most people who visited parks were, as ever, dog-walkers, mothers with children and children on bicycles (fig. 4.4).[6] Leisure time did not increase markedly, certainly not for those in work.

Figure 4.6 *Environmental controls seek to limit logging to sustainable forests and to curb illegal trade, such as this rosewood being extracted from a national park on Madagascar.*

Landscape designers who remembered themselves as the idealists of the 1960s were left wondering why the world had stopped applauding them. They had once felt needed as the common perception of large-scale environmental problems had moved away from, for example, London smog, which was eradicated by the Clean Air Acts, and on to questions requiring design solutions, such as the new universities and the eradication of derelict land (fig. 4.5). During the 1980s, though, environmental issues returned to the realm of taxation, regulation and public awareness (fig. 4.6), as the public began to concern themselves with the side-effects of food production, cosmetics, transport and refrigeration upon the atmosphere and other life forms.

In this process the social, economic and artistic prescriptions set by the design professions between the 1940s and the 1960s had become significantly less relevant to politicians. The social responsibility that inspired the functionalism of Pevsner, Tunnard and Eckbo had been overshadowed by the ecological imperatives insisted on by the ecologists. Designers ruefully observed that the rise of environmentalism eclipsed the landscape professions in the public consciousness, not just by being more prominent in the media, but also by elevating the significance of conservation in its broadest sense and contracting the contribution that design could make.

Shattered dreams **95**

Uncertainty and practical knowledge

The failure of so many of the modernists' planning ventures had given the lie to their faith in inevitable progress. The failure had been exacerbated partly by an unwillingness to acknowledge the complexity of the real world, or to accept a new mindset which could accommodate uncertainty.

Contrasting responses to the disappointment could be observed. On the one hand, the late 1960s had seen a rearguard action by architects to cover all eventualities. 'Flexibility' had been the rage, even ideas of plug-in towns where the only fixed element was the infrastructure. However, most uncertainty stemmed from unpredictable changes in the immaterial, so the difficulties arising were too fundamental to be solved by the clever technical wizardry of what is now termed 'late modernism'.

Uncertainty required a shift to a different mindset. First, beliefs in dualism (or polarities, or binary oppositions), genius and the unconscious, which merely served to obfuscate, deserved to be consigned to the dustbin of ideas. The science of problem-solving had become ever more sophisticated as operational researchers suggested ways to manage and cope with uncertainty.[7] Then lateral thinking encouraged more fundamental questions to be addressed; before answers were attempted, the question was looked at; and before the question was looked at, the questioner was. This process was slow, but it meant that people wanted to know themselves better, and one proverb at least approved of that.

Second, belief was often supplanted by conviction. Religions and some political doctrines demanded faith in a particular version of the world's origins and workings, but scepticism was rife. A more pragmatic approach to the truth, combined with a readiness to review one's understanding, was adopted.[8] Hence 'practical knowledge', a reliance on convictions derived from observation and reflection which enable sensible everyday assumptions, was proposed.[9]

Faith could be greatly comforting, though. Peter Fuller, the art critic, without finding it, observed that psychologically 'we need a secular equivalent of the religious illusion'.[10] He mocked those with belief, and yet envied their certitude. Faith could, though, be a great obstacle to practical knowledge, when it denied human beings that most precious asset, rationality. None the less, the greatest misery of all was for faith to be shattered. Those who put their trust in faith instead of practical knowledge faced painful realisations.

'Practical knowledge', and the invitation to embrace desirable change, may have meant that old beliefs were thrown out, but they were not an invitation to spinelessness or pragmatism. It was an alternative route to a new sense of ethics, often addressing the current issues rather better than older systems of faith. A recognition of the interconnectedness of all things, and the understanding that the individual, was simply a node in a much wider social and cultural world, was given fresh relevance. Complex issues were seen with wider, conscious, vision. In fact those who operated from a basis in practical knowledge developed morals not so wildly different from those of faith.

Karl Popper had proposed to suspend the expectation that all aspects of society could be modelled or controlled, and to take an experimental approach.[11] Developing public policy would be a process. The goals would be set. Various solutions to problems would be tested, and the results monitored carefully. Both ends and means would then be held up to scrutiny. Policy-makers would constantly be probing and testing, seeking improvements and experience. This approach encouraged constant but minor and incremental changes. Handling policy in this way was not seen as necessarily leading to an unravelling of complexity, but it did encourage an understanding of the behaviour of complex systems. This was not the 'disjointed incrementalism' dreaded by the so-called 'rational-comprehensive' planning theorists of the 1960s, but a very joined-up version. By acknowledging the limitations of understanding of complex systems, and the uncertainty of predictions as to the consequences of action, it addressed the problems of planning more modestly and realistically than the high-flown aims of the socialists and utopians.

Complexity and chaos

Closely linked and part causal to the modernists' failure to project accurately had been their inadequate appreciation of complexity. It had become clear that their simplistic analyses and solutions were almost invariably wrong. Short answers were merely trite. The world was always more complex than at first thought.

Some religions had provided positive ways to view complexity. Indeed, a spiritual understanding of it and the interaction of all things had been an age-old philosophical goal, and had been integral to several branches of Eastern metaphysics. Another attitude for which Zen, among other philosophies, was known, was that individuals only imagine themselves to be such; in reality they were centres of consciousness in an infinitely complex web of connections. It is remarkable how frequently such attitudes have re-occurred amongst contemplative minds through the ages. It was only the Western 'enlightenment' that improbably imagined that all mysteries except God Himself could be mastered by a lone mind.

The speculative thoughts on complexity and process by James Lovelock and Ian McHarg began to be supplemented since the 1970s by more scientific ones by mathematicians and climatographers. Their work suggested that although the universe was unpredictable in detail, several of its systems were in fact self-ordering and predictable as a whole. The inner qualities of isolated objects were less revealing and significant than connections between them. The mathematicians developed ideas on chaos, in which positive feedback made predictions of future conditions, as in weather, very sensitive to initial conditions, though always staying within limits. Fractals followed in 1975;[12] these geometrical shapes, when magnified, reappear in the detail. Examples include fancy cauliflowers (fig. 4.7), ferns and types of tree in which the twigs look like the whole. Computer graphics using fractal geometry could simulate mountains and coastlines, and it was even used to develop some of the scenes in *Star Trek II: The Wrath of Khan*.

Figure 4.7 *An example of fractals in the vegetable world – a Romanesco broccoli.*

Richard Dawkins, the evolutionist who saw no need to invoke God in explaining the design of the universe, emphasised complexity as a characteristic of self-perpetuating organisms in a theory of species evolution that was strikingly similar to Lovelock's for the planet.[13]

One architectural critic, Charles Jencks, went so far as to claim that these developments, coupled with the new understanding of the structure of matter and of the origins of the universe, amounted to 'the first Post-Christian synthesis of a new world view'. They 'are likely to change every area of life. Religion, society, politics, art, the environment and architecture will not be the same again'. He saw the universe as an unfolding event, jumping unpredictably to higher levels of organisation, as if destined to generate 'human-like-stuff'. Jencks's 'cosmogenic' world view would 'refute the nihilistic view, developed because of modern determinism and materialism, that our place in the universe is accidental, tangential, absurd and discontinuous with the rest of nature' and reinstate humans, as sentient creatures with intelligence, as the very essence of the new nature (fig. 4.8).[14]

Figure 4.8 *One of the ceramic serpents by Beverley Pepper in the Parc de l'Estacio del Nord in Barcelona 1991. Jencks (1995) thought they were naturalistic in the sense that they resemble fractals, ocean waves, clouds, and the rising and falling of the surrounding earth.*

Complexity and chaos

Cognition

There was much debate about how the mind worked and how it perceived the world, but the most influential thinking has been the 'cognitive theory' of perception. When it emerged after the Second World War, the dominant approach in psychology was 'behaviourism' which, as the name implies, sought to define and predict behaviour by empirical observation, largely without any insight into the reasons for it. 'Cognition', by contrast, focused on the mental processes that gave meaning to human action. The then current understanding was rehearsed by a British psychologist, Richard Gregory, in his *Eye and Brain: the Psychology of Seeing* (1966), so that by the 1970s cognitivism was beginning to overhaul behaviourism as the prevailing approach. Cognition seems to hold good across different cultures, helps to explain perception in the visually impaired, and is relevant in contracted form to non-human higher animals. It also tallies with neuroscience, another way to penetrate the workings of the mind.

The theory did not presuppose anything about the world beyond the assumptions that it is out there and to be engaged. The mind, using its evolved faculties of memory and reasoning powers, will grope and explore till sense is made of the visual and other sensory signals of the outside world. Indeed, it is constantly seeking situation-reports on the world of real objects outside.[15] If the mind is prevented from exploring the outside world, it appeared to speculate or run wild, producing fantasies and hallucinations. Similarly, and contra Carl Jung, dreams signified merely spontaneous activity by the brain, unchecked by sensory data. The most that could be said about them was that they might indicate something of recently invoked motives and fears.

A further gloss is that the mind forms 'representations' (analogous to a specification) or schema of objects.[16] They are symbolic and abstract, rather than just visual, and they stand for or represent to the mind concepts and ideas including those of objects in the outside world. Any and all forms of information, including emotions, are employed in assembling them. Not all the senses are needed in order to form an adequate picture of the outside world: unsighted people assemble their mental maps anyway. The mind then has this idea, rather than a purely photographic image, so that it can recognise the object once again in different conditions or circumstances. For example, the general idea of a table is re-employed when it comes to different tables. The characteristics and behaviour of similar objects already encountered, including non-sensory data such as information on use and material, flesh out the representation.

Sensory stimuli, perception, memory, attention, reasoning, and emotion all have their place in the explanation of cognition. The sensory stimuli – seeing, touching, hearing, smelling and tasting – are just the raw materials for situation reports on the world. When developing, the brains of apes, including humans, have a huge number of potential pathways to connect centres of input and processing, but none well defined. So sensory stimuli would just seem chaotic until the mind had learned to order, compare, identify and assess them. This not only requires a databank on objects and events in the outside world, but impressive computing power. Most psychologists presume a general-purpose intelligence in higher life forms, giving a capacity for learning by trial and error, and associative memory, in other words enabling knowledge of the world around.

The next step is to recall what associations can legitimately be made about the behaviour of the object perceived. Is it food? Is it dangerous? Finally the mind reaches the point of the whole exercise; what action needs to be taken? Knowing the behaviour of objects allows prediction of the consequences of action. Intelligent decisions can then be made. Two forms of cognition are sometimes distinguished. One is 'explicit', being a deliberate, conscious, process; the other is 'implicit', such as automatic activity completed with hardly any conscious awareness, like walking.

Thus far, humans largely conform to general rules for apes, but the human is more than just a very clever animal. The discussion needed to be extended because humans have acquired particular mental faculties – social, natural history, technical and linguistic – the combination of which is unique in the animal world. Evolutionary psychologists had described how humans have highly developed special adaptations thought to have developed through evolution in Pleistocene times, in other words the last two million years spent by *Homo habilis, H. erectus* and *H. sapiens* as hunter-gatherers. Psychological adaptations evolved gradually, awaiting deployment at birth, and these determine that many behavioural tendencies of the species are partly determined genetically.[17]

The archaeological record of early hominid sites was meanwhile interpreted to give a speculative account of the nature of these adaptations and the timetable for their emergence.[18] About two million years ago, *H. habilis* stood upright, had a much better developed social intelligence than ape-like ancestors and had added

Figure 4.9 *A diorama at the Nairobi National Museum portrays early hominids; a technical intelligence through tool-making combined with social and other skills led to self-consciousness.*

a technical intelligence through tool-making (fig. 4.9). *H. erectus* followed 1.8 million years ago, and probably had some linguistic intelligence to supplement the social one, as well as a much improved intuition, enabling complex hunting strategies and technical abilities that led to making hand-axes. Neanderthals and archaic *H. sapiens*, from about 0.4 million years ago, had brain sizes and probably linguistic potentials approaching those of modern humans.

Consciousness and creativity

Evolutionary psychologists, however, said there was more. With archaic *H. sapiens*, the mental faculties were not deployed at the same time, but independently, as and when required. Humans were thought to do this still in particular circumstances. The thinking of infants went like this. Some tribal customs led to animals or objects being treated in different ways, depending on which faculty was being deployed; and craftsmen tended to demonstrate advanced technical skills to enquirers, rather than verbalising them, thereby maintaining their attention within the realm of technical intelligence.

Figure 4.10 *Aurochs, horses, and rhinoceroses, a wall painting in the Chauvet Cave, Vallon-Pont-d'Arc, France, c. 30,000-28,000 or c.15,000-13,000 BCE, were an outcome of joined-up thinking.*

The great and defining innovation by the modern human was joined-up thinking. Humans began to apply knowledge and thoughts from one mental faculty to flow into others. Metaphor and analogy were employed as new ways to represent the world. An example of this would be when thinking about people in one's social intelligence, and thinking about animals in one's natural-history intelligence, became mixed as thinking about animals as people ('anthropo-morphism'), or thinking about people as animals ('totemism'). A 'cultural explosion' accompanying joined-up thinking has been noted by archaeologists, in which ivory statuettes and wall paintings appear for the first time, and the technology of hunting and seafaring become sophisticated, exploiting materials to the full (fig. 4.10). The fully modern mind, in the evolutionary sense, had been formed.

Ironically, bearing in mind that this was a theory of human inheritance, the main opposition came from geneticists. They saw human behaviour as predominantly the product of genes, but there were two camps poles apart – some pointed to shared genes within the species and others to an individual's own mix. The former party said, rather as the old human ecologists had, that humans had inherited genes that compelled them

Consciousness and creativity **103**

en masse towards certain behaviours, which were therefore broadly standardised, and that cultural practices were merely a superficial overlay. In 1975 one biologist specialising in the study of ants proposed this doctrine as 'sociobiology' (applicable to humans as well as insects).[19]

The other party claimed that genes could be found to explain differences in behaviour between individuals. As geneticists discovered the function of more and more genes, they seemed increasingly to be placed at the centre of culture, behaviour and morality. It might not have been someone's fault that they committed crimes, for example: their genes impelled them to do so. At the extreme, because all mysteries of creation would be laid bare, this would deny any scope for religious belief.[20] Did this imply that human nature was fixed at conception? Could humans escape from their biological destiny? How much free will do we have?

The evolutionary psychologists' answer started with the proposition that while natural selection has left each species with inborn traits, predispositions, susceptibilities, capacities or faculties latent in every individual, there would also be a variation within a species, as individuals might have slightly differing capacities, as well as different life histories which would shape how these capacities developed.[21] Hence, whilst the broad description of a species was set by inherited traits, this variation meant that there was no inevitability about the development of any individual. Causal chains are long and experiences are complex so that, spiritually, humans could feel untrammelled by their genetic imperatives.[22] The position that most evolutionary psychologists came to adopt was that while basic human nature was shared by all, it existed only at the level of evolved mental faculties, not of actual cultural behaviours.[23]

Consciousness was seen as an evolved faculty to predict the behaviour of others by examining the self's thoughts and feelings.[24] Concepts of social organisation and convention could thus become much more sophisticated, giving rise eventually to those like money, ethical values and politics. A shared culture had obvious advantages in that every new member had access to received wisdom, which could be seen as a codification of useful information about environmental and social matters, instead of needing to carry out trial and error afresh. Culture came about through one person's observation of another's knowledge and mindset.[25]

The development of consciousness helped explain why biology would never explain human behaviour fully, for it was behind the development of joined-up thinking. Early hominid species probably developed it slowly as a feature of social intelligence. It then became a powerful tool in integrating information and ideas across the various mental faculties. When information about technical and natural-history matters was brought into the social sphere, it could then be transmitted through language. Furthermore, it was brought into consciousness, and this resulted in imaginative leaps that connected thoughts in the social sphere with those in the other faculties. These connections in turn permitted improved management of information, as new knowledge could be tested and appropriately stored. Such knowledge could be about abstract matters, those independent of personal experience, a unique ability of the modern human amongst animals. Consciousness was thus thought to promote much greater flexibility, sensitivity and creativity in the handling of social and non-social information alike. An essential feature of creativity was the ability to relate seemingly unconnected frames of thought to synthesise new constructions.[26]

Imaginative leaps of consciousness, combined with a sense of belonging to a community, suggested forms of shared communication that are nowadays interpreted as art and spirituality. In art social communication was conducted through the creation of artefacts with iconographic meanings (fig. 4.11).[27] These may have referred to events or objects possibly far away in time or place, but social conventions gave the key to understanding. Spirituality concerned communication with supernatural beings, such as in ancestor-worship. It was thought that the non-physical component of people, their spirits, had an afterlife. These had supernatural powers in that they could in certain respects disobey everyday intuitive knowledge of how the world works. To gain access to and influence such powers, for example to increase fertility or to make it rain, the spirits needed to be invoked, which was performed through shamans and/or rituals. Again, certain conventional understandings were required as the background to this communication, for example a cosmology that explained the position and function of the several spirits.

Joined-up thinking was thus regarded as giving humans the power to imagine things that cannot be seen, and which are quite independent of human existence. Transcendent thoughts detached humans from the business of being human and transported them into the realms of free will, of spirituality and of pure intellect. Geneticists might have seen people as behaving in conformity with biological imperatives, yet humans largely thought and acted as if they were free. Humans had acquired the means to transcend their biology.

Figure 4.11 *Willendorf Venus, a statuette of c.27,000 BC in the Naturhistorisches Museum, Vienna, an example of artefacts with iconographic meanings.*

It might have been that early brain development was 'plastic', in the sense that universal intuitive mental faculties provided the raw material for the construction of yet more specialised skills in individuals, say in mathematics, under cultural pressures.[28] The development of animal faculties was sometimes influenced by early environmental conditions. Hence human nature and creativity could well be an amalgam of inherited and cultural forces. The standard social-scientific model of the mind crafted by cultural conditioning might have had some application after all.

An aesthetic experience

Philosophers tend to think less in terms of art and more in terms of the 'aesthetic experience'. John Dewey described a particular and intense form that was not everyday – 'an experience', rather than just 'experience':

> An experience occurs when a work is finished in a satisfactory way, a problem solved, a game is played through, a conversation is rounded out, and fulfillment and consummation conclude the experience. In an experience, every successive part flows freely. An experience has a unity and episodes fuse into a unity, as in a work of art.[29]

The proposal by Dewey was to see an aesthetic experience as characterised by challenges and rewards. The more challenging it was, and the more skill that was required to tackle it, the greater the reward in terms of mind-expanding insights. Those with practical knowledge would thus see art appreciation as a test of connoisseurship, and as the joy of spiritual communion between one human and another through the medium of an artwork.

No one disputed that the purpose of art was to test people's preconceptions (fig. 4.12). Benefits would occur as a result of an intellectual interchange between art object and observer:

> If the qualities of the work of art cannot be described purely in themselves, independently of the mind which perceives and orders and appreciates them, neither, in this view, does the human subject stand apart from her experiences ... Where art exists, it must change the human being who has entered into relation with it ... a new self, new possibilities, are created in each encounter.[30]

An American philosopher, Jerome Stolnitz, described a similar sensation in the art gallery:

> The aesthetic experience, at its best, seems to isolate both us and the object from the flow of experience. The object, in being admired for itself, is divorced from its interrelations with other things. And we feel as though life had suddenly been arrested, for we are absorbed wholly in the object before us ... [31]

Likewise David Pole, who nevertheless argued that aesthetic moments could be as short as an instantaneous response or as long as reading *War and Peace*, noted that 'An aesthetic reaction ... implies a certain heightening of, of dwelling in, our experience'.[32]

Some empirical research described this heightening of consciousness. Concentration might be so intense that a certain detachment from other

Figure 4.12 *Shaking preconceptions: one of Igor Miteraj's giant masks is a simple example.*

matters occurs. In such cases of total absorption or fascination, the sense of time can be lost, as could be the sense of self. An intense aesthetic experience might follow, perhaps from engaging with an 'art object', but maybe when rock-climbing, playing chess, or even reading a book.[33] Such intense experiences cannot be conjured up at will. However, they required prior analytical and technical skills, together with receptivity. Yet, when they did occur, the glow of achievement was immensely satisfying to the mind, as well as providing the comfort of closer personal convergence with the parameters governing the condition of humanity.

The use of history

The post-modern, 'post-structuralist', view was that nothing could be produced or interpreted in an unbiased way. For example, the traditional writing of history as that of nations, great leaders and battles was flawed: there was no real homogeneity in society; social and economic differences were always more significant to the individual than matters shared.[34] History is generated as narratives from single viewpoints, and is inevitably an abstraction from the complexity of past events to suit the prejudices of the narrator. Not all narrators are equally influential, though, and certain versions of the past come to dominate its popular understanding. A society gets the history it deserves.

There are two implications from this, both reasons for the conservationist's attention. First, history will continue to be re-written for as long as it appears relevant. The study of the past should thus explore the context for the construction of versions of history. Studies of cultural heritage and conservation are indispensable in revealing the ways in which versions of history are value-laden. The second reason is that some objective check on re-workings of the past, through documents and physical remains, is vital lest it descend to mere fiction. The idealism, passion, greed and anger of historical events may have been real enough, but they remain only as memory, captured fragmentarily as contemporary and subsequent interpretations in annals, newspapers and papers of all sorts. The physical circumstances in which historical figures found themselves, or which they created for themselves, have value as a powerful aide-memoire, and often serve as the one truly objective testimony to the circumstances of history.

Could lessons be derived from political history, then? In the past it had been supposed that a 'trained mind' was able to do so. However, historic parallels were usually chimeras; history does not repeat itself meaningfully. The value of history was rather the reverse; it stripped away falsity. In everyday thought propositions were put forward constantly, with little analysis of the assumptions underlying them. These needed to be challenged for factual correctness and clarity of meaning. In other words, the study of history guided judgement, but it could not help predict the future or devise historical laws.

It was far better to acknowledge that it was numerous individuals and their good, selfless, greedy, relevant or clever ideas that determined events, played out in particular contexts of the natural world and a society's political and social conditions. History, then, shows the human race in all its guises, shakes people out of their preconceptions, and frees them from the intellectual blinkers of their time. It provides perspective and insights upon the present, sharpens informed analysis of events, deconstructs predictions of the consequences of action, and encourages lateral thinking. History, as a source of real example and illustrative material, can thus be a considerable philosophical aid.

History holds fascination because people are curious about who they are and where they come from. Great personalities of the past, ancestors or a person's locality, might spark the interest, but before long questions such as 'what did they know and believe about themselves and the world?' would be asked. This could be more interesting than looking at alternative twentieth-century cultures, because who or what was significant for posterity could be seen in hindsight, and each query could have an answer. In answer to 'why did they make such gardens?', for example, it would be discovered that many views have been expressed through garden design, such as political power, or objection to its abuse, the dignity of craftsmanship, theories of colour and vision, and so forth. Hence gardens were often more than just beautiful; they allowed those who understand them to penetrate the minds of their makers.

Those historians and philosophers who had been fond of postulating laws of historical development were referred to as 'historicists'.[35] At its crudest level, their thinking took the form of comparing present situations to past ones with some appearance of similarity, often in order to reinvoke old hopes or fears. Selective choices of historical events could be employed in attempts to underpin a viewpoint with an historical justification.[36] Such sleight of hand has been used to convince others of some moral, of the impossibility of any further refinement of an art form, or of the inexorability of sociological or artistic processes. This use of history has about as much validity as recalling that, say, a certain horse has never won at a particular racecourse on a Tuesday.

Many historians, however, developed beliefs in the tide of history. Marxists, for example, espoused laws of evolutionary social progress, with capitalism being a lower form of civilisation, and socialism being a further development which society will, some day, reach. This historicist style of thought was perhaps understandable from Karl Marx as a devotee of Georg Hegel's doctrines about evolutionary social progress towards 'the great Idea'. He was also vastly impressed by Charles Darwin's *Origin of Species* (1859), which explained that primordial species had evolved by stages until *Homo sapiens* was reached. Marx, who was seeking to explain the mechanisms by which his utopian ideas could be realised, found Hegel's and Darwin's ideas inspirational, and in fact wished to dedicate his book to the latter.

Yet a belief in the inevitability of progress towards the ideal is dangerous.[37] Social goals that differ from the chosen version of the ideal are seen as a threat, and their espousers as deviant and reactionary. Normal ethics are discarded, and rights are forfeited, often with dire consequences. Historical analysis is perverted too. Events are seen as steps on the path to the final conclusion: and judged to be good when they are a step in the ordained direction or bad when they do not. The attempt to fit events into a stream of progress was characteristic of the supporters of the modern movement. An obvious example was Pevsner's *Pioneers of Modern Design* (1936). The very word 'pioneers' in the title suggested that people like William Morris had been unconsciously groping for the Holy Grail.[38] A milder danger was 'prolepsis', the assessment of an historical period in terms of present knowledge or standards. How often have historians heard of a style being 'transitional'!

The historicist frame of mind that had believed in a tide of social progress would, very likely, also have accepted the metaphysical doctrine of zeitgeist – the spirit of the age – supposedly acting as the unseen force translating political, economic and social forces into the artistic productions of the day.[39]

In fact some garden styles have quite literally been the product of a state of mind. An example would be the walled yard of Middle Eastern cultures over the millennia (fig. 4.13), grandly referred to as the *hortus*

Figure 4.13 *Gardens as a state of mind: the enclosed yard derives from the desire to protect property: Al-Qasr, Ottoman Village near Dakhla Oasis, Egypt.*

The use of history

Figure 4.14 *An example of style revealing mentality; the Tudor style at New College, Oxford, with its mount and intricate knot garden below betray a love of conceits.*

conclusus by garden historians. The motive for building the walls was not aesthetic, of course, but the protection of property. The poorest Arab yard has these walls in breeze blocks, and the palace gardens of the Alhambra were an expression of the same mentality writ large. Other examples of garden style being literal translations of mentality were the Tudor conceits, such as mazes (fig. 4.14), and the arrangement of specimens in the arboreta formed by botanical classifiers from about 1800.

Moving beyond these simple examples, though, the higher claims for zeitgeist, that it is a force that can translate abstract philosophical thoughts into form appears improbable (fig. 4.15). The idea that 'absolutism' was the inspiration for the great regular gardens of France was to abstract the royal examples from the innumerable other regular gardens of the time: and it didn't explain why absolutism should produce regular designs. The same doubts about the role of a moving spirit occurred when the Picturesque, nineteenth-century parterres, Robinsonian wild gardens and the Lutyens/Jekyll style are examined as indicators of the political, spiritual or intellectual climate of the time. There can indeed be a connection between intellectual climate and design (see 'The sociology of criticism' below), but the zeitgeist was not it.

Figure 4.15 *Seek the zeitgeist; what higher abstract philosophical idea was being translated into form when Percy Cane designed this plan for a small garden? In his* Garden Design *(1936), p.53*

First, the zeitgeist failed to work at the simple and obvious level; many influential concepts connected with the environment have failed to generate specific artistic responses in architecture or landscape design. This is not infrequently the fate of ideas on nature. Jean-Jacques Rousseau's idea of Julie's garden was a fantasised world, suggested by the discovery of some uninhabited islands in the Pacific by Captain George Anson in 1741 (fig. 4.16).[40] An untouched natural garden, savage but gentle, was the right setting for a human being of similar description. An attractive idea, but no fashion for Rousseauesque gardens followed. In the late twentieth century, Louis le Roy was against design, preferring that pressures from human use would shape the amorphous planted areas into useful form; unfortunately his landscapes, made in the early 1970s in The Netherlands, became jungles or mud patches within a few years: not very useful at all. The lesson was that it needs more than a worthy sentiment to create a designed style.

The use of history

Figure 4.16 *'A View of the Watering Place at TENIAN' (1748), copperplate from A voyage round the world, in the years MDCCXL, I, II, III, IV by George Anson, Esq. by Richard Walter, the inspiration for Rousseau's 'Julie's garden'.*

Second, if the zeitgeist operated, it might be supposed that there would be only one true style among those sharing the same philosophy. It could not be denied that when new orthodoxies have sprung up in the past they have often led to one style only, but it had also happened that two or three styles sprang simultaneously from the same philosophy. Indeed this was so with the modern movement in gardens. Designers in France like the brothers André and Paul Vera shared the ideals and aspirations of the Swedish Baron Sven Hermelin, Christopher Tunnard from England, Thomas Church from California and Roberto Burle Marx from Brazil. Yet the Veras had a parterre in their own garden in Saint-Germain-en-Laye, whilst Hermelin and Tunnard preferred the gentle, subdued informality much like the eighteenth-century English Park; Church and Burle Marx chose unfamiliar materials in exuberant shapes and colours.

Third, if the zeitgeist did not work at these obvious levels, perhaps it worked in less obvious ways via a web of connected principles? Indeed Pevsner attempted to demonstrate this possibility. In the early 1940s he thought he had singled out the vital intellectual spark that set off the English landscape garden in the 1730s.[41] The politics of the Whigs emphasised freedom. So did the asymmetrical garden forms of Lord Burlington and William Kent. The connection between politics and garden style was thus established through the unifying concept of freedom. Unfortunately for this idea, it has recently been pointed out that Lord Burlington's Whiggery was a mask of convenience; having broken with the Whig-dominated Court in 1733, he reverted to his true views in backing Tory candidates for Yorkshire in the 1734 and 1741 elections, which happens also to be when he allowed Kent to create an area of naturalistic garden at Chiswick.[42] Pevsner had perceived a parallel between the eighteenth-century concept of freedom and the utilitarian mindset behind the modern movement, in that the latter was expressed politically by a socialist ethic and in terms of design by the functionalism of his own time. As Frank Clark found, though, a connection between the socialist ideals of the 1930s and a suitable outward expression in garden style was hard to discover, just as Pevsner was never able to define his unifying idea between the zeitgeist and design style more precisely.

The sociology of criticism

So, if the zeitgeist will not suffice as an explanation for creative forces, how do intellectual ideas connect with style in landscape design? The mechanisms may be close to the classical model of creativity, and the key is the interaction between the designer, supplying innovation, and the client (this term being shorthand for whoever commissions work), selecting innovations on the basis of relevance to requirements.[43] Clients' choices were generally for explicable reasons, even if not very well articulated. A client might consider an innovation irrelevant, so it will fall by the wayside, but another might be thought relevant, so would be carried forward and contribute to the vocabulary of future design.

The best conditions for a good design are when the roles of client and designer are carefully distinguished but complementary. The client's responsibility is to define the aims and principles prompting a commission. It is the designer's duty to offer a suitable design. It would generally be unhelpful for the client to interfere during the design process, as this might restrict the designer's experimentation and inventiveness. Conversely, the designer would best have stood back while the client's judgement on whether the design meets aspirations was being exercised. Thus artistic creation needed a dynamic balance of message and style. This was not a novel idea. Alexander Pope wrote much the same in his *Epistle to Burlington* (1731). Instead of 'principle' and 'expression', he used the words 'sense' and 'taste':

Oft have you hinted to your brother Peer
A certain truth, which many buy too dear:
Something there is more needful than Expense,
And something previous ev'n to Taste –'tis Sense ...
A Light, which in yourself you must perceive;
Jones and Le Nôtre have it not to give.

A single act of artistic creation has never stood alone, but in a moving crowd of commissions. The critic (this term is shorthand for those who express informed judgements) is an observer, interpreter and opinion-former. The critic's role is that of catalyst, an enabler of the wider public's appreciation through knowledgeable explanation. Standing aside from the relationship between client and designer, the critic can disinterestedly identify which designs, or aspects of designs, are worthy of notice, draw the public's attention to them, and hasten the appreciation of good new ideas.

The preferences of the designers themselves, while they may be of anecdotal interest, are not relevant in assessing finished work. Designers have no uniquely privileged status among the critics of their work. Indeed they might be prejudiced and idiosyncratic in their opinions, and can be so bound up in their own preoccupations as to be uninterested in the work of others.[44] On the other hand, the client's perceptions will be of great interest to the critic. There would also be the reaction of the user and visitor to take into account, as they would probably see the design in a different light to the client's. The critic will then synthesise a personal reaction with these others, and say in what ways the design gave satisfactions.

Such views will of course be essentially subjective. They cannot be dissociated from the particular experiences and circumstances of the individual critic. Also there is scope for subjectivity, waywardness and quirkishness in the case of any assessor. So can judgements on works of art be more than 'all a matter of taste'? Yes, in a social scientific sense. The 'facts' would be judgements by respected critics. Verification of aesthetic judgements would likely become gradual and cumulative, with those whose judgements are respected providing a growing consensus of opinion. Furthermore their judgements are verified or faulted by the consensus of a wider informed public, so that aesthetic judgements can be depersonalised and become collective wisdom in the light of the accumulated experience of many assessors.

That is not to say that the collective judgement will necessarily remain stable for all time. Artists and designers can be rediscovered when a new age uncovers fresh relevance in their work. This has often happened in architectural style. Palladian, Greek, Indian, 'Jacobethan', Tudor and cottage styles were successively revived in the eighteenth and nineteenth centuries as their protagonists consciously looked to their favoured past eras as embodying virtue. Then Victorian architecture came to be despised, only to be rediscovered in the late twentieth century. Art deco and the modern movement were rediscovered in the 1980s. There have been examples in landscape too. Capability Brown's reputation was smeared towards the end of his lifetime and thereafter sank ever deeper until rescued by Dorothy Stroud in the 1950s.

Every design will have an internal consistency, order, logic, fitness, and other qualities that give a distinctive solution. At the same time, critics will notice that designs share common characteristics with others. They will assume that they are based on similar aims and ideas, and will characterise them collectively before detecting nuances between them. This is a well-understood activity on the part of the architectural and landscape historian, and is a strategy to handle the complexity of reality by sifting and ordering information. The process of assessing the vernacular cultural landscape is the same; areas of similar landscape character are identified before local distinctiveness can be pinpointed.

Design characteristics, that will come to be referred to as style, emerge when designers strive to find form that satisfies the brief, is enabled by the available technology and materials, and carries the relevant associations. A designer can invent a motif, but cannot simply invent a whole style as an exercise of logic, as if inevitably determined by the wishes of clients, the goals of society, or ethical or aesthetic convictions. Instead designers must see what others are doing, offer their own solution, see it tested by criticism and public reaction, and then engage in further experimentation.[45] Certain characteristics will come to be associated with subsequent design objectives, and designers make those that find favour more recognisable and distinct in subsequent commissions, and may even exaggerate them in order to parody their own work for emphasis. In this way style is selected, sometimes unpredictably and unexpectedly, from the stream of work.

Designers themselves almost always try to resist their style being categorised. They have a point; all simplifications can cause distortions and loose ends. None the less, style is far too useful a concept for the critic and historian ever to give up. Take the modernist stepping-stone path, for example, which stems from the desire for an uninterrupted

The sociology of criticism

Figure 4.17 *Style: stepping-stone paths were characteristic of modernist landscapes; here at Woluwe, Belgium, by Jean Canneel-Claes, 1947. In Shepheard, plate 16.*

landscape swirling around the building, and is the compromise required when access across the landscape is required (fig. 4.17). The form is characteristic and enables the knowledgeable eye to attribute work to the period, design tradition or even an individual designer. Additionally, all designs are statements to those who can read the messages, even designs that are attempts to eschew all style. Style may thus signify deeper motives, and provide a quick visual cue to the more important underlying imperatives, opportunities, ideals and values.

NOTES AND REFERENCES

1. One only had to see the garden-design section at the Chelsea Flower Show every year to see this illustrated in the most literal terms; conservatism in British garden design was discussed in Lucinda Greswell, 'A muffled modernism', *Landscape Design* (September 1990), 38-9.

2. Peirce Lewis, 'American landscape tastes', in Marc Treib (ed), *Modern Landscape Architecture: a critical review* (Cambridge, MA, 1993), pp. 8-10.

3. Nikolaus Pevsner, *The Englishness of English Art*. Reith lecture (London, 1955).

4. English Heritage landscape architects found this to their cost – the howl of public opposition against some fairly modest restoration at Marble Hill and Chiswick House Grounds in the late 1980s showed a pretty unhealthy belief in conspiracy theory among some members of the general public.

5. Louis le Roy, quoted in Allan R. Ruff, *Holland and the Ecological Landscape* (Stockport, Cheshire, 1979), pp. 28-33.

6. The question now arises whether parks need to be redesigned, or whether the older layouts simply need to be well repaired. The modernist would now be surprised to hear of restoration at Battersea Park in central London, Victoria Park in Hackney, east London, and Sefton Park in south Liverpool, with a return largely to the mid-nineteenth century layouts being judged to be in the residents' interests.

7. J.K. Friend & W.N. Jessop, *Local Government and Strategic Choice* (London, 1969); operational research was developed in the Second World War as the application of scientific method to decisions in warfare, and after the war was employed to assist managers by giving them a quantitative and logical basis for many of their more difficult decisions.

8. John Searle, *Mind, Language and Society* (London, 1999), p. 10; this was his proposed basic tenet of his 'default positions' on how to view the world.

9. Roger Scruton, *The Aesthetics of Architecture* (London, 1979), p. 35.

10 Peter Fuller, 'The Geography of Mother Nature', in Denis Cosgrove & Stephen Daniels (eds), *The Iconography of Landscape: Essays on the Symbolic Representation, Design and Use of Past Environments* (Cambridge, 1988), p. 25.

11 Karl R. Popper, *The Poverty of Historicism,* 2nd edn (London, 1961), pp. 64-70.

12 Benoit Mandelbrot, 'Fractals – a Geometry of Nature', in Nina Hall (ed), *The New Scientist Guide to Chaos* (London, 1992), p. 123.

13 Richard Dawkins, *The Blind Watchmaker* (London, 1986), pp. 4 *et seq.*

14 Charles Jencks, *The Architecture of the Jumping Universe: a polemic – how complexity science is changing architecture and culture* (London, 1995), pp. 9 & 125.

15 Richard L. Gregory, *Eye and Brain: the Psychology of Seeing*, 3rd ed. (Princeton NJ, 1977).

16 Stephen & Rachel Kaplan (eds), *Humanscape: Environments for People* (North Scituate MA, 1978), p. 53.

17 Jerome H. Barkow, Lena Cosmides & John Tooby, *The Adapted Mind* (New York, 1992), pp. 5 & 25-49.

18 Stephen Mithen, *The Prehistory of the Mind* (New York, 1996), p. 211.

19 Edward O. Wilson, *Sociobiology: the New Synthesis* (Cambridge MA, 1975), p. 4.

20 Brian Appleyard, *Brave New Worlds* (London, 1999), p. 119.

21 A useful introduction is provided by Robert A. Hinde & Joan Stevenson-Hinde, *Instinct and intelligence.* Carolina Biology Reader No. 63 (Burlington NC, 1987).

22 Appleyard, op. cit., p. 155.

23 Barkow, *et al.*, op. cit., p. 5.

24 Nicholas Humphrey, *A History of the Mind* (London, 1992), p. 179.

25 Barkow, *et al.*, op. cit., p. 118.

26 Margaret Boden, *The Creative Mind* (London, 1990), pp. 23-4, 117.

27 Mithen, op. cit., pp. 158 & 174.

28 Annette Karmiloff-Smith, *Beyond Modularity: a Developmental Perspective on Cognitive Science* (Cambridge MA, 1992).

29 John Dewey, *Art as Experience* (New York, 1934), chapter 3.

30 Mara Miller, *The Garden as an Art* (Albany NY, 1993), p. 109.

31 Jerome Stolnitz, *Aethetics and the Philosophy of Art Criticsm: a critical introduction* (Boston 1960), pp. 49 & 52.

32 David Pole, *Aesthetics, Form and Emotion* (London, 1983), p. 29.

33 Mihály Csíkszentmihályi & Rick E. Robinson, *The Art of Seeing: an interpretation of the aesthetic encounter* (Malibu CA, 1990); they refer to this state of mind as 'flow activity'.

34 I am grateful to Dr Kathleen Watt for inducting me into post-structuralist thinking in conservation.

35 David Watkin, *The Rise of Architectural History* (London, 1980), pp. 2-4, briefly explained the origins of ideas on the spirit of the age in the writings of Johann Joachim Winckelmann (1717-1768) and of history seen as a step-by-step progress towards the Ideal in the writings of Georg Wilhelm Friedrich Hegel (1770-1831). Watkin in *Morality and Architecture* (London, 1977) and Scruton, op. cit., are among modern writers to criticise Hegelian thought as it applies to architectural history.

36 An eighteenth-century example of prolepsis in garden history is provided by Horace Walpole's account of the founding of the English landscape garden, *On Modern Gardening* (1782). In this he places William Kent firmly in the role as hero, and treats Alexander Pope, Charles Bridgeman and others only in so far as they provided the stepping-stones across which Kent would pass to Elysium. A more recent example is Christopher Tunnard who, when he came to write the historical section of *Gardens in the Modern Landscape* (1938), made judgements on how wrong Joseph Addison had been, and how tasteless the Victorian period had been, clearly judging them by his own standards, not by the standards of the time.

37 Popper, op. cit., was a devastating attack on the historicist mentality, including Marxism and Nazism, by someone who had real cause to question it.

38 In a later edition Pevsner, op. cit., who had reviled Art Nouveau and Art Deco because he had regarded them as departures from right thinking, conceded that he had been too damning in his judgement.

39 Watkin 1977, op.cit., pp. 80 *et seq.*, discusses the zeitgeist, especially as manifested in Pevsner's writings.

40 Christopher Thacker, ' "O Tinian!" "O Juan-Fernandez!": Rousseau's "Elysée" and Anson's islands', *Garden History*: V/2 (Summer 1977), 42.

41 Nikolaus Pevsner, 'The Genesis of the Picturesque', *Architectural Review*, 96 (1944), 139-46.

42 The Third Earl of Burlington's politics were examined in detail by Dr Eveline Cruikshanks at a symposium at the Society of Antiquaries, organised by the Friends of Chiswick House, on 22 February 1991.

43 Hugo A. Meynell, *The Nature of Aesthetic Value* (London, 1986), has been a useful guide in this section on criticism.

44 Jacob W. Getzels, & Mihály Csíkszentmihályi, *The Creative Vision: a Longitudinal Study of Problem Finding in Art* (New York, 1976), p. 110.

45 John Hopkins, 'Critics' forum', *Landscape Design* (February 1994), 24-5, argued for more and better criticism of projects.

Figure 4.18 *Charles Darwin, a cartoon by Leslie Starke, 1940s.*

CHAPTER 5

FACTS, VALUE AND IDEOLOGY

The emerging new approach to landscape, replacing the disillusionment and uncertainty from the collapse of modernism, was built upon the theoretical foundations set out in the chapter above. A good analogy for this process was that of the mind (see Chapter 4 – 'Cognition'). When disorientated, it struggles to ascertain the situation and uses its pre-assembled knowledge to make sense once again.

The most far-reaching change was in the recognition that meanings and values in the landscape stemmed from the observer. They were accepted as culturally-determined and subjective, so that meaning and value were laid upon the landscape by people. This was a radical change to the former assumption that values were objectively present in the landscape itself.

There can be many forms of value, and many can relate to the same landscape. Values may change over time or be re-evaluated in the light of new knowledge or changing value-systems. Values can always be added. Designers seek to introduce new qualities that add value to the landscape, and these may come to be appreciated then or over time. They could also usually be seen to be linked:

> Often the various values derive from some determinant inherent in the landscape or its history, such as topography or past land-use management. A remarkable mountain may have attracted spiritual value to itself, which may have led to an architecturally important monastery being built. An historic park may, because of its history of continuous grazing, have preserved the archaeological remains of a medieval village and have led to a floristically rich turf … A cherished landscape is not just the cumulative sum of the constituent interests; it is a complex bundle of interrelated interests.

Many disciplines and interests would then have a legitimate interest in the landscape:

> So we have the aesthetes, the archaeologists, the cultural historians, the garden historians, nature conservationists and ecologists, all adhering to distinctive values, and all interested in the landscape for what they would all regard as 'conservation' reasons.[1]

Every conservation interest could be seen as cultural, but this idea was resisted by some ecologists who maintained that there was something special about nature conservation value. They were inspired by a fresh

Facts, value and ideology **123**

round of ecocentric theories and philosophies, and could point to national and international institutions, the World Heritage Committee for example, which at the time required the heritage to be distinguished between 'cultural' and 'natural'.

This chapter first looks at cultural geography which drove the 'post-structuralist' points home through historical analysis, dissecting the meanings and values to be found in landscape. It continues with the recognition of human values in landscape, and the story of the rise of cultural landscapes which embodied many of the characteristics of the new thinking. The morality and politics behind environmental ethics since the 1970s are then briefly described. Meanwhile ecocentrism provided an alternative world view for many academics and ecologists, and so the logic behind that way of thinking is set out, followed by a section addressing ecocentrism as metaphysics.

Reading the landscape

A brief discussion of some of the fashions in academic geography following 'environmental determinism' is necessary to provide the background to 'cultural geography'. Carl Sauer was a geographer at the University of California at Berkeley who thought that the former approach was unbalanced in placing undue emphasis upon the role of ecology, and the geographer 'must guard well against acclaiming as "scientific" verities of adaptation', that is of the human to the environment. He noticed the tendencies of its protagonists, observing: 'The aim, therefore, is to make of geography a part of biophysics, concerned with human tropisms.' He felt he had an explanation in the desire to find a God-like explanation for life: 'Geography under the banner of environmentalism represents a dogma, the assertion of a faith that brings rest to a spirit vexed by the riddle of the universe.'

Sauer certainly did not disagree that the natural environment was a determinant in landscapes, but he felt that the role of culture needed emphasising much more:

> Geography is distinctly anthropocentric, in the sense of value or use of the earth to man. We are interested in that part of the areal scene which concerns us as human beings because we are part of it, live with it, are limited by it, and modify it.[2]

His view of the environment was not the pristine wilderness imagined by the preservationists, but the lived-in landscape of field and meadow. Climate and terrain did not alter human genes; rather they influenced human culture, which in turn reshaped the land.

Another change in cultural geography was seen after the Second World War. Whereas Sauer had been interested in the landscape itself, a new generation, with literally a new perspective from aerial photography, was interested in 'reading' it for its meaning. John Brinkerhof Jackson, when with the US Air Force conducting wartime aerial-photographic interpretation, learned that there are many sets of eyes – military, geographical, recreational, etc. – through which landscapes can be seen. This led to a passion for observation of the everyday, and then in 1951 to his much admired journal, *Landscape*, an inspiration to younger cultural geographers.[3] Aerial photography also provided enormous benefits to field archaeology. The considerable rise in interest in garden history in the 1970s and the early 1980s in Britain was to no small degree spurred on by a flood of discoveries made through interpretation of aerial photos (fig. 5.1).[4] In the 1990s the landscape of western America, as seen from high-level photography and Landsat satellite imagery, has been described as a vast engine of 'time, network, event and production'.[5]

Meanwhile historians and geographers had taken to using literary analogies. A landscape was a 'text', and one of many overlays is referred to as a 'palimpsest' (a parchment written on many times), that can be

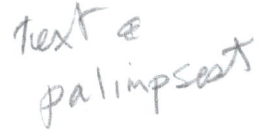

Figure 5.1 *The King's Knot, Stirling Castle; the interpretation of oblique and aerial photographs in the 1970s informed geography, local history and garden history.*

Reading the landscape **125**

Figure 5.2 *This 'ridge-and-furrow' landscape at Dumbleton, Gloucestershire, has been 'written' on many times – ridge and furrow, plantation, sheep grazing: such landscapes are sometimes referred to as 'palimpsests'.*

'read' and provide 'meaning' (fig. 5.2). In England, Thomas Sharp and W.A. Eden had made studies of rural settlements, demonstrating how human activity had made the country.[6] A golden age of local history, sometimes coming under the heading of 'economic history', followed post-war with the recognition of deserted medieval villages, moated sites and the layers of the English countryside. Bill Hoskins then at Oxford University asserted in *The Making of the English Landscape* (1955) that: 'The English landscape itself, to those who know how to read it aright, is the richest historical record we possess.' Jackson commenced his first issue of *Landscape* with: 'A rich and beautiful book is always open before us. We have but to learn to read it.'

It actually took some time for these publications to have an impact. Hoskins's became popular only in the 1970s, with a TV programme in 1973 and republication. Jackson gave up *Landscape* in 1968 to write his highly acclaimed books about the American landscape. Meanwhile, in the 1960s two geographers from University College London, David Lowenthal and Hugh Prince, became interested in the tastes for English landscape:

> People in any country see their terrain through preferred and accustomed spectacles, and tend to make it over as they see it. The English landscape ... mirrors a long succession of such idealized images and visual prejudices ... The types of landscape the English prefer, preserve, and reproduce they regard as uniquely English, embodying the past and present virtues of the inhabitants ... Among a people so appreciative of their landscape, the range of taste is bound to be great.[7]

By the 1970s this way of writing of insightful observation and analysing the meanings and significance of landscape features remained popular despite the analytical, scientific tendencies then dominating academic discipline. In 1979 Donald Meinig, a professor at New York State University at Syracuse, brought together Jackson, Lowenthal, and other well-known writers including Peirce Lewis and Yi-Fu Tuan in a sort of lap of honour.[8] Meinig wrote:

> We regard all landscapes as symbolic, as expressions of cultural values, social behaviour, and individual actions worked upon particular localities over a span of time ... And every landscape is a code, and its study may be undertaken as a deciphering of meaning, of the cultural and social significance of ordinary but diagnostic features.

He regarded 'the nine essays ... an exhibit of the vitality of the topic 'landscape'.[9]

Within a few years of his writing this, though, a new movement was underway, dissatisfied with what was seen as lyrical description of physical artefacts obscuring its thin theoretical basis. It is true that the cultural geographers tended to be dispassionate about the values they found and tended to avoid the city. Their critics, those of the 'new cultural geography', wished to set a new agenda firmly in the context of contemporary social and cultural theory. For this some had turned to the radical French philosophers. The theories on the relationship between power and knowledge, and how the former is used to control and define the latter, by Michel Foucault, for example, were cited.

Two cultural critics were especially influential in this academic stream in England. John Berger, painter, art critic and novelist, had been unhappy with the blandness and high-art orientation of the *Civilization* television series by Sir Kenneth Clark, and with the presentation of social class and colonialism in the media generally. He wrote a BBC television series in 1972, *Ways of Seeing*, in which he criticized traditional Western cultural aesthetics by examining the hidden ideologies in visual images. His contemporary, Raymond Williams, presented a Marxist critique of images of the country and the city in English literature since the sixteenth century.[10] These images were chosen for their depiction of

Figure 5.3 *Rural poverty in Leinster, Ireland, in the 1840s, depicted picturesquely by Robert Thomas Landells; the reality was often romanticised by poets and painters.*

social and economic forces associated with capitalism in England. He debunked the notion of rural life as simple, natural and unadulterated, leaving an image of the country as a Golden Age (fig. 5.3). This idea had become embedded in the writings of English poets and novelists, but it was, according to Williams, 'a myth functioning as a memory', glossing over injustices and class conflicts.

For the 'new' cultural geographers of the 1980s, then, meanings and significance were still to be drawn from the landscape, but they were more interested in exploring the political symbolism of their elite and popular cultures, and issues of gender and sexuality, race, language, identity and ideology. In *Social Formation and Symbolic Landscape* (1984), Denis Cosgrove took the view that the old cultural geography of Sauer and his followers 'remains unconvincing as an account of landscape to the extent that it ignores such symbolic dimensions – the symbolic and cultural meaning invested in these forms by those who have produced and sustained them ...'

He was redefining the ways in which culture invests the world with meanings. Nobody could boast of an entirely neutral, objective, view of the landscape, and, as Foucault would have done, Cosgrove had 'the feeling that in landscape we are dealing with an ideologically-charged and very complex cultural product'. He wished to excavate the often-concealed reasons for its representation. Hence he did not treat the land as such, but the 'idea of landscape' in the mind: 'Landscape is not merely the world we see, it is a construction, a composition of that world. Landscape is a way of seeing that world.'[11] The art-historical term 'iconography' was borrowed and used mercilessly.[12]

Cosgrove's book was an historical sketch of ideas about landscape in Europe and North America since the fifteenth century. His case studies were on the Veneto, the English countryside, Washington DC and elsewhere. He probably read more meanings into such landscapes than was strictly justified – there were no surveys of public taste, preferences or attitudes – and the reader just had to trust his judgement that the readings were correct. One could imagine the inhabitants of those landscapes being bemused that Cosgrove would presume to interrogate their inner motives, but then the point of the book was to present a Marxist interpretation of history with an emphasis on tracking the transition from feudalism to capitalism and modern social formation.

Cosgrove joined Stephen Daniels of the University of Nottingham in 1988 in editing a reader on cultural geography. They explained that they viewed landscape as a cultural image, 'a pictorial way of representing, structuring or symbolising surroundings'.[13] Contributors examined how landscape could be made to signify social, cultural and political issues, and found a variety of meanings on paper or canvas, in literary form or on its ground. For example, one piece 'read' maps to examine how societies saw themselves. Another was the exhumation of John Ruskin as a prophet of the iconographical approach to landscape studies. The iconographers amply demonstrated that art and literature about landscape could serve unstated political or economic interests. Indeed they had unwittingly shown it in their own writings.[14]

The ideological slant seen at the beginnings of the 'new' cultural geography was largely a result of the persuasions of the particular proponents. David Pepper, an ex-student of Cosgrove's at Oxford Polytechnic, with two colleagues, produced in *The Roots of Modern Environmentalism* (1984) a rebuttal of both the technocentric (capitalist) and ecocentric (environmental) positions. His analysis of ecocentrism's intellectual antecedents was exhaustive, as was his point-by-point critique. Deploring the romantic and escapist underpinnings of bioethics, he concluded that: 'Modern ecocentrics must, in the Marxist view, follow Marx in rejecting both the despoilation of nature under capitalism, and the deification of nature.'[15]

There were other geographers who did not feel the urge to offer analyses in terms of the transition to capitalism, exploitation or social conflict. They continued the examination of meanings, beliefs and tastes towards the landscape in more dispassionate terms. David Lowenthal, an American by birth, had stayed in London and, using his historical skills, developed a critique of conservation and tourism in *The Past is a Foreign Country* (1985).[16] His arguments were ironic and often very amusing, pointing out contradictions and curious logic. One lecture he gave was on 'England-Land', pointing to the way that the tourist industry was marketing England as an olde-worlde caricature of itself, akin to 'Disney-Land'. Stephen Daniels explored identity in *Fields of Vision: Landscape Imagery and National Identity in England and the United States* (1993), and also became an accomplished scholar of garden history, particularly on Humphry Repton.

The older interest in interpreting the landscape for insights into human history at the local scale was seen again when Oliver Rackham applied his skills as an historical ecologist to the English countryside: 'the landscape is a record of our roots and the growth of civilisation. Each individual historic wood, heath, etc. is uniquely different from every other, and each has something to tell us.' The picture that emerged of the care and skill in woodsmanship required to operate medieval systems of coppicing, wood pasture and pollarding gave him a strong preference for such woodlands over the industrialised monoculture of timber plantations.[17]

Knowledge gives value

The variety of values in the landscape requires some explication. The 'post-structuralist' position was that all values are cultural and so values in the landscape stem from humans alone. Places mean something. Aesthetic values are by association against a pre-formed idealised image in the mind. Natural-history values are not inherently scientific, but arise from commitment to the cause of ecology.

The terminology could be confusing, for while values were felt and held by individuals, the word was given another meaning when applied to objects and landscapes perceived by the individual. Strictly speaking, objects and landscapes could only have attributes or qualities – and these could be described more-or-less objectively – and it was these that appeal to people's internal values, and so in this sense could be said to have 'value'. It was an unsatisfactory lack of clarity, but it was common usage. Alternative words for such 'value' in objects have been used, such as 'worth', or 'significance', the latter being very often preferred despite its clumsiness. 'Evaluation' was the systematic determination of an object's or landscape's merit using an agreed set of criteria. Alternative terms were 'appraisal' or 'assessment'. Good practice would require that assessment was systematic, competent, honest, and adhered strictly to the agreed standards.

When the 'rational-comprehensive' plans were being composed in the 1960s, and sieve maps were being sketched out, the principal values in the countryside were seen as economic (more specifically, agricultural land quality), natural (wildlife interest), and scenic (i.e. its landscape beauty). These were amenable to objective assessment, it was thought. National Parks, Archaeological Monuments and designated Sites of Special Scientific Interest (principally for rare flora and fauna) were treated as sacrosanct and were blocked in on the maps of constraints.

Cultural geographers exploring some of the meanings of landscapes through 'iconography' and the skill of 'reading' a work of art 'by ascertaining those underlying attitudes of a nation, a period, a class, a religious or philosophical persuasion' opened the possibility that the range of values could be much, much wider. However, if values in the landscape are not objectively there, but laid upon it by humans, how do they come to be generated and recognised? It is a process, starting when someone who is acquainted with a particular place points out its qualities, maybe at first in a neutral way. A value-judgement may then be applied, in other words an individual's assessment of worth. If a sufficient number of people agree, a movement for their protection could be started.

Knowledge gives value. Dedicated observers examine fossils, archaeological remains, painters, even cigarette packets, and their insights give enlightenment and delight to others. Objects that might seem inconsequential to the ignorant, sparkle afresh in the light of comprehension:[18] the skill of the makers of Pulhamite rockwork must be admired, derelict land is a record of mighty processes, and monstrous football-ground stands are redolent in social history. Knowledge turns iconoclasts into admirers: J.C. Loudon, was converted from a rival to an admirer of Humphry Repton's skill, and

Knowledge gives value **131**

Christopher Tunnard came round to appreciating nineteenth century landscape design.[19] Perhaps everything acquires value the more that is known about it.

Allen Carlson, a philosopher from the University of Alberta, was pursuing his theme that knowledge brings value in the 1980s. He pointed out that aesthetic appreciation of works of art is most rewarding when taken in the light of knowledge of their real natures. So, for example, appreciation of a work such as Picasso's 'Guernica' (1937) would be enhanced in the light of knowledge of paintings in general and of cubist paintings in particular. Likewise, in appreciating natural scenery, an expert understanding of geological processes, trees and natural vegetation, and the local ecology would highlight its values.[20] The same principle might be applied to designed landscapes, and quite possibly any valued place – the more one knows about it, the more special it becomes.[21]

Landscapes have been recycled constantly as emblems of personal values: whatever the motives of its creators, a landscape comes to represent a multitude of further meanings to others, for example nationhood, class interests, childhood happiness or efficiency. It can also be that while a landscape may remain unaltered, the understanding or interpretation improves. Changes of policy or theory often derive from a different way of looking at the problem, or by reinterpreting what has always been known, so the same facts may support competing versions of 'truth'. Witty observations that each generation reinvented the landscape in its own way contain essential truth.[22]

This was the case also with conservation thinking. Its precepts were not fixed for all time, but moved on as a reflection of the passions and preoccupations of each succeeding generation, and the onward march of knowledge and skills. They were just our best thoughts at that date, and we could not have predicted how they would change in the future. Hence it was disingenuous to claim that conservation was about 'negotiating the transition from the past to future in such a way as to secure the transfer of maximum significance'.[23] Those protecting the heritage ought to have been honest that they were doing so in accord with their own values.

In the list below are many of the more commonly perceived qualities or attributes in landscapes, though others may well have been or will be identified.

A List of some Landscape Qualities that have been valued:

1. Expression of design tastes, aesthetic ideas or intellectual ideals;
2. Skill and scale in the management, design and construction of landscape elements;
3. Topography and landscape features of a particular character;
4. Conformity with idealised notions of landscape;   — *imaginaries*
5. Habitat for plant and animal species;
6. Minerals, rocks and geological formations;
7. Testimony to a distinctive culture, its way of life or its artefacts;
8. Testimony of technologies or particular social organisation;
9. Association of a place with artists, writers, painters or musicians;
10. Association of a place with myth, folklore, historical events or traditions;
11. Association of a place with spiritual and/or religious life or history;
12. Association with individual or group memory or remembrance;
13. Association of a place with formative intellectual, philosophical and metaphysical ideas or movements;
14. Associated artefacts such as records or objects generated by, or associated with, the landscape;
15. Suitability for the generation of emotional responses, e.g. awe, wonder, terror, fear or well-being, composure, order, appropriateness to human scale;   — *peri-urban edgeland*
16. Suitability to accommodate sought-after physical activities;
17. Functionality, with interrelated, or interdependent, elements;
18. Connection with other places, making a group;
19. Degree of knowledge.

These are all neutral qualities upon which most people could agree, but the value of the landscape arises because they will appreciate them maybe for a variety of reasons, often differing according to culture, profession and experiences. Qualities are the nouns and values are the adjectives. In the list below are many of the more commonly cited reasons given for value-judgements.

Knowledge gives value

A List of Reasons for Value Judgements:

1. Excellent in artistic terms;
2. Rare: a scarce example;
3. Abundant: of a particular quality;
4. Complex;
5. Influential: has influenced developments elsewhere;
6. Exemplar: a notable example of its type, style, or the work of a particular designer;
7. Sequential: the outcome of an interesting sequence of events or phases;
8. Grouped: part of a group of places illustrating the same or related phenomena;
9. Authentic: the genuine original, not a replacement or a restoration;
10. Entire: maintains its extent and completeness;
11. Vulnerable: degree to which the qualities are at risk;
12. Accessible: provides significant intellectual and recreational opportunities;
13. Distinctive: expressive of local customs and preferences or a unique creation;
14. Socially valuable: linked with sense of community or national identity;
15. Popular: providing a resource for a large number of people;
16. Economically valuable: associated with monetary value, either intrinsically or through products.

Once a collective value-judgement enters the realm of politics and policy, it will be pointed out that not all landscapes with these desirable qualities can be protected, and choices have to be made. Criteria are asked for that set a threshold of significance. More 'objective' methods for determining relative value often use a points system which turns out to be subjectively devised. Hence evaluation is usually carried out by a committee that has long experience in such matters. National and international criteria for landscapes were established by UNESCO, the UK Government, the US Secretary of State, and governments around the world, all reflecting a complex and nuanced approach to defining value. Terms were often enshrined in legislation, and while conflicts of terminology exist between countries and disciplines, the same criteria recurred, suggesting that aesthetic values are moderately consistent across Western countries. Rather different criteria can be found in other cultures.

The rise of cultural landscapes

In studies of landscape the phenomenon that was particularly symptomatic of the 1990s mindset was the rise of cultural landscapes. Conventional disciplines provided the academic understanding of topography, geomorphology, ecology and human settlement, but they were brought together when the subject began to address the values imbued in the landscape. Its starting point was that these derive from human judgement, and its contribution has been to describe them in their variety and complexity. All landscape is within its scope, so it embraces designed landscapes, agricultural ones, relict ones, national parks, urban landscapes, and the rich associations that they often have.

Carl Sauer stated the basics back in 1925: 'Culture is the agent, the natural area is the medium, the cultural landscape the result'.[24] His school of geography ensured that many of the pioneers of the subject were on the west coast of America.[25] Meanwhile the German tradition of landscape ecology was strong before, during and after the Second World War.[26]

Cultural landscapes are the record of human struggles and achievements, in the context of organisation, technology, natural factors – history written on the land instead of upon the page. The extraordinary achievements of farming communities in having created the rice terraces of the Philippines and China (fig. 5.4), the mountain-top citadel and terraces at Machu Picchu (fig. 5.5), the vineyards of the Rhine gorge, the sixteenth-century drainage of the Veneto and the Roman field systems of southern Italy and north Africa, are amongst

Figure 5.4 *Honghe Hani rice terraces, Yunnan Province, China; an achievement both of the available technology and social organisation.*

The rise of cultural landscapes

Figure 5.5 *Machu Picchu, Peru, a 15th century Inca citadel and centre of an agricultural estate high in the Andes.*

the examples. The spiritual association with land is pointed out, from Stonehenge, Mont St Michel and Monserrat (fig. 5.6) in Europe, to the folkloric sites of aboriginal and native communities in Australia and the Americas. The Australians discovered evidence for over 60,000 years of habitation of the continent by the Aborigines, and were impressed by their beliefs and traditions of living in the landscape. The traditions of North American 'First Peoples' are similarly being looked upon with fresh interest by those of European descent. With the incorporation of such human values, the scientific approach of landscape ecology has thereby blossomed into cultural landscapes.[27]

Increasingly, this new lens was the way through which landscapes came to be viewed. The outstanding consequence of this was that academics and practitioners became aware of, and enjoyed, the complexity of landscape and the human values invested in it. Several abutting disciplines began to pool their ideas to this end. Archaeologists realised that they could understand ancient cultures better if they looked at the wider scene; landscape architects recognised that the appearance of the landscape is determined by its history and use; ecologists likewise recognised that an area's ecology is often critically determined by human intervention; anthropologists listened to the

136 *Facts, value and ideology*

Figure 5.6 *Spiritual values attached to a mountain: the monastery high up on Monserrat is thought of as the spiritual centre of Catalonia, Spain.*

oral traditions of native peoples celebrating the landscape; and cultural historians and geographers explored the associations between the landscape and the mind.

The rise of cultural landscapes as a subject was a signal of deep undercurrents. It promoted a workable practical knowledge of the dynamic between human activity and the Earth. The landscape was seen as an archive of the consequences of value-systems as they have interacted with their physical environments, the record of the human race's struggle, intellectual and physical, etched upon the Earth's surface. Insights gained could help humans behave more rationally, using judgement informed by intimations of what consequences are likely to flow from action. The landscape thus became a potential aid to shaping the future.

Morality and action

Having convictions was not just about whether the earth is flat or round, a matter that has no moral consequence, but encompassed the way things ought to have been. The uncertainties about almost everything (see Chapter 4) suggested that the only defensible starting point was that the individual had to decide on what was right and how

Figure 5.7 *An etching of 'King John signing Magna Carta'; a public expression of private views converted into law, depicted by John Leech in* The Comic History of England *(1855).*

to act. In the 1970s it was increasingly common to find people making reference to their personal values rather than beliefs ordained by some higher religious or political power. These values would provide internal references for what was good, beneficial, important, useful, beautiful, desirable and constructive. They formed the standard when individuals acted according to conscience. One could not abnegate responsibility for one's actions.

This possibly obvious point is made because for most of the twentieth century many people adopted some ideology that predetermined their decisions ('normative ethics'). Acting in certain ways to conform to one's higher beliefs, though, did not help in all cases when responses to unpredictable or particular issues were required. Regrettably, by postulating behaviour supposedly inherited genetically, human ecology and Jungian psychology focused on programmed behaviour rather than the role of free will. They thereby served the human race ill at a time of fundamental social, economic and environmental change, and when answers that are essentially moral by nature were urgently required.

One test for whether people feel value in the landscape would be that they may regret the loss of some of its qualities. The public expression of personal values might lead the individual to align with like-minded groups

138 *Facts, value and ideology*

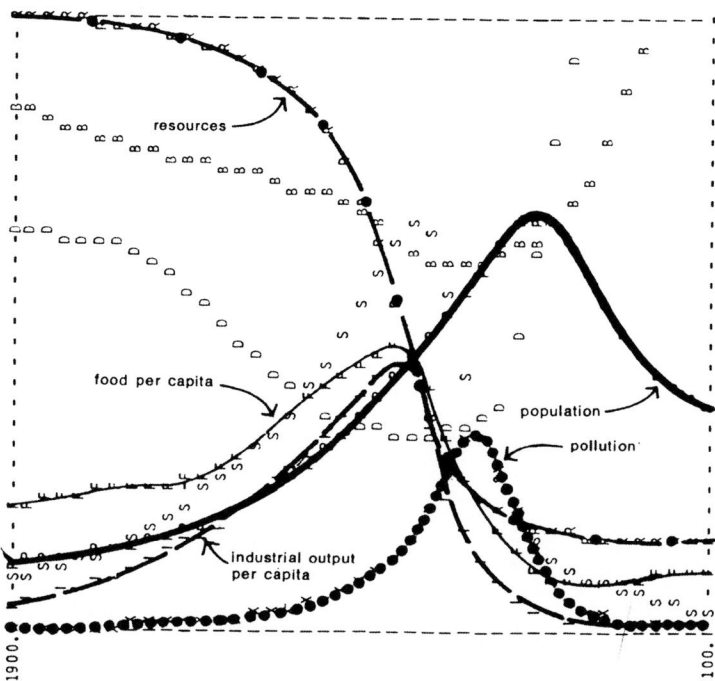

The "standard" world model run assumes no major change in the physical, economic, or social relationships that have historically governed the development of the world system. All variables plotted here follow historical values from 1900 to 1970. Food, industrial output, and population grow exponentially until the rapidly diminishing resource base forces a slowdown in industrial growth. Because of natural delays in the system, both population and pollution continue to increase for some time after the peak of industrialization. Population growth is finally halted by a rise in the death rate due to decreased food and medical services.

Figure 5.8 *The Club of Rome's predictions in 1972: using modelling, they predicted global disaster unless population and/or the consumption of resources were controlled.*

of people, and this would lead to mass action. Conservationists seek to forestall a threat by recognition and definition of values so that they may be protected. Historically, this process laid the foundations of law, custom and tradition. Rights could be advocated and passed into law, starting from the Magna Carta of 1215 (fig. 5.7). Any such rights, being essentially political decisions, could be taken away as well as granted.

Some of the well-known examples of environmental action taken in the late twentieth century are outlined hereunder. The population and standards of living were continually rising, but this implied much greater consumption of resources. Alarm bells began to sound, and in 1970 the Club of Rome reminded all that the Earth's resources were finite, and that if humanity's consumption of them continued to rise intolerable pollution and economic collapse could be the result (fig. 5.8).[28] Its first report, *The Limits to Growth* (1972), received

Morality and action **139**

Figure 5.9 *The* Phyllis Cormack, *later renamed* Greenpeace, *sailing to Alaska in 1971 to prevent atomic testing.*

considerable public attention. Fears were expressed that politicians seemed unwilling to avert the imminent catastrophes, at first from nuclear war, and then from pollution.[29] It was an exciting time: it seemed that politics and economics would never be the same again.

Greenpeace was founded in 1971 in Vancouver, Canada, when a small group of activists, with a conviction that a few individuals could make a difference, set sail from that city in an old fishing boat, the *Phyllis Cormack*, renamed *Greenpeace* (fig. 5.9). Their mission was to sail into a nuclear testing ground at Amchitka, a tiny island off the coast of Alaska, to forestall a nuclear detonation. The island, in one of the world's most earthquake-prone regions, happened to be the last refuge for 3,000 endangered sea otters, and home to bald eagles, peregrine falcons and other wildlife. The boat was intercepted before reaching Amchitka, and the United States Government detonated the device anyway, but Greenpeace had achieved its aim of worldwide publicity. Nuclear testing on Amchitka was terminated later that year, and it became a bird sanctuary.

Greenpeace's principles had been inspired by the Quaker practice of 'bearing witness'. Every member took personal responsibility for their actions based on conscience, and was committed to non-violent action. There were many other global environmental issues to confront – commercial whaling, grey seal culling, dumping of nuclear and toxic waste – and as it tackled them Greenpeace's ambition grew to that of altering the outlook of governments, industry and the public so that they would stop viewing the Earth as an inexhaustible resource and start treating it as something precious that needed sustainable and careful management. By taking sometimes quite risky direct action Greenpeace generated sympathy for its causes and had an impact far beyond its numbers. The message spread like wildfire across the developed nations until it had offices in over 40 countries.[30]

The second example of global action concerned the principle of conservation that a resource should not be exploited beyond its powers of recuperation. John Muir, the founder of the Sierra Club in the United States, had argued for 'use without impairment' in the 1910s, and this principle had been strongly promoted since, but the difficulty was in implementing it at a global scale. Many landscape designers, perhaps most, were inclined to be sympathetic, yet were unable to see how landscape design could help in any meaningful way. Many ideas were put forward, in particular designing for low energy-consumption and by specifying low-maintenance regimes of care.[31] It was difficult to see the relevance of an individual's contribution, though, when the issues were global. Did 'think globally, act locally' sound like a compelling rallying cry? Hardly. The only way to tackle a problem like global warming was for governments world-wide to collaborate in setting laws and regulations to which all were obliged to comply.[32]

There was, however, a clash between increasing globalized economic growth, which individual governments were loath to arrest, and accelerating global environmental degradation. One of the first uses of the term 'sustainable' to describe the conservation principle was by the Club of Rome in 1972 in *Limits to Growth*: 'we are searching for a model output that represents a world system that is sustainable without sudden and uncontrolled collapse and capable of satisfying the basic material requirements of all of its people'. In 1983 the United Nations requested a former Prime Minister of Norway, Gro Harlem Brundtland, to create a body independent of the UN to address this question. The Brundtland Commission reported in 1987 through a document entitled *Our Common Future*. This defined the concept of 'Sustainable Development' as: 'development that meets the needs of the present without compromising the ability of future generations to meet their own needs'. In 1992 this became 'Agenda 21' (for the 21st Century), and the world's nations were invited to subscribe to its principles and implement measures.

Another successful international agreement was the banning of volatile chlorofluorocarbons (CFCs) which were being widely used as refrigerants, propellants (as aerosols), and solvents. Unfortunately they had caused the depletion of the ozone layer over the Antarctic and were strong greenhouse gases. Unless action was taken the problem would become more widespread, and so the Montreal Protocol 1987 led to the phasing out of their production worldwide. Over time the ozone hole in Antarctica slowly recovered, and projections indicated that the ozone layer would return to 1980 levels between 2050 and 2070. This initiative and that for sustainability have been hailed as examples of exceptional international co-operation that pressured governments to pass laws, and set regulations for the benefit of all mankind.

The logic of ecocentrism

Although this book is about changes to landscape theory, seen as an aspect of modern culture, it would be very deficient as a book about landscape, if it did not also mention the impetus to a fresh round of ecocentrism given by the rise of environmentalism at much the same time.

Deep ecology and ecosophy

The term 'deep ecology' was coined by Arne Naess, a Norwegian philosopher (fig. 5.10). Inspired by Rachel Carson's book, *Silent Spring* (1962), a critique of the use of pesticides, he resigned from his professorship to devote himself full time to environmental matters. In 1976 his theoretical work, *Økologi, Samfunn og Livsstil* (*Ecology, Community and Lifestyle*), proposed a fundamentally altered conception of how things ought to be. Instead of the modernist anthropocentric outlook, reinforcing the dualism of man and nature, the one seeking mastery over the other, he reaffirmed the ecological perspective in which humans were necessarily part of, and dependent on, the environment. The realization of the 'ecological self' was to accept that a seeming individual was all one with everything else that existed. His identity would be defined not as an individual but in terms of the whole.

Naess put forward the term 'deep ecology' as the radical environmentalist's approach to the world's problems. It started from the premise that all forms of life had value in their own right, and this was irrespective of their usefulness for human purposes. Richness and diversity contributed to the fulfilment of these values and were also values in themselves. Humans had no right to reduce these values except to satisfy vital human needs, though human interference with

Figure 5.10 *Arne Naess, the prophet of Deep Ecology, by Andres Musta.*

the nonhuman world had already become excessive. Public policy therefore needed changing, and this would necessarily result in quite different prescriptions for economic, technological, and ideological matters.[33] There had been arguments in *Limits to Growth* about the need to limit the world's population. Naess is said to have suggested that 100 million would be about right. The remaining people would have an improved quality of life at the price of a lower standard of living as measured by consumption.

The logic of ecocentrism

The 'deep ecology' approach was differentiated from 'shallow ecology'; whilst the former would involve deep questioning, right down to fundamental root causes, the latter was well-meaning but without its insights, and would not inspire a change in the way people perceive the world around them. For example, a shallow approach might seek a technological fix, say purifying air or water, though this might be through expensive equipment and consuming quantities of electricity. Laws might seek to limit permissible pollution as a compromise with the interests of industry. Sustainability was clearly a shallow ecological concept, as it did not prescribe radical solutions. Deep ecology, by contrast, would combat the causes of pollution, not merely its superficial short-range effects.

The root of environmental problems had been misdirected conceptions of the place of humans in nature. If, though, environmentalists made value-judgements in favour of the biosphere as a whole, and conceived of the world and themselves in such a way that the intrinsic value of life forms were fully regarded, 'self-realisation' had been reached, and would flower into a personal 'ecosophy' (ecological philosophy). High standards of personal responsibility would consequently be expected. Naess believed that environmental problems would be solved when enough individuals had seen the light and started acting in concert.

These ideas were being expressed at the same time as another philosopher, the New Zealander Richard Routley, was likewise calling for a new ethic. This was a development from Aldo Leopold's plea for a sense of stewardship, though went further in arguing for the intrinsic value of animals, plants and ecosystems and for the moral qualities of naturalness.[34] These two philosophers' arguments subsequently dominated environmental ethics. They inspired environmentalists, ecologists and green movements, and gave strength to the advocacy of preservation of wilderness, human population control and simple living. One biologist saw the arguments as so compelling that he wrote: 'The time has come for ethics to be removed temporarily from the hands of the philosophers and biologicized.'[35]

Direct realism

Over matters such as perception, behaviour and aesthetics, the ecocentric mindset referred to the holistic relationship that an individual had with everything else that existed. Holism, which is mentioned above (Chapter 3), proposed that the properties of a system cannot be explained by the sum of its component parts; rather, the system as a whole determines how the parts behave. Any attempt to reduce the whole to its constituent parts will eliminate some aspects that are present only when seen as a whole.

On the other hand, if supposed parts are artificially brought together they will not make a meaningful whole. Ecocentrists were convinced that their holistic scheme had no such flaws.

Many referred to the theories set out by the Cornell professor, James Gibson, in *The Ecological Approach to Visual Perception* (1979), proclaimed by him as 'ecological psychology'. He was much influenced by systems theory and by the holistic principles of gestalt (whole form) psychology, namely that the individual forms a whole view of the world rather than through its disaggregated elements.[36]

Gibson preferred the concept of 'perceptual systems' over that of the senses. Seeing, perceiving, evaluating and acting were all one unified act of appraising the world for its 'affordances', the benefits that the environment could afford the individual. Seeing was simply the information-gathering component. It was not that the eye was passive, awaiting stimulus, but that the mind engaged with the environment around by using the eye as one means to hunt for comprehension and clarity in building up a picture of it. The human had evolved to scan the environment in order to be at one with it. 'I realized that perceiving is an act, not a response, an act of attention, not a triggered impression, an achievement, not a reflex.'

He presumed that a human would know his world by moving about in it, and that the individual was not constrained to what could be seen, but had a constantly adjusted, three-dimensional construct in the head of a place with objects seen and unseen, heard and smelt (fig. 5.11). He noted that the horizon, objects and other aspects of a view have an existence independent of the perceiver, and persisted whether being observed or not, and in whatever light conditions prevailed. Such 'invariants' were used in forming mental maps and depth perception. These 'facts' were assembled by 'a process of information pickup that involved the exploratory activity of looking around, getting around, and looking at things'.[37]

Gibson's hypothesis was classed as 'direct, or common sense', perception unmediated by cognition and producing a 'direct realism' knowledge of reality. The world, its beauty, its perception, appropriate ethics and human behaviour were all one seamless gestalt whole. It opposed the growing assumption in social science of 'indirect realism', the understanding of perception whereby the eye received neural signals only, and the mind engaged in cognitive processes to determine the nature of reality. He would not agree with cognition:

> The belief of empiricists that the perceived meanings and values of things are supplied from the past experience of the observer will not do.[38]

The logic of ecocentrism

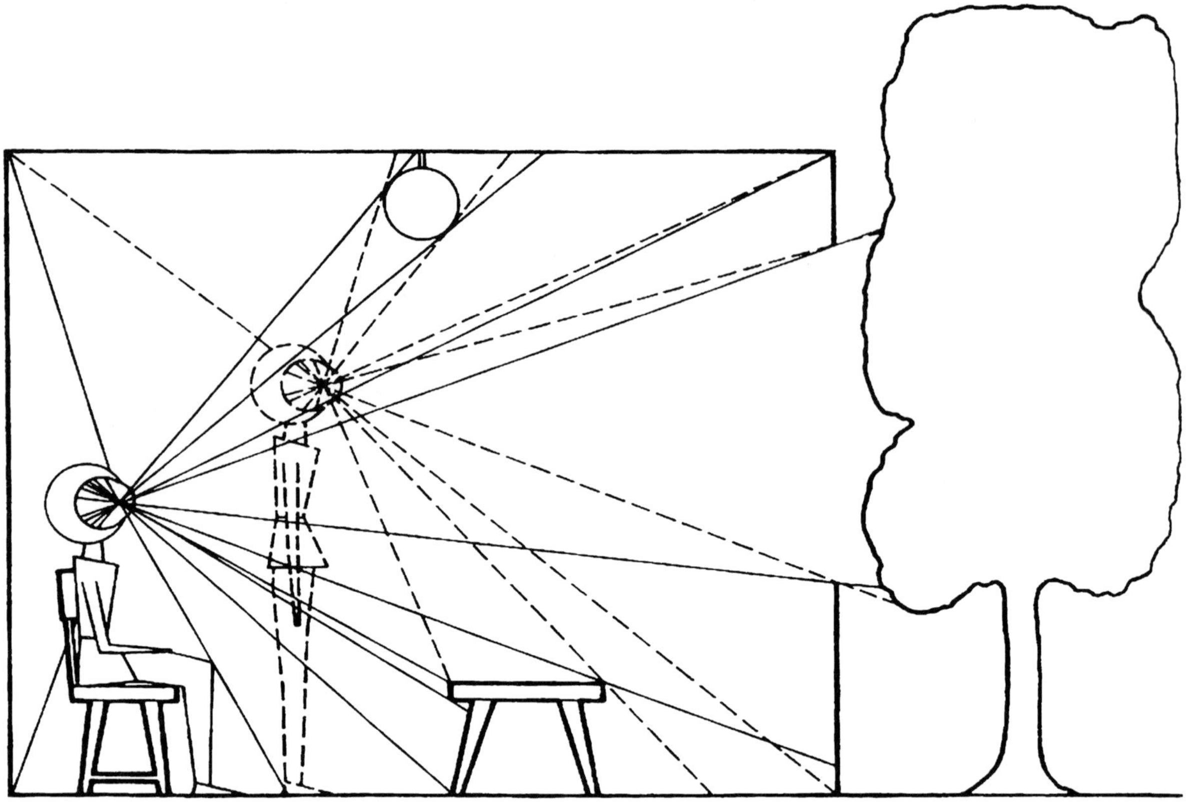

Figure 5.11 *James Gibson pointed out that motion (here standing from sitting) leads to the shape and distance of fixed objects being defined. His argument was that vision builds a picture of the world without cognition, but he could not satisfactorily explain how objects are identified and evaluated, i.e. fully perceived.*

His rejection of cognitive perception was shared by many in artistic circles at the time, particularly those primitivists and abstract expressionists who believed in a direct sense of feeling, such as Henry Moore and Jackson Pollock. Phenomenologists also tended to favour direct perception over cognition.

One such was Arnold Berleant, whose doctoral thesis had been on John Dewey, and whose *The Aesthetic Field: A Phenomenology of Aesthetic Experience* (1970) gave a critique of the fine-art aesthetic theory, especially of disinterestedness, and proposed to investigate aesthetic experience phenomenologically. Soon he became attuned to the rise of ecocentrism in the 1970s, which reinforced his gestalt or holistic frame of mind:

> ... there is no outside world. There is no outside. Nor is there an inner sanctum in which I can take refuge from inimical external forces. The perceiver (mind) is an aspect of the perceived (body) and conversely; person and environment are continuous.[39]

Berleant's conception of 'environment' was not just of the physical world, as his holistic approach embraced 'cultural influences' such as memories, beliefs, and associations. 'Because we live as part of a

146 *Facts, value and ideology*

cultural environment,' he explained, 'our aesthetic perception and judgement are inevitably cultural.' Judgement introduces values, and these 'originate in experience as an inseparable part of being human' and lay at the centre of the aesthetic. This expanded definition of the environment was not only the basis of Berleant's approach to aesthetics, but it gave a rounded hypothesis that included ethics. It 'profoundly affects our moral understanding of human relationships and our social ethics' so that:

> Aesthetics, then, is no illusory escape from the moral realm but ultimately becomes both its guide and its fulfillment.

Meanwhile his commitment to 'direct realism' was seen in statements like: 'perceptual directness, with its strong focus on immediacy and presence, becomes pre-eminent.' He was to write that we perceive the environment with all our senses including the kinasthetic, that 'perception is not passive but an active, reciprocal engagement with environment', and that 'the philosophic concepts of sense data ... are now cognitively obsolete'.[40] These parallels with Gibson's 'ecological psychology' were striking.

In 1993 another theory of 'direct reality' was put forward that fully dispensed with the role of culture. A professor of film studies from the University of Wisconsin-Madison, Noël Carroll, argued that one form of appreciation was simply a matter of people opening themselves to being immersed in an experience, and allowing themselves to respond emotionally and enjoy as they felt fit. This 'arousal model' saw the more visceral responses to nature as an actual form of appreciation known to many that did not require any previous knowledge or cultural interpretation, something that was 'bred in the bone'. He described 'being moved by nature' as a respectable form of nature appreciation, for example:

> ... standing near a towering cascade, our ears reverberating with the roar of falling water, we are overwhelmed and excited by its grandeur ... Moreover, when caught up in such experiences our attention is fixed on certain aspects of the natural expanse rather than others – the palpable force of the cascade, its height, the volume of the water, the way it alters the surrounding atmosphere, etc.[41]

It was interesting that a specialist in film studies should propose a theory of total immersion that was closest to the holistic viewpoint. He added that this form of emotional response 'will involve some sort of selective attention', echoing the nature of 'significant form' as described by Clive Bell (see Chapter 4).

The logic of ecocentrism **147**

What if the logic is flawed?

Most writers on deep ecology were seeking to establish their subject and so chose assertive terminology – they referred to 'deep' ecology and 'strong' ecocentrism. 'Environment' was promoted at the expense of value-laden 'landscape'. Berleant thought that 'The very word "landscape", for example, institutionalizes the conventional objectification of environment'.[42]

The cultural landscape became dehumanised and redefined as in the definition: 'a landscape is a heterogeneous land area composed of a cluster of interacting ecosystems that is repeated in similar form throughout.'[43] Landscape had become land, preferably wilderness.

The ecologists were anxious to highlight the 'new' against a background of the 'traditional'. Berleant, in a somewhat historicist mood, implied that any cultural analysis, labelled as 'anthropocentric', would inevitably be overtaken by ecocentrism:

> The ecological conception of environment required a major conceptual shift whose acceptance is slow and painful. Even today, more than a century later, it remains locked in conflict with anthropocentric attitudes that still regard environment as a place that is essentially opposed and hostile to human interests or at least separate and apart, and so properly subject to domination and exploitation.
>
> Yet the ecological view continues to develop and gain in influence as part of the present-day emergence of widespread environmental consciousness.[44]

It was certainly true that the ecological approach was becoming so dominant by the 1990s that a cognitive voice was hard to discern.

There were, though, unanswered questions about ecocentrism. The general tenor in philosophy had been 'post-structuralism' which was the questioning of the overarching 'grand narratives' (science, Marxism, progress, etc.), and their purpose of deriving truth over greater matters, but here was ecosophy, in the manner of a new religion, reintroducing a new 'structure' all of its own. It seemed to be out of step with all other fields of learning.

Another area of doubt concerned the fundamentals of perception. James Gibson, as we have seen, promoted 'direct realism'. In the opposing theory of 'indirect realism' the raw data from the senses is ordered into shapes, forms and qualities in order to be classified, then compared to knowledge in the memory to identify what that object may be. It suggested that the individual developed 'internal representations', or the mental imagery of objects that could be stored in memory (see Chapter 4 – 'Cognition'). Some theorists proposed that the individual developed 'schemata', a matrix of preconceived ideas whereby new information could be compared, organized and perceived, and some even that we develop a miniature virtual-reality replica of the world. The common theme, though, was that information was absorbed by being compared to existing knowledge.

'Direct realism', on the other hand, took the 'common-sense' view that objects exist independently of the mind, and that it was possible to perceive them without invoking this complex chain of cognitive processes. Its difficulty was to explain how objects could be perceived from the raw sensory data made available through the eye. In Gibson's theory the mind instructed the eye to pick up information on 'invariants', or permanent features. The eye accordingly scanned, following which 'the inputs of the receptors have to be processed, of course'. This processing would involve 'the extracting and abstracting of the invariants that specify the environment'. Gibson's theory gave no means to do this, nor did he explain how perception of the invariants became knowledge of them. Perhaps he did not feel the need, as:

> To perceive the environment and to conceive it are different in degree but not in kind. One is continuous with the other. Knowing is an extension of perceiving.[45]

His justification for asserting this appeared to go back to his reliance on gestalt theory with its holistic concept of the whole having a reality of its own, independent of the parts.

On the question of ethics, there was an array of criticisms of the ecocentrists' views that all organisms are of equal moral worth and that the role of the human being in the future of the planet should be downplayed. Its ethics demanded 'intrinsic' rights for non-human life, but developing a non-anthropocentric set of values was a self-contradiction, and might be suspected as a concealment of the writers' own ideologies.[46]

By no means all environmentalists were ecocentric. There were anthropocentric ones who were pressing for a 'project of social reconstruction' as the solution to the environmental crisis. One such took a dim view of the new thinking challenging his long-standing anarchist critique of capitalism and exploitation, and wrote excoriating criticism of 'a vague, formless, often self-contradictory, and invertebrate thing called deep ecology':

> ... deep ecology, despite all its social rhetoric, has virtually no real sense that our ecological problems have their ultimate roots in society and in social problems. It preaches a gospel of a kind of 'original sin' that accurses a vague species called humanity ...

He was particularly troubled by the implications of rapid reduction of population, which could be achieved only through 'eco-fascism' of the most lethal kind. Basically, he thought, ecocentrists were anti-human:

> Deep ecologists see this vague and undifferentiated humanity essentially as an ugly 'anthropocentric' thing ... presumably a malignant product of natural evolution ... that is 'overpopulating' the planet, 'devouring' its resources, and destroying its wildlife and the biosphere ...
>
> Deep ecology, formulated largely by privileged male white academics, has managed to bring sincere naturalists like Paul Shepard into the same company as patently antihumanist and macho mountain men like David Foreman of Earth First! who preach a gospel that humanity is some kind of cancer in the world of life.[47]

Militant ecocentrists may indeed have been too eager to exclude the involvement of humans, saying that the Earth would function very well without them.

Any such dogma was of course irreconcilable with a viewpoint that the world is known through our experience of it – and we see it through human eyes and with a human mind. Dewey himself doubted that it was possible for an artist (or presumably anybody else) 'to approach a scene with no interests and attitudes, no background of values, drawn from his prior experience'.[48]

Cultural geographers were reminded of the dark days of environmental determinism:

> It is an ideology which had a major impact upon ... the early stages of human ecology and anthropogeography. The central working concept was 'environmentalism' in one form or another ... The general concept is not only still alive, it is rapidly gathering strength in somewhat more sophisticated form. It lurks in various guises within much of the recent literature on ecology and environment.[49]

After hearing the views of Gordon Orians, a professor of zoology at the University of Washington, Seattle, on the evolutionary origin of landscape aesthetics relating to their resources, Denis Cosgrove responded:

> Frankly, I have very little sympathy with this paper. I do not doubt that as part of nature we intuit strong links between processes and forms and those of our own bodies ... but such intuitions are so transformed, overlain and mediated by social, cultural and economic as well as personal meanings historically, that to trace the bio-physiological bases of environmental (not landscape) response seems largely futile at best, and at worst pandering to the most dangerously ideological interpretation of 'human nature'.[50]

The 'new' cultural geographers had impressed on their readers that human history is one of constant environmental modification, manipulation, destruction and creation, both material and imaginative. Their focus on abstract ideas brought tensions with the ecologists as above, and also with other geographers whose conception of the land was more than just a palimpsest onto which political and ideological narratives had been inscribed through history: they were places where people lived, enjoyed and felt passionate about them. Maybe the 'way of seeing' approach did seem too detached, too superior.

That said, the desire and capacity to enquire into cherished notions, to see where they came from and whether they remain valid, is fundamental to landscape studies. Such enquiries were continued by the 'environmental historians' who applied their forensic skills to the ecological approach in the same way that the 'new' cultural geographers had done to paintings and literature. Bill McKibben, an American environmental activist and journalist, aware that there is no true wilderness any more, investigated this ecological nirvana in *The End of Nature* (1989). The historian William Cronon expanded on this thought in *Uncommon Ground: Toward Reinventing Nature* (1995). This traced the concept of wilderness through 300 years of American history, and concluded that untouched, pristine, wilderness was mythical, and indeed impossible, as nature was never something apart from humans. Furthermore, the very idea of 'nature' had been reinvented several times and was thus clearly a cultural construct. Cronon upset many ecocentrists!

Doubts about the logic and tenor of ecocentrism led many to reject its most ardent formulations. There was, though, common ground with the anthropocentrists over more than each side cared to admit. One does not need to be an ecocentrist to agree with the desirability of individuals taking personal responsibility, nor of the general principle of 'engagement'.

The logic of ecocentrism

The metaphysics of nature

Holism was concisely summarized by Aristotle in his *Metaphysics*: 'The whole is more than the sum of its parts'. This was restated by the gestalt theorist that inspired Gibson as 'The whole is other than the sum of the parts'. Aristotle, it can be noted, was clear that what later became known as 'holism' was metaphysics, the area of higher-level truths beyond the boundaries of verifiable scientific knowledge.

We have seen that Carl Sauer considered environmental determinism to be an 'assertion of a faith'. It was perhaps unfortunate that Jim Lovelock, in postulating his Gaia hypothesis, chose to name the Earth after a goddess.[51] He himself warned that the Earth had no mind and no morals; it was just a mighty biological system that adapted to have multiple checks and balances that returned the whole to an equilibrium. Nevertheless the metaphor was compelling to some, and a mystic reverence for Gaia took on a religious flavour as She was seen to proffer the answers to many fundamental questions about life. Lovelock afterwards added the gloss that the Earth would recover after the extinction of humans by themselves.[52]

By the 1990s deep ecology had become a social movement with religious and mystical undertones. Murray Bookchin related that when George Sessions, co-author of *Deep Ecology: Living as if Nature Mattered* (1985), was asked at an ecofeminist conference about the differences between deep ecology and social ecology, he identified it as one between spiritualism and Marxism. Clearly, ecology had stepped over the line from science to religion.

The spiritualism referred to was the worship of a new God, one as far from the anthropomorphic God of the *Bible* as could be found, namely nature, the mindless but yet self-ordering system from which all life had sprung. Self-realization meant primarily one's self-subjugation to this God that needed no followers. Morality became the defence of nature which did not care anyway. Non-ecocentrists saw such a religion as perverse, and held that morality's purpose was primarily to guide relations between human beings. Environmental problems would have to be solved without returning the human race to a former geological age.

The adoption of deep ecology as a quasi-religion was far from being the first case of the metaphysics of nature. There had in fact been a succession of them since the rise of Romanticism in the early nineteenth century. By far the most prolific source of misconceptions about the landscape was that the fundamental laws of the universe were sensed unconsciously through long and intimate exposure to nature which is the fount of all that is good and worthy, in contrast to the city which was artificial and a barren soil for the soul and its inspiration. Getting away to the mountains, nature or rural life was thought to purify the senses and to expose the soul to the more refreshing truths inherent in Creation. The Scandinavian nature worshipers promoted the purification of body and mind through close contact with nature. The French-American environmentalist, René Dubos, wrote: 'man eventually rejects excessive abstraction and mechanisation in order to re-establish contact with natural forces from which he derives the awareness of his own existence and to which he owes his very sense of being'.[53]

The inspirational value of communion with nature was once very widely supposed. Professor Joad had asserted that contact with the country, especially mountains, was necessary for the human being to rediscover the soul and creativity. A common assumption by those advocating this view was that nature herself is the greatest creative force of all. Creativity in the individual was achieved only by integration into nature's rhythms and continuum of purpose. A belief in one's self as a minor stroke in an infinitely grand design provides great solace. The problem with submerging the individual in this way, though, was that any feelings of lack of achievement, bad luck, or frustration at the unsolved mysteries of life could be excused on the basis that they must have been pre-ordained. This would encourage 'fatalism', suppressing the desire to be inventive or to achieve, which, of course, would defeat the object of communing with nature.

Closely allied to the concept of the inspirational role of nature was that of nature as automatically and inherently beautiful. This idea had a long pedigree in enlightenment thought. Jean-Jacques Rousseau was one of its most famous promulgators. His case was that nature was truth, and truth was beauty, hence nature was beauty. A century later John Ruskin, whose work predominantly concerned nature, expressed the equation of truth and beauty again, though from his overtly religious standpoint. 'Beauty,' he said, 'is a gift of God; a gift not necessary to our being, but added to, and elevating it'. He felt that the truth of his art would surely reveal beauty, which was thus a matter of moral perception, more than sensual or intellectual. A century on from Ruskin, Peter Fuller still felt 'the impulse in the human breast to affirm beauty in and unity with the natural world'.[54] As the equation of nature and beauty came increasingly to be the orthodox view, the connecting part of the logic concerned with truth had come to be overlooked.

The metaphysics of nature **153**

Figure 5.12 *Le Roy's 'eco-cathedral' in Heerenveen, the Netherlands: piles of stone and the giant hogweed has mostly died.*

Allan Ruff, a British landscape manager, equated nature with beauty. He was among those arguing for a style of treatment of open spaces modelled more closely upon ecological principles, being much inspired by the theory and practice of Jacobus Thijsse and Louis le Roy in The Netherlands. Ruff shared the Dutch assumption of 'naturalness eventually bringing its own aesthetic quality',[55] and waxed lyrical about Le Roy's work at the Kennedylaan in Heerenveen (fig. 5.12) in the late 1960s which had:

> ... a quality that derives from the aesthetic of nature. As one enters, all the stress and strain of the surrounding town falls [sic] away and is replaced by the sound of birds, the flight of dragonflies, the sight of snails on the hogweed stems. In the shelter of the trees the sun's warmth is pleasant and free from glare whilst the trees make pleasing patterns on the path. The senses come alive ... As Le Roy had said, harmony in nature brings a closeness to nature and between people, so that people stop to talk in a way that would never happen on the pavements to either side.

This passage associated nature with aesthetic, even moral, value.

It is worth expanding on the idea of 'harmony', sometimes called 'harmonious balance', as it became central to the ethics of human ecology, and its visual confirmation was said to bring a sense of beauty. The idea of the harmony of the spheres went back many centuries, and concepts of the biological community, succession, climax and self-regulating biomes, all emphasising equilibrium and the balance of nature, dominated ecological theory for most of the twentieth century. A supposedly scientific theory proposed that there is an inbuilt human impulse to respect nature and reach harmony with it. 'Biophilia', promoted in E.O. Wilson's *Biophilia* (1984) as 'the urge to affiliate with other forms of life', supposedly makes the human sensitive to the qualities of natural objects. According to this proposition, an automatic appreciation of the natural world is the legacy of hundreds of thousands of years living in and with it. For these various reasons harmony seemed to be a worthy aim in the relations between humans and their environment, and human ecologists considered that, if achieved, it would bring automatic social as well as aesthetic bliss.

In ancient Greek mysticism, harmony was fundamental to the sense of world order, music and geometry. It is commonly associated with Pythagoras and Heraclites. In Renaissance Europe, from Dante onwards, the theme was encountered in literature, such as when Jonathan Swift made Gulliver visit a wonderful country where the land was fruitful and the people wise. When Jean-Jacques Rousseau's fictional heroine, Julie, created a beautiful natural garden called 'Elysée' (which Rousseau had modelled on descriptions of uninhabited Pacific islands) where she recovered her virtue.[57] In the 1790s, Thomas Johnes started to create a paradise in a Welsh valley, where peasantry and landscape would smile in unison (fig. 5.13). Edwin Landseer, in his paintings of Queen Victoria at Balmoral, depicted a tranquil natural order in which animals and highlanders alike acted deferentially to their sovereign.[58]

Jens Jensen argued that a key tenet of landscape design was that it should promote harmony:

> We shall never produce an art of landscaping worth while until we have learned to love the soil and the beauty of our homeland, and fit man's accomplishments into its infinite harmony.[59]

All these writers and practitioners saw harmony in terms of a stable balance. The ecologically harmonious landscape was such a powerful idea, pandering to romantic dreams of rural paradise to which all urbanised people, at least the economically conservative, seemed prone.

The metaphysics of nature

Figure 5.13 *Hafod House by John Warwick Smith, a vision of a landscape in harmony from the late eighteenth century. In George Cumberland,* An Attempt to Describe Hafod *(1796).*

More contemporary still was the claim by ecocentrists that all forms of life had intrinsic rights, especially that of survival. There were obvious philosophical problems with such assertions. If they cannot take on obligations, can they be said to have rights? Would the environment or a species have value if human beings did not exist? Furthermore, rights are bestowed by consent or the law by a decision of the people, and can be taken away. This could take place regarding species, say, but nobody and nothing can have intrinsic rights. In response, deep ecologists claimed to identify with and speak for non-human nature. This sounded much like human values dressed up to appear selfless.

NOTES AND REFERENCES

1. David Jacques, 'The Welcome Complexity of Cherished Landscapes', *Paysage et Amenagement*, 21, Special issue - Blois Conference, 'Landscapes in a new Europe: unity in diversity', (October 1992), 83-91.

2. Carl Sauer, 'The Morphology of Landscape', *University of California Publications in Geography* 2.2 (1925), 29 & 51-2.

3. Robert Melnick from the University of Oregon, well known for his studies of Hawaiian landscapes and their populations, was among the most respected experts on cultural landscapes in the USA in the 1990s.

4. Christopher Taylor, *The Archaeology of Gardens* (Princes Risborough, Bucks, 1983) explained this topic almost wholly in terms of aerial photography.

5. James Corner, 'The Obscene (American) Landscape', in Michael Spens (ed), *Landscape Transformed* (London, 1996), p. 10.

6. The phrase 'cultural landscape' may have been used first in Britain in Thomas Sharp, *Town Planning* (London, 1940), p. 19.

7. David Lowenthal & Hugh Prince, 'English Landscape Tastes', *Geographical Review* 55 (April 1965), 186-222.

8. For example, Yi-fu Tuan, *Topophilia: A Study of Environmental Perception, Attitudes and Values* (New York, 1974).

9. Donald W. Meinig (ed), *The Interpretation of Ordinary Landscapes* (New York, 1979), pp. v & 6.

10. Raymond Williams, *The Country and the City* (London, 1973).

11. Denis Cosgrove, *Social Formation and Symbolic Landscape* (London, 1984), pp. 11, 13 & 18.

12. Erwin Panofsky, quoted in Cosgrove, Ibid., p.17.

13. Denis Cosgrove & Stephen Daniels (eds), *The Iconography of Landscape: Essays on the Symbolic Representation of Past Environments* (Cambridge, 1988).

14. The bounds of what could reasonably be deduced from images by individual artists were sometimes transgressed, and such clues, together with the thrust, delivery and conclusion of analyses can

provide examples of how discourse on literature, painting, even landscape design, inevitably serves philosophical or political motives outside the supposed scope of the work.

15   David Pepper, *The Roots of Modern Environmentalism* (London, 1984), p. 166.

16   Lowenthal served on the English Heritage gardens committee in the early 1990s at the invitation of this author when cultural landscapes were being discussed.

17   Oliver Rackham, *The History of the Countryside* (London, 1986), pp. xiii, 26, 28, etc.

18   I once found myself appreciative of derelict land after a spell working with it, a taste that has not dimmed over the years.

19   Christopher Tunnard, *Gardens in the Modern Landscape* 1st edn (London, 1938), p. 5.

20   Allen Carlson, 'Appreciation and the Natural Environment', *Journal of Aesthetics and Art Criticism*, 37 (Spring 1979), 274.

21   David Jacques, 'Knowledge is a Value', *Landscape Research*, 17:2 (Summer 1992), 90-4.

22   Lowenthal was fond of saying this.

23   Alan Holland & Kate Rawles, 'Values in conservation', *ECOS*, 14 : 1 (1993), 14-9. The authors were from Lancaster University on a contract from the Countryside Council for Wales to examine the ethics of conservation.

24   Carl Sauer, op. cit., p. 46.

25   A tradition continued by Robert Melnick, who was already advising on evaluating, registering and managing cultural landscapes in the National Park System in 1984.

26   The pre-war German tradition included Otto Schlüter, and Walter Christaller, whose name every geography student knows, and later Wolfgang Haber, professor at Munich, and Mechtild Rössler whose doctorate was on Christaller, and who has had responsibility for cultural landscapes at the UNESCO World Heritage Centre from 1992.

27   David Jacques, 'The Rise of Cultural Landscapes', *International Journal of Heritage Studies*, 1: 2 (Winter 1994), 91-101.

28 Dennis L. Meadows *et al.*, *The Limits to Growth: A Report for the Club of Rome's Project on the Predicament of Mankind* (New York, 1972).

29 Early examples were the 'Blueprint for survival' issue of *The Ecologist*, 2: 1 (January 1972), and the report of the Club of Rome.

30 This author remembers attending Greenpeace meetings in Sheffield in 1973.

31 Catherine Findlay, 'Bio-power', *Landscape Design* (December 1996), 41-5.

32 Roger Levett, 'Feedback Loops – Part 2', *Landscape Design* (November 1991), 24-5, is an example of the calls to government to apply environmental measures, using the classic argument that what may be perceived as bad by the individual may be for the greater good if everyone acted the same.

33 Arne Naess, 'The Shallow and the Deep, Long-Range Ecology Movement. A Summary', *Inquiry*, 16 : 1 (1973), 95-100; this article was based on a lecture to the 3rd World Future Research Conference in 1972.

34 Richard Routley, 'Is There a Need for a New, an Environmental, Ethic?', in *Proceedings of the 15th World Congress of Philosophy*, 1 (Sophia, 1973), pp. 205-10.

35 Edward O Wilson, *Sociobiology, the New Synthesis* (Cambridge MA, 1975), p. 562.

36 James Gibson, *The Ecological Approach to Visual Perception* (Ithaca NY, 1979), pp. 138 & 140: in particular Kurt Koffka.

37 Ibid., pp. 147 & 244-59.

38 Ibid., p. 238.

39 Arnold Berleant, *The Aesthetics of Environment* (Philadelphia PA, 1992), pp. 4, 12 & 21-3.

40 Ibid., 16-18.

41 Noël Carroll, 'On Being Moved by Nature: Between Religion and Natural History', in Salim Kemal & Ivan Gaskell (eds), *Landscape, Natural Beauty and the Arts* (Cambridge, 1993), pp. 244-266; pp. 245 & 250-2.

42 Berleant, op. cit., p. 5.

43   Richard T.T. Forman and Michel Godron, *Landscape Ecology* (New York, 1986), p. 11.

44   Berleant, op. cit., pp. 4-5.

45   Gibson, op. cit., pp. 219, 250 & 258.

46   Tony Lynch, 'Deep Ecology as an Aesthetic Movement', *Environmental Values*, 5:2 (May 1996), 147-160.

47   Murray Bookchin, 'Social Ecology versus Deep Ecology: A Challenge for the Ecology Movement', *Green Perspectives: Newsletter of the Green Program Project* (Summer 1987), 4-5.

48   Dewey, op. cit., p. 93.

49   Meinig, op. cit., p. 36.

50   Edmund C. Penning-Rowsell & David Lowenthal (eds), *Landscape Meanings and Values* (London, 1986), p. 23.

51   James Lovelock & Sidney Epton, 'The Quest for Gaia', *New Scientist*, 65 (6 February 1975), 304.

52   Michael Allaby, *Guide to Gaia* (London, 1989) is a readable exposition of Gaian ideas by someone closely involved in their development.

53   René Dubos, 'So Human an Animal' (London, 1973), quoted by Allan R. Ruff, *Holland and the Ecological Landscape* (Stockport, 1979), p. 1.

54   John Ruskin, *Modern Painters*, Part III, 2nd American Edn (New York, 1849), p. 15.

55   Ruff, op. cit., pp. 18 & 32.

56   Peter Fuller, 'The Geography of Mother Nature', in Cosgrove and Daniels (eds) op. cit., p. 29.

57   Christopher Thacker, ' "O Tinian!" "O Juan-Fernandez": Rousseau's "Elysée" and Anson's Desert Islands', *Garden History*, V/2 (Summer 1977), 42.

58   Trevor Pringle, 'The Privation of History: Landseer, Victoria and the Highland Myth', in Cosgrove & Daniels (eds), op. cit., pp. 142-61.

59   Jens Jensen, *Siftings* (Chicago, 1939), p. 104.

CHAPTER 6

LANDSCAPE PREFERENCES

Several of the foundation stones of the theories on landscape beauty from the 1960s were undermined by the late-century world view, as demonstrated in the first three sections below. The 'big' ideas on the laws of the cosmos, the collective unconscious and the significance of form gave way to uncertainty coupled with a desire to explore ideas that did not start with these overarching theories but with the individual's experience.

The implications were many: the state of consciousness became a new focus in psychology, sidelining theories of the unconscious; a landscape's meaning was more relevant than its form; its appreciation was seen as deriving from values and preferences, rather than an instantaneous reaction; participatory aesthetics was the trend as the belief in the disinterested expert waned; and plurality accorded with reality better than assumed consensus.

The new starting point was with the individual, and his values and preferences. The recognition of place was a new departure. The chapter concludes with a look at the officially-sanctioned methods of landscape assessment and how they were modified as the new thinking took hold.

An unconscious recognition of beauty?

The 'workings of the cosmos' had been a mystifying incantation, implying both a divine plan, and that it had become manifest through physical means. However, they were ordained by universal laws of such a profundity that, in a conscious state, humans could at best only dimly perceive their outlines. Geoffrey Jellicoe had thought that these laws were nevertheless implanted in the structure of the human unconscious mind (see Chapter 1). He intended to tap the endless resources of the unconscious, and thus raise landscape design to undreamed-of heights.

Carl Jung's claims that aspects of the unconscious were inherited, and 'the undeniable common inheritance of all mankind' was impossible to disprove, though it was also, by definition, unprovable by the conscious mind. Unconscious mental states have to be consciously thinkable.[1] The observation that some mental processes take place without full consciousness of them (see Chapter 4 – 'Cognition') is no proof, and 'implicit' cognition accepts that people learn without seeking to, and objects may seem familiar without people realising exactly why. The explanation derived from the constant making of associations between sensory stimuli and ideas as part of the normal process of perception.

So whilst it was conceded that there are unconscious states – dreams, petit mals, the passing awareness of mechanical tasks when the mind is elsewhere, etc. – it was pointless to believe in the hidden powers of the unconscious mind. Without proof or even solid evidence, either way, believing in the existence of a Jungian common unconscious was a matter of faith and, as it became decreasingly helpful in explanations of how the mind works, it passed into irrelevance.

It was consciousness, not unconsciousness, that came to provide the deep insights to feed the human spirit (see Chapter 4). Consciousness was seen as an essential means for joined-up thinking to allow humans to function creatively. It was an hypothesis that made Jellicoe's appeals to the 'subconscious' redundant, whilst there were doubts as to whether his ideas were even based on a correct interpretation of Jung's. The first point to clear up was the confusion of terms. Jellicoe used the term 'subconscious'. Generally, Freud and Jung kept to the term 'unconscious', though Jung did describe a state of 'subconsciousness' which acts as a channel between the unconscious and the conscious, for example in dreams, and which was unique to each person because, in this state, personal experience mingled with the unconscious. Jellicoe's theory, though, only made sense if it referred to a supposed common unconscious; otherwise design would be meaningless to all but the designer. Besides, his description of the 'subconscious' as the source of inspirational ideas leading to artistic achievement was clearly Jung's claim for the unconscious.

Jellicoe chose to believe in a language of design using the symbols of the unconscious. He believed that certain shapes universally evoked certain reactions, for example fear, and connections to ideas such as dominant king and subdominant consort. 'Three to four days later the significance of what you have seen will be apparent ... the subconscious will work it out', he once said hopefully.[2] Jung had not sanctioned this. He had envisaged that while abstract symbols were general and inherited, their expression was personal to each individual and so could take many forms. The closest that symbols came to universality was when archetypal ideas were commonly represented in similar ways.

The assumed ease of sprinkling symbols around a design as if it were a paper chase for the unconscious would have seemed ludicrous to Jung. Those who have written about the Jungian view of art have not suggested that the artists they discuss were consciously manipulating symbols; rather the evidence for the intervention of their unconsciousness was apparent only after the creative act. The essence of the collective unconscious could not be bottled, even if it existed.

This did not mean that cultural symbolism, sometimes referred to as 'iconography', could not validly be employed in design, and it was useful to distinguish between these two types of symbolism. Jung himself did so by referring to cultural symbols as 'signs': 'Man ... employs signs ... Although these are meaningless in themselves, they have acquired a recognisable meaning through common usage or deliberate intent. Such things are not symbols'. 'Symbols' noticed by the unconscious, on the other hand, 'are natural and spontaneous products. No genius has ever sat down with a pen or brush in his hand and said: "Now I am going to invent a symbol".'[3]

Figure 6.1 *Geoffrey Jellicoe later in* The Guelph Lectures *(1983) rationalised his design for the Hemel Hempstead water garden of 1957 in terms of a water serpent of which people would be subconsciously aware.*

An unconscious recognition of beauty?

Figure 6.2 *The Kennedy memorial of 1964 at Runnymede, Surrey, showing the crowd of granite setts representing a multitude of pilgrims swarming up to the catafalque of J.F. Kennedy.*

This distinction between symbols and signs is useful in considering Jellicoe's design ideas, for it becomes clear that he was not using Jungian symbols at all, but signs. His explanation of the shape of the lake in the Hemel Hempstead Water Gardens was that it represented a serpent (fig. 6.1). The twin hillocks at the Rutherford Laboratory at Harwell represented Zeus and one of his wives, Themis. The granite sets at Runnymede represented a multitude of pilgrims (fig. 6.2). In fact Jellicoe's devices were unintelligible to either the conscious or the unconscious until they were explained. He himself pointed out that at Runnymede it was 'only when the craftsman laying the setts appreciated the analogy could he break away from the uniformity and regimentation to which he was conditioned',[4] and the earth-moving operators at Harwell floundered until the ideas behind the design were explained. Jellicoe's motifs were not spontaneously understood, and acquired recognisable meaning only through analogy and association.

164 *Landscape preferences*

An hereditary feel for beauty?

An unassuaged desire for an explanation of landscape aesthetics had driven Jay Appleton to his own highly creative theory expounded in *The Experience of Landscape* (1975) (see Chapter 3).[5] In brief, he postulated that, during the hunting phase of evolution, humans had acquired a preference for environments where one could see without being seen. These environments, Appleton argued, were still assessed by inherited instinct; although they had become symbolic rather than functional, and the satisfaction was aesthetic rather than gastronomic.

Appleton thereby plucked his readers out of the mysteries of neo-Platonism, and plunged them into the murky metaphysics of nature. Nevertheless, most readers had garnered a smattering of human ecology from Sylvia Crowe and Ian McHarg, and animal behaviourism from such writers as Konrad Lorenz and Desmond Morris. The 'prospect-refuge theory' gained quite a following.

It is worth prefacing the remarks below by observing that Appleton's theory was actually several propositions stitched together. He drew on John Dewey who had contended that beauty is sensed through the nature of human experience of landscape, and that the explanation of landscape aesthetics should be sought in the 'primitive relationships' between the human and its environment. Appleton drew on zoological studies of inherited behaviour in animals, or instincts, and agreed with Colvin's views on aesthetic enjoyment through the lens of human ecology. He passed on to Lorenz's observations that certain environments were favoured for their suitability for human behaviour. He then produced his own propositions that the key behaviour was hunting, and that such instincts were sublimated into aesthetic enjoyment in the modern human.

'Evolutionary Psychology' (see Chapter 4) suggested some years after Appleton's book, that faculties for social interaction, including consciousness and speech, and for others natural history and technology, lay behind many traits among humans. Cultural traits were not seen as inheritable, but learned.[6] Appleton, though, claimed that humans had inherited instinctual hunting behaviour (fig. 6.3).[7] This would run counter to evolutionary psychology on the grounds that hunting skills are a classic acquired behaviour permitted by the human's considerable learning powers within the technical and natural history faculties, and enhanced by social behaviour. Furthermore 'instincts' were no longer felt to be a useful concept in biology. The general understanding of them had been as 'hard-wired' behaviour initiated without any previous

Figure 6.3 *'Primitive Man Hunting Animals', mural at the Museum of Vietnamese History; Appleton thought that the modern human had inherited hunting instincts.*

experience, and by definition stereotyped and resistant to modification. However, the great imagination and adaptability that humans have shown are the very antithesis. Superior memory and learning abilities have enabled the perfection of a range of behaviours appropriate to a vast range of environments, preys and lifestyles.[8]

The idea that aesthetic preferences were an evolved version of hunting behaviour introduced some absurdities. At least in historical times, hunting has been predominantly by men. Did only men inherit the supposed hunting instinct, and thus a capacity for perceiving beauty, or did women too? Even if it were true that *Homo sapiens* has inherited hunting instincts, it was very unclear how they could be transmuted into aesthetic appreciation. Appleton simply asked his readers to accept that humans gain satisfaction from an environment that seems to be conducive to satisfying the basic drives such as eating, sleeping, mating and escaping from danger. He then asked that it be allowed that humans are born with a tendency to be spontaneously aware of the survival value of the physical environment, postulating, on unknown grounds, that this is one of the basic drives.

166 *Landscape preferences*

Appleton's book appeared slightly prior to James Gibson's *The Ecological Approach to Visual Perception*, though the assumption of spontaneous assessment would have placed Appleton in the 'direct realism' camp. A link between biological advantage and aesthetics was claimed: 'habitat theory' asserted that gratification, when released from necessity, became the sense of beauty. Appleton argued that humans had such control of their environment that instincts had become redundant, but instead of dying out had sublimated into aesthetic enjoyment. This was so metaphysical that it was impossible to verify or refute. What was certain, though, was that the example provided – that sexual activity was worthwhile as an aesthetic experience despite contraception making it biologically unnecessary – was inappropriate because, until the advent of test-tube conception and cloning, sexual drive could hardly have been a redundant aspect of human behaviour.

It was perhaps strange that the aesthetic identified by 'habitat theory' and 'prospect-refuge theory' concerned only one out of the five senses, and <u>only one</u> of the biological drives. Surely there would have been submerged instincts other than the appreciation of a good hunting scene that could have given aesthetic satisfaction? It was also strange that no examples were given of the beauty of those places that are actually good as hunting grounds (fig. 6.4).

Figure 6.4 *A deer park with weak prospect-and-refuge symbolism: according to the theory, parkland like this imaginary 'improved' one should have few beauties; Appleton was unable to explain why Capability Brown was so widely admired. This view by Thomas Hearne represented a landscape under the influence of a 'modern' improver.*

Instead 'prospect-refuge theory' involved a convoluted reasoning for explaining why the places which one would have thought are among the least suitable for hunting with stone tools, that is mountains, were the most favoured aesthetically.

Part of that reasoning was that the elements of the landscape were seen as symbols stimulating an unconscious recognition of prospect, refuge and hazard. Indeed most of Appleton's book concerned the ways in which the infinite variety of landscape elements could be read by the unconscious. There must then have been a ready-made set of symbols, part of the instinctual baggage, though this was difficult to square with the assertion that 'an object may represent more than one idea and conversely one idea may require a number of associated objects through which to be represented',[9] a position that would have suggested signs understood through learning and association. Here, then, was a mix-up between instinctual and stereotyped symbolism on the one hand, and the understanding of landscape as cultural association, image or sign, sometimes described as 'iconography', on the other.[10]

The final, and most glaring omission, from 'habitat theory' and its derivatives was an explanation for the aesthetics of things and places made by humans. The argument used to explain the beauty of a formal garden was that its parts symbolised prospect and refuge. This came as a surprise to garden historians who had many explanations, but none like that. 'Habitat theory' asked the reader to 'accept the validity of the symbolic link even when reason tells us that it is invalid'. Answers like this were even more clearly inadequate when considering non-landscapes. How did pleasures taken in industrial design, furniture, sculpture and so on arise? If there was a separate cause for such pleasures, what was it, and why didn't it apply to natural landscapes as well?

The long chain of assertions, any one of which could have been a weak link, and the assumptions on direct reality and instincts, did make it seem unlikely that Appleton's theory could survive detailed examination. Nevertheless it filled a gap in theory with fashionable talk of human inheritance. Gordon Orians was broadly supportive at a Landscape Research Group conference in 1984 with his 'habitat selection theory'.[11] However, when Steven Bourassa, of the Australian National University, came to summarise his extensive reading around the topic, whilst being in part sympathetic, pointed out several problems including Appleton's extreme reductionism in explaining culture as biology.

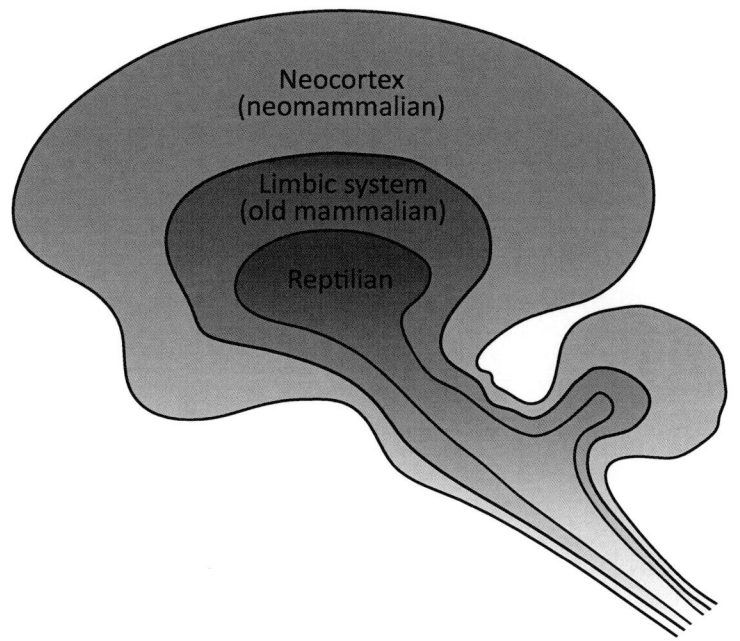

Figure 6.5 *The supposed triune structure of the human brain; a theory that the brain had evolved with higher functions but had not lost its instinctual, reptilian, core.*

Bourassa's own approach was an ingenious tripartite theory in which human inheritance was one of three influences on aesthetics, the other two being a person's cultural heritage and personal predelictions. He likened this to Carl Jung's three levels of the mind – consciousness, the personal unconscious and the collective unconscious. He afterwards read that neuroscience was describing the different parts of the human brain via a 1960s theory that postulated three layers of the 'triune' human brain, added sequentially through evolution: the inner 'reptilian' zone giving instincts, the 'paleomammalian', or limbic, giving feelings, and the 'neomammalian' outer cortex permitting language and culture (fig. 6.5). He suggested then that an experience could be processed simultaneously in these various ways, giving a triple-level reaction, which would account for the complexity of aesthetic responses.[12] In this way he seemed to have nicely reconciled the ecocentric and cultural positions, though in due course the Triune Brain theory was shown to be simplistic and generally misconceived.

Form revealing idea?

The methodology of 'component analysis', and the underlying assumption of the mind as a passive receptor of beauty originating in the object of view (see Chapter 4 and 'Place and pleasure' below), had skirted round inconvenient aspects of theory. Notably, public consensus was just assumed to exist until researchers were

An hereditary feel for beauty?

challenged, and then great pains were taken to sift out the preferences of individuals. There was very little treatment of ugliness; was it just the absence of beauty, or were there qualities of ugliness that could be measured too?[13]

Planners had been led only too willingly down this path by the prospect of 'visual quality' being made susceptible to measurement and mapping. Despite component analysis's veneer of mathematical respectability, the 1960s had actually been a time of simplistic belief in cosmic forces, and was even anti-intellectual with respect to ascertaining the causes of appreciation of art and landscape. The presumptions of the artists and the experts had been elitist; and it had required the faith of the public in the artist and expert for the whole charade to be plausible.

The conviction among modernists that beauty derived, in a neo-Platonic way, from a landscape's or a landscape design's 'formal qualities', was usually coupled with the notion that forms were themselves expressions of significant ideas. This doctrine of formal qualities as applied to landscape aesthetics did face several theoretical problems, though. First, the claim that beauty was inherent in an object or landscape, and thus objective and permanent, could not be reconciled with the historians' and geographers' observations that appreciations change between ages and cultures. Second, there was no possibility that underlying landform could derive from ideas (unless its detailed shapes had been individually sculpted by God). That might preclude experiences from being 'aesthetic'.

Third, verification of the 'formal qualities' of aesthetics was never achieved even on modernism's own home ground, functional architecture. Functionality per se had not proved a significant determinant of landscape beauty, either in the 'undesigned', or the designed landscape. Those gardens most admired for their beauty could seldom be thought of as functional. Avowedly functional landscape design, such as works to cut down noise or reduce visibility of unsightly objects, have not been considered particularly beautiful. The most that such ameliorative measures can hope for was to be accepted if bland and recessive (fig. 6.6). It is difficult to escape the conclusion that satisfaction of functional requirements brings no automatic aesthetic reward, at least in landscape.

Perhaps ideas other than functionalism could generate beauty in form? Frank Clark's quest for the forms that would express the spirit of the late twentieth century (see Chapter 1) had been premised on the hope that noble ideas could be suggested by form through an

Figure 6.6 *Ameliorative landscape: acceptable in reducing the impact of the road, but not a thing of beauty in itself: the M25 Motorway near Byfleet, Surrey.*

appeal to the imagination, awareness through Zen, and generally through association between form and thought. The unfortunate fact, though, was that landscape design in the 1950s and 1960s did not develop highly distinctive forms that were particularly associated with the ethos of modernism. Instead, neo-Georgian and Continental functionalist motifs mingled to give as weak a style as has ever been seen in landscape design.

Meanwhile an alternative explanation existed for the beauty that people find in the wider landscape: morphology by natural processes. All processes produce form, and good form will be 'fit' and meaningful. DNA, crystal structure, the adaptation of birds' beaks, plant communities, geomorphology, and of course the Earth itself, all tend to perfect fitness. One of Ian McHarg's more original insights had been that 'we can dispose of the old canard, 'form follows function': 'form follows nothing – it is integral with all processes'. He claimed for morphology that it was 'the essence of the graphic and plastic arts'.[14]

As the cultural geographers pointed out, morphology is not just that by natural processes, but results from the agricultural, industrial and other cultural processes at work. The humanisation of the landscape starts with ideas and creates form, and it is the fine grain of the humanised landscape rather than the underlying landform that is chiefly admired. The patterns that emerged from the interplay of people and nature can be quite striking. All landscapes

Form revealing idea?

with individuality and character have their admirers. The popularity of landscape photography is a testimony to an urge to illustrate ideas and values through landscape that never seems to wane: in fact the older and more wrinkled it is, the richer its possibilities.

How preferences arise

Which function or functions of the mind determine aesthetic assessments? Joseph Addison thought that beauty was accessed through the imagination, by bringing to mind ideal (and thus necessarily beautiful) forms. Edmund Burke and Uvedale Price saw the source in the emotions, which were instantaneously prompted by external stimuli. Archibald Alison argued that aesthetic satisfactions are generated through a process of pleasurable association through memory. In modern times some functionalists like Christopher Tunnard emphasised the sense of something well-designed for relevance and use, which transcended mere beauty. Then Henry Moore, Geoffrey Jellicoe, Brenda Colvin and Jay Appleton felt that a sense of beauty lay in a common unconscious memory, stimulated by external objects displaying intrinsic harmony, or symbolic form.

As we have seen, this last explanation was the prevailing assumption in studies to assess beauty (or 'visual quality') in the 1960s and 1970s. One feature, a weakness, of all these theories was that variations in people's preferences were declared to be invalid. In a different context, viz. the United States parks and forests services, theories took second place to empirical research designed to reveal preferences. A large number of studies on landscapes were commissioned, seeing their role as serving the general public as well as ecology, including the Visual Management System of the US Forest Service in 1973, Landscape Resource Management from the US Soil Conservation Service in 1979 and the Visual Resource Management of the Bureau of Land Management in 1980. Several addressed scenic beauty, but others were not primarily concerned with that topic, being wider in scope and directed at all sensory experience in the landscape.

Amongst those involved were the environmental psychologists Rachel and Stephen Kaplan. Their work related to people's preferences in nature rather than to visual quality per se. They argued that preferences are not necessarily random or frivolous, and could be analyzed en masse. They spent much effort on the identification of the content and qualities of views that could be used as 'predictors' of preference. Through regression analysis they then built predictive models of preferences, so that their method looked outwardly much like the 'formal qualities' models. However, whilst the latter were based on theory, the Kaplans sought to be empirical, and afterwards they speculated on possibly applicable theory that fitted their results. Their information-processing theory that suggested coherence, diversity, mystery and legibility (see Chapter 3 – 'Prospect, refuge and hazard symbolism') might have suggested that they were in the cognitive camp. Yet they did not dismiss Appleton's evolutionary-based theory, and saw similarities between their ideas on evolutionary-determined 'predictors' and Gibson's 'affordances'. In order to reconcile these positions they entertained 'the possibility of a biological substrate underlying what people prefer'.[15]

There was also a purely cultural approach at hand. David Lowenthal and Hugh Prince had written in 1965 of 'idealized images and visual prejudices' that the English carried in their heads, an idea that would have been perfectly understandable to anyone who had studied the history of landscape appreciation through the beautiful, the sublime and the picturesque, through 'associations', and then into the tourist literature of the late eighteenth and early nineteenth centuries. This present author was one such person.[16] Tastes could be multiple and changeable:

> There is no reason why a single person may not have a number of idealised landscapes in his mind, which will be appropriate to a greater or lesser extent in different landscape types ... The history of landscape appraisal is the story of shifting aesthetic tastes as values have changed throughout time and across space. Landscapes have been idealised according to literary tastes, physical requirements and pleasurable associations.

In such a view, any method seeking to elucidate preferences should accept that 'cultural attitudes are a strong, if not overriding, determinant.' Discussion would then be in terms of values:

> ... we should look to our own values as the source of beauty rather than 'intrinsic qualities' of the landscape ... The distinction between 'value' and 'quality' is meaningless, since both terms refer to the comparison of the landscape in front of your eyes to an idealised landscape in one's mind.[17]

During the 1980s several psychologists, cultural geographers and historians were refuting holism and instead formulating cognitive explanations of perception. Terry Purcell from the Architecture Faculty at the University of Sydney, for example, proposed that people store 'schemata', that is representations of the environment, in memory (see Chapter 4 – 'Cognition'). The experience of any particular landscape would stem from a matching or otherwise between its sensory perception and attributes of the prototypical example.[18] William Cronon likewise observed:

> The material nature we inhabit and the ideal nature we carry in our heads exist always in complex relationship with each other, and we will misunderstand both ourselves and the world if we fail to explore that relationship in all its rich and contradictory complexity.[19]

These assertions of cognitive engagement could have been extended to a consideration of the intensity of experience, the obvious determinants of which would have been the clarity of the observer's interpretation of signs, and personal preferences for what was signified. Instead of generating 'normal' and predictable assessments, cognitive processes would manifest themselves in a unique way in each individual, being influenced by culture, experience, ideology and other factors specific to them.

Two additional thoughts on cognitive aesthetic assessment were advanced by Allen Carlson and Ronald Hepburn. The former considered that knowledge and understanding of the object being perceived was a considerable stimulus to interestedness and thus a view of worth. Furthermore:

> To aesthetically appreciate nature we must have knowledge of the different environments of nature and of the systems and elements within those environments ... the naturalist and the ecologist are well equipped to aesthetically appreciate nature.[20]

Hepburn, the Professor of Moral Philosophy at the University of Edinburgh, gave a reminder that landscapes are not simply places to respond to, but were places particularly suited to contemplation, spiritual thought, the transcendental and the sublime.[21] Theories based on non-cognitive 'engagement' were often quite mechanistic in character, and disassociating landscape aesthetics from artistic modes of appreciation could inadvertently overlook the potential of the imagination and metaphysical speculation.

Place and pleasure

One of the factors that the component-analysis methods had difficulty in explaining was that many people place a high premium on landscapes that are simply familiar to them. This must, then, have been another form of satisfaction separate from 'visual quality'. Chapter 4 describes a third form of satisfaction, the intense experiences generated by the total immersion of the appreciator in the object of appreciation. Indeed there were possibly many forms of satisfaction.

This introduces the unruly topic of satisfactions. 'Unruly' because there are very few rules, and so most would not be accepted by philosophers as meeting the requirements of being 'aesthetic'. Almost all who have written on this topic agreed that everyday landscapes could be appreciated only through the individual's engagement or interaction with them, but further than that the topic is as diverse as the subject matter. There was John Dewey, who expounded upon 'our everyday enjoyment of scenes and situations', to be followed by Arnold Berleant, who took a more ecological and phenomenological approach. There were also geographers and psychologists much more closely allied to cultural explanations of place and preference.

Action/Place

The twentieth century version of the 'Principle of Association' was that of 'action/place' promulgated in environmental psychology. This approach rejected the 'environment/behaviour' relationship between an individual and the world in which simply responding to environmental stimuli was seen as placing the person in too passive a role. Instead, 'action/place' identified the individual as the active player, with self-will and the ability to interpret the world in a variety of ways according to relevance.

Seeing the relationship this way round, a particular garden design or landscape would acquire distinctiveness and become appreciated because it had meaning. The world was made real by what each individual knew, did and felt about it. Places were not made significant by some objective standpoint, but by how people involved themselves, created, managed, used, and made emotional investments in such places, and how they observed this also in others. Nor were places just locations; they were where people sought to achieve their ends, and to explore and intervene in places in the fulfilment of these ends. Action would be taken based on a forecast of what it would achieve. Whether the forecast was correct or false, a bit more was learnt about the world. It was by acting upon their surroundings that people made sense of them and learnt to mould them.[22]

As groups or individuals, people wanted influence over the decisions that were of immediate relevance to them. Social scientists and market researchers observed the general correspondence between a person's role and that person's perceptions. A group of people with similar objectives, such as farmers, would associate the landscape with a particular set of meanings. Walkers, on the other hand, would see another. The spread of countryside organisations since 1970 illustrated the variety of viewpoints.

Place and pleasure **175**

Place and Identity

> The near landscape is valuable and lovable because of its nearness, not something to be disregarded and shrugged off; it is where children are reared and what they take away in their minds to their long future. What ground could be more hallowed? [23]

Several surveys found that most people had no definite views on which landscapes are most beautiful, but instead valued familiarity, so that, for example, the beaches at Torquay in Devon (fig. 6.7) might have been more highly valued overall than the mountains of the Brecon Beacons, in a National Park. The awkward finding that familiarity was a major factor in landscape preferences should have been explored more fully.

Popular tastes in landscape were evident for all to observe. In twentieth century Britain there was a strong tradition of writing on the countryside, for example the *Shell Guides* and posters (fig. 6.8), and other celebrations of local-character differences. The landscape profession, whether driven by nostalgia or Colvin's imperative of climate and soil, was united in its concern to reflect the unique qualities of each place.

David Lowenthal had asserted long ago that, tasteless though they may often have seemed, public preferences revealed 'a deeply

Figure 6.7 *A postcard of Anstey's Cove, Torquay, Devon, by Raphael Tuck & Sons, 1952: more preferred than mountains because more familiar to users.*

held and deeply rooted system of shared beliefs'.²⁴ Peirce Lewis, a professor of geography at Pennsylvania State University, had been interested in landscape tastes because 'they were part of a larger value-system through which people identified themselves as members of a community'. He postulated three 'canons' of popular landscape taste:

> **Canon 1:** Popular taste is not a trivial matter; it is a fundamental part of all cultures, and a crucial means by which nations and cultures identify themselves and separate themselves from other nations and cultures.
>
> **Canon 2:** Landscape taste, like all taste, reveals itself at two quite different levels within any given culture. One level is fundamental; the other is ephemeral.
>
> **Canon 3:** The cultural landscape is divided into two large spatial categories: areas where standards of taste are routinely invoked, and areas where they are not. ²⁵

Lewis was being assiduously non-judgemental. He just tried to understand landscape as an aspect of culture, not to examine standards of taste.

Figure 6.8 *The Shell Guides and posters were part of the campaign by the petrol company to encourage drivers to explore the British countryside; this poster was painted by Paul Nash.*

Place and pleasure

In North America the word 'place' was in currency; for example, the US National Park Service started assembling its National Register of Historic Places, that is historic and archaeological sites, from 1966. In the early 1970s, a geography PhD student in Toronto, Ted Relph, was dissatisfied with the imprecise way in which the word was generally used, and decided to devote his thesis, later a book, to this single word. His chief interest in place was as a venue for human subjective experience, and he described his study as 'a phenomenology of place'.[26] Places played an integral part in the lives of human beings, he asserted, and he noted that places provided many different types of experience, for different people, in different situations, in varying intensities. Places could take on different qualities of feeling, meaning, and ambience, and in turn directed and focused human intentions, experiences, and actions spatially.

Relph was interested in the connections between people's identity and place through 'its persistent sameness and unity which allows that [place] to be differentiated from others'. The identity with place was strong when the individual was an 'insider': the degree of 'insideness' determined the degree of attachment, involvement, and concern that a person (or group) had for a particular place.[27] The strongest sense of 'place experience' is what Relph called 'existential insideness', a profound and unself-conscious immersion in place.

Figure 6.9 *Common Ground's cider table, a representation of the community orchards project of the late 1970s.*

In the UK the forces for homogenisation had been running strongly through the modernist project, 'rational-comprehensive' planning, the Common Market, a common currency, and in many other ways. A reaction set in against the assumption of consensus, and, as noted above (see Chapter 4 – 'Shattered dreams'), acceptance of the validity of pluralism became conventional during the 1970s. Individuality began to be prized again. Although Relph's book was a rare (and therefore useful) expression of the value of identity, there were many others who felt in a similar way. One early official sanction of diversity in the UK was the Countryside Commission's sponsorship of Common Ground, an organisation 'to promote the importance of our common cultural heritage ... local distinctiveness and our links with the past', a topic which it pursued assiduously (figs. 6.9 & 6.10).[28] A grant of 75 per cent was given to research and writing *Holding Your Ground* (1985).

A Canadian landscape architect made a similarly strong appeal for restoring a sense of place and distinctiveness to city landscapes.[29] It looked as if 'identity' was not just a matter of perception and appreciation, but was becoming part of the ethos of the landscape professional. Meanwhile, heritage protection, which was very largely about national and local identity, was on the rise in the 1980s in many countries.

Figure 6.10 *Celebrating local identity: a sculpture project in Dorset using local limestone by Peter Randall-Page.*

The concept of the *lieu de mémoire* has been promoted by Pierre Nora, a French historian known for his work on identity and memory. He reminded that a culture collects and shapes its memories into narratives that define identity and the national myth. This is quite different from composing histories which conventionally rely upon analysis of more objective sources such as administrative documents and which attempt to identify the motivations and intentions of 'great men' as explanations for historical events. Nora thus promotes his approach as *nouvelle histoire*.

A *lieu de mémoire* may be a physical place, or it may be a non-material tradition, so long as it has become a symbolic element of the collective memory of a community. It may be a monument, a landmark, a museum, an event, a symbol like a flag, or even a sound or a colour that has resonance (the red flag of left politics, for instance). It would not include prehistoric and archaeological sites as no collective memories attach to them. Sites of memory can be identified and described. Nora proved this in a great four-volume work, *Les Lieux de Mémoire* (1999-2010).

Landscape and emotion

When places come to be used and associated with events and a person's aesthetic and intellectual development, they become emotionally charged in that person's mind. Visiting the place again would be the trigger to remember and re-live past events and pleasures and offer the promise of experiencing new ones. Place becomes part of the self.

Some places can gain particular meaning for their individuality and timelessness. Geographers and historians, with their specialists' understanding, could imbue landscapes with special character, unseen order or rich history. Such insights, or even just a personal involvement in a landscape, could make it special. Everyone was seeking some reassurance that life had meaning and that one lived on afterwards in some form. The good feeling when one was part of something timeless allowed mortality to be subsumed within something immortal.[30] Affection for mountains was a rather literal example of attaching oneself to something greater. Landowners and residents too liked to think that those places with which they were particularly associated were unique and personal. This made them feel individual, more than just nameless cogs, and having a special contribution to make.

Emotional attachments to landscapes should not be dismissed as mere sentimentality; while they were held they stimulated memory and awareness of self. Loss of familiar landscape caused disorientation as treasured memory was negated. Margaret Drabble, the writer, saw that:

> The landscape ... is a living link between what we were and what we have become. This is one of the reasons why we feel such profound and apparently disproportionate anguish when a loved landscape is altered out of recognition; we lose not only a place, but part of ourselves, a continuity between the shifting phases of our life.[31]

People indeed craved continuity in their surroundings, unless it was they themselves that changed them (fig. 6.11).[32] They liked to think that places remained intact, 'unspoiled', to allow their enjoyment to be repeated. It was a commonplace to observe the phenomenon of a community radicalised by the threat of a nearby highway because it would negate the self-image of people who resided in the countryside. Then how many people have been saddened to visit old haunts, only to discover disconcertingly that they no longer exist? It would have been better not to have visited, for at least the place remained unsullied in memory. Protests against change could be seen as emotional pain.

Public open spaces were typically replete with personal and social meanings.[33] The most valued areas were often the intimate and familiar ones that played a part in people's daily lives, rather than the distant parks and outstanding landscapes far from home. The social contact at such places was important, but so too were the direct sensuous encounters with nature, such as being outside in open space, enjoying the changing seasons, feeling the sun, the wind and the rain, being able to run or walk, or just sitting down and enjoying the view. Simple contact with nature could suffice; ordinary plants, and any birds or animals were good to see. Successful parks combined formal flowerbeds and naturalistic areas with a mix of recreational facilities and a variety of congenial social settings. They were best able to provide both associative and material access to a better world through providing a high-quality sensory and natural experience, a world of adventure play, and a more supportive social community where common experiences were shared.

Place and pleasure

Figure 6.11 *Pain at the loss of place; the objectors to the removal of this splendid monkey puzzle tree at Brockhole, in the English Lake District.*

Everyday satisfactions

Everyday satisfactions should not be overlooked. Seeing wildlife; the colours from oil on a puddle; leaves in the wind and the crunch as they are walked on; the scents of the rose garden – and there are innumerable other small delights for everyone to enjoy in their own way. Thinking of beauty addressed only one posssible layer in the world of outdoor pleasures. A gently modulated variety of sensations from colour, touch, sound and taste could be perfectly satisfying.

Below are quotations from quite different writers – one rural, the other urban and over a century later – that illustrated their appreciations of small events and minor sights. The first, by Uvedale Price is a description of a picturesque landscape, imagined as on a gentle stroll around a lush garden exploring the qualities and odours of the plants:

> ... suppose ... a glade, or a small valley of the softest turf and finest verdure; the ground on each side swelling gently into knolls, with other glades and recesses stealing in between them; the whole adorned with trees of the smoothest and tenderest bark, and most elegant forms, mixed with tufts of various evergreens and flowering shrubs: all these growing as luxuriantly as in a garden mould, yet disposed in as loose and artless groups as those in forests; whilst a natural pathway led the eye amidst these intricacies, and towards the other glades and recesses. Suppose a clear and gentle stream to flow through this retirement, on a bed of the purest gravel or pebbles; its bank sometimes smooth and level, sometimes indented and varied in height and form ... [34]

The grandfather of the theoreticians in environmental aesthetics, including the aesthetic of everyday landscapes, was John Dewey who had argued that the human being thought and acted in wholeness and unity with the world about in aesthetics as in everyday life. The roots of aesthetic experience lay, Dewey argued, in commonplace experience. He proposed that there was a sort of spectrum between everyday activities and events and the refined experience of works of art, but in order to understand the aesthetic one must begin with the events and scenes of daily life:

> In order to understand the esthetic in its ultimate and approved forms, one must begin with it in the raw; in the events and scenes that hold the attentive eye and ear of man, arousing his interest and affording him enjoyment as he looks and listens: the sights that hold the crowd – the fire-engine rushing by; the machines excavating enormous holes in the earth; the human-fly climbing the steeple-side; the men perched high in air on girders, throwing and catching red-hot bolts. The sources of art in human experience will be learned by him who sees how the tense grace of the ball-player infects the onlooking crowd; who notes the delight of the housewife in tending her plants, the zest of the spectator in poking the wood burning on the hearth and in watching the darting flames and crumbling coals ... He does not remain a cold spectator.[35]

Everyday satisfactions were just that – part of everyday life for everyone – but they were only very rarely the subject of serious consideration. Academically they appeared trivial, and what would be the value of pursuing this matter? They were not symbolic of social or political beliefs, impossible to describe en masse as they were personal to each citizen, and it was difficult to see how design could create them. Perhaps, though, the value of recognising their existence could potentially lead to a world which is not scraped clean, or 'made pure', but is knowingly allowed to be complex, messy and irrational.

Place and pleasure **183**

Landscape assessment methods

With the major exception of human ecology, the pre-1980s approaches to the assessment of the aesthetic value of landscape were generally artistic, psychological and technical, in other words expert-driven, whilst the valued qualities in the landscape became restricted in a rather unimaginative and inflexible manner to just its ecology, scenic qualities and heritage.

With revisions to theories on how preferences arise, and indeed the widening of preferences beyond simply the aesthetic, radical changes took place, nowhere more so than in Britain.[36] In academic and government circles the assessment of aesthetic value was coming to be seen less as a matter of intrinsic beauty that can be judged only by experts, and more one of diverse meanings for individuals. These meanings could be their associations, support of self-image or intellectual reward. One needed to look to cherished ideas, the ideal state of affairs in people's minds, or some other subjective viewpoint for the source of emotional reaction. The methodology threatened to become complex and costly, and there were few studies purely of 'visual quality' after the early 1980s. Meanwhile there was a dislike of designations and their maps, and landscape character sounded like a more objective approach.

Landscape beauty

David Lowenthal, who had long been interesting himself in the history of ideas and tastes relating to the landscape,[37] was firmly of the persuasion that any assessment of the landscape was necessarily personal, and thus subjective. In 1978 he took the planners to task. His chief criticism was their refusal to admit to the subjectivity that underlay the design of studies and assessments. 'Evaluators themselves generally assumed that they were dealing with scientific facts about landscape esthetics, not just with their own scenic values'. Wittingly or unwittingly, 'academics as well as planners parade their own tastes as survey results'. Unfortunately, 'many readers erroneously conclude that the quantified technical apparatus of landscape evaluation connotes scholarly respectability', but in fact 'the information that landscape evaluation yields on favoured landscapes is thus trivial and expectable'.

Another complaint was that 'landscape evaluation studies neither ascertain landscape tastes nor assess public preferences; they tell us nothing about what landscapes the public values or why. Indeed they are not a form of research at all ...'.[38] Some researchers had already expressed grave doubts about the assumption that trained specialists could be relied upon to provide disinterested 'judgements' of landscape beauty, and the corollary that hoi-poloi appreciation of the landscape was far too distorted by subjectivities such as memories, impressions, and associations for their mere 'preferences' to have any credibility. The views of the general public began to be looked at and accorded more standing than the opinions of narrow professional sub-groups.[39]

A shift in methodology from those who had attempted to be 'objective', to approaches that accepted that they needed to start with the 'subjective', took place mostly around 1980. Allen Carlson argued that the expert's judgement could never be replaced by mathematical modelling.[40] One landscape planner, on the other hand, stressed that it was the public's subjective preferences that mattered, and argued for a new methodology starting from the premise that 'an individual's satisfaction derived from a view will be entirely subjective'. There would be variability in taste and in depth of feeling, with some people having no firm tastes as such, maybe just feeling comfortable in familiar places, while others would care very much. A consensus in taste amongst the population could not be assumed, and there would be no 'normal' or 'standard' assessments. It was pointed out that:

> Many studies suppress these varying patterns of preference by different groups by aggregation, and proceed on the more convenient basis of a broad consensus towards deriving a predictive model of landscape 'quality'.

In order to allow for a wide range of tastes among the public, 'the numbers of respondents that would have to be involved would be substantially in excess of most current evaluation work'. The reliance of 'objective' methods on the 'elitist views of a professional subgroup' was objectionable on democratic grounds.[41] If a quantitative method of appraisal was required, a very different approach was needed, starting with basic fact-finding about the landscape tastes of the public.[42]

Such criticisms irretrievably undermined the methods of 'objective' landscape evaluation, and the emphasis was anyway swinging towards subjective assessment based upon contemporary and historical descriptions, classification of landscape types, and surveys of public taste. Almost no major statistical exercises on objective 'landscape value' were commenced after 1980.

The US Soil Conservation Service's landscape architect was writing in the mid-1980s that 'most visual assessment professionals agree that a solitary practitioner can no longer make professional visual judgements in isolation and expect that these will be implemented or withstand legal scrutiny ... the user – the public – should be the key player from the beginning.' Evaluation of 'quality' was downplayed in her advice, and she nominated character, uniqueness, fragility, fitness, structure and information as the domain of experts, and preference and meaning as 'public input': there was no talk of mathematical modelling.[43]

In the UK a public inquiry in 1985 into the proposed designation of the North Pennines Area of Outstanding Natural Beauty made it necessary for the Countryside Commission to clarify its approach. When it came to summarise 'landscape assessment' in 1987, it was by then 'not solely concerned with the appearance of land, but with people's reactions to and the pleasure which they gain from the landscape'. Hence the Commission was advocating that a whole scene was more than the sum of its components, that the historic landscape and human artefacts gave 'a link with our past and a better understanding of our place in the world and in time', and that associations and national sentiment could be significant. In effect, the old component-analysis modelling had been dropped.

The favoured approach was for skilled assessors to make their own 'multi-criteria' judgements having carefully considered the 'objective' factors derived from survey and description, the 'subjective' responses of writers, artists, the public and the assessors themselves, and the purpose to which the findings would be put. A checklist thus covered physiographic factors ranging from geology and landform through to ecology, land use and archaeology, and also allowed for historical and cultural associations.[44]

The role of the professional was thus shifting from being the 'expert', giving detached but objective evaluations, to that of interpreter of the public's perceptions. Typically the professional was presented with a mass of viewpoints and other data, perhaps resulting from a public consultation, which needed somehow to be structured in a form that is comprehensible and useful to decision-makers.

Landscape character

In the early 1990s another change in British methodology came about: a renewed attempt at objectivity through the determination of landscape character.[45] Referring to the discussion of values above (see Chapter 5 – 'Knowledge gives value'), this form of assessment addressed the landscape's qualities, but stopped short of defining its aesthetic value.

'Landscape assessment', just discussed, had retained an emphasis on the identification of areas of high aesthetic value as a tool for protection, though this purpose now came into question. Whilst designations and their boundaries continued to be in the mainstream of protection, they were being seen by some officials as a residual usage pending the eventual abolition of such crude planning tools in favour of case-by-case consideration appropriate to the nature and strength of the values present.

Maps showing boundaries of designated areas may have seemed old-fashioned, but any planning tool would need to be based on factual or widely-agreed assessments. Landscape character could be determined in large part by physiographic factors and landscape elements, and could be mapped at a fairly fine grain (fig. 6.12). Descriptions of character could be backed up by detailed descriptive information on landscape elements. The assessment of proposals for development or new policies could, then, be in terms of changes to landscape elements, and hence character. Thus the professional's input to the political process of judging proposals would not need to extend to arguable assessments of scenic quality, but could be confined to the analysis of character.

It was convenient to differentiate landscape character areas at various scales. Since the English landscape was broken into moderately clear zones by numerous differences in geology, for example chalk downland as against clay lowlands, broad generic types could be defined. At a more local level there were differences of character within one of these types which might depend upon, say, altitude, proportion of built-up area or land-use history. Each local character area could then be described in terms of the elements that provide the character such as woodlands, field walls, or the layout of traditional farm complexes (fig. 6.13). At each level, actual names are usually to be found for specific geographical units, so local councillors, farmers, and in fact everyone familiar with their localities could readily relate to this approach.[46]

Assessment of character was well received for a variety of reasons. First, it would render landscape assessment inherently less arguable and contentious, and in view of the changing role of 'the expert', methods that could achieve a moderate degree of consensus were badly needed. Second, studies of character recognised local distinctiveness and the sense of place, whereas earlier methods had assessed values against absolute or national standards. Third, character-studies held out the prospect of assessment of the whole countryside, rather than just designated areas.[47] This tied in with the idea that every part of England, beautiful or otherwise, required a landscape policy that could guide change in the countryside. Fourth, assessment of character could be relatively quick.

Now that the focus was upon landscape character, the question of what made a landscape scenic had been somewhat sidelined, one might

Landscape assessment methods **187**

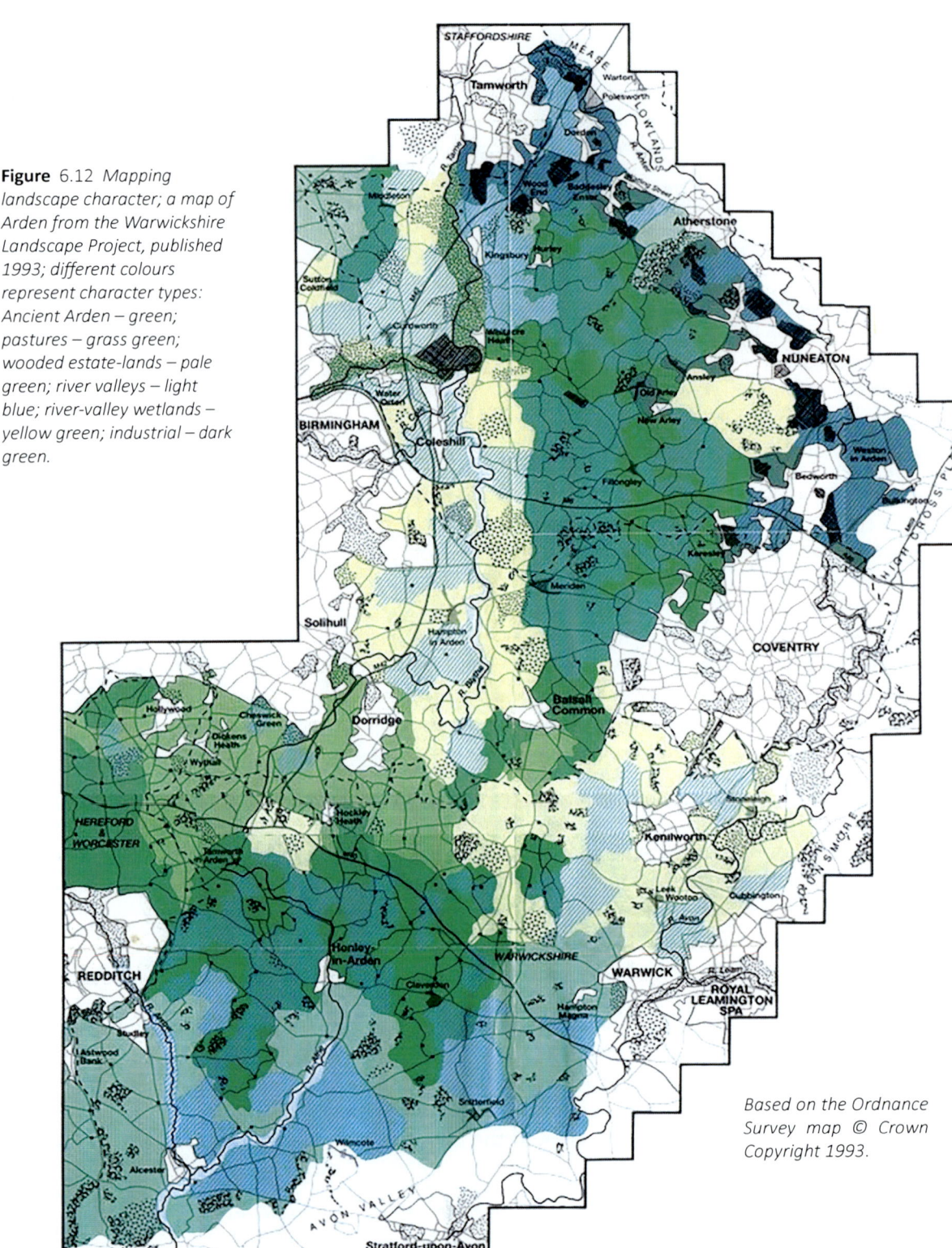

Figure 6.12 *Mapping landscape character; a map of Arden from the Warwickshire Landscape Project, published 1993; different colours represent character types: Ancient Arden – green; pastures – grass green; wooded estate-lands – pale green; river valleys – light blue; river-valley wetlands – yellow green; industrial – dark green.*

Based on the Ordnance Survey map © Crown Copyright 1993.

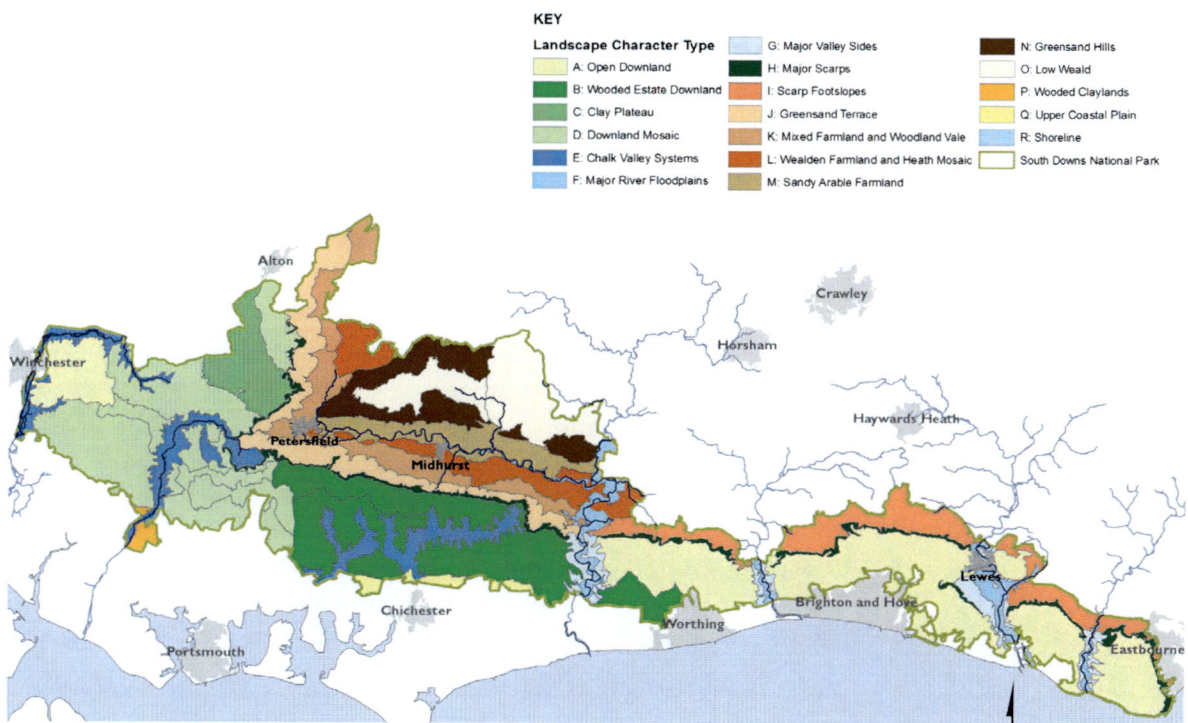

Figure 6.13 *Landscape character zones in the South Downs, in East and West Sussex westwards to Hampshire; the aim is to inform landscape policy generally, rather than to pick out areas of high scenic value, though the Downs were declared a National Park in 2011.*

almost say gratefully set to one side. The Countryside Commission felt in 1993 that it should again revise its advice on landscape assessment. The criteria for appraising a landscape were expanding and could be picked from the following:

- it is an important 'resource ... for reasons of rarity or representativeness';
- it is of high scenic quality, with pleasing patterns and combinations of features, and important aesthetic or intangible factors;
- unspoilt by inharmonious development;
- it should have a distinctive sense of place;
- it should include other conservation interests (i.e. historic, archaeological, nature-conservation); and
- there should be a consensus on its importance by poets, painters, the public and professionals.[48]

The choice of criteria, and the evaluation of one against another, would have to be a matter of local or national politics. The idea was floated of unifying conservation criteria across the board. Those for archaeological and nature-conservation designations, for example, were not so very far apart over the questions of rarity and representativeness.

Landscape assessment methods **189**

It was a question of who was going to be bold enough to take a lead – the national bodies, or the local planning authorities? At national level, dispensing with the need to worry about such a tricky subject as scenic beauty had its obvious attractions and might be elided by talk of identity and distinctiveness if the issue was strictly localised. However, the latter, and grant-giving arms of the various bodies, wanted definite guidance, and liked maps showing areas of high value for whatever quality was under consideration.

When regional or county assessments were needed for developing policy and designations, national or international standards were necessary for evaluations. Character-assessment took the question as far as analysis could go, but progress thereafter would depend on willingness to tackle the questions of public landscape tastes and preferences. In the case of wider issues of policy, such as over new forests or wind farms, this could not be avoided. The Countryside Stewardship Scheme in Britain, for example, had quite clear aims in increasing the 'beauty and diversity of the landscape'.

On the positive side, the historical and archaeological analysis of all landscape, as a culmination of the work of the cultural geographers, held great potential for understanding. Furthermore, character assessment could help to some degree in debates on specific conservation-issues when these were a question of comparing 'before' and 'after'. It could characterise the 'before', and envision the 'after', and so suggest the effect of any particular change upon the qualities represented in the landscape. The final judgement would still have to be based on values, though.

Meanwhile, what had happened to the work on landscape beauty? After all, landscape beauty was not simply a visual matter, as many at the time preferred to assume, but it arose from meanings and ideologies. These are an integral and essential aspect of culture, and it is these that are tested and laid bare in political decisions.

Figure 6.14 *Landscape near Swansea, Wales, by James Ward, c. 1805. How would your preference change if you appreciated that the smoke was from industrial processes?*

NOTES AND REFERENCES

1 John Searle, *Mind, Language and Society* (London, 1999), p. 76.

2 Sir Geoffrey Jellicoe, at a lecture at the Architectural Association, London, on 2 February 1989.

3 Carl Jung, *Man and his Symbols* (London, 1964), pp. 20, 55 & 67.

4 Geoffrey Jellicoe, *The Guelph Lectures on Landscape Design* (Guelph ON, 1983), p. 91.

5 The 'theoretical vacuum' was bemoaned in Jay Appleton, 'Landscape Evaluation: the Theoretical Vacuum', *Transactions of the Institute of British Geographers*, 66 (1975), 120-3.

6 Jerome H. Barkow *et al.*, *The Adapted Mind* (New York, 1992), p. 5.

7 I am grateful to Brent Elliott, RHS Librarian, for exchanging thoughts on the concepts of the unconscious and instinctive behaviour; they helped greatly in considering Appleton's ideas. It is only fair to report that Appleton latterly acknowledged more strongly the role of cultural influences in terms of the landscape as theatre and illusion in *The Symbolism of Habitat* (Seattle WA, 1990).

8 The last 100,000 years of human evolution have taken place in a wide variety of local environments across several continents, making a shared unconscious preference for the same type of prospect-refuge environment improbable. One of Appleton's earliest critics raised this point: see Ian Brotherton, 'Prospect-Refuge Theory: Is it Hazardous?' *Landscape Research*, 4 : 3 (Autumn 1979), 13-4.

9 Jay Appleton, *The Experience of Landscape* (London, 1975); compare pp. 69 & 81.

10 Appleton (1990), op. cit., p. 8. differentiated between the 'natural' symbolism of instincts and the unconscious, and 'cultural' symbolism of learned signs.

11 Gordon H. Orians, 'An Ecological and Evolutionary Approach to Landscape Aesthetics', in Edmund C. Penning-Rowsell & David Lowenthal (eds), *Landscape Meanings and Values* (London, 1986), pp. 3-22.

12 Stephen C. Bourassa, *The Aesthetics of Landscape* (London, 1991), pp. 51, 57 & 59.

13 Clifford Tandy's point-scoring method of landscape evaluation, presented to the Landscape Research Group's symposium on 'Methods of Landscape Analysis' in May 1967, allowed for 'undesirable' elements, such as derelict factories, but the later mathematical models never addressed the factors that make some landscapes disliked.

14 Ian McHarg, *Design with Nature* (Garden City NY, 1969), pp. 163 & 173.

15 Stephen Kaplan, 'Aesthetics, Affect, and Cognition: Environmental Preference from an Evolutionary Perspective', *Environment and Behaviour*, 19:1 (1987), 3-32, 3-4, 17 & 26.

16 This author was commissioned in 1979 to write *Georgian Gardens: the Reign of Nature* (London, 1983).

17 David Jacques, 'Landscape Appraisal: the Case for a Subjective Theory', *Journal of Environmental Management* (1980), 109-10.

18 A. Terry Purcell, 'Landscape Perception, Preference and Schema Discrepancy', *Environment and Planning*, 14 : 1 (1987), 67-92.

19 William Cronon (ed), *Uncommon Ground: Rethinking the Human Place in Nature* (New York, 1996), p. 22.

20 Allen Carlson, 'Appreciation and the Natural Environment', *Journal of Aesthetics and Art Criticism* (Spring 1979), 267-76.

21 Ronald Hepburn, 'Landscape and the Metaphysical Imagination', *Environmental Values,* 5:3 (1996), 197.

22 David Canter, 'Action and Place: an Existential Dialectic', in David Canter *et a*l. (eds), *Ethnoscapes, Vol 1: Environmental Perspectives* (Aldershot, Hants, 1988), pp. xix & 1-17.

23 Frank Fraser Darling, *Wilderness and Plenty.* 1969 BBC Reith Lecture, cited in Jane Brown, *The Everywhere Landscape* (London, 1982), p. 12.

24 David Lowenthal, 'The American Scene', *Geographical Review*, 58 (1968), 61.

25 Peirce Lewis, 'American Landscape Tastes', in Marc Treib (ed), *Modern Landscape Architecture: a critical review* (Cambridge MA, 1993), pp. 2-17.

26 Edward Relph, *Place and Placelessnes* (London, 1976), pp. 4-7.

27 Ibid., pp. 45 & 141.

28 Sue Clifford & Angela King (eds), *Local Distinctiveness: Place, Particularity and Identity* (London, 1993).

29 Michael Hough, *Out of Place: Restoring Identity to the Regional Landscape* (New Haven CT, 1990).

30 Walter Pater's writings on 'the aesthetic moment' were based on this concept of the purpose of art.

31 Margaret Drabble, *A Writer's Britain; Landscape in Literature* (London, 1979), p. 270.

32 John J. Costonis, *Icons and Aliens: Law, Aesthetics, and Environmental Change* (Urbana IL, 1989); written by a legal theorist who put forward a 'cultural stability-identity' hypothesis by which communities apply aesthetic controls in order to protect their identities through stabilising their environments.

33 Jacqueline Burgess *et al.*, 'People, Parks and the Urban Green: A Study of Popular Meanings and Values for Open Spaces in the City', *Urban Studies*, 25 (1988), 455-73. Dr Burgess further developed her valuable work on what parks mean for people, and it became one of the justifications for the Heritage Lottery Fund's initiative on public parks, launched in 1996.

34 Uvedale Price, 'A letter to H. Repton, Esq.', in *Essays on the Picturesque, III* (London/ Hereford, 1795), p. 158.

35 John Dewey, *Art as Experience* (New York, 1934), p. 3.

36 David L. Uzzell, 'Environmental Psychological Perspectives on Landscape', *Landscape Research*, 16 : 1 (Spring 1991), 3-10, gave a valuable overview of approaches to landscape assessment, and provided pointers towards some which he terms 'semiotics', 'social representations', 'functional use' and 'action research'.

37 Most notably in David Lowenthal & Hugh Prince, 'English Landscape Tastes', *Geographical Review*, 55 (April 1965) 186-222.

38 David Lowenthal, 'Finding Valued Landscapes', *Progress in Human Geography*, 2 : 3 (1978), 373-418.

39 P.E. Clamp, 'Evaluation of the Impact of Roads on the Visual Amenity of Rural Areas' (Report by Ralph Hopkinson, Newton Watson and Partners), *Department of the Environment Research Report 7* (London, 1976): and E.C. Penning Rowsell, G.H. Gullett,

G.H. Searle & S.A. Witham, 'Public Evaluation of Landscape Quality', *Middlesex Polytechnic Planning Research Group Report 13* (1977).

40   Allen Carlson, 'On the Possibility of Quantifying Scenic Beauty', *Landscape Planning*, 4:2 (1977), 131-72.

41   Jacques (1980), op. cit., 109 & 112.

42   Bourassa, op. cit., pp. 94-109; though he still clung to a partly biological basis for aesthetics, he did expand usefully on the question of how landscape tastes might be related to the 'cultural rules' of societal groups.

43   Sally Schauman, 'Countryside Landscape Visual Assessment', in Richard C. Smardon, James F. Palmer & John P. Felleman (eds), *Foundations for Visual Project Analysis* (New York, 1986), pp. 103-114; 109-111.

44   Jo Meredith, *Landscape Assessment: A Countryside Commission Approach*, CCD18 (Cheltenham, Glos, 1987). She was assisted in this by the Landscape Research Group which prepared *A Review of Recent Practice and Research in Landscape Assessment*, CCD25 (Cheltenham, Glos, 1988).

45   The idea is not altogether new, for example in the little book, *Countryside Character* (London, 1946) compiled by Richard Harman. Dutch and German precedents for landscape-character work were quoted by Land Use Consultants when they undertook the study, 'A Planning Classification of Scottish Landscape Resources', *Countryside Commission for Scotland Occasional Paper* No. 1 (Redgorton, Perth, 1971).

46   Countryside Commission, *Assessment and Conservation of Landscape Character: the Warwickshire Landscapes Project Approach*, CCP332 (Cheltenham, Glos, 1991).

47   Cobham Resource Consultants, *Landscape Assessment Guidance*, CCP423 (Northampton, 1993).

48   As a postscript, Graham Fairclough, Ingrid Sarlöv Herlin and Carys Swanwick, *Routledge Handbook of Landscape Character Assessment* (London, 2018) looked back on 30 years of Landscape Character Assessment and Historic Landscape Characterisation, and how the favourable climate for their spread was created through the European Landscape Convention.

CHAPTER 7

MEMORY MAKETH HUMANITY

Many horrendous mistakes were made in restoring historic gardens and landscapes, as has been frequently acknowledged in retrospect. Garden restoration was not thought to be a serious topic until the late twentieth century, but then governments, which had agreed to support it, insisted on proper guidelines. At first those for architectural monuments, which had been in development for over a century, were referred to, but some notable difficulties, arising from a garden's relative ephemerality became apparent. The classification of designed landscapes as a form of cultural landscape offered some resolution through its handling of change, resulting in a distinctive philosophy for garden and landscape restoration.

A good part of this chapter is a blow-by-blow account of the several steps in the emergence of this philosophy, first those taken by government agencies, particularly in the USA and the UK, and then at the international level by ICOMOS and the World Heritage system.

Figure 7.1 *A period garden at New Place, Stratford-upon-Avon: made in the 1920s to reinvoke the flavour of Elizabethan times, here depicted by A. Forestier.*

Restoration tragedies

The absence of a widely accepted philosophy for conserving landscapes gave free reign to 'restoration' of various kinds. Motives were various: ideologies; practical circumstances; the desire to impress visitors or to improve presentation to the public; and many others. 'Reconstruction' re-made designs, with or without the benefit of archival information, and without the inclusion of adequate original fabric to qualify as authentic. 'Restoration-in-spirit' had the primary aim of realising the presumed original design intentions anew, with attention to original fabric being secondary. Last, 'period-style gardens' were avowedly imaginative re-creations mimicking a style from the past (fig. 7.1).

All such work was essentially new work, pastiches of a former style, and presenting bogus scenes. Honest attempts to enliven a designed landscape became, wittingly or unwittingly, misrepresentation of the 'document'. However, the preconceptions of the time could not be escaped, and these became embodied in reconstructions or period-style gardens. This meant that such gardens would not only be untruthful, but they would give an untruthful impression. In other words, the whole reason for an historic garden being retained would have been subverted.

Figure 7.2 *Asynchrony: Real Jardin Botanico, Madrid, a housing development intruding into a nationally important scenic and historic area.*

Another common experience was that a recovered design could not be reconciled to its new surroundings. There was an adjective for this: 'asynchronous', used when two objects which could never have co-existed together in history became juxtaposed (fig. 7.2). The resulting awkwardness was to the detriment of both. A classic example would be the reconstruction of the gardens attached to a ruined castle or abbey. Vistas and views off site may have been altered, so that either they must be blanked off, or redesigned, or some anachronistic scene accepted.

In the 1870s, Félix Roguet, the architect working on the Château de Chenonceau in the Loire valley, proposed a full restoration to the days of Diane de Poitiers in the 1550s. This was not accomplished in full because the owner baulked at removing the famous and spectacular gallery on the bridge dated 1577, but the philosophy was applied in respect of the gardens. The part that had been converted into a *jardin anglais* in the 1790s was doomed. Since there was insufficient evidence of what this area had been like beforehand, the architect simply invented a period-style garden, named the Jardin de Catherine de Médici after Diane's successor at the place. The genuinely ancient Jardin de Diane de Poitiers still retained some elements of Diane's Renaissance garden, though the architect did not realise this, and remodelled it as a *parterre de broderie* (fig. 7.3). This

Figure 7.3 *A falsification of the evidence: the Jardin de Diane de Poitiers at Chenonceau, part of the* jardin anglais *but 'restored' in the 1860s to an architect's conception of what it might have looked like as a parterre.*

parterre was an extremely poor interpretation both in terms of design and use of materials, and anyway this sort of parterre had not been invented till half a century after Diane de Poitiers' death. Hence garden overlays of interest and merit had been removed in ignorance in order that a faulty pastiche of the architect's preferred period could be installed.

Other examples of misrepresentation could be seen when restorers, or interpreters, have carried out a reconstruction in order to freshen up the story of a place, or even issued false information for the same purpose. This might be seen as deception. Some Victorian garden restorations, usually involving yews, fooled visitors for a while. Reginald Blomfield wrote warmly about the topiary at Levens Hall in his *Formal Garden in England* (1st edn, 1891). He believed that the gardens were the work of the early eighteenth century:

> ... the curious cut work in the gardens of Levens Hall, in Westmoreland, is a well known instance, but the most remarkable instance still exists at Packwood, in Warwickshire, where the Sermon on the Mount is literally represented in clipped yew ... At the top of the mount is an arbour formed in a great yew-tree called the 'pinnacle of the temple', which was supposed to represent Christ on the Mount overlooking the evangelists, apostles, and the multitude below; at least, this account of it was given by the gardener.[1]

Figure 7.4 *The crime of deception; the 'sermon-on-the-mount' at Packwood House, Warwickshire, was passed off in the late 19th century as dating from the 17th century, though it was in fact only a few decades old.*

In fact half of the topiary at Levens dated from the 1810s, which is when the fantastic shapes probably dated from, whilst the multitude at Packwood dated from only twenty years prior to Blomfield's visit (fig. 7.4).

Several gardens within monastic or castle ruins were 'restored' in order to satisfy the craving for Tudor and Stuart gardens, for example Edzell Castle in Scotland in the 1930s (fig. 7.5). The new garden was an imaginative design, quite unlike the gardens of the period from which it purported to come. There were clues that would alert the expert to the fraud, such as stylistic improbabilities, and the asynchronous association between the ruined castles and the pristine gardens. There was a danger, though, that if the true history of these gardens were not to be properly revealed in the guidebooks, they could seriously mislead the unwary visitor.

A similar process took place at Kirby Hall, in Northamptonshire. This garden was abandoned to sheep early in the eighteenth century, before being landscaped with planting and a pool a century after that. In 1932 an architect, George Chettle, was asked by the Office of Works to reinstate the seventeenth-century layout. He located the paths in the Great Garden by primitive means, designed a garden

Figure 7.5 *Edzell Castle garden, Angus, in Scotland, 'restored' in the 1930s to a conception of what the garden of 1604 might have been like. The outcome looked more like a 1930s garden than what we would now recognise as a Stuart one.*

Restoration tragedies **199**

around them which was intended to simulate the mid-seventeenth century style, replaced the top six inches of ground with fresh soil, depositing the stripped material in the pool, and constructed a new garden (fig. 7.6). Not only had he destroyed a component of the early nineteenth-century overlay, but the top six inches he had removed had most likely contained evidence of the actual seventeenth-century garden.[2] Chettle's version of the seventeenth century was coloured by his Arts and Crafts training, and his invented detail was stylistically inaccurate. Once again, historic overlays had been removed for a mere period-style garden.[3]

Post-war, the prevailing ethos was modernism which emphasised redesign for modern living. The very idea of restoration was seen as reactionary (i.e. harking after earlier epochs) and deadening (suppressing the creativity of modern designers). There was sometimes scope for restoration at national monuments where it could be justified as a means to display important artistic achievement, meaningful for all time. Usually this meant intervention that made the higher artistic qualities, with which the places in question were imbued, potentially accessible to the modern person. This was often with a modernist slant.

Figure 7.6 *Destructive reconstruction at Kirby Hall, Northamptonshire: George Chettle's scheme in the early 1930s unwittingly eliminated the shallow remains of the 1680s garden in favour of this rose garden, then thought to be moderately authentic.*

Figure 7.7 *Drottningholm Palace, Sweden, Chinese Pavilion: the new setting in the 1950s designed for perceived modern needs and which ignored historic plans.*

Figure 7.8 *Wilanow Palace, outside Warsaw. Details – tarmac, concrete edgings, inauthentic planting – because the form, and not the detail, mattered.*

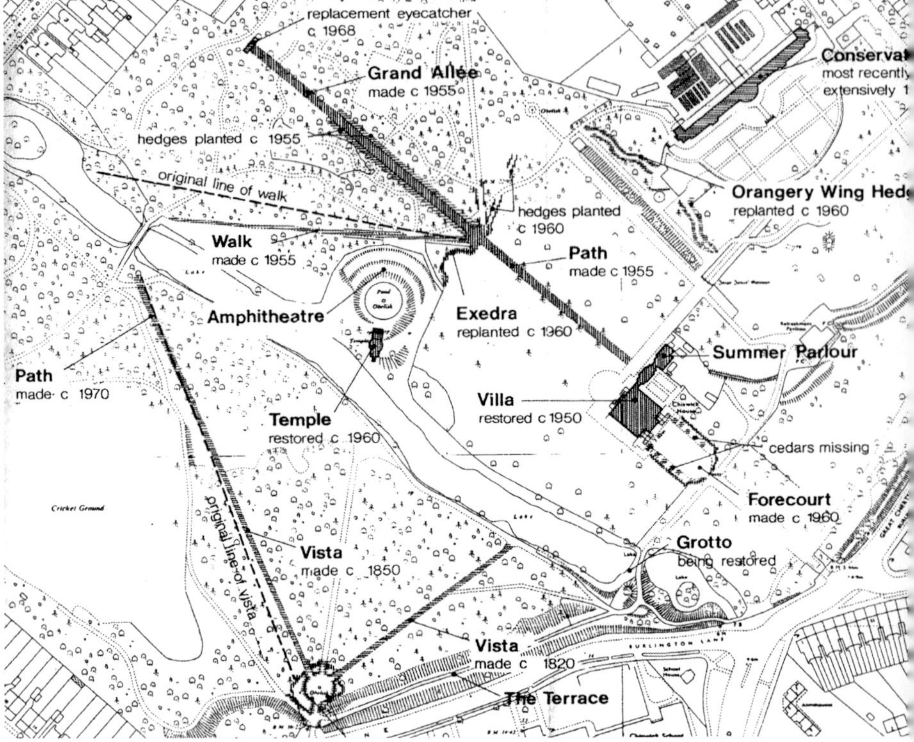

Figure 7.9 *Restoration-in-spirit: this analysis of restored features at Chiswick House grounds, west London, in 1983 showed that all the garden features 'restored' in 1955-1970 had been on non-historic lines; the general impression had been sought, and accuracy would have been 'pedantic'.*

At Drottningholm Palace, outside Stockholm, the landscape architect Walter Bauer was commissioned in 1950 to renovate the groves around the Chinese house (fig. 7.7). He ignored historic plans and implemented a new design that was more open but nothing to do with historical truth. The designer had reinterpreted the needs of the visitor and the place and produced a modernist vision of light and space. There was often a deliberate disregard for the accuracy of details in favour of modern materials. At Wilanów, outside Warsaw, the parterres were restored by Professor Gerard Ciołek in the 1970s with paths of asphalt instead of gravel, edgings of concrete rather than stone, and thuja in the *plates bandes* instead of yews (fig. 7.8).

In reflecting on the 1950s restoration at Chiswick House, near London, Frank Clark argued that it was ideas behind designs that were important, not the designs per se. Hence he considered that the restoration of the garden should seek to reinstate the essential ideas by work 'in the spirit' of the original (fig. 7.9). This permitted *allées* to be replanted on non-historic lines and the dimensions and materials to be inauthentic. Similar ideas were given even more scope in Czechoslovakia from the 1950s, where the landscape architect Otakar Kuča was asked

202 *Memory maketh humanity*

Figure 7.10 *Kratochvíle, in Netolice, Czech Republic, a 'modern analogy of the original concept', and one that caused massive damage to archaeological potential.*

to restore several of the Republic's finest Renaissance and Baroque gardens (fig. 7.10). His approach has been described as 'the search for the essential compositional structure and the spatial relations which he then tries to restore ... in particular situations, conservation or renovation is chosen, with renovation understood as a fine suggestion or modern analogy of "the original concept" '. His own interpretations of style did not closely follow the historic features found there, and in the process of restoration much archaeological evidence was destroyed.

In the UK, as the edifice of modernism crumbled in the 1970s and 1980s, a revived respect for historic buildings was kindled, and along with buildings came their settings, that is their associated designed landscapes. Garden history was taken seriously and became an academic topic, and alongside was the desire to conserve them.[4] The question arose as to what principles should guide this endeavour.

Conservation and interpretation

The subject of conservation is broad: buildings, textiles, paintings, and landscapes amongst other topics. The principles are the same; the application differs according to the nature of the material.

Conservations and interpretation **203**

Figure 7.11 *Hohenzollern Castle, Baden-Würtemberg, the family home of the Kaisers, as rebuilt between 1846 and 1867 to create as much drama as possible in recalling historical associations.*

There have been vigorous debates on the purpose and practice of restoration which can be summed up as restoration versus repair. Restoration, or what might today be seen as partial 'reconstruction', was felt by architects inspired by architectural history to be desirable to allow the qualities of architectural monuments to be fully expressed. Architectural style was not seen neutrally by the nineteenth-century historian; it had serious meaning. The Gothic style was associated with Romantic nationalism, especially in Germany (fig. 7.11). In Britain, Augustus Pugin saw the Gothic Catholic past as a natural and organic outgrowth of a people at a particular time. The Renaissance was seen as representing the rational, and having a language of true or perfect types of everlasting validity. Most passion was devoted to the Gothic, and expressed thousands of times in church restoration, the more famous exponents being Eugène Viollet-le-Duc in France (fig. 7.12) and Sir Gilbert Scott in Britain.

Such restorations may have brought buildings back to the coherence and aesthetic qualities presumed to have been intended but would often require the removal of later changes and additions. In his *The Seven Lamps of Architecture* (1849), John Ruskin objected

Figure 7.12 *Notre-Dame Paris, under restoration by Eugène Viollet-le-Duc from 1844 to enhance its Gothic style; here in a photograph by Bisson Frères c. 1858-60.*

to returning a building to some idealised state from the past, 'scraped and patched up into smugness and smoothness more tragic than uttermost ruin'. He argued for repair instead:

> Take proper care of your monuments, and you will not need to restore them ... Watch an old building with an anxious care; guard it as best you may, and at any cost, from every influence of dilapidation.[5]

Ruskin was joined by William Morris, who was likewise outraged by the stripping away of genuinely old features, which they had dubbed the 'Scrape' approach. He saw all parts of a building as contributing to its interest as a document of the past, and advocated 'Anti-Scrape'. He set up the Society for the Protection of Ancient Buildings (SPAB) in 1877 which promoted this cause.

The 'Anti-Scrape' approach steadily gained ground, and in 1964 the Second International Congress of Architects and Specialists of Historic Buildings drew up the 'Venice Charter'. This contained a clause that stated that the intention of conserving monuments 'is to safeguard them no less as works of art than as historical evidence'. A SPAB-type approach can be seen in other clauses that argued that 'the valid contributions of all periods to the building of a monument must be respected, since unity of style is not the

Conservations and interpretation **205**

aim of a restoration'. The Charter sternly opposed any conjectural repairs as perverting the story told by the fabric, and absolutely proscribed reconstruction.[6]

Conservation was a crusade in the UK in the 1980s, often resulting in hardline attitudes. The new English Heritage advice on historic buildings, as might be expected, took the SPAB-inspired position, stating that 'the primary purpose of repair is to restrain the process of decay'. Works of repair:

> ... must be kept to the minimum required to stabilise and conserve buildings and monuments, with the aim of achieving a sufficiently sound structural condition to ensure their long-term survival.

The potential harm from the replacement of fabric was pointed out:

> The unnecessary replacement of historic fabric, no matter how carefully the work is carried out ... will seriously diminish its authenticity, and will significantly reduce its value as a source of historical information.[7]

Many architects found restoration hard to resist in practice, so that tension between a building as a work of art and as evidence persisted. The arguments had been expressed in terms of the treatment of historic fabric, though underlain by a complementary line of argument in terms of values (see Chapter 5 – 'Knowledge gives value'). The ICOMOS Nara Document on Authenticity, for example, stated that 'The conservation of cultural heritage in all its forms and historical periods is rooted in the values attributed to the heritage'.[8] There was in fact a precedent though it was not well known in English-speaking countries until translated in 1982. Aloïs Riegl, an Austrian art historian, seeking a rationale for the preservation of art, architecture and monuments from the ravages of time, listed historical value, artistic value, age value, commemorative value, use value, and newness value. The first two we have seen above, and 'age value' gave a sense of 'the life cycle of the artefact, and of culture as a whole'.[9]

The ultimate purpose of preserving or restoring a building was not, of course, merely its retention, but to make it available for appreciation, education and information. In North America, politicians keen to promote the national identity chose sites for 'preservation' because of their capacity to illustrate the story they wished to be told; hence the interest in battlefields, presidents' houses and even the 'trails' that opened up the West. The point of conservation was lost if the story was not then literally told by trained interpreters (fig. 7.13). Not surprisingly, the national parks services of North America led the world in methods of interpretation.

Memory maketh humanity

Figure 7.13 *Telling the story: interpreters at the John Dickinson Plantation near Dover, Delaware, outside the smokehouse. A demonstration inside showed visitors how smoked, pickled and salted meats helped stretch food reserves in the winter.*

Interpretation raised far from simple questions, though. For whose benefit was the physical testimony of historic events conserved? Who decided on what is important? Few people in Britain accepted the idea of the old Office of Works that monuments were protected 'for their own sake', as objects of beauty, awe and wonder, available to anyone with enough prior knowledge to appreciate. The Office and its post-war successors offered scholarly guidebooks on the background history and on the archaeological interest of the monument, which were incomprehensible to most of the visiting public.

The potential role of historians and interpreters could be compared to that of art critics (see Chapter 4 – 'The Sociology of Criticism').[10] They might be seen as enablers, using their knowledge to identify the pertinent, and often difficult and uncomfortable, questions raised by the monuments. The places themselves were often evocative and a useful template for reconstructing the historical events and scenes of importance in the imagination. The imagination could be further stimulated by educational packs for schools, posters, children's books, guidebooks, artist's impressions, models and videos. By such means, relatively unknowledgeable but interested visitors could reconstruct events or scenes, and seek enlightenment through their own observation and reflection.

Conservations and interpretation

Figure 7.14 *Abbotsford House, Visitor Centre, Scotland, catering for the visitors to Sir Walter Scott's home. Such grandiose structures become another overlay on the site.*

Interpreters who either intended their monuments to provide a simple political message, or were looking to accommodate the public's imagined intellectual passivity, would tend to provide literal interpretations of some former preferred period by reconstructing its physical forms. Meanwhile the requirements of presentation would ideally involve no intervention with the fabric, but in practice, through visitor facilities and reconstruction, presentation often became de facto a further overlay in the history of the site (fig. 7.14).

Change and ephemerality

The conservation of landscapes and gardens has a very distinctive character amongst the broad family of conservation disciplines. As one set of ICOMOS guidelines from 1994 observed:

> Landscapes are dynamic and complex. They require an holistic approach that will safeguard their cultural value, retain their historic character and still accommodate change.[11]

It was difficult to envision a type of landscape that did not undergo change, either by natural forces or through design or management. Change did seem to be of the very essence of landscape.

208 *Memory maketh humanity*

Figure 7.15 *David Garrick as Gloucester in* Richard III *by William Shakespeare, performing in Drury Lane. Painting by Francis Hayman, 1760, intended to capture Garrick's notable performances.*

The conservation of gardens and landscapes thus differed in important respects from the conservation of buildings which were usually assumed to be more-or-less permanent, given sufficient repairs. At the other end of the scale, representing maximum impermanence, were the performing arts: music and drama. There was no substance and no impression, apart from that on human memory. No wonder that a desire to capture the moment, to bottle the experience, has accompanied the ephemeral arts. David Garrick, the great eighteenth-century Shakespearean actor, conceitedly wanted some memorial of his art, and so commissioned paintings to remind the world of special moments of his career (fig. 7.15). In more modern times music and drama have been recorded electronically.

Cookery was a case of relatively impermanent, though physical, creation. Horace Walpole reported on a very extravagant example of the confectioner's art:

Change and ephemerality

Jellies, biscuits, sugarplumbs and creams have long given way to harlequins, gondoliers, Turks, Chinese, and shepherdesses of Saxon-china. But these, unconnected, and only seeming to wander among the groves of curled paper and silk flowers, were soon discovered to be too insipid and unmeaning. By degrees whole meadows of cattle, of the same brittle materials, spread themselves over the whole table; cottages rose in sugar, and temples in barley-sugar; pigmy Neptunes in cars of cockle-shells, triumphed over oceans of looking-glass, or seas of silver tissue ... It is known that a celebrated confectioner (so the architects of our desserts still humbly call themselves) complained, that after having prepared a middle dish of gods and goddesses, eighteen feet high, his lord would not cause the ceiling of his parlour to be demolished to facilitate their entrée.[12]

It would defeat the object of the art to forego consumption, but nevertheless strategies for preservation were practised through committing recipes to paper (fig. 7.16). Hence the glimmering wedding cake and the great ice sculptures of Edwardian days that were drawn for Mrs Beeton before they melted (fig. 7.17). Hence recipes form the enduring record of the cook's art, allowing successors to repeat the culinary achievements of the past.

Figure 7.16 *Mrs Beeton - a 'supper table with floral decorations, arranged for 16 persons'; artistic but ephemeral.*

210 *Memory maketh humanity*

Figure 7.17 *Ephemerality: Finnish folk tales at the Harbin International Ice and Snow Sculpture Festival in China, 2009.*

As plantsmen are fond of pointing out to architectural conservationists, their medium is living organisms that grow and then die. Possibly they over-simplified matters by singling out vegetation as the only medium of the gardener – Japanese sand and rock gardens, to take an extreme, mostly eschewed plants – but they were certainly right to emphasise the relative ephemerality of landscape as a whole.

Neither fleeting nor permanent, the various elements of the landscape occupy a large range between the eight weeks of the bedding-out display and the timelessness of the archaeological earthwork. The architectural component could last as long as other buildings, but very often not: pergolas were easily damaged and many garden buildings were thrown up in cheap materials including wood. Retaining walls and ha-has tended to succumb to hydrostatic pressure eventually. Dams developed fissures and needed repair. Avenues would last a couple of hundred years, shrubbery a few decades, and the fine effects of an herbaceous border a few years only. Paths needed periodic patching. Hence those who cared for landscapes found that their major task was to grapple with the perishability of vegetation and human construction.

Change and ephemerality **211**

Because of landscapes' ephemerality, recording was the *sine qua non*, the very essence, of their conservation. It could take place:

- at the earliest feasible moment;
- when decisions were made at the beginning of the restoration process;
- when the works of restoration were completed; and
- during the cyclical monitoring process.

An initial survey would provide a baseline against which those making decisions in the future could evaluate success or failure of the tactics chosen in the past or the objectives of care since. It was thus never too soon to carry out such a survey of a property. Various types of record might be desired: measured drawings, tree surveys, photographs and oral history.

Successive minor alterations could result in almost imperceptible, though cumulative, departures from a design. The accuracy of repairs depended crucially upon the record of the fabric. Without good records what might have been repairs became speculative reconstruction of limited historical value. Conversely, good repair reliably replicated original detail.

Historians and conservationists were acutely aware of the value of surveys, photographs, old files and the like in illuminating both the broader picture and the detail; with this in mind, they were conscious of the responsibility of providing future researchers with their historical materials.

Every project was a candidate for a site archive, a collection of all technical information generated by the project, including photography, survey work, committee papers and minutes, research reports, archaeological reports, design drawings and monitoring reports. A policy for a site archive from the start of a project was recommended as beneficial.

Conservation guidelines for landscape

Almost every paragraph above in this chapter has added weight to the case for settling some principles for the conservation and restoration of landscapes. The difficulty was that, relative to the architectural profession, the landscape profession was slow in establishing itself, and remained poorly organised at both national and international level. For such reasons attempts to develop guidelines for the conservation of designed landscapes had to wait till the 1980s.

Florence Charter 1981

The International Council for Monuments and Sites (ICOMOS), which had been founded at the same time that the Venice Charter was signed in 1964, acquired an International Scientific Committee on Historic Gardens and Sites a few years later. The moving spirit and its first president was René Pechère, a modernist landscape architect from Belgium closely aligned to French traditions. He had been president of the International Federation of Landscape Architects (IFLA) 1956-8. Having received encouragement from Geoffrey Jellicoe, who had been the founding president 1948-54, Pechère formed an IFLA committee on historic gardens. It was agreed at a meeting in Fontainebleau in 1971 that this should also become an ICOMOS committee, and it took on art historians and conservation practitioners to complement the designers.

In the late 1970s Pechère decided that his committee should create an ICOMOS-IFLA charter for historic gardens. He worked up a draft with Jean Feray, a French *architecte-en-chef* whose career was in handling many of the great French châteaux on behalf of the State. They were *monuments*, a term of special significance in French conservation denoting high art rather than the building being seen merely as a record. Substantial alterations were often sanctioned to bring out the artistic achievements of the original designer 'for the glory of France'. Maybe it was Feray who pressed for their gardens to be treated as *monuments* too. The pair saw the garden as an 'architectural and horticultural composition' which could largely follow architectural principles. Both were creative individuals who saw their mission as restoring gardens to make them beautiful and useful. Pechère's modernist perspective emerged in the declarations that a garden was 'the expression of the direct affinity between civilization and nature', and that 'the garden thus acquires the cosmic significance of an idealized image of the world'.

The charter included many valuable principles but there were some wrinkles too. First, as the British representative argued, the charter allowed for formal gardens only, and should have included landscape parks such as those by Capability Brown. Second, and although Pechère claimed that his draft was in furtherance of the Venice Charter, and stated the 'desire of the artist and craftsman to keep it permanently unchanged', the text did betray the authors' ambivalence over the purpose of restoration. To them, gardens were a 'testimony', not so much as fabric, but to 'a culture, a style, an age, and often to the originality of a creative artist'. They advised that 'reconstruction work might be undertaken more particularly on the parts of the garden nearest to the building it contains in order to bring out their significance in the design', confirming that the authors favoured work for aesthetic reasons. Hence the charter permitted reconstructions of gardens, provided that 'thorough prior research to ensure that such work is scientifically executed and which will involve everything from excavation to the assembling of records' had been undertaken.

The Italian ministry had a rather different, and very strict, approach to monuments as 'documents', each a 'limited, perishable, non-reproducible unicum'. The Italian Charter of Restoration of 1972 did not admit re-creations or reconstructions on the grounds that to 're-create it all over again, to the detriment of the subsequent steps, would cause a reduction in resources and it would moreover result in a restrictive and definitely anti-historic attitude'. The Italians set up their own historic gardens committee which took exception to the ICOMOS-IFLA approach and within months drew up its own charter for historic gardens.[13] These differences were an echo of the debate over the designer's sense of aesthetics versus the ethic of retaining fabric as historical evidence.

Figure 7.18 *Kloster Kamp terraced garden, Kamp-Lintfort, North Rhine-Westphalia, restored 2004 to recover the design intent, but so thoroughly that it effectively became a new garden.*

Nevertheless, the Florence Charter was welcomed in many countries, and nowhere more so than Germany where numerous Baroque gardens were subsequently reconstructed (fig. 7.18). One view was that the meaning and significance of any monument relates to immaterial values, and that the fabric is just the means to describe them. While this may be argued, going one step further by downgrading the importance of retaining genuine historic fabric led in several cases to massive physical losses and thus its associated evidence. The Charter had stated that the materials of a garden were primarily 'vegetal', which meant that they were 'perishable and renewable', and this may have given the impression that trees were not viewed as fabric to be protected in the same way as built structures. This promoted recklessness in specifying replanting. Yet trees very often embodied the history of their own planting and maintenance in their genetics, position, cut marks, and branching patterns. Mass felling and replanting would destroy all potential for research.

Not surprisingly, reconstruction and mass clear-felling became increasingly controversial in Germany. From the 1990s, a much greater acknowledgement was made of the value of trees and other plants as documents, and attention given to research and protection. The Italian position came to be shared by many professionals outside Italy.

Figure 7.19 *Westbury Court, Gloucestershire; the pavilion and canal restored 1967-72, but the bobbles and spikes, and the hedge they rise from, derive from a faulty interpretation of an historic print.*

Conservation guidelines for landscape

The desire for accuracy

Where reconstruction prevailed, the purpose of recovering the design naturally led to a concern for accuracy. This was the case with German restorations, and in Britain there had been a rush of them by the National Trust starting with Westbury Court in 1967 to 1972 (fig. 7.19), and then at Ham House and Claremont in 1974. The exercise at Het Loo in The Netherlands from 1977 to 1984 reproduced an historic plan to stunning visual effect. The Privy Garden at Hampton Court was restored in 1995 with the benefit of exceptional archaeological and documentary findings, backed up by research on contemporary detailing and historical plant varieties (fig. 7.20).[14] An increasing emphasis on accuracy of restoration could be seen over this period. Whereas garden restoration in the early 1970s tended to be pristine but inaccurate, the 1990s equivalent sought accuracy of detail, even at the price of looking strange to the modern eye.

Archaeology was often a great aid to accurate restoration, and was employed with spectacular results at several historic formal gardens. Much of their information on paths and parterres was in the top half metre. Formerly it was assumed that this zone would almost certainly be irretrievably disturbed. However, excavations at Monticello, Bacon's Castle and Williamsburg in Virginia, and at Audley End, Kirby Hall, Castle Bromwich and Hampton Court in England, revealed how

Figure 7.20 *Hampton Court, Middlesex, the Privy Garden restored 1994-5, the acme of accuracy; yet still only an approximation to the garden of 1714.*

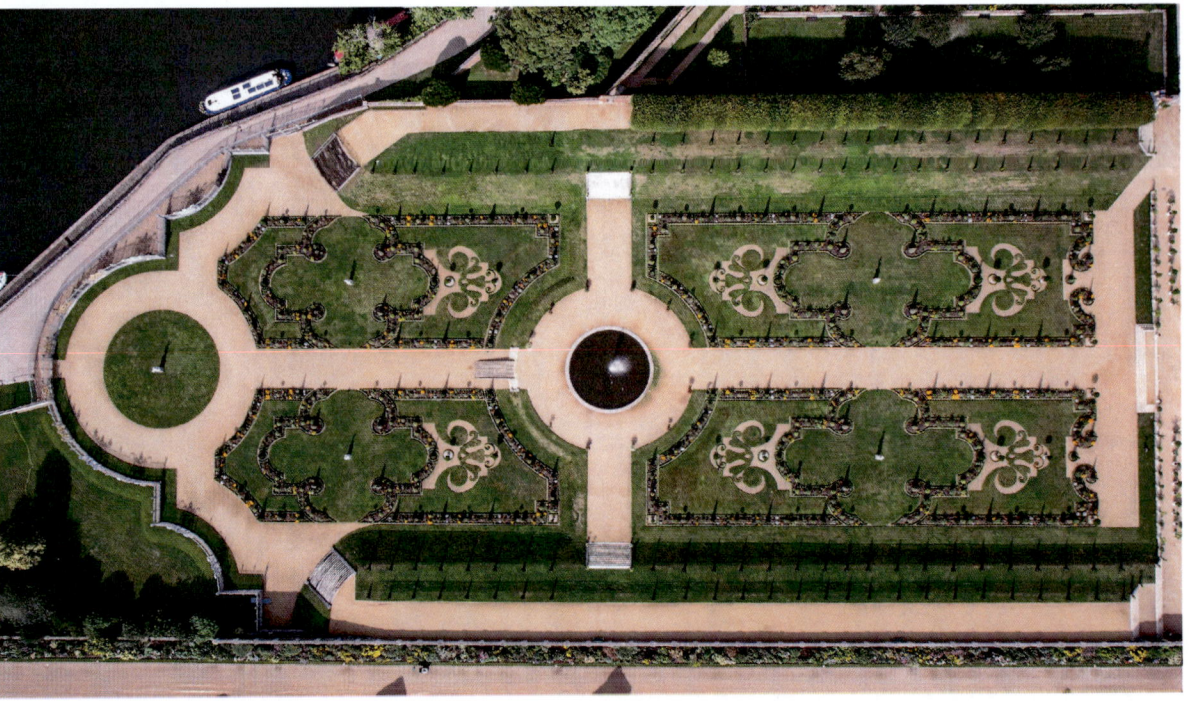

216 *Memory maketh humanity*

wrong that assumption could be. These examples could not be taken as the general case – undoubtedly many sites had lost the bulk of their archaeological interest – but excavation was only one among the archaeologists' armoury of techniques including environmental archaeology (macrofossils, pollen, chemical analysis), resistivity testing, magnetometers, and ground-penetrating radar. A minor revolution took place in historic garden survey.

A comparison between Het Loo and the Privy Garden at Hampton Court illustrated how the concern for accuracy had moved on. Both gardens had been made for William of Orange, and the driving force behind the restorations was much the same, as curators at both places

Figure 7.21 *Hampton Court, Middlesex; the Privy Garden excavations of 1994, giving exceptional evidence for the former layout.*

aimed to present the gardens as they would have been in their heyday. At Het Loo, great reliance was placed upon the architect in charge of the restoration to interpret historic plans, and archaeology principally amounted to recording elements uncovered in the restoration. However, the Hampton Court project was preceded by intensive archaeological investigation (fig. 7.21). Strenuous efforts were made to ensure that the design as thus revealed was reinstated as accurately as feasible, and that the surface and above-ground elements that had to be reinvented were based on the best available background research. The result was an even more accurate representation of the Williamite garden.

The mood was to want to know precisely what historic gardens looked like in their heyday, and to undertake restorations accordingly. They were often promoted as museum pieces, and indeed several examples were carried out by curators seeking to recover the settings of their houses and palaces. At this date, though, reconstruction was generally frowned upon as a matter of principle by English Heritage (see above).

US guidelines for the treatment of cultural landscapes 1996

Similar thoughts might recur in many places, though each country had its own terminology. An example of English-speaking countries being 'divided by a common language' was the use of 'preservation' in the United States. Elsewhere the term was thought to represent the discredited idea that something can be protected simply by leaving it alone, and 'conservation' had come to be preferred. However, the term was embedded in US legislation, and was to remain unaltered.

The US Secretary of the Interior had in 1976 published *Standards for the Treatment of Historic Properties*, a quasi-legal statement of principles and desirable practice within government agencies, in particular State Historic Preservation Boards and the National Park Service. These standards were revised in 1992 so that they could be applied to all forms of heritage site, now including landscapes. All 'treatment' came under one of four heads: 'preservation', 'restoration', 'rehabilitation', and 'reconstruction'.

Preservation came closest to the spirit of the Venice Charter, while restoration, in 'preserving materials from the period of significance and removing materials from other periods', came close to the nineteenth-century church architect's concept of restoration seeking stylistic coherence. Whereas preservation's view of the structure as a document would argue for the retention of all periods, restoration could countenance one period being privileged as the 'high point' in the structure's history. 'Rehabilitation' (sometimes 'adaptation') sought changes for new uses, while 'reconstruction' was the replacement of vanished structures primarily for interpretive purposes.

The 'Guidelines for the Treatment of Cultural Landscapes' became a subset within these Standards. In preparation since 1990, publication took place in 1996.[15] The Guidelines had to be based on the principles in the Standards, and their purpose was not to present an argued case but to give practical advice. They were illustrated by 'recommended' and 'not recommended' examples, and looked and felt like an instruction manual. Perhaps their real significance was simply their existence. They acknowledged in effect that interest in designed landscapes, especially public parks, as well as the cultural landscapes of native Americans, had expanded substantially during the 1980s, sufficient for the need for special consideration.

Architectural principles in gardens

In the UK, as in the US, conservation had proceeded largely without reference to international standards. Conservation architects, used to having their judgement trusted, had no official guidance on what was expected of them until 1991. In landscape design, meanwhile, the long-standing formula of 'Survey-Analysis-Design', which omitted any reference to values or aims, was deemed inadequate in a new age of managerial planning.

Following the Great Storm that ravaged the south-east of England in October 1987 (fig. 7.22), money was found for English Heritage, which was responsible for parks and gardens, to assist owners in clearance and replanting of trees. A rationale for its distribution was needed, as was guidance on the principles of conservation which were formalised in 1989.[16] These events resulted in the world's first purpose-made grant scheme for parks and gardens in 1988.

In many ways, English Heritage saw parks and gardens as an extension of historic buildings, and that the principles of architectural repair could be carried outwards to their landscapes. The central concern was preserving the non-renewable information embodied in the authentic fabric. However, the relative ephemerality of gardens had important practical implications and made adjustments to the traditional 'conserve-as-found' philosophy necessary. The inevitable growth and decay would mean that normal repairs, in the architectural sense, would eventually become ineffective in preserving the fabric overall. The priorities of garden conservation thus needed redefining: they became, in order, the protection of the historic fabric, recording of fabric, and then restoration to conserve the design.[17]

Figure 7.22 *Emmetts, Kent: the devastation wrought by the great storm of October 1987.*

Also, English Heritage made a distinction between the more permanent elements of a garden, which would include avenues, hedges, topiary and other semi-permanent planting, which could be treated and funded similarly to architectural features, on the one hand, and the gardening involving shorter-lived plants likely to be replaced in less than 40 years on the other. In these ways the tensions between preserving the fabric and the desire to keep and update a garden were slackened considerably, if not eliminated entirely.

Restoration in the British context generally meant parks and gardens at the country houses of the aristocracy and the trusts that had in many cases replaced them. They had been owned and developed over several centuries, leading usually to several phases or 'overlays' (fig. 7.23). There would also be several types of fabric: parterres with bedding, terraces, paths, avenues, tree belts, 'rivers' and so forth. Very often decay had set in during the early to mid-twentieth century. The question then arose as to what state should be aimed for in restoration.

At first the vision was that the garden should be unchanged from its last great manifestation. The all-important accuracy was principally promoted by increasing technical sophistication in survey, historical research and the use of archaeology. These aims were familiar from

220 *Memory maketh humanity*

Figure 7.23 *Weston Park, Staffordshire, view looking south. The earlier formal gardens were expunged for the park by Capability Brown, but the parterres reintroduced formality in Victorian times.*

architectural conservation, and represented a rejection of the vague objectives, often incompetently and destructively implemented, of modernist attitudes to restoration. English Heritage had an axiom that parks and gardens should be restored to the last significant change.[18] This would ensure that all surviving fabric could be restored with coherence. There was also a pragmatic reason, which was that national mapping at 1:2,500 was excellent from the late nineteenth century onwards, and this would give an objective blueprint at a scale useful for parkland and larger gardens.

Restoration would be based on a management plan that involved survey of the landscape elements, historical research to clarify the 'overlays', consideration of managing practices, identification of cultural and natural values and whether these were vulnerable, and the proposed aims of the restoration. This process was considered to be so essential to the conservation of the landscape, both in the short and long term, that English Heritage offered grants of 75 per cent to have them commissioned. This became the accepted norm when the Countryside Commission funded replanting in the wider countryside, and then later when the Heritage Lottery Fund started to fund the restoration of public parks.

Conservation guidelines for landscape

The integrated approach

For too long the various agencies in most countries had battled for their own interests exclusively, which militated against unified assessments. Often it was found that the range of values in a landscape derived from common determinants, such as topography or past land-use management. An historic park, because of its history of continuous grazing, may have preserved the archaeological remains of a medieval village and have led to a floristically rich turf. Mountainous land like the Lake District had led, through generations of struggle, to a remarkable cultural landscape which was celebrated by even more remarkable poets. A prominent mountain may have attracted spiritual value to itself, which may have led to an architecturally important monastery being built. Such examples illustrated that cherished landscapes were not just the cumulative sum of the constituent interests; but complex bundles of related interests.

An example about which this author was once acutely aware was the recurring conflict between the interests of historic gardens and those of nature conservation. The latter had designated areas and the force of law, and saw no merit in restoration to recover historic designs; indeed, the more unkempt, derelict, wild (choose an adjective) the better. The English Heritage historic parks and gardens team could only observe that the two interests served each other more than they conflicted, and the problematic questions were generally quite limited. Hence sparring between the interest groups was largely unnecessary and it was sensible to seek some accommodation whereby the most overall benefit could be reached.

When plans for management began to be produced in any numbers in the 1980s the force of such observations became manifest, and single-issue plans were discouraged in favour of those addressing all values, whatever the nature of the client or funding agency. Planners, too, liked to be made aware of the full range of values, and this began to be acknowledged in wider studies.[19] The existing designations were not about to be disbanded, but at least they could be considered alongside each other. In England, the three main government agencies concerned, the Countryside Commission, English Nature and English Heritage, mounted an attempt at a truly integrated approach to countryside conservation. They collaborated in advising local authorities on how to prepare conservation policies for their development plans.[20]

The cultural landscapes approach

The changes to the World Heritage Convention in 1993 (see below) had included the acknowledgement of 'cultural landscapes', one category of them being 'designed landscapes'. Although this did not signify a great conceptual change in the conservation of gardens at the time, it was a reminder that the topic did not need to be seen as just an offshoot of architectural conservation. Indeed, some concepts from cultural landscapes, especially of change being inherent to all landscape, and in the treatment of value, became helpful in achieving a more rounded and realistic approach.[21]

The early international charters shared the tendency with the theories of the 1960s of stating propositions as if they were unchanging universal truths. In the 1990s that mindset was giving way to a greater acknowledgement of relativity, for example to accommodate non-Western concepts of conservation. It is described above how value came to be seen not as something inherent in objects, but as deriving from a complex and potentially variable set of qualities evaluated through people's culture, expectations and preferences (see Chapter 5 – 'How preferences arise'). Instead of a reliance on experts for their opinions, a wider range of bodies and individuals could contribute to deciding upon aims and priorities so that pluralism was entering the conservation world.

That attitude led bodies and governments to assure their ends through explaining to owners and persuading public bodies, rather than by inflexible prescriptions. Guidance recognized the possibility of debate and alternative outcomes and was preferred to the absolutes of laws and charters. Awareness of issues in conservation was rising amongst a new generation of conservation professionals and officials, who were better equipped to exercise their judgement and not just rely on fixed prescriptions.

The primary qualities in historic gardens recognized by English Heritage, for instance, were still art-historical, with several factors relevant to aesthetic appreciation being specified, while significance was qualified by rarity and condition. In addition, there were the 'natural' qualities relating to geology, ecology and biodiversity, and the benefits of physical and intellectual public access, to add to the mix. The focus on the great monuments as proof of genius was paralleled by an interest in the vernacular and the cultural landscape as informing us as much, or even more, about the history of mankind.

Conservation guidelines for landscape **223**

The suggestion that a park or garden should be returned to its state at the date of the last significant change had been close to the old aim of architectural restoration for aesthetic purposes. A conserver's approach to protect historical fabric would more properly have been to respect the landscape as received by our generation, defects and all, and attending to repairs. It was better not to look back, just forward, and emphasise taking heritage into the future by putting the garden into good order.

As landscapes cannot be preserved indefinitely through repairs, the management of change emerges as an increasingly insistent theme. Any landscape could have many qualities overlying each other, each being valued in different ways, and each with its own vulnerability and resilience. Various forms of change might be acceptable so long as the essential cultural qualities had been identified and adequately protected. Although landscape-managers had been well aware that each landscape had its own dynamic, and required active management for protection of their historic interest, the discussion of change had only just been raised by conservationists in the late 1990s.

In summary, the conservation approach had moved some way towards human values instead of universal principles; an acceptance of change; and attention to its dynamics. Professionals were advised to accept a landscape as inherited and merely put it into good order. Exercise of judgement was expected, rather than reliance on fixed prescriptions.

Figure 7.24 *Château de Fontainebleau, south-eastern aspect. This garden was part of the World Heritage Site centred on the palace.*

Figure 7.25 *Studley Royal, Yorkshire; the Temple of Filial Piety and the water garden; the gardens were included in the World Heritage Site with Fountains Abbey.*

The World Heritage criteria

The World Heritage Convention had been signed by most of the world's governments by the 1980s.[22] Its committee oversaw the 'World Heritage List' for which there were criteria embodied in the Convention. UNESCO provided the secretariat. Article 1 of the Convention defined the scope of the cultural heritage as monuments, groups of buildings and sites, and 'sites' which were:

> ... the works of man, or the combined works of nature and of man, and areas including archaeological sites which are of outstanding universal value from the historic, aesthetic, ethnological or anthropological points of view.[23]

Cultural landscapes – landscapes that showed traces of interaction with humans – were easily accommodated in the above definition as 'the combined works of nature and of man'. Some very fine gardens had already been inscribed on the World Heritage List as part of nominations for important buildings. In France the palaces and estates of Chambord, Fontainebleau (fig. 7.24) and Versailles were included. In Britain, there was Blenheim Palace with its park, and Studley Royal and Fountains Abbey (fig. 7.25). In the United States, Monticello (fig. 7.26) (with the University of Virginia at Charlottesville, Virginia) was inscribed.

Figure 7.26 *Monticello, Virginia, west front; the home of Thomas Jefferson, the third President of the United States. The garden and house were within a World Heritage Site that also included the University of Virginia.*

The list included archaeological cultural landscapes too, including the Avebury/Stonehenge complex (fig. 7.27) and the industrial heritage of the Ironbridge Gorge in the UK, the Chaco Culture National Historic Park in the US, and in Canada the Head-Smashed-In Buffalo Jump in Alberta was accepted for its evidence of the sophisticated manipulation of the natural environment by the 'first peoples' over millennia (fig. 7.28). So there were landscapes on the List, though landscapes without associated architectural monuments or archaeological remains had rarely been assessed in their own right.

La Petite Pierre 1992

The rise of cultural landscapes in the 1980s and 1990s was a complicated story. It started, in fact, with the attempt by the nature-conservation community to have what they termed 'protected landscapes' (in effect cultural landscapes with high nature conservation interest) included. At the time (the early 1980s) there were no criteria for assessing cultural or 'Protected' landscapes. The omission was first addressed in 1984, and the next year some draft guidelines for evaluating landscapes were drawn up, suggesting that cultural landscapes could be regarded as 'mixed' sites. Then in 1987 UNESCO met with ICOMOS and IUCN and the participants agreed that in future evaluations of mixed sites should be prepared jointly by both bodies. Keen to test this working arrangement, UNESCO encouraged the United Kingdom to nominate its Lake District.

226 *Memory maketh humanity*

Figure 7.27 *Avebury, Wiltshire; the ditch and standing stones dating from sometime between 3000 BC to 2400 BC; an example of an extensive archaeological site inscribed as a World Heritage Site.*

This area consists of some small-scale glaciated mountains with lakes. It has also been inhabited for millennia, and visitors notice the handiwork of generations of farmers, giving a richness and diversity of colour and pattern to the landscape (see fig. 7.34 on p. 240). The Lake District was a principal locus for a revolution in aesthetic sensibility towards the natural majesty of mountains wrought by poets such as William Wordsworth in the late eighteenth and early nineteenth centuries (fig. 7.29). It was central to the establishment of the conservation and national-park movements in the English-speaking world from the mid-nineteenth century and which have been influential globally.

When IUCN came to measure the Lake District against their criteria it came to the view that there are many better examples of glaciation, and the wildlife was not of world-wide significance. Uneasy at making non-scientific judgements on 'natural beauty', it declined to pronounce on that aspect. It found three reasons to defer a decision, two concerning the need to clarify guidelines for evaluation. ICOMOS, meanwhile, was not nearly so reluctant to give a judgement. It was, if anything, prepared to stretch the existing cultural guidelines to make way for what it considered was an obvious case for inscription. Nevertheless the World Heritage Committee agreed with IUCN to defer. Its reluctance to accept or refuse was partly because the perceptions of the Western nations

The world heritage criteria **227**

Figure 7.28 *Representation of the buffalo leaps operated by the Blackfoot Indians; painting by Alfred Jacob Miller, 'Hunting Buffalo', 1858, which illustrated the very ancient practice of driving the animals over a cliff.*

could not easily be reconciled with those of the Third World. The latter were not so ready to accept the concept of a 'mixed site', and questioned the importance of Wordsworth's poetry, for example, in world terms.[24]

In their own ways both ICOMOS and IUCN had confirmed the continuing deficiencies of the World Heritage criteria – ICOMOS by bending them, and IUCN by refusing to do so. In retrospect the Lake District was not a very suitable test case. First, its acceptance depended fundamentally upon a perception of the world-wide significance of nineteenth-century British literature, which cannot be taken for granted in all parts of the world. Second, it was not a clear test of the concept of a 'mixed site' which would have been better provided by a landscape like the terraced rice paddies of the Philippines, with neither natural nor cultural attributes conventionally remarkable, but nevertheless outstanding as a 'combined work of nature and of man'.

The Countryside Commission for England and Wales held an international symposium on Protected Landscapes in the Lake District in October 1987, and made a declaration that the biological

Figure 7.29 *How should the Lake District in Cumbria be viewed: as small-scale glaciated mountains, as the handiwork of farmers for millennia, or the inspiration for romantic poets? George Barratt's* Winnandermere-Lake, *1784.*

diversity and value of such areas had developed and continued because of human intervention. Some protected landscapes, it was said, were predominantly of nature-conservation interest, whilst others were of interest in displaying long-standing harmony between human society and the natural world. This latter type preserved the evidence of human history in structures and the traces of past land-use practices; provided a livelihood for indigenous populations following traditional values and ways of life; made an important contribution to the physical and mental health; offered beauty, pleasure and recreation to many; gave inspiration to writers and artists; and were living models of the sustainable use of the land and natural resources.[25]

In 1991 UNESCO presented new ideas on revisions to the World Heritage Guidelines designed to allow the guidelines to accommodate protected, otherwise cultural, landscapes. The paper proposed that a new criterion should be added, but adopted the Protected Landscapes approach in phrasing it as 'testimony of an outstandingly harmonious balance between nature and human beings over a long period of time'.

The world heritage criteria **229**

At this point the cultural-landscape specialists in ICOMOS entered the discussion. Some resolutions by the Alliance for Historic Landscape Preservation in 1990 had suggested criteria by which landscapes of high cultural significance could be assessed.[26] ICOMOS UK set up the ICOMOS Landscapes Working Group in early 1991 in order to co-ordinate the views of ICOMOS members world-wide.[27]

The 'protected-landscape' approach was thought unsuitable for a number of reasons. First, a poetic state of grace between a traditional life-style and consequently beautiful landscape seems to have been envisaged by its advocates. There was a need for a tighter and less idealistic definition. Conservation can work only if it relates to concrete, definable, artefacts, and the concept of harmony is so vague that it would have led to uncertainties and difficulties in definition and identification. No system of protection of landscapes could have been devised to conserve some possibly ephemeral state of harmony.

Second, there were problems in borrowing concepts and terminology from ecology like 'harmonious evolution'. The concept of the 'super-organism' evolving towards a stable 'climax' had just been debunked in *Discordant Harmonies* by Daniel Botkin. Even areas subject to environmental management to provide an appearance of stability and harmony, could not necessarily be regarded as stable. Without the usual occasional disasters, like fire, the processes of long-term regeneration could be interrupted so that the appearance of stability was illusory. Hence 'we have not abandoned ... Leopold's ethic, but have redefined "harmony" '.[28]

Even more serious were the political implications. The surest means of perpetuating the balance of people and nature in many ancient landscapes would be to keep the 'traditional' society and its culture in a state of arrested development. It was as if the ideal stage of development for Western Europe was the Middle Ages, before the rise of finance and industry, and when almost everybody lived at levels of subsistence. This would imply relative poverty in the twentieth century, so it was deemed undesirable and impractical to consider this method of management. In sum, harmony could not be defined, measured, imposed or monitored, and a more robust concept of protecting cultural landscapes had to be found.

The ICOMOS approach started with the recognition that cultural landscapes were an integral part of the cultural heritage. Second, based on an analysis of cultural types of landscape, ICOMOS was confident that they could be judged by UNESCO's cultural criteria alone. This meant that the concept of 'mixed' criteria, and any suggestion of special criteria for landscapes, was redundant. Last, and as the Alliance resolutions had suggested, the existing World Heritage cultural criteria could suffice if the wording of each criterion was tweaked with cultural landscapes in mind.[29] This approach was incremental and achievable in terms of acceptance by the World Heritage Committee and was agreed by UNESCO on these and philosophical grounds. Revised proposals were requested, a form of words was developed at a meeting at La Petite Pierre, in the Vosges, in October 1992,[30] and the Committee adopted these a few months after.[31]

The broad classification of cultural landscapes was simple – 'designed', 'continuing landscapes' (principally agricultural), and associative ones. The adjusted criteria accommodated all recognised values perceived in landscapes, though omitted any on beauty. As argued strongly elsewhere (see Chapter 5 – 'How preferences arise'), this is a cultural, rather than a natural value, yet by quirk of historical accident, was amongst the 'natural' criteria, though infrequently applied.

Many 'associative' places of high value were remarkable for their topography, and had been adopted by humans for religious purposes, often resulting in outstandingly spiritual places. Some categories of them might be suggested:

- religious – having acquired the sense of being a holy place for a religious tradition;
- patriotic – being the location of an event or tradition, a source of pride to a national or regional culture;
- artistic – being the source, or at least the location, of inspiration for literature and painting;
- aesthetic – conforming to an ideal of beauty.

Finally, there were the settings of important monuments or towns.

The first cultural landscape to be inscribed (in December 1993) under the revised criteria was Tonga-riro in New Zealand, a Maori sacred mountain (fig. 7.30). Ayer's Rock in Australia was re-inscribed using its aboriginal name as Uluru. Whilst both were associative landscapes, some 'continuing' landscapes like rice terraces and vineyards followed.

The world heritage criteria

Figure 7.30 *Value depending upon cultural association: Tonga Riro, a sacred Maori site, made a World Heritage Site in 1993.*

Czerniejewo Guidelines 1994

The next logical step after identification was to consider the conservation of cultural landscapes. This had been carried out in a very few countries, an example being the Countryside Commission UK's funding of repairs to walls and barns and replanting of woodlands. The French Government had supported *terroirs*, that is areas known for particular named foods, and the landscapes associated with them.

The Polish Ministry of Culture hosted a small meeting at the Czerniejewo manor house in western Poland in 1994 to start the process of considering general principles.[32] Guidelines were composed to encapsulate discussions. Landscapes were viewed as the tangible evidence of the historical, social, technological, economic and natural processes that have shaped today's world. This was an early opportunity to express the multiplicity of values found applied to landscapes (see Chapter 5 – 'Knowledge gives value'). It was accepted that an approach that integrated the many values was preferable in order to safeguard them, retain their historic character and still accommodate change. This would require an understanding of the dynamics of each landscape, and this would potentially include its many layers of history, and thus accretion of values over time.

The short-term nature of plant materials had been acknowledged in all doctrinal texts on gardens, and had been woven into restoration philosophies, but the Czerniejewo text went further in implying that change was not a process to be counteracted or minimised, but was an inherent aspect of cultural landscapes. So 'physical changes constantly occur in cultural landscapes', and landscapes are 'dynamic and complex'. Therefore 'cultural landscapes cannot be frozen in time'. Although change could cause losses of some values, it could also bring gains, and both needed to be appreciated.

Conservation of landscapes was seen in terms of preparing and implementing a management plan; the steps being perception/initiation, research, inventory, assessment of overlays, significance, impact of changes, then the proposals. It was also seen that collaboration between scholars and professionals on the one hand, and the community on the other, was the way for a lasting approach supported by inhabitants.[33]

Burra Charter 1999

The first version of the Burra Charter had been produced by Australia ICOMOS in 1979 in order to expand upon the Venice Charter for the Australian context. It wanted an all-embracing document, and so avoided the terms 'building' or 'archaeological site', and chose the useful term 'place' instead. Likewise 'historic' and 'aesthetic' were avoided, and 'cultural significance' was used instead. These seemingly unimportant semantic decisions would pay off when other forms of site, like landscapes, came to be included.

The term 'restoration' was not given the traditional meaning of achieving aesthetic unity, but was 'returning the existing fabric of a place to a known earlier state by removing accretions or by reassembling existing components without the introduction of new material'. This last phrase is virtually impossible in practice, but the definition would otherwise have been recognized in the UK as 'repair'. 'Conservation' was used in a general way to mean looking after a place to retain its cultural significance. Americans would have said 'treatment'.

The charter tackled ethical matters more fully than other similar documents. The professional should be:

> ... committed to care and clarity at all stages of conservation action ... care with the terms used, clarity about the options available and why one is chosen for the particular occasion, and clarity about decisions made along the way.[34]

In 1988 a new version included landscapes within the definition of 'place', but did not elaborate on this.

In 1999 a new and much-expanded version appeared after a decade of increasing recognition of the aboriginal cultural landscapes as well as the parks and gardens of those of European descent. The revised explanatory notes on the definition of 'place' included 'memorials, trees, gardens, parks, places of historical events, urban areas, towns, industrial places, archaeological sites and spiritual and religious places'.

A paragraph on the 'Cautious approach' mentioned respect for associations and meanings, in addition to fabric. Associations 'may include social or spiritual values and cultural responsibilities for a place', whilst meanings 'generally relate to intangible aspects such as symbolic qualities and memories'. New articles appeared on 'values', to include natural significance; and on 'participation'; 'change'; 'maintenance'; 'new work'; and 'managing change'. This new version of the Charter may be said to have fully embraced new thinking on cultural landscapes including designed ones.

Unifying the criteria

One long-standing issue connected with the World Heritage Criteria had been the division of the heritage into cultural and natural aspects. This was understandable in view of the great divide along these lines academically and institutionally. In UNESCO circles 'natural beauty' was understood as the aesthetic appreciation of natural areas, to be distinguished from 'cultural beauty' which referred to the qualities of cultural environments or artefacts. IUCN had responsibility for assessing 'natural beauty', and ICOMOS was not asked to advise on this aspect.

The sorts of places that IUCN had in mind were desert landforms, like those at Wadi Rum in Jordan, a spectacular series of sandstone mountains and valleys, natural arches, narrow gorges, high cliffs, and where cavernous weathering forms are to be found (fig. 7.31).[35] Looking from outside the constraints of the World Heritage Convention, 'superlative natural phenomena', which can often be objectively measured and assessed, would be preferable to the phrase 'natural beauty', for many would have argued that the appreciation of all beauty in landscape is in the subjective realm of culture, even when contemplating deserts or volcanoes. What makes such places of interest is that a number of people have decided, on the basis of their own systems of value, that certain qualities of the landscape make them valuable.

Figure 7.31 *The Jabal Umm Fruth rock bridge in the Wadi Rum Protected Area, Jordan – natural beauty with superlative forms.*

Distinctions between natural and cultural beauty were becoming increasingly unclear conceptually. 'Post-structuralist' thinking from the 1970s opposed the use of binary oppositions like 'nature versus culture'. The cultural-landscapes initiative was ideologically attuned to the integrated approach in the handling of values, and thus to the unification of the World Heritage criteria. William Cronon had predicted that 'given the universalizing tendencies that lie at the very core of this human

The world heritage criteria **235**

construct called 'nature' divisions would inevitably result.³⁶ Indeed, a view opposing unification, taken by the followers of 'deep ecology' and wilderness ideology, was that natural qualities have an intrinsic value in their own right, should not be classed with the cultural, and so should remain distinct.

Nevertheless, a 'global strategy' meeting for cultural and natural heritage experts, meeting in Amsterdam in March 1998, considered that the unification of World Heritage criteria would improve the logic and coverage of the guidelines. Their proposals were implemented through a revision of the Operational Guidelines.³⁷ This outcome probably owed as much to administrative convenience as to ideology. When a site was nominated for both cultural and natural reasons, as the Lake District had been, it had to go to both ICOMOS and IUCN. It would be referred to as a 'mixed' site. When cultural landscapes were made eligible, the task of assessment was given solely to ICOMOS, even when natural values were involved, which provoked IUCN to start work on a paper on 'Natural values in cultural landscapes'. However, if all criteria were on the same list, the nomination needed to go to only one advisory body, with that body consulting the other as needed. This would also encourage more rounded argumentation in the nomination dossiers.

Figure 7.32 *Panorama of Wadi Rum, Jordan; an area of weather-worn sandstone outcrops of 'natural beauty'.*

NOTES AND REFERENCES

1. Reginald Blomfield, *The Formal Garden in England* 3rd edn (London, 1901), pp. 72 & 74.

2. The Northamptonshire Archaeology Unit suspected this after carrying out excavations for English Heritage in 1988-1990.

3. Arguably, Chettle's garden, as the earliest serious attempt in England at garden restoration, had by 1990 acquired historic interest in its own right. English Heritage rejected this argument, thinking that it should attempt a new restoration, and demolished Chettle's garden. However, since Chettle had destroyed much of the earlier layers, the new design could not be based on archaeological findings and was as much guesswork as Chettle's; in the event, at this author's suggestion, a cutwork parterre based on that by George London at Longleat in the 1690s, was re-created.

4. The Garden History Society was founded in 1965, and this author joined its Conservation Committee in 1976, becoming chairman in 1986, though resigning in 1987 to become the Inspector at English Heritage.

5. John Ruskin, *The Seven Lamps of Architecture*, 4th ed. (Orpington, Kent, 1883), pp. v & 196.

6. ICOMOS, *Venice Charter* (1964), articles 3, 11 & 15. Digital version: https://www.icomos.org/charters/venice_e.pdf

7. Christopher Brereton, *The Repair of Historic Buildings: Advice on Principles and Methods* (London, 1991), pp. 7 & 8.

8. ICOMOS, *Nara Document on Authenticity* (ICOMOS, 1994), article 9.

9. Aloïs Riegl, 'The Modern Cult of Monuments: Its Character and Its Origin', trans. Kurt W. Forster & Diane Ghirardo, *Oppositions*, 25 (Fall 1982), 21-51.

10. David Jacques, 'Landscape Interpretation in the United Kingdom: An Historical Perspective and Outlook', *CRM Bulletin*, 17:7 (1994), 7-9.

11. ICOMOS-IFLA International Scientific Committee on Cultural Landscapes, 'Guidelines for the Conservation of Cultural Landscapes', devised at Czerniejewo, Poland (April 1994), article 4. These were produced as an internal ICOMOS-IFLA paper.

12 Horace Walpole, [letter], in Adam Fitz-Adam (pseud.) (ed), *The World*, 6 (8 February 1753).

13 Information from Lionella Scazzosi.

14 Simon Thurley (ed), *The King's Privy Garden at Hampton Court Palace 1689-1995* (London, 1995).

15 Charles A. Birnbaum, *Guidelines for the Treatment of Cultural Landscapes* (Washington DC, 1996). He was at Czerniejewo, and afterwards established the Landscape Foundation.

16 In an English Heritage committee paper, 'Historical Aims in the Treatment of Parks and Gardens' by this author in 1989: this was proposed and accepted as policy.

17 The English Heritage principles were reworked and published as David Jacques, 'The Treatment of Historic Parks and Gardens', *Journal of Architectural Conservation*, 1 : 2 (July 1995), 21-35.

18 David Jacques, 'The Great Reconstruction Debate: the Moment in Time', *CRM Bulletin*, 13 : 4 (1990), 25-26.

19 An example of multi-issue guidance to planners at this time was the Countryside Commission's *Strategic Guidance for Heritage Land in London*, CCD28 (London, 1988), prepared by this author.

20 *Conservation Issues in Strategic Plans*, CCP 420 (Cheltenham, 1993), and *Conservation Issues in Local Plans*, CCP 485 (London, 1996).

21 The thoughts hereafter were developed in 1998 whilst preparing for teaching on the MA course on Conservation (Landscapes & Gardens) at the Architectural Association, London.

22 This body was formed in 1972, largely at the instigation of the United States. The Convention appoints 21 of its members to a Committee serviced by UNESCO, and the committee decides which sites nominated by national governments are of 'outstanding universal value', and thus should be on the 'World Heritage List'. Recommendations are provided beforehand by ICOMOS if the site is 'cultural', and by IUCN if 'natural'. The criteria are both the site's intrinsic merit, and the degree of protection being afforded. The Committee had, by the end of 1999, declared 630 World Heritage Sites.

23 UNESCO, *World Heritage Convention* (Paris, 1972) Updated digital version: https://whc.unesco.org/en/convention/

24 As a postscript, the Lake District was eventually inscribed on the List in 2017 on purely cultural grounds, though 'harmonious beauty' (a 'natural' criterion) was in the nomination document.

25 John Foster (ed), *Protected Landscapes*. Summary Proceedings of an International Symposium, 5-10 October 1987 (Manchester, 1988).

26 Susan Buggey (ICOMOS Canada), Nora Mitchell (ICOMOS USA) and David Jacques (ICOMOS UK) drew up the resolutions at the Alliance meeting in the Olympic National Park in June 1990.

27 The main medium for discussion within ICOMOS was the Landscapes Working Group newsletter, edited by this author as 'co-ordinator' of the Group, and circulated to 13 national 'correspondents' and about 20 other interested persons from UNESCO, ICOMOS, etc. Five issues came out between June 1991 and January 1993. Thereafter, the circulation was widened considerably and guest editors prepared issues concentrating on different parts of the world. The first under this system, in September 1993, was Patricia O'Donnell's North American issue, and the second was Ken Taylor's and Val Kirby's Australia and New Zealand issue.

28 Daniel B. Botkin, *Discordant Harmonies: A New Ecology for the Twenty-First Century* (Oxford, 1990), pp. 70, 98 & 191.

29 Apart from the Alliance resolutions, both Herb Stovel, who had taken a keen interest in the whole cultural landscapes issue as Secretary General of ICOMOS, and Peter Goodchild made suggestions for modifications which demonstrated that they need only be slight.

30 These included additions to the World Heritage guidelines agreed by participants including Senake Bandaranayake (Sri Lanka), Susan Buggey (Canada), Henry Cleere (ICOMOS), Peter Fowler (United Kingdom), Bing Lucas (New Zealand), Isobel MacBryde (Australia) and Mechtild Rössler (UNESCO), and this author chaired part of the meeting.

31 At Santa Fe, New Mexico, in 1993.

32 The host was Andreij Michaelowski, and the participants were Thomas Zwiek, one of his staff specialising in the subject; Charles Birnbaum from the US National Park Service who had been working on the Guidelines for Cultural Landscape Conservation; Ken Taylor from the University of Canberra; and this author. The topic was

raised again in the 2010s resulting in the ICOMOS-IFLA, *Principles Concerning Rural Landscapes as Heritage* being adopted.

33 ICOMOS-IFLA International Scientific Committee on Cultural Landscapes, op. cit., articles 5 & 14.

34 ICOMOS Australia, *Burra Charter* (1979), chairman's message. Digital 2013 version: https://australia.icomos.org/wp-content/uploads/The-Burra-Charter-2013-Adopted-31.10.2013.pdf

35 Nora Mitchell, *Study on the Application of Criterion VII: Considering Superlative Natural Phenomena and Exceptional Natural Beauty within the World Heritage Convention*, IUCN World Heritage Study № 10 (Gland, Switzerland, 2013), pp. 25 & 42.

36 William Cronon, 'Introduction: in search of nature', in William Cronon (ed), *Uncommon Ground: Rethinking the Human Place in Nature* (New York, 1996), pp. 23–56.

37 UNESCO, *Report of the 23rd Session of the World Heritage Committee at Marrakesh, Morocco, December 1999* (2000), section XIII.

Figure 7.33 *Wasdale Head in the English Lake District; both a natural and man-made landscape initially refused World Heritage status (see pp. 227 & 228).*

CHAPTER 8

POST-MODERN DESIGNS

Innovative landscape designs of the last quarter of the twentieth century reflected, in some cases and to a certain degree, the guiding principles of the post-1970 mindset. Locality and identity were expressed by 'contextualism', the celebration of engagement and everyday satisfactions was seen in 'land art', and observation and knowledge of the land and its vegetation promised a low-input and high-value ecological technique. Less successful were the self-conscious attempts to be 'post-modern'. Another delusion was to imagine that a landscape could express great spiritual ideas by association or by some congruity of forms. Whilst the motive in attempting this may have been noble, it was difficult not to feel that the results were contrived.

Post-modernism was less a style in itself than the feeling that modernism was certainly not the way forward. It embraced a range of responses but came to be characterised by the pastiche of historical motif used in architectural detailing. Sometimes this was done wittily, to good effect, but the impact wore off when others tried the same, and the result was depressing when large-scale development attempted to disguise its crude forms by the use of irrelevant frill. The rapidity with which one historic style after another was raided illustrated the general malaise of a lack of certainty and conviction, and a bored society which engendered egocentrism, hedonism, consumerism and superficiality.

Perhaps the archetypal post-modernist landscapes were the garden festivals in Britain. Temporary, flippant and populist, they suggested that in the 1980s instant gratification was the only available substitute for design based on conviction. Post-modern architectural detail was freely introduced. There were even instant historic gardens at Stoke-on-Trent (fig. 8.1). The idea was common at revamped public parks and gardens generally, so that visitors to Wolseley Park, Staffordshire,[1] would find a post-modern pergola, and those going to Crystal Palace, in London, will find post-modern neo-Victorian gate piers (fig. 8.2).

The designs that are not discussed below are the large private gardens laid out in England from the 1980s. Inspired by Rosemary Verey's knot designs, and embracing topiary and lengthy straight hedges and paths

Figure 8.1 *Stoke-on-Trent garden festival 1986: temporary and flippant, representing 1980s post-modernism.*

Figure 8.2 *Crystal Palace, south London; a post-modernist version of Victorian gate piers.*

242 Post-modern designs

Figure 8.3 *Barnsley House, Gloucestershire; Rosemary Verey's 1970s interlacing knot garden based on a 17th century design.*

once again, there were several dozen major gardens in that decade in what might be described as a New Classical style, picking up from where Hidcote and Sissinghurst left off when they were sidelined by the advent of modernism in all public work (fig. 8.3).

Contextualism

Landscape design always had a greater awareness of geographical, climatic and environmental context than architecture. The sense of the social context and a willingness to see existing features as part of the history of a city led to some interesting designs with derelict land and structures, with often heavily polluted soils and groundwater. Generally speaking, former workers, remembering the bad old days, were not keen to acknowledge the relics of the industrial past, while those who were trying to improve the appearance and image of their post-industrial cities wanted to expunge them as beacons of ugliness.

An early example of a city deciding the reverse – that industrial relics were attached to memories that defined the identity of a place – was the city of Seattle in the United States. An area that contained the remnants of the sole remaining coal-gasification plant in that country was acquired for a public park, and the landscape architect, Richard Haag, researched the history of the site and discovered its significance (fig. 8.4). In his Master Plan of 1971 he recommended preservation of portions of the plant for its 'historic, esthetic and utilitarian value'. The Gas Works Park was initially going to be called Myrtle Edwards Park, after the local politician who had campaigned for it. Her family, however, finding that the design proposed the retention of much of the plant, thought that that did not represent her intentions and requested that her name be removed. The die was cast, though, and the retention and re-use of the most striking structures drew attention to the exceptional history of the site. Although not all of them were saved, the more character-defining and prominent pieces of the old plant were retained, some as ruins, but others were painted, reconditioned, and given new uses such as a children's 'play barn'.

The same sort of transformation took place in Stoke-on-Trent in Staffordshire (known locally as The Potteries), also in the 1970s, though on a much wider scale. There had been potteries, ironworks, coal mines, spoil heaps, clay pits, pottery-waste grounds, gas works, mineral lines and canals in a confusing array, and mostly abandoned

Figure 8.4 *Gasworks Park, Seattle, designed by Richard Haag, 1970s; one of the first projects to recycle dereliction into public open space.*

by 1970. In fact, the city had the dubious distinction of having the highest proportion of derelict land of anywhere in Britain. Work started on flattening out and revegetating the spoil heaps around 1970, and the local politicians wanted the colliery winding gear to be removed. Through the 1970s something interesting happened. Cliff Tandy, Richard Flenley and their colleagues at Land Use Consultants turned mineral lines into footpaths and cycle routes, converted a flooded area of subsidence into a recreational lake and even discussed saving some spoil heaps for their industrial heritage.[2] Gradually the city's embarrassment with its deformities turned into a proud statement of its past (fig. 8.5).

Ten years later a similar story unfolded in the Ruhr valley in Germany, though at a yet larger scale than at Stoke. One element of the huge regional Emscher Park was the former blast furnace plant of the industrial giant, the Thyssen-Meiderich company. This was designed as the Duisberg Nord Landscape Park in 1991 by Peter Latz and his team. Placing great emphasis on the value of memory, his approach was to heal and understand the industrial past, rather than trying to erase it. The remains of the plant were recycled: the concrete bunkers created a space for a series of intimate gardens,

Figure 8.5 *Making a statement: Central Forest Park in Stoke-on-Trent, at the planting stage; the aim in the early 1970s was to expunge the mining past; over time this changed to acknowledgement of industrial heritage.*

Contextualism

concrete walls were given over to rock climbing, the old gas tanks became pools for scuba divers, and a central space within the steel mill was made into a piazza (fig. 8.6).

When the Canadian Center for Architecture (CCA) was built in Montreal, another form of contextualism based on off-site features was tried. The southern part of the site, unpromisingly wedged between two four-lane highways, was allocated for use as a garden. Melvin Charney, its designer, was determined to make the best of the situation, and make a garden that was of the city, and not apart from it (fig. 8.7). He attempted this through contextualism in both time and place:

Figure 8.6 *Duisberg Nord Landscape Park, Germany, by Peter Latz and team in 1991; an attempt to understand and embrace the industrial past rather than to expunge it.*

Figure 8.7 *Relating new work to its historic context: an attempt to do this in the garden at the Canadian Center for Architecture in Montreal with representations of buildings once seen.*

Each constituent of the garden was set up as the direct counterpart of an existing element of the city that could be seen, or could be made to be 'seen', from the site – for example, a 'façade' is placed in the garden in relation to an existing façade on an opposite street.³

This *façade* was a folly mimicking the ground floor of the building standing across the highway and now incorporated into the CCA. Charney planted apple trees to the sides because the area had been shown on a mid-nineteenth century map as one of orchards. Finally, he placed metal models of the buildings that had once been visible from the site on poles on a viewing 'esplanade' at the rear of the site. This interesting attempt at contextualism might have worked in differing circumstances: as it was, the site was so awful environmentally that it was hardly visited, and even if it had been, the references to place and time were just too far removed from the existing to be readily comprehensible.

Contextualism **247**

Philosophy becomes design

One of the more famous examples of the philosophical garden was that in the Pentland Hills near Edinburgh by the poet Ian Hamilton Finlay. This took shape in the 1970s, was renamed 'Little Sparta' in 1983, and was continually added to for over 30 years (fig. 8.8). In the same way that William Shenstone attached little inscriptions to his garden seats at The Leasowes, in Shropshire, in the mid-eighteenth century, Finlay in the 1970s placed inscribed tablets in his garden with such epithets as 'See POUSSIN Hear LORRAIN' and 'Et in Arcadia ego'. These were reminders of moral and philosophical themes through history that underlay the emergence of modern society. The French Revolution, nuclear submarines, and the sea and its fishing fleets were amongst them. Little Sparta was not a garden of the senses, for it had little structure or plantsmanship, but was one of meaning by association, and much admired by literary historians and classicists.

Figure 8.8 *The attempt to express spiritual ideas through association: Little Sparta, Lanarkshire, Scotland, by Ian Hamilton Finlay.*

An interesting example from 1984 of an attempt to convert philosophy literally into concrete form was that by Bernard Tschumi at Parc de la Villette, in Paris, where he attempted to design according to the principles of deconstruction. As a philosophy, 'deconstruction' has much to commend itself; it acknowledges that there is no ultimate truth, it is an attempt to redeem through questioning, it exposes myth, and contextualism is implicit. However, the attempt to use deconstructive principles in physical design ended in farce. 'Interrogative exchange' between visual and textual elements had been a characteristic of the drawings by Valerio Adami. At Parc de la Villette the attempt was made at another such exchange by superimposing three systems (surfaces, lines and points) upon each other.[4] The idea failed because the scale of the park meant that the design could not be read on the ground, because there was a lack of anything like a text, and because it was unclear what would be the nature and purpose of the interrogation anyway (fig. 8.9). The features most appreciated were the bamboo garden by a different designer and the various eccentric architectural constructions painted red. Perhaps it was a warning that meaning cannot be artificially injected into design.[5]

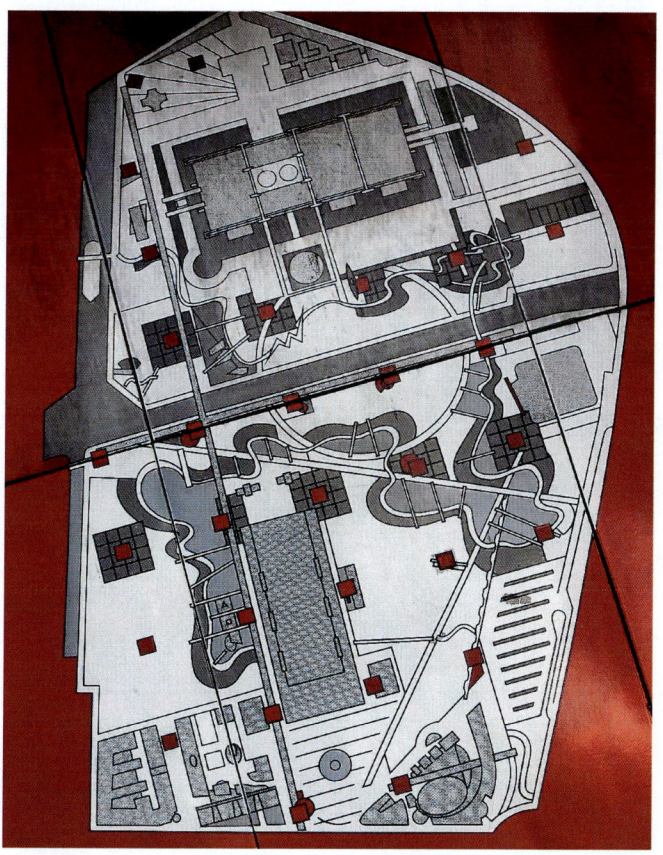

Figure 8.9 *Deconstruction misapplied as a philosophy of design: Parc de la Villette in Paris.*

Philosophy becomes design **249**

Another example, started in 1988, was Charles Jencks's 'Garden of Cosmic Speculation' at Portrack House in Dumfriesshire, where he designed landform 'snakes' replicating the forms of diagrams of catastrophe theorists (fig. 8.10). He proposed rules for architecture that he tried to apply to landscape.[6] First, he suggested 'building close to nature and natural languages'. By espousing 'the rhetoric of natural systems' seen in 'crystals, bones, slime-mould and clouds', humans could be 'the originators of a second nature'. Second, he would have designs reflect 'self-organisation, emergence and jumps to a higher level'. This stems from his insight, influenced by chaos theory, that the 'direction' of evolution was towards greater complexity, though via unpredictability and surprise. Buildings could reflect such ideas in their form. Next he advocated organisational depth underlying the complexity. The 'ecological imperative and political pluralism' argued for green solutions and local styles, though the effect here would be principally symbolic. Last, Jencks would keep searching for 'the cosmic code', or the 'transcendant laws which science reveals', thereby encouraging the emergence of a 'cosmogenic architecture'. These ideas were an attempt to fashion a new style of garden design from a theory in another field; and were felt by some to be somewhat contrived.[7] Jencks's lasting legacy was an upsurge of interest in earthworks, many designed by himself.

Figure 8.10 *Portrack House, Dumfries & Galloway; snail and snake mounds in the 'Garden of Cosmic Speculation', started 1988 by Charles Jencks.*

250 *Post-modern designs*

Designer ecology

Conventional horticulture had demanded great resources to maintain a designer's principally aesthetic concept of a composition of plants that would perform in the same manner year-to-year. Planting design would specify mainly exotic species formed into a stable, or static, plant assemblage, though not one that would be recognised as a functioning plant community by ecologists.

The naturalists' desire to recover former plant communities had led, where these had been expunged, to habitat re-creation with native plants, which was of course a completely different approach from the horticultural. Conceptual and practical difficulties (for example what counted as native, and the complexities of designing a native community) abounded, though, and made exact re-creations infeasible. If the literal recovery of nature was not possible, the next best that the plantsman could aim for would be 'nature-like' vegetation.

'Nature-like' was as various as its proponents, though, each hoping to achieve an optimum balance between the use of native species, the desirability of being attractive in colour and form, and being economic to maintain. The Mid-West 'prairie style' promulgated by Jens Jensen, for example, attempted to give some feel for the lost grasslands of America by using indigenous plants. Though the prairie was recalled only in an idealised form, the movement was an understandable response at a time when only a few fragments of a once-rich flora had evaded being ploughed up. The twentieth-century 'flowery mead' sought to embellish grassland with native herbs that could survive if mowing was left till after seed-setting, and thereby recalled the medieval practice of transplanting plugs from the fields into the herber. The *heem* parks of The Netherlands were conceived as an educational tool to introduce students to the native flora and suggest that a garden can be a demonstration of the nature-conservation potential of a place. Many other more recent variations could be mentioned. The cumulative effect of the 'nature-like' approaches was an emerging aesthetic, one that meant that garden plantings could be somewhat wild-looking, or 'naturalistic'.

Nevertheless, none of these forms of plant assemblage could be considered as a functioning plant community that reproduced and looked after itself as natural plant communities do. Hence they were essentially gardens with a selected, and thus limited, species list and which still needed significant intervention by humans in order to make them conform to the design intentions. Indeed they were not necessarily cheaper to maintain than traditional gardens. Amongst the *heem* parks was the Jac. P. Thijssepark in Amstelveen (fig. 8.11), made from 1949 on former dune sand. Its planting was designed for low fertility, and the truth of its management was that the ground was turned over to the depth of a metre every few years, at great expense, in order to maintain the low pH.

The aim of a lightly managed, self-perpetuating, plant community could be seen in practice in several agricultural systems, principally grazing lands. It had also been achieved in a select few gardens, if they could be called 'gardens', at which the owners or managers gained their ends by an intimate understanding of the site through trial and observation. Amongst these was Geoffrey Dutton, a medical scientist at the University of Dundee, and who at the weekends from about 1960 worked on his few acres near Bridge of Cally in the Perthshire hills (fig. 8.12).[8] He had always wanted a normal garden with the usual plants, and bought a copy of Sylvia Crowe's *Garden Design* for this purpose. However, he faced severe problems with the impoverished moorland soil strewn with large boulders, wickedly cold winters of that part of Scotland, and very little money. In due course he learned to work with the place, rather than against it.[9]

Figure 8.11 *Jac. P. Thijssepark in Amstelveen, The Netherlands, created in 1949 for didactic purposes in demonstrating the nature-conservation potential of any place.*

Figure 8.12 *Expressing ideals in the relationship between humans and nature: Professor Dutton in his garden in Perthshire, a demonstration of the creative role of intelligent intervention in natural systems.*

The extreme contrast between summer and winter, the invasion of his garden by moorland species, the different areas of wood and moor, and the natural components including a gorge and waterfall were aspects that he came to appreciate and make use of. He also found that the extreme weather conditions hampered plant growth to such an extent that even his small energy could have a significant effect. He would weed out or cut back, wait and see, assess good and bad, and go through the process again, coaxing and guiding the favoured aspect of the natural processes. Hence, for example, he found that his push mower could satisfactorily mark out grass paths between the rocks and ferns, and he could create an area of vivid purple heather that needed his attention only once every ten years. The greatest demands upon him were time, observation and patience.

Dutton's garden became a practical application of several principles, and was a model for the method that all landscape treatment should have aimed at: the gardener with the mentality of a shepherd; the intimate engagement with the land and the processes taking place; the glad use of the materials provided naturally; the exploitation of naturally occurring diversity; the very low consumption of resources other than

Designer ecology

Figure 8.13 *The gardener with the mentality of a shepherd: Philip Fry discusses how he encouraged the native flora to revisit his garden near Kemptville, Ontario.*

his own time; the integration of his skills as both scientist and artist; the discipline; all points echo those made in a different context by the land artists (see below).

Similar ideas to Dutton's were tried by Philip Fry at his garden at Kemptville, Ontario (fig. 8.13).[10] The soil was a glacial boulder clay with granite erratics, overlying limestone about eight feet down (roughly 2.5 metres). In places the clay was itself overlain by sand drifts. The property had once been farmland, and stones had been cleared to field edges. Its poor soils, and the long and terrible winters, were presumably the reason why it was abandoned about 1938. Fry purchased the property in 1984. Part of his challenge, he felt, was to show a way forward for land that had been regarded as almost worthless. Like Dutton, he was able, through trial and error, to manipulate an unpromising situation to achieve some interesting results.

'The 'field' was an open area around the house. Fry just removed the self-seeded saplings, so that the birds could disturb the soil in the spring. The result was a fairly open sward, with a variety of meadow flowers. It was never mowed; in fact, mowers were banned from the garden. Around the edges Fry introduced some more interesting plants, such as the rare Canadian lily, and added a variety of manures to speed them on their way. In an area of planted spruce woodland the canopy was opened up enough to admit some light to the woodland floor. Fry added some soil, and many woodland plants were thriving after only a few years. The old sand dunes had virtually no soil, and Fry developed his 'desert' there. He even had cacti from Manitoba.

Towards the end of the twentieth century another approach was conceived which meant abandoning the requirement to work within the native flora. Because Britain was cut off from Europe during the ice ages, its flora is relatively limited. Many previously unseen plant communities could be possible if the full range of temperate-zone species were permitted. They could be suitable for British circumstances and compatible with others, allowing for viable plant communities tailor-made for a range of niches. They would be guided only lightly by humans for them to be kept on the path to use and beauty. Such systems would bring the great benefit of much reduced maintenance.

Whether the theory would work in practice or not, the thinking behind it might be said to share several characteristics with new approaches to landscape mentioned in chapters above. It was a rejection of a great overarching theory (in this case ecocentrism and its insistence on 'native' flora); it acknowledged and welcomed the complexity of natural systems (and species richness); it had a philosophy of change (as plant communities adjusted themselves); it furthered sustainability (in being less demanding on time, water and nutrients); it was pragmatic and experimental (the technique is discussed below); and it even came to be labelled 'anthropogenic landscape'.

Extending the aim of a lightly managed, self-perpetuating plant community would have great benefits if extended into public parks and other urban spaces. Designers could not wait to discover the inherent dynamics of a particular rural spot, and, in any case, they were frequently working with heavily altered soils and artificial microclimates. The sub-discipline of urban ecology had developed in Britain since the 1970s as curious mixes of spontaneous vegetation arose amongst the dereliction of post-industrial cities.[11] This provided useful lessons, among which was the redundancy of any preconceptions of what species ought to have colonised and the unworkability of any plans for habitat re-creation.

Designer ecology

The planting envisaged would achieve not just a fully naturalistic effect, but would actually work as a plant community into the indefinite future. It could be designed also with the visual effects of colour, form and seasonal change (including winter) in mind. The result would be not quite garden-like nor nature-like, but a new range of bespoke types of vegetation that would act like natural ones, self-propagating and evolving, whilst being attractive, even if unfamiliar, to the eye.

The hopes for earlier 'nature-like' designs had been hindered by shaky theoretical underpinnings and a fundamental lack of technique. This had been recognised by various people in various places. At the University of Sheffield, Philip Grime of the Department of Botany was working from the 1970s on the theoretical underpinnings of plant ecology. One such concerned the adaptation of plant communities to stress; few species could deal with high levels, whilst a few thugs dominated in conditions of low stress, and the maximum diversity was found in between. Similarly, the Intermediate 'Disturbance Hypothesis' suggested that *species diversity* was maximized when *ecological disturbance* was neither too rare nor too frequent. Grime's 'Universal Adaptive Strategy Theory' described the evolved *trade-off* for organisms between growth, maintenance and regeneration. Each plant species would have its own blend of these three strategies which broadly defined them as C (competitive), S (stress tolerant) or R (ruderal, or rapid propagation).

Meanwhile Richard Hansen, who had set up an institute for perennials, shrubs and applied plant sociology at the University of Weihenstephan in Bavaria in 1948, had carried out many trials over decades. These sought to blend native and non-native perennials, and to discover how different plants could be associated together in stylised types of vegetation on ecological, rather than aesthetic, principles. He published his findings and ideas in 1981, and this was made available in English as *Perennials and their Garden Habitats* (1993). One landscape architect, introducing Hansen's ideas, noted that many German parks and festivals displayed low-maintenance designs of herbaceous perennials based on them.[12]

In the same publication James Hitchmough, a horticulturalist, also promoted herbaceous perennials used in a similar manner, seeing a clear break from the traditional British herbaceous border. He had no ideological inclination towards the use of native plants, and was pragmatic, responding to the declining resources for public open space experienced in Britain in the early 1990s. The American practice of Wolfgang Oehme and James van Sweden had demonstrated that

Figure 8.14 *Garden at the Slifka Beach House, Sagaponack NY, by Oehme and Van Sweden; an example of the new wave of naturalistic planting.*

perennials can give colour and interesting foliage, and even die beautifully (fig. 8.14). Why, then, plant traditional annual bedding that 'has been estimated to be 15 to 30 times more expensive than intelligently managed plantings of herbaceous perennials'?[13]

Hitchmough had Hansen's large body of experience to draw upon, but wanted to understand not just how to select herbaceous plants, but why: he wanted a rationale. He was grateful for Grime's distinctions between the plant strategies of competitors, stress-tolerators and ruderals, though 'little progress has been made to date in applying these ideas to the cultivation of landscape plants'. Most of his article was an examination of the factors to consider. Noel Kingsbury soon afterwards produced an influential work on *The New Perennial Garden* (1996).

Nigel Dunnett.

In the mid-1990s, Hitchmough transferred to the Department of Landscape Architecture at Sheffield, and thus became a colleague of Nigel Dunnett who had undertaken a PhD in ecology under Grime. Dunnett wrote inspiringly about naturalistic planting, highlighting some of the salient factors – dynamism, intricacy, suitability to site, unity, sustainability, structure and diversity. He advocated paying attention to plants, the 'great interpreters of site conditions ... they mirror minute changes in soil type, topography, climate and management', and expanded on the rewards that came from tracking 'the progressing year', as observing 'seasonal plant highlights is a thrill'.[14]

Figure 8.15 *Eden Project, Cornwall: the slopes were almost pure sand, so James Hitchmough introduced a 'prairie' cover with grasses and flowering herbaceous plants to revegetate the sides of the former quarry.*

The research carried out by these two complemented each other's. Hitchmough carried out trials and felt sufficiently informed to devise plant lists and seed lists for a range of habitats (fig. 8.15). Dunnett was more theoretical, concentrating upon dynamics like succession, patterns and process that would be the mark of genuine plant communities. At the end of the century it was too soon to check whether the theory

would be borne out in practice. Would they achieve designed plant communities that would settle down to persist and regenerate *in situ* given minor but appropriate (skilled) management, and would this be without additional inputs of water and nutrients, and pest and disease control?[15] Would their plant compositions differ in essence from those inspired by Hansen, or devised by Oehme and Van Sweden, or Piet Oudolf, or Noel Kingsbury? Would their approach end up, in practice, being their own variation of the balance of aesthetics, ecology and resources, as it was with the others, or could they establish a new tradition of scientifically-based designer ecologies? Aiming high, though, they had raised hopes for just that.

Land art

Land art attracted much attention since the 1970s.[16] Though several more could be mentioned, and many American exponents too, the work of a trio of English sculptors, Richard Long,[17] David Nash[18] and Andy Goldsworthy[19] was worthy of special notice.

Long was interested in the reaction of the individual to the landscape, and what happened when human sensibilities engage with natural forces and patterns. His work was a celebration of places, his feelings of journeying through them, and the objects he encountered along the way. The energy to carry out a work came from being in a place, and since every place was different his creations reflected the change and complexity of natural phenomena. Long's works were not conceptual. They were not references, and sought to be no more than they actually were. Stones were to be seen simply as stones. He intended, by being practical and using simple ideas, to let the outcome of his interaction with nature be clear. Too much theory would destroy his freedom to do what came to mind, and being able to adapt to circumstances.

He set himself a task such as walking in a circle around the countryside, or in a line across the Sahara, and recorded exactly what he felt, moment to moment, whether it was the sight of something or an inner thought. At times he felt the impulse to interact with the landscape, by arranging stones in a line, or a cairn, or removing them to clear a circle. Some work was extremely ephemeral, such as grass marks or watermarks, and he would stand down stones after having photographed them. The circle and the straight line had no special significance to him, but he found such obvious shapes to be convenient in allowing him to concentrate upon the nature of his interaction with the materials of the place. The form of his creations was not their chief point (fig. 8.16).

Figure 8.16 *Interaction of the human mind with the landscape: the work of Richard Long concerns process not product; here is his 'A Line in Ireland', 1974.*

Long hoped his work tied up with the aims of the green movement, for example in seeing the world as one place and using materials with respect. He was reluctant to fix the meaning of his work beyond that, but it was not difficult to see in it a metaphor for the human condition. The moment of human impact, which should be considered but not considerable, became a noteworthy event on an otherwise unrecorded journey. The act of engagement by eyes, ears and mind, as well as by hand, was specific to time and place. It could not be frozen or repeated, but it could be recorded.[20] The correspondences with the present understanding of cultural landscapes were striking, and the message that the art was in the interaction itself, not the product, was surely worth pondering. Furthermore, Long's ability to celebrate place in such diverse ways, even with great self-imposed restraints, or perhaps partly because of them, was an inspiration for all that work with the landscape.

Figure 8.17 *One of David Nash's sculptures in Kew Gardens; his concern to avoid wastefulness extended to making his own charcoal.*

David Nash's lifelong work was to explore the potential of wood. He started when he constructed towers and other large and elaborate creations by using timber that others had discarded. Then, during the 1970s he took to exploiting the quirks of wood to express, in a gentle and humorous way, the metamorphic possibilities of branches and twigs. Hence unseasoned wood was used so that the effects of cracking and warping could be exploited and formal shapes such as balls and boxes would turn into something else. The anthropomorphic theme could be played through branches becoming arms and legs. One piece was two trunks, with two branches each, pinned together in opposing directions to form a 'running table'.

From the late 1970s, though, Nash started developing more serious ideas on timber as a resource through its planting, felling and use. In 1977 he planted a bower 30 feet in diameter called 'Ash Dome', which he intended to manage over a thirty-year period. Two years later he started felling trees for his own use. His approach was unsentimental, in that he accepted that trees were a crop, but ecologically aware when he determined to use the whole tree, wasting none if possible. He thus stayed with the tree, finding a purpose for every part, and camping nearby, until he had consumed it totally. Even the twigs could be found a purpose; he burnt these to make the charcoal he needed for his drawings. His interest in stoves was a by-product of this process (fig. 8.17).

Figure 8.18 *Beauty can be found in the commonplace: an example of Andy Goldsworthy's walling.*

In saying that humans must use resources, but must do so respectfully and not wastefully, Nash made a clear statement on the relationship that humans should adopt towards natural resources. His approach echoed that of many cultures that live intimately with nature, and pride themselves on using every part of an animal. It is especially close to some North American Native Peoples who will apologise to the spirit of a tree before felling it, promising that it will be well used. As with Long's art, Nash's is partly in the process, which is restrained and respectful. The significance of his work lay just as much in what he eschewed as in what he actually produced.

Andy Goldsworthy allied himself to Long when indulging in ephemeral art, with snow and leaves for example, and Nash in his deliberately local and inexpensive constructions. He always used the materials he found at a place, and would seek to express some aspect of it, whether it was the flowers in the grass, the trees in the forest, or the local stone with which field walls were made (fig. 8.18). He enjoyed re-ordering such materials into more formal geometry, exploring the endless possibilities.

Land art pointed to the satisfactions through landscape art as being twofold. First, it was an exploration of the operation of ethics in the planned and more permanent aspects. The appreciation of landscape art should be through engagement with it, and in considering the first of these satisfactions the designer's ideas should be understood as well, to give insights into how process and form interlocked and how interconnectedness operated on change.

The second satisfaction was the poetic surprise of the unplanned effect, the flash of fresh light, enhancing people's perception and imagination in their interaction with the landscape. Ephemerality of effects should be welcomed, with the accidental new pleasures. This was something to which art could help everyone be receptive. The land artists' work led the way for every citizen to find interest in the commonplace through the exercise of imagination, and the observation of nature's infinite variation.

New work in historic contexts

One of the more contentious issues in conservation was the incorporation of new work. Many conservationists in Britain were better described as 'preservationists' in the European sense, and unable to see the worth of new work, or to conceive the possibilities in terms of design and aesthetics, of careful mingling of old with the new. Meanwhile architects and developers saw conservationists as reactionary and the enemies of progress. Both sides were at fault.

The long-standing simplistic opposition between 'progress' and 'protection' needed breaking down, but there was a history to this. Modernism required 'history' to act as a problematic counterpart against which it could be contrasted in a good light: modernism represented the future, and history was a brake on progress. Modernism thus occupied the high ground, and conservationists, forced on the defensive, found that they had to champion a caricature of the 'traditional' that was defined within the framework of the modern.[21] In creating designations, enforcing stasis, they merely served to confirm that the dead hand of history had no meaningful place in the changing everyday world.

A common misconception was that because conservationists protect old objects, their motive was the worship of the ancient for its own sake. In fact history and conservation were about ideas, not objects per se. The criticism was that conservationists concentrated upon the negative aspects of change, whilst change clearly cannot always be bad, because the existing mix of value in the townscape and landscape was the result of past change. Nowhere is this clearer than in historic designed landscapes which might be the accumulations of many layers.

A more constructive approach was proposed, with values being the common ground. Rather than use the crude measure of whether there was visible change, conservationists were asked to think more in terms of adding a layer to the already valuable. The stewardship of values in the landscape suggested a guiding principle that any new work must be of more lasting quality than that which it replaces. The sum of human achievement should not be diminished by change. Furthermore the onus is upon those who would destroy in the cause of progress to demonstrate that the change is for the good overall.

Where the value, or mix of values, in a landscape is already high, the emphasis of treatment is, rightly, protection and repair. Where existing value is less pronounced, it might not be difficult to argue that change would be beneficial. Even so, the scope for completely new design on a clean drawing board is extremely limited today. That suits the mood of the time; grandiose empty gestures are less relevant than incremental interventions, solidly based upon an understanding of the landscape and the demands upon it. Cultivated persons who understand and welcome complexity, who seek the good of many interests but recognise that the balance will be different in each locality, are at a premium.

Concepts of the past are merely value-laden present-day abstractions, just like visions of the future, and should be open to scrutiny and debate. Furthermore, the traditional and the modern are not mutually exclusive, but connected and interpenetrating. The past is with us today in many forms and still subject to change. Conservation is thus about the present, not the past, about the wise use of resources, and about how a culture takes what it inherits into the future. Conservation should have a creative involvement in mapping out a complex and uncertain future.

NOTES AND REFERENCES

1. Wolseley Park Garden, the creation of Sir Charles Wolseley, B[art], and his consultants, Cobham Resource Consultants, was an expensive and carefully-conceived project. It is interesting in being very characteristic of the style of the late 1980s, although being a privately-funded project.

2. This author had a minor part in this. He undertook some research into the industrial history of the Apedale valley in Newcastle-under Lyme, particularly the criss-crossing mineral lines, and remembers being surprised when it was well received.

3. Melvin Charney, 'A Garden for the Canadian Center for Architecture', in Larry Richards (ed), *Canadian Center for Architecture: Building and Gardens* (Montreal, 1989), pp. 87-102.

4. Bernard Tschumi, 'Parc de la Villette, Paris', in Andreas Papadakis *et al.* (eds), *Deconstruction: Omnibus Volume* (London, 1989), pp. 175-83.

5. A point made by Marc Treib in his essay, 'Must Landscapes Mean? Approaches to Significance in Recent Landscape Architecture', *Landscape Journal*, 14 (1995), 46-62.

6. Charles Jencks, *The Architecture of the Jumping Universe* (London, 1995), p. 167.

7. Kevin Thwaites, 'In Search of the Designer's New Mind', *Landscape Design* (September 1996), 13-18.

8. Geoffrey Dutton, 'A Marginal Garden', *Journal of the Royal Horticultural Society*, 2 Part 2 (February 1988), 81-7.

9. Geoffrey Dutton, *Harvesting the Edge: Some Personal Explorations from a Marginal Garden* (London, 1995).

10. The author visited Philip Fry on 17 July 1994 in company with Linda Dicaire.

11. Among the foremost was Tony Bradshaw (1926-2008) of the University of Liverpool, who specialised in plants for the restoration of polluted land, and Oliver Gilbert (1936-2005) of the University of Sheffield, whose exploration of post-industrial landscape led to his *The Ecology of Urban Habitats* (1989).

12 Brita von Schoenaich, 'The End of the Border', *Landscape Design*, 229 (April 1994), 9-14.

13 James Hitchmough, 'Natural Neighbours', *Landscape Design* 229 (April 1994), 15-22.

14 Nigel Dunnett, 'Harnessing Anarchy', *Landscape Design*, 245 (November 1995), 25-9.

15 Further research was reported upon in Nigel Dunnett & Hitchmough, James, *The Dynamic Landscape: Design, Ecology and Management of Naturalistic Urban Planting* (London, 2004).

16 Sutherland Lyall, *Designing the New Landscape* (London, 1991), p. 20, provides a brief overview of the topic.

17 Richard Long (b. 1945) is from Bristol, and while a student of art was much influenced by the Earth Art movement of the late 1960s. He developed the practice, usually whilst taking long walks, of expressing his reaction to the landscape through simple and ephemeral adjustments of the natural elements and through notes and jottings. Though his work does not transfer to galleries well, such is the interest in it that he has frequently been asked to exhibit from 1967 to the present.

18 David Nash (b. 1945) is from Esher, Surrey, though he moved to a deserted chapel in Blaenau Ffestiniog, a Welsh slate town, in 1967. He has explored how timber, as an inexpensive and renewable material, can be used in diverse and interesting ways.

19 Andy Goldsworthy (b. 1956) is from Cheshire, but based in Dumfriesshire. His work with materials found in the landscape has received very wide publicity since about 1985.

20 Richard Long, *Richard Long: Walking in Circles* (London, 1991), p. 252.

21 Kathleen Watt, 'On the Need to Re-theorise Tradition'. Unpublished Paper (University of Hull School of Architecture, 1996).

PART C

REFLECTIONS

Up to this point, the book has charted how a characteristic modernist landscape theory of the third quarter of the twentieth century was reworked, strand by strand, in its last quarter on quite different lines. Whilst the theory of landscape architecture has advanced in more recent decades,[1] the theory of landscape appreciation has been characterised by adjustments in detail and emphasis, rather than by new fundamentals. The genealogy of most current landscape appreciation has thus already been drawn out above. Rather than carry the examination forward to the present with diminishing reward, this final part is comprised of reflections on certain themes in landscape theory past, present and future.

First the shift in theory around the 1970s, here called a 'cultural turn', is reviewed retrospectively in Chapter 9 under 'Metanarratives', together with thoughts on modern cosmology and the background to the revived interest in phenomenology. Second, the modern sub-discipline of 'environmental aesthetics' is reviewed in Chapter 10, in order to see whether and how it throws light on our concerns. Its sections provide context for Chapter 11 on 'satisfactions', a wider term than just 'aesthetics'. Some forms of satisfaction are described, necessarily from a personal point of view, before notes are made on designed landscapes and assessing aesthetic value.

Notwithstanding the blizzard of ecocentric writings from the 1980s onwards, their theories of how environmental ethics transfer to environmental aesthetics reach no conclusion. Arnold Berleant's contribution, from his holistic viewpoint, was that 'the moral is entangled with the aesthetic' because 'it is mistaken to think that one can consider ethical, religious, political, or aesthetic values apart from all the others'.[2] Such a viewpoint was airily unspecific.

In order to pin down viewpoints, Ian Thompson, a philosopher who taught landscape architecture at Newcastle University, carried out a survey of the attitudes of leading British landscape architects, as described in *Ecology, Community and Delight* (2000). On the strength of that he was invited to contribute to *The Routledge Companion to Landscape Studies* (1st ed., 2000). As he explained,

An argument over anthropocentric versus non-anthropocentric theories of value, and a fixation upon non-humanized environments (supposed wildernesses) has, until recently, pushed consideration of landscapes and the built environment to the periphery of ethicists' concerns.[3]

Thompson's chapter was 38 out of 39 – a hint of where ethics come in the priorities of landscape studies. In America Andrew Light edited seminal papers on environmental ethics, mostly from the previous 20 years, as *Environmental Ethics: An Anthology* (2002) before being diverted towards issues of climate. Also in 2002, the 19th International Social Philosophy Conference was held on the topic of Environmental Philosophy, but the transactions, only a selection of the papers, had to wait till 2018 for publication.[4]

Overall there is little new to report on environmental ethics, or at least 'Environmental Ethics' as defined by ecocentrist philosophers. Being heavily skewed towards non-anthropocentrism, it has missed the ethics of human values, and the moulding of aesthetic sensibilities through association and meaning. It was not always so. Immanuel Kant pointed out that people associate other people and objects with qualities, and thereby, by collective consent, make judgement on aesthetic and moral worth, each bolstered by the other. In this way:

> The beautiful is the symbol of the morally good ... whereupon the mind becomes conscious of a certain ennoblement and elevation above mere sensibility to pleasure from impressions of sense.[5]

Roger Scruton argued that aesthetics is a matter of 'practical reasoning', using critical judgement on appropriateness. Warning against the symbolism of the 'medicinal' aesthetics of Scandinavian functionalism, he preferred forms honed by long use and gradual adaptation for their specific use:

> If the appropriate form is the one that looks right a man must, if he is to be able to reason fully about practical matters, acquire the sense of visual validity ... and in acquiring it he will see his activities as part of an order greater than himself; he will think of himself as responding to imperatives which have their origin in a rational and objective point of view.[6]

For someone with an education or experience in aesthetic matters (which is all of us to a greater or lesser extent) this 'visual validity' may be apparent from practical considerations, but by extension it could be from other forms of worth such as conformity with values. If appreciation concerns meanings, as argued below, beneficial associations will make the scene more attractive and vice-versa. Emily Brady considered that the sublime response can 'have real moral significance', and repeated the question of what makes ugliness.[7]

A recent and promising approach in environmental ethics has been 'environmental hermeneutics', the interpretation of beliefs in environmentalism. It examines and questions the almost theological origins of ecocentrism, and inevitably various terms such as 'nature' and 'anthropocentrism' are put under the spotlight. Hopefully this endeavour will inform a new sense of practical environmental ethics, and could find common ground with culturally-orientated thinking. Its proponents warn that there are limits to the contribution that philosophical 'ethical theory' can make, a similar point to that made below with respect to environmental aesthetics. Their topic extends beyond it into the subjectivities of obligations and convictions – what we *should* do – with respect to both human and non-human affairs.[8]

As yet, the linkage between ethics and aesthetics has been left largely undeveloped by the theorists, and so these Reflections will pass straight on to topics that feed into our account of satisfactions and how to assess them.

Figure 9.1 Claude Monet's painting of the Gare St Lazare in Paris: a scene that one would normally consider ugly, but where he found interest and beauty.

NOTES AND REFERENCES

1. Marc Treib, *Modern Landscape Architecture: A Critical Review* (1993), Michael Spens, *Landscape Transformed*, (1996), James Corner (ed), *Recovering Landscape: Essays in Contemporary Landscape Architecture* (1999), Simon Swaffield (ed), *Theory in Landscape Architecture: A Reader* (2002), Michael D. Murphy, *Landscape Architecture Theory: An Evolving Body of Thought* (2005), and Kathryn Moore, *Overlooking the Visual: Demystifying the Art of Design* (2010), to name but a few of the English-language works.

2. Arnold Berleant, *The Aesthetics of Environment* (Philadelphia, 1992), p. 182; a theme briefly returned to in Arnold Berleant, *The Aesthetics of Human Environments* (Peterborough ON, 2007), pp. 86 & 148.

3. Ian Thompson, 'Landscape and environmental ethics', in Peter Howard, Ian Thompson & Emma Waterton (eds), *The Routledge Companion to Environmental Studies*. 1st edn. (Abingdon, Oxon, 2000), pp. 450-60.

4. Andrew Light (ed), 'Environmental Philosophy as Social Philosophy', *Social Philosophy Today* 19 (Charlottesville VA, 2018).

5. Immanuel Kant, *Critique of Aesthetic Judgement* (1790), trans. J. C. Meredith (Oxford, 1911), pp. 223-4, as cited by Stephen Bourassa, *The Aesthetics of Landscape* (London, 1991), p. 36.

6. Roger Scruton, *The Aesthetics of Architecture* (London, 1979), p. 240.

7. Emily Brady, *The Sublime in Modern Philosophy: Aesthetics, Ethics, and Nature* (Cambridge, 2013), pp. 174-9 & 200-6.

8. Forrest Clingerman, *et al.*, (eds), *Interpreting Nature: The Emerging Field of Environmental Hermeneutics* (New York, 2014), pp. 2, 6, 8 & 297.

CHAPTER 9

PHILOSOPHICAL MOVEMENTS

Metanarratives

This book has 'Cultural Turn' in its title. Though the expression came into general usage only after the millennium, it came to suggest the shift, beginning in the 1970s, among scholars in the humanities and social sciences to emphasise culture as the focus of their inquiry.

In philosophy one found 'post-structuralism' with its breaking down of grand overarching explanations ('metanarratives') and opposition to dualisms (or 'polarities', or 'binary oppositions'). Famously, Jean-François Lyotard, in *The Postmodern Condition: A Report on Knowledge* (1979) expressed his scepticism of the grand narratives (Progress, Enlightenment, Marxism) that had been integral to a sense of modernity with their assertions of some greater and universal truths. When these great structures crumbled, there was a sense of freedom as thinkers no longer needed to fit their conclusions to them and could study topics in their own right. Many standpoints could exist, and this promoted the acknowledgement of a diversity of human experience and identities. Relativism, anti-colonialism, feminism, and many other '-isms' thereby came to greater prominence.

The new thinking particularly affected sociology and anthropology, from which emerged 'cultural studies'. In geography 'cultural geography' came to prominence. It often meant a new emphasis on what landscapes meant to people and moved away from attempts at understanding through exclusively scientific channels. Denis Cosgrove, the 'new' cultural geographer, considered that the early stages of 'a profound collapse of long-established scholarly assumptions about disciplinary coherence, scientific method and verification, objectivity and the politics of knowledge' had already affected his discipline by the early 1980s. In his view, 'no single, coherent set of theories, concepts and methods – regardless of their moral or political appeal – can hope to provide a certain and progressive path towards truth'.[1]

When working on Long Acre, not far from Leicester Square in London, I witnessed the birth of British post-modernism in architecture when noticing Terry Farrell's greenhouse in a corner of Covent Garden (fig. 9.2). This structure was a Clifton Nurseries shop built in 1980-1 on land that was vacant while the Royal Opera House was planning its great extension. Farrell offered a relatively inexpensive lean-to

Figure 9.2 *Clifton Nurseries' shop in Covent Garden by Terry Farrell, 1980; one of the early British post-modernist buildings.*

structure, but he dressed up the end as a Doric temple with columns, entablature and pediment. On closer inspection one could see that the right-hand side of the pediment concealed the lean-to – the other half was just a sham. Some apparently squat and solid columns were actually made in trellis. Such playful tricks, mocking the seriousness of the modernist idiom, were supposed at the time to be the very essence of architectural post-modernism.

There was a new phenomenon in British garden design too. Just as the Covent Garden greenhouse was shocking to many architects, landscape architects looked askance upon the new formal gardens of the 1980s. The response varied from no response – virtually nothing was written about them in the official journal, *Landscape Design* – to mocking the likes of Rosemary Verey, Roy Strong and Prince Charles, though in fact the reincarnations of Hidcote and Sissinghurst, with their hedges, topiary and knots, was the style of choice by the most passionate garden-makers from 1980 onwards (fig. 9.3).

Another factor that made the 1970s and 1980s interesting for the landscape profession was that the environmental crisis of the early 1970s gave rise to some innovative, if not necessarily co-ordinated, thinking. This was the time of deep ecology, ecological psychology and

272 *Philosophical movements*

Figure 9.3 *The Lasket, Herefordshire, where from the 1970s Roy Strong and his wife Julia created a grand formal garden, shockingly non-modernist at the time.*

sustainability. Although these cannot be thought of as part of the cultural turn – they might instead be described as outcomes of an ecocentric turn – they gave rise to great divergences, and thus much debate, which continues today.

It is remarkable how ecocentrist thought overwhelmed much of landscape theory. Being itself a metanarrative, it is impossible to prove or disprove. Deep Ecology had a 'religious component' – Arne Naess said so[2] – and it has many disciples, and even more followers. There was hardly any challenge to it. Just at the time (the 1980s) when a proper debate on the merits of rival positions would have been of much benefit, the new high priest of culture in landscape, Denis Cosgrove, saw off those of his colleagues in cultural geography whom he thought were insufficiently theoretical and too innocent politically. He turned his dais into a platform for his political views. He saw only the traces of political and social exploitation in the landscape, and completely missed any aesthetic or phenomenological encounters.

Ever since, there has been a procession of academics, many in philosophy, busy at work in finding reasons why the ecocentric norm was good and correct. Nevertheless, not everyone was won over, particularly in the landscape profession itself.[3]

Metanarratives **273**

Cosmology

The Foreword of this book made a point of contrasting two versions of how to arrive at the higher-level truths that govern our existence, that is a cosmology. Karl Popper saw the term as 'the problem of understanding the world – including ourselves, and our knowledge, as part of the world'.[4] Every individual has his own cosmology, whether they be empiricists believing in the efficacy of science, phenomenologists or holists like deep ecologists.

In the consideration of matters external to the body, the distinction between the appearance of objects in the world (as understood through psychology or phenomenology) and the supposed reality underlying appearances (as framed by science) has been a battleground for debate. We trust our own experience, in that we know that it has happened, but how far do we trust ourselves to have interpreted it right, and how far can we trust the findings of science? The psychological study of experience posed a challenge to conventional science, for some parts of consciousness are forever internal, and outside the realm of natural science: these include subjective feelings, emotions, convictions, poetic thoughts.

Another challenge is 'idealism', a way of thinking which holds that the source of all knowledge and truth is a higher belief held in the mind, a metanarrative. The believer enforces it through faith, spirit or will. The existence and nature of a world independent of the mind is not denied, though cosmologies that emanate from an absolute belief in God, Marxism or deep ecology will judge all experience, science and rational thinking against the yardstick and will recast understandings to ensure that they reflect the higher truth. This is the characteristic of totalitarian politics, and was once seen in minor ways in the narratives of the unconscious and in formalism. It has been prominent in environmental thought in the various forms of biological determinism, first with the doctrine of survival of the fittest, then with human ecology, eugenics, sociobiology, and latterly deep ecology. When combined with holism – another idealism – some of these trains of thought were expanded to the power of two.

The tensions between the holistic tendency (ecocentrism) and the view of humans as essentially cultural beings (anthropocentrism) have been explored in Chapter 5 and will be again below. Meanwhile there is neither a need just yet to adjust the conventional mind-environment duality, nor to seek a reconfiguration of the natural sciences or social sciences.

Phenomenology

The cultural geographer, John Wylie, has drawn attention to Carl Sauer's use of the term back in the 1930s when stating that the task of geography was:

> ... conceived as the establishment of a critical system which embraces the phenomenology of landscape, in order to grasp in all of its meaning and color the varied terrestrial scene.[5]

Sauer's understanding of phenomenology appears to have been through Hermann von Keyserling's *Prolegomena zur Naturphilosophie* (1910), which was itself an introduction to the ideas of the circle around Georg Hegel, notably his work translated as *The Phenomenology of Mind: Science of the Experience of Consciousness*. Their idea was to re-lay the foundations for the natural sciences. Their 'phenomena' were whatever we perceive in the natural world and seek to explain, a meaning that remains in common usage till today. Hence Sauer could write: 'All science may be regarded as phenomenology'.[6]

The North American tradition of cultural geographers exploring the cultural landscape inspired by John Brinkerhof Jackson could likewise be regarded as phenomenologists in this original sense. One of the foremost amongst them in the 1970s and 1980s was Tuan Yi-Fu. He once stated that phenomenologists and existential phenomenologists had influenced his approach to describing landscape.[7] Against the trend in his profession at the time (i.e. its 'quantitative revolution' that led to mathematical modelling), Tuan saw human geography as the study of human-environment relations in the quest to unravel geographical processes. He explored what it is to be human and became increasingly interested in the emotional and intimate engagement of people in their environment and particularly place. Tuan's personal, descriptive, approach was criticised in a re-run of the general arguments against phenomenology – political naivety and lack of scientific rigour. His work was said to be 'highly subjective', 'valid only as "criticism" of more scientific geography', and that he thus failed to pin down causal relations.

Alongside this tradition in geography a new version of phenomenology had commenced with the publication of *Logische Untersuchungen* (1900/1901) ['Logical Investigations'], by Edmund Husserl, a docent at the University of Halle, in Germany. He took phenomena to be whatever we are conscious of, including ourselves, and our own conscious experiences. The aim of phenomenology became to reveal the world as perceived through direct experience, unmediated by cognition, and prior to any theorization about it. He had thus changed the question from 'what can we observe?' to 'how does it feel?'.

Hence he did not aim at scientific knowledge as such, but was seeking, through systematic reflection on experiences of phenomena by groups of people, to reach consensus on their 'essences', or essential properties to give a 'descriptive psychology' of the 'things themselves'. Because his researches concerned the individual's impressions, and could not share the concepts and terms of the natural sciences, he had to develop a purpose-made method, concepts for description, and language, including 'intentionality', or focus of interest, 'life-world', and 'structures of experience'.

The primacy of subjectivity in Husserl's phenomenology was agreed by the existentialists who became prominent immediately after the Second World War. That school likewise centred upon the rationalisation of existence, but they were more concerned with the way humans seek to find their true natures, and the meaning of life, from conditions of confusion and uncertainty. Individuals were presumed to have free will, that is not automatically subject to the rules of society or faith systems, and would discover who and what they are through choices, acknowledging their consequences and taking personal responsibility.

Many phenomenologists saw themselves privately as existentialists, while in professional terms they saw themselves as following but yet expanding upon Husserl, and pursuing the quest to establish a phenomenological body of knowledge. Martin Heidegger had a central idea in the 'foundational analyses of human being as a "dwelling" in the world'. Maurice Merleau-Ponty proposed that regarding the body and its organs as the primary means to know the world would be more fruitful than starting with consciousness, and had a 'conception of the lived body, entwined with the world in everyday perception and movement'.[8] He rejected most of the assumptions of science, in particular that the world exists as a ready-made and fully objective reality. He also disliked idealism and mistrusted any constructs of the mind. As he emphasised: 'The world is not what I think, but what I live through'.

Although his intention was 'to give a direct description of our experience as it is, without taking account of its psychological origin and the causal explanations which the scientist, the historian or the sociologist may be able to provide', he had evidently studied psychological works and so perhaps went beyond his own restrictions. He was, though, writing at a time when psychology was a contest between behaviourism and gestalt thinking, and before the rise of cognitive theory or ecological psychology. On perception, he simply saw it as the communication between the mind and the world, imbuing it with meanings and values: 'Our own body is in the world as the heart is in the organism; it keeps the visible spectacle constantly alive, it breathes life into it and sustains it inwardly, and with it forms a system'. An aspect of perception, he noted, illustrated by his own experience of arriving in Paris from his village, was that an initial experience would supply the 'atmosphere' or 'style' of the place. Specific objects or buildings would tend to remain 'ambiguous', though afterwards attention would be directed towards them. These ambiguous perceptions then 'emerge as explicit acts: perceptions, that is, to which we ourselves give a significance'.

Because their investigations were so subjective, phenomenologists had great difficulty in even fixing on a definition. Merleau-Ponty apologised that phenomenology 'as for so long remained at an initial stage, as a problem to be solved and a hope to be realised'. He forgave the reader who 'will wonder whether a philosophy which cannot define its scope deserves all the discussion which has gone on around it, and whether he is not faced rather by a myth or a fashion'.[9] Karl Popper's conclusion after examining one of the technical aspects of the methodology was that: 'For this reason, and for many other reasons, I do not think that there is any chance of rescuing phenomenalism by this method'.[10]

So the phenomenologist takes his open-topped sports car for a spin, and enjoys the lived experience of the roar of its engine, the power to pull up the hills, the wind rushing through his hair and the redness of his car's bonnet as it slices through the ever-changing greens of the landscape outside. But the car breaks down. That is when the phenomenologist lifts up the bonnet, scratches his head, and calls the logical positivist vehicle recovery firm.

There were objections to phenomenology's individualism from left-wing theorists. The 'whole effort of man shaping himself and his world' was seen as 'being dictated by consciousness, and an individual consciousness at that'. The Marxists believed that it was only through engaging with nature's laws and the means of production that the individual became useful to society. Instead, in phenomenology, 'man is removed from his social and natural context, yet it is via society, through particular forms of production, that his relationship to nature is formulated'.[11]

Merleau-Ponty had a chapter on 'Temporality' in which he referred to 'the world as we have tried to show it, as standing on the horizon of our life as the primordial unity of all our experiences'.[12] That was understandable from a phenomenologist, but Tim Ingold, a British anthropologist supporting a different form of idealism – human ecology – objected to the image of the world being on the horizon. He saw the world as enveloping, and that the human-environment relation was one of intimacy. His article on 'The Temporality of Landscape' (1993) had a holistic approach whereby 'life and landscape were one and the same'. His own 'dwelling perspective' set out people's active, perceptual engagement in the world. Meanwhile he covered his other flank by implicitly criticising the 'way of seeing' approach of the 'new' cultural geographers for not acknowledging oneness.[13]

Meanwhile the 'new' cultural geography had already become dominant in Britain, dissuading its own discipline from further phenomenology, and so the archaeologists expanded their horizons and quickly filled the void. Henry Cleere, Peter Fowler, Graham Fairclough and Timothy Darvill were all prominent in British thinking on cultural landscapes in the 1990s, nationally and internationally. There probably always will be a call for fact-finding and analysis of the historical and contemporary relationships between humans and their landscapes.

An archaeologist, Christopher Tilley, gave a customary nod to Heidegger and Merleau-Ponty in his *A Phenomenology of Landscape: Places, Paths and Monuments* (1994). He proceeded to speculate on the role that tumuli played in ancestor-worship practices amongst Neolithic peoples in Wales and southern England by re-imagining their landscapes. Projecting his thoughts across the millennia like that drew criticism for its unscientific approach, but archaeology was not short of such guessing games, and his was an interesting new one that may have provided insights.

The interest in landscape phenomenology grew significantly from the late 1990s, with studies on walking, looking and spectating, writing, gardening, touching and feeling, spiritual or therapeutic retreat and contemplation, angling and watercraft, cycling and train travel.[14] These address the question: 'what is it like to be human in this world'?

What might the recent interest in phenomenology signify? Is it a few academics seeking to impress with selective quotations, but who do not, or perhaps find that they cannot, follow through fully in testing the theory? Or is there a return to the observational phenomenology of Tuan? Hopefully the latter, because there is no reason why a scientific study of real landscapes should not be complementary to a cultural understanding and appreciation.

The human mind entertains a world of perceptions, memories, emotions and disembodied thoughts, known only to the mind itself, and seeks to perceive, make sense of, and find relationships with, the environment – by contrast very physical and comparatively constant in nature, and which sustains the body in very many senses. This may be a duality, but one that is ineluctably with us always by the nature of ourselves and of the world, and one that is the wellspring for much poetry, literature, philosophy, aesthetics and art that we would be immeasurably poorer if denied.

NOTES AND REFERENCES

1. Denis Cosgrove, *Social Formation and Symbolic Landscape* (London, 1984; new pb edn Madison WI, 1998), p. xv.

2. Bill Devall & George Sessions, *Deep Ecology* (Layton UT, 1985), p. 76.

3. Ian H. Thompson, *Ecology, Community and Delight* (London, 2000), p. 163.

4. Karl R. Popper, *The Logic of Scientific Discovery* (London, 1972), p. 15.

5. Carl O. Sauer, 'The Morphology of Landscape', *University of California Publications in Geography* 2 : 2 (1925), 25.

6. Ibid, 20.

7. Yi-Fu Tuan, 'Humanistic Geography', *Annals of the Association of American Geographers*, 66 (1976), 275n.

8. John Wylie, 'Landscape and Phenomenology', in Howard *et al.*, *The Routledge Companion to Environmental Studies*. 1st edn. (Abingdon, Oxon, 2000), pp. 54-65; p. 56.

9. Maurice Merleau-Ponty, *The Phenomenology of Perception*, trans. Colin Smith (London, 1962), pp. vii-viii, xvi, 203 & 281.

10. Popper, op. cit., p. 440.

11. David Pepper, *The Roots of Modern Environmentalism* (London, 1984), p. 161.

12. Merleau-Ponty, op. cit., p. 430.

13. Timothy Ingold, 'The Temporality of Landscape', *World Archaeology* 25/2 (1993), 152-171.

14. John Wylie, op. cit., pp. 54-65; p. 61.

CHAPTER 10

ENVIRONMENTAL AESTHETICS

British philosophers of aesthetics in the eighteenth and nineteenth centuries had often seen their subject in landscape terms. Landscape was then sidelined and ignored for most of the twentieth, in part because art critics like Clive Bell argued that aesthetic appreciation sprang from significant form, seen in abstract art. The sub-discipline of 'environmental aesthetics', given point and relevance by the landscape-evaluation projects of the 1960s and 1970s for countryside-planning purposes, and then the environmental movement of the 1970s, thus had to be reinvented almost from scratch.

The modern philosophers of environmental aesthetics are first and foremost academic philosophers: they just happen to have chosen landscape (or environment, or nature) as a speciality. Their task is to propose a theory of aesthetic experience that can be said to be 'true', having passed rigorous philosophical examination. Describing the actual experience of landscape appreciations, and devising a method for determining landscape beauty in practice, is for the writers and phenomenologists on the one hand, and the landscape planners and countryside officers on the other.

Several theories were put forward with none of them gaining general acceptance, reflecting some wide divergences of approach. Each theory tended to highlight an aspect of the act of appreciation. Hence Ronald Hepburn's more metaphysical approach drew attention to the 'imaginative possibilities in appreciation of nature'. Arnold Berleant, in his ecocentric approach, argued for an appreciative experience of nature, not by just passing through, but by communing with it. Emily Brady, who considered that almost anything perceived could be 'relevant' to the aesthetic experience wrote that:

> ... appreciation comes about through the subject's appreciative capacities – perception, imagination and so on, coupled with open, sympathetic attention to qualities of the aesthetic object.[1]

She noted that appreciation can take place in sequential views, and in all weather conditions, making it 'more like a happening'.

Ronald Hepburn

Environmental aestheticians point to a chapter by Ronald Hepburn in *British Analytical Philosophy* (1966) as marking the re-emergence of the topic. It was the last but one in this survey of contemporary philosophical thinking, and did not come to the notice of landscape practitioners at the time. It was only when environmental aesthetics later sought its own origins that the chapter's significance became apparent. In fact by far the more important contribution to the volume was one by its co-editor, the moral philosopher Alan Montefiore, on 'Fact, Value and Ideology'. The distinction between facts and values was being discussed on postgraduate town-planning courses by the early 1970s, and had ramifications in planning, cultural geography, political science and indeed any subject that touched on values.

Montefiore's task was to show that value-judgements were a legitimate philosophical concept. The prevailing view at the time was that truth derived either from analytic propositions, whose truth depended on the meanings of their wording, or empirical propositions, so long as they were scientifically verifiable. Value-judgements by themselves were regarded as logically meaningless, and merely expressed the feelings of the author. Alternatively, they were particular expressions of universal principles, such as religion or political dogma, believed by believers to be true. Montefiore argued that value statements were based on principles of universal import, were shared publicly, and were subscribed to by an individual's act of free will. They thus stood in logical independence, and were beyond being merely someone's personal preferences.[2]

Hepburn's chapter noted how aesthetics had transferred attention away from the landscape and towards paintings and sculpture in art galleries, and had developed fairly specific rules of engagement that were not appropriate in contemplating nature. He cited several differences between the appreciation of art and of nature, including that nature would 'envelop him on all sides', that 'motion may be an important element in his aesthetic experience', and that 'the spectator experiences himself in an unusual and vivid way'. However, the main difference was that 'we are in nature and a part of nature', so that 'I am both actor and spectator'. Nature thus provided 'distinctive and valuable types of aesthetic experience ... that art cannot provide'.

He was cautious about holistic claims for 'oneness' with nature :

> ... accounts of natural beauty that take 'unity' as their central concept are often metaphysically extravagant, and are chronically unperceptive of ambiguities in their claims [so that] we would be ill-advised to take this cluster of unity-concepts as by itself adequate for all explanatory purposes.

He thought that there could be a range of possible interactions with nature, ranging from 'detachment' at one extreme through to 'involvement' and 'oneness with nature' at the other.

Hepburn's task was to propose that judgements of nature could be made equivalent in seriousness to those of art. This would not be easy, for those of nature, because it was constantly changing and had flexible boundaries, were 'always provisional, correctible by reference to a different, perhaps wider, context, or to a narrower one realized in greater detail'. He wrote of landscape appealing to the metaphysical imagination, by being the prompt to some fundamental questions on the nature and purpose of one's short habitation on Earth and suchlike. He fixed on the human response of 'realizing', which meant 'making, or becoming, vivid to perception, or to the imagination'. He thought that a person's 'coming-to-be-aware' was one of the chief activities in the aesthetic experiencing of nature'. The important point was that 'to realize' implies a 'built-in reference to truth', so that informed aesthetic judgements should be repeatable and have stability.[3]

Hepburn was predicting much of the agenda of the debates in environmental aesthetics: the nature of perception (cognitive versus noncognitive), detachment versus involvement (which became disinterestedness versus engagement), and the rules for correct judgement (necessary for a philosophical assertion of truth).

Cognitive vs non-cognitive perception

The first item of agenda here is the form which the human-world relationship takes, as understood in theories of perception. On the one hand there are those who recognise that aesthetics is a cultural question, in which perception passes through cognitive processes, or 'cultural filter', to the point that the mind can form a judgement. This was argued by George Santayana in his *The Sense of Beauty* (1896):

> ... the whole machinery of our intelligence, our general ideas and laws, fixed and external objects, principles, persons, and gods, are so many symbolic, algebraic expressions. They stand for experience; experience which we are incapable of retaining and surveying in its multitudinous immediacy. We should flounder hopelessly, like the animals, did we not keep ourselves afloat and direct our course by these intellectual devices.[4]

Richard Gregory's exposition of cognitive theory in his *Eye and Brain: the Psychology of Seeing* (1966) is outlined in Chapter 4. To him, perception was not a passive acceptance of stimuli, but an active process involving looking, memory and imagination as the mind assembles a coherent view of the world outside.

One prominent environmental aestheticist, Allen Carlson, defined a 'natural environmental model' of appreciation which is informed by knowledge provided by the natural sciences. For him, 'knowledge and intelligence transform raw experience by making it determinate, harmonious, and meaningful', which is clearly a description of the cognitive process, and he added that his 'emphasis on scientific knowledge gives such appreciation a highly cognitive and what might be judged an overly intellectual quality'.[5]

On the other hand, there are those that follow James Gibson and his 'ecological psychology', which refused to accept the need for cognition, instead preferring the perceptual system of 'affordances' (see Chapter 5 – 'The logic of ecocentrism'). In this theory unmediated linkage between the mind and external experience was supposed, giving instantaneous perception. He held his distrust of cognitive theory in common with the phenomenologists of that time. Meanwhile many ecocentrists found in Gibson's holism a convenient prop for presuming that 'engagement' describes the human being not just living in the world, but being at one with it; what was happening in the world was indistinguishable from what was happening in its perceivers.

Most environmental aestheticians were inclined to adopt Gibson's 'direct realism': there appears to have been a general feeling that one's environmentalist credentials started with accepting 'ecological psychology'. If you were an ecocentrist that was sufficient, for judgements and actions were supposed to flow forth seamlessly. If not, you needed some mental mechanism to connect sensual perception to appreciation, and cognitive thought was the only available model. There was sometimes partial acceptance of ecological psychology. Stephen Kaplan, himself a psychologist, was interested in 'affordances', but did not mention direct realism, and was happy to discuss 'the cognitive domain' and its role in forming preferences.[6]

Arnold Berleant revelled in 'a direct grasp of the sights and sounds of the world, an immediate apprehension of its tastes and smells, the textures and resistance of things', but went on to observe that 'sensation ... fuses with cultural influences. This is, in fact, the only way a cultural organism can experience', and that 'human perception blends memories, beliefs, and associations, and this range of meanings deepens experience'.[7] Emily Brady wrote that 'I identify with the non-cognitivists', but imagination, emotion/expression and the role of thought and knowledge were accommodated in her 'integrated aesthetics'. So while Berleant and Brady declined to accept cognition as the explanation for the perception of beauty in nature, they reserved a role for knowledge, meaning and cultural influences. Brady considered that Berleant's 'emphasis on culture suggests an overly human-orientated view towards the natural world', and we might agree that he and she appear to be de-facto cognitivists over questions of landscape perception.[8]

Disinterestedness and engagement

This debate on perception has carried over into another on the mode of appreciation of nature. Is 'engagement' different from 'disinterestedness', and if so, is it more appropriate when contemplating nature? The latter had been cited as desirable for achieving the right frame of mind to make serious aesthetic judgements on art objects. Jerome Stolnitz, famously described 'the aesthetic attitude' as a 'disinterested and sympathetic attention to and contemplation of any object of awareness whatever, for its own sake alone'. By 'sympathetic' Stolnitz meant being fully prepared intellectually and mentally, and 'disinterested' meant disengaging from all thoughts of utility to 'isolate both us and the object from the flow of experience'. We see the object 'for its own sake alone', stripped of all the baggage that may come with it or with us. That would enable 'the object to come fully alive in our experience',[9] so that we could 'savour fully the distinctive value of the object'. Note that 'disinterest' means intellectual neutrality; it does not imply mental or physical detachment.

The word 'attention' might be taken to imply that the object is the active agent in this relationship – such that it emanates its qualities and we give our attention. That may have been accepted at a time when people believed that objects had intrinsic qualities, and the human was the passive observer, but the relationship is now generally reversed (see Chapter 6 – 'Action/place'). Another meaning could be attributed to 'attention' in cognitive theory, that is the ability to select some aspects of the world presented to our senses for further processing, and thus to ignore other aspects. This may indeed be part of the landscape experience, for otherwise why does one choose to look one way rather than another? For both reasons, 'appraisal' might be a better word today.

Monroe Beardsley was writing about aesthetics at much the same date, and implying a cognitive approach. Brady mentioned his thoughts about aesthetic experience because he gave not so much a definition, but a list of criteria for whether it had taken place.[10] They were:

(1) 'object directedness', similar to Stolnitz's 'attention';

(2) 'felt freedom', a release from distractions, permitting disinterestedness;

(3) 'detached affect', setting the object at a slight emotional distance;

(4) 'active discovery', making connections and imaginative engagement; and/or

(5) 'wholeness', feelings of satisfaction or contentment on completion.

There are few better descriptions of the aspects of satisfactory aesthetic encounters.

Carlson sought some slight amendments to the Stolnitz model. He suggested that in the absence of artistic design in nature, the observer has to work collaboratively with it: 'our appreciation is guided by the nature of the object of appreciation'. In effect, 'we become designers of our own experience, working with the properties of the environment, but for proper appreciation, appropriate preparation is still necessary.[11] In other words, he was devising an equivalent to the disinterestedness mode for use in the natural environment.

Other philosophers would have nothing to do with a mode from fine art. Berleant recalled that Dewey had much disliked the commercialisation of art and wanted to demystify the fine art conspiracy to make it more accessible. Pompous museums were 'memorials of the rise of nationalism and imperialism', and:

> The nouveaux riches, who are an important byproduct of the capitalist system, have felt especially bound to surround themselves with works of fine art which, being rare, are also costly.[12]

Mindful of Dewey's concept of an everyday art of people interacting with their environments, Berleant felt that the aesthetics of landscape cannot be treated in the same rarefied manner as that for fine art. He first suggested that the term 'engagement' should supplant 'disinterestedness' when developing his phenomenological approach in the late 1960s.[13] As his interest in ecocentrism developed he found the term becoming more central to his thinking. 'What is it to experience environment aesthetically? Foremost is the quality of engagement,' he wrote, and 'appreciative engagement must replace the customary contemplative admiration'.[14] In this way he constructed an 'aesthetics of engagement' based on 'mutual interaction' so that we 'engage with it in ways that intensify and enlarge our awareness'. His proposed method of study was to be 'descriptive aesthetics' that may be 'partly narrative, partly phenomenological, partly evocative, and sometimes even revelatory'.

The general view among environmental aestheticians was to differentiate between fine art, as seen in a picture frame, from the everyday experience from engagement with the environment. For Berleant and his followers, it was important that 'engagement' should drive out the term 'disinterestedness' from discourse on nature and wilderness areas. The distinction was sometimes emphasised by suggestions that disinterestedness implied a lack of the necessary physical engagement. 'Disinterestedness' was often misinterpreted as meaning, by inference, non-engagement and non-interest:

> When theory insists upon distance and disinterest as a precondition for art and the aesthetic, then art and the aesthetic become means of alienation and objectification'.[15]

'Engagement' itself was seen in quite physical terms, for example walking through a landscape. This was another parallel to Gibson's 'ecological psychology'. Berleant, though, encountered difficulties in fully melding it with the aesthetics of engagement, for Gibson had nothing to say about aesthetics, beauty or culture. Furthermore, his theory concerned people, and what 'affordances' the outside world could render to them: there was no scope for nature having its own voice. He himself dismissed any such thoughts: 'The environment does not communicate with the observers who inhabit it. Why should the world speak to us?'[16] It might even be suggested that he was anthropocentric.

Struggling to reconcile his 'cultural influences' with Gibson's 'direct realism', we find Berleant complaining perplexedly:

> The difficulty of trying to express the idea of environment as a seamless unity of organism, perception, and place, all suffused with values, is almost impossible to overcome in the English language.[17]

Berleant did usefully describe four 'stages' on the path of enlightenment from the 'Lockean notion of nature as something apart from humans', to the 'Spinozistic conception of nature as all-inclusive'.[18] They can here be restated with the addition of *disinterest* as rungs on the ladder of engagement.

- *Competition*: nature is seen as powerful and unforgiving, leading humans to resist its forces, and ultimately to control and conquer it.

- *Disinterest:* the human being views the landscape neutrally at first, but is prepared and open to the emotions of beauty, the sublime and the picturesque being stirred.

- *Co-existence*: nature and mankind are essentially different, yet they are entwined and act reciprocally, resulting in cultural landscapes and identity of place.

- *Assimilation*: the human sees himself as embedded and part of the natural world, as in the animism of the native Americans.

- *Integration*: a holistic view of the human and nature, whereby nothing is other than nature, and humans are simply an aspect of an all-inclusive seamless existence.

Brady referred to the archetypal fine-art mode as 'aesthetic attitude theory', its hallmark being 'the attitude of the subject that demarcates the experience or response as aesthetic'.[19] She trod a middle line, seeking to amend Stolnitz's model in order to answer criticisms, noting for example the critique of disinterestedness by Berleant. Her softer approach was for 'not a full-blown engagement or holistic account such as Berleant's', but one from the 'the environing experience of nature' that promoted 'relationship, rather than becoming one with nature'. This relationship was premised on the 'recognition of nature's otherness', and hence 'some distance is maintained'. While she supported the 'concept of disinterestedness', the observer's 'appreciative capacities' were as causal to an aesthetic experience as the object's qualities. The interplay became her 'integrated aesthetic'.[20] Other writers have agreed, preferring 'involvement' or some other term to suggest respect and appreciation by the human for his habitation. The English philosopher, David Cooper, has hardened up a 'deep' form of 'co-existence' in his *A Philosophy of Gardens* – 'co-dependence'.[21]

The desirability of some form of 'engagement' was taken as a given in most modern landscape studies. It became almost obligatory for theoreticians to state that they were non-cognitive engagers. Not all environmental aestheticians followed Berleant all the way: for example, some accepted that there were rules for fine art, and saw their subject as embracing everything that was not fine art. Most agreed, though, that purist fine-art appreciation was inapplicable in the wider landscape, and they rejected several forms of landscape evaluation of 'scenic beauty' based on artistic ideas such as the Picturesque or formalism.

Relevance and preparation

If disinterestedness gives you entry to the scenic route, as it were, you need to be sure that the windows are clean and the driver is awake. In 'aesthetic attitude theory' the various possible inputs need to be considered for 'relevance' to the process, and the subject/perceiver examined for his preparation.

In order for an experience to be judged as aesthetic, discipline was required to exclude extraneous artefacts or information so that the object itself could be focused upon. If the appreciation was to be of the form, shapes, lines and colours of the object, nothing except the object mattered. If the assessment was going to be relative to other objects, or placed within an artist's canon, knowledge of the artist's intentions and the history of the object might be relevant. However, strict limits were still desirable, and Stolnitz queried whether it is:

> ... ever 'relevant' to aesthetic experience to have thoughts and images or bits of knowledge which are not present within the object itself? If these are ever relevant, under what conditions are they so?

That would depend on the nature of the object and of the appreciation: 'accept the object 'on its own terms'... follow the lead of the object and respond in concert with it'.[22] We might be considering an association of a place with an artist: then the reminders of the scenery of that place in the artist's work is relevant; the identities of the friends or lovers he had to stay are probably not.

Allen Carlson set out his advice in terms of the appreciation of the environment. Obviously, some of the circumstances would differ from those in an art gallery, but the central principle could be followed. Nature may not have been created by an artist, but there would still be information about it relevant to its appreciation:

> The basic idea of the objectivist point of view is that our appreciation is guided by the nature of the object of appreciation. Thus, information about the object's nature, about its genesis, type, and properties, is necessary for appropriate aesthetic appreciation.

If appreciation of nature was to be 'for its own sake alone', one had to appreciate nature as what it in fact is, that is, as natural and as an environment. This was his 'natural environmental model' of appreciation, in which we should:

> ... appreciate nature in light of our knowledge of what it is, that is, in light of knowledge provided by the natural sciences, especially the environmental sciences such as geology, biology, and ecology.[23]

If the perceiver's judgements were guided by science, they might be said to be 'true'. However, this might imply that only geologists and ecologists were knowledgeable and discriminating enough to be suitable as appreciators, a point challenged by Brady:

> Given that the context is an aesthetic one, why turn to the experience and knowledge of scientists, rather than the aesthetic experience of poets, painters, photographers, environmental artists and other, such as indigenous people living in the land, or even visitors to their local natural areas?[24]

She considered that 'the cognitive models run into problems when they make science a necessary framework and the only correct one', and suggested pluralism in drawing on several types of appreciator, as long as they are informed and reasonably objective.

Brady's 'integrated aesthetics' allows for that vast storehouse of memories and learning in the mind to be available to a value-judgement, awakening new thoughts, knowledge and imaginative possibilities. Without the questioning and reflection, the visitor to a landscape, along with maybe the majority of people, may have no particular preferences, or has accepted without question those ingrained through the endless pre-formed images and sentiments in the media. Robust preferences are not given to us automatically; we learn to develop judgement. Experience in judging past enjoyable encounters helps us improve our faculties.

Objective vs subjective

Jerome Stolnitz had rejected both 'objectivism' – the claim that beauty resides in the object, allowing objective evaluations – and 'subjectivism' – the assertion that beauty is a purely personal preference that is not binding on anyone else. His method sought 'objective relativism', in which:

> ... aesthetic value ... is that property of objects which is a 'potentiality' or 'capacity' for causing experiences of intrinsic value in the percipient ... one of those properties which belong to a thing because of what it does in interaction with a human organism.[25]

Reference to the 'potentiality' of an object (analogous to 'qualities' or 'attributes' in Chapter 5) implies that whatever is being judged will be 'a stable object with enduring properties' which can be examined publicly. The percipient will state that he had a good, bad or indifferent reaction to it, and give a thoughtful analysis of why. Others will give their reactions and their reasons. The process of dialogue will arrive at a judgement that commands most respect. In this sense evaluations can be shared, though not necessarily permanent, much as described under 'The Sociology of Criticism' in Chapter 4. Note, incidentally, that Stolnitz's method did not exclude natural objects: 'we apprehend aesthetically not only works of art but also objects in nature'.[26]

Berleant saw talk of subject/object interaction as an unfortunate example of a 'dualism'. 'Subjective' and 'objective' became meaningless in a holistic philosophy. However, he had to explain how perception of the environment could be turned into aesthetic appreciation. Being a holist, this presented no great difficulty, as he could just make the assertion:

> Moreover, this act of perception, this process of integrated experience, because it is perceived, has an aesthetic dimension... For the fully engaged participant, an aesthetic factor is always present.[27]

Carlson and Brady, though, had taken pains to devise models that passed the tests of disinterestedness, sympathetic attention, and relevance, which would permit appreciations to be accepted as 'true' or 'objective'. The prize was to have their models adopted by practitioners as the 'correct' bases for carrying out appreciations of nature and, assuming the models were true, this would be so for all time.

Carlson laid down strict conditions for ensuring relevant attention, for example a narrow class of suitable assessors. Brady's concept of relevance admitted a wide range of cultural factors. Aware that this might undermine the objectivity of any individual's judgements, she proposed a social-science approach of 'practical objectivity':

> The case I make here is for objectivity in terms of the intersubjective validity of aesthetic judgements, rather than a rigid objectivity that would leave out the subjective dimension of aesthetic experience altogether.

Appreciators would then canvass their judgements with the public:

> Appreciators are trying to show others that the aesthetic qualities are there by getting people to see those qualities for themselves. This kind of public, persuasive method is a type of proof, laying claim to objectivity, yet of course very unlike other kinds of proofs...'

Carlson's 'natural environmental model' and Brady's 'practical objectivity' were both devices to argue for disinterestedness, which in turn would answer any charge of subjectivity. Brady made this point thus:

> ... disinterestedness... will help filter out idiosyncratic features of the appreciator... distinguish aesthetic appreciation as a shared activity from the personal activity of expressing preferences.

She thought that mere preferences led to attention on irrelevant matters, and could and should be screened out:

> Of course, there will be cases of personal experience and imaginative or emotional linkages that are irrelevant or eccentric, but these can be excluded through the critical process.[28]

Assessors were supposed to be 'suitably qualified' (Brady suggested education for 'competent judges ... with developed aesthetic sensibilities and experience') and 'disinterested', and thus 'objective' in their judgements. This would clear the way to objectivity:

> If aesthetic value is to be taken seriously in the practical context of environmental planning and policy-making, objectivity, of some degree at least, is essential. Aesthetic value is often viewed as reflecting mere personal preferences rather than rational aesthetic judgements.

Carlson's experience went back to the 1970s and he was well aware of the so-called 'objective' evaluations being devised then, but it is unclear whether Brady appreciated that she was replicating the argumentation deployed in those projects (see Chapters 2 and 6). All her propositions for ensuring objectivity, it may be noted, had been rejected back in the 1980s.

Philosophy, always seeking universal 'truth', will abhor the chaos of diverse preferences. Among the models of appreciation that Carlson listed was the 'post-modern'. That term may sound a bit quaint today, but in the 1990s post-modernism was being hotly debated. What he had in mind was the post-structural refusal to accept overarching theories and the view that one person's values and opinions had as much right to be heard as the next person's. The problem for Carlson was that no theory could be developed under these conditions: the exasperating 'post-modernist' model could be 'of no relevance as it has no rules of appreciation'.[29]

Brady too was uneasy with post-modernism and sought to counter:

> ... the common assumption among environmental conservationists and decision-makers that aesthetic appreciation is a subjective matter which involves personal preferences rather than rational judgement and debate.

and

> I rejected the belief that aesthetic judgements express personal preferences and argued that perceptual rather than deductive or inductive proof supports our judgements ... I would argue that the assumption that aesthetic valuing is a subjective matter is based on an unreflective understanding of aesthetics.

Objective vs subjective

Without some theoretical framework to identify judgements grounded in some kind of objectivity 'there is no way to arbitrate between personal opinions'.[30] Such dismissals of the hard-won experience over 30 years make the practitioner question how grounded the aestheticians were.

This determination to find the one, true, way of assessing environments was questioned by Jonathan Maskit. Instead of rehearsing the old debates of cognitive versus non-cognitive, he wished to focus on the divide between the 'universalists' like Brady together with most other established theoreticians on the one hand, and 'cultural historicists' who hold that the role of culture and history in judgement should be emphasised more on the other. He cited German philosophers who had observed that 'the nature dealt with in an aesthetics of nature, is a threatened region *within* the human world', and that 'it is human beings who encounter nature and of course we do so using *our* senses, *our* language, and *our* concepts'.[31]

Berleant, also in contrast to Brady, came to acknowledge the validity of preferences. Despite his holistic leanings (which led most writers towards assumptions of the universality of human response), he had always argued that aesthetic appreciations were partly cultural, and in 2010 expanded on the implications of this.[32] He started with the thought that:

> ... time, experience and individual variability introduce irreducible differences, and because no two occasions are exact duplicates, judgments of them will thus rarely be unanimous.

He thus rejected the universality of aesthetic judgement and all consequent methods of appraisal that claimed to be objective. He argued, in a strikingly similar fashion to those on consensus in Britain 30 years beforehand, that: 'universality cannot merely be assumed or claimed: it is precisely what needs to be proved.'

He implied that much of environmental aesthetics had been promising what it could never have delivered, and observed that:

> It is not the first time that philosophy has tied itself up in knots of its own making, and this is nowhere more evident than in attempts to objectify the world.

With Maskit approaching the 'way of seeing' approach, and Berleant's repudiation of the possibility of objectivity, serious doubts were being raised about the underlying normative assumptions of philosophical 'environmental aesthetics', at least in the form it took between 1990 and 2010.

NOTES AND REFERENCES

1. Emily Brady, *Aesthetics of the Natural Environment* (Edinburgh, 2003), pp. 120-3.

2. Alan Montefiore, 'Facts, Values and Ideology', in Bernard Williams & Alan Montefiore (eds), *British Analytical Philosophy* (London, 1966), pp. 179-203, p. 198.

3. Ronald Hepburn 'Contemporary Aesthetics and the Neglect of Natural Beauty', in Williams & Montefiore, op. cit., pp. 285-310; pp. 303-4.

4. George Santayana, *The Sense of Beauty: Being the Outlines of Aesthetic Theory* (New York, 1896), p. 122.

5. Allen Carlson, *Aesthetics and the Environment* (London, 2000), pp. 6 & 50.

6. Stephen Kaplan, 'Perception and landscape: conceptions and misconceptions', in Jack Nasar (ed), *Environmental Aesthetics: Theory, Research and Applications* (Cambridge, 1988), p. 45.

7. Arnold Berleant, *The Aesthetics of Environment* (Philadelphia PA, 1992), pp. 16, 19 & 23.

8. Brady, op. cit., pp. 106 & 120.

9. Jerome Stolnitz, *Aesthetics and the Philosophy of Art Criticism: a Critical Introduction* (Boston MA, 1960), pp. 35, 36 & 52.

10. Brady, op. cit., p. 13.

11. Carlson, op. cit., pp. xix & 50.

12. John Dewey, *Art as Experience* (New York, 1934), p. 7.

13. Arnold Berleant, 'The Experience and Criticism of Art', *Sarah Lawrence Journal* (Winter 1967), 55–64.

14. Berleant 1992, op. cit., pp. 27 & 131.

15. Mara Miller, *The Garden as an Art* (Albany NY, 1993), p. 180; she provided her detailed critique of disinterestedness on pp. 93-105.

16   James Gibson, *The Ecological Approach to Visual Perception* (Boston MA, 1979), p. 63.

17   Berleant 1992, op. cit., p. 10.

18   Ibid, pp. 4, 7-8, 14, 16, 26 & 150.

19   Brady, op. cit., pp. 9 & 13.

20   Ibid., pp. 106 & 121.

21   David Cooper, *A Philosophy of Gardens* (Oxford, 2006), p. 142.

22   Stolnitz, op. cit., pp. 36 & 53.

23   Carlson, op. cit., pp. xix & 6.

24   Brady, op. cit., p. 94.

25   Stolnitz, op. cit., p. 421.

26   Ibid., pp. 23 & 35.

27   Berleant 1992, op. cit., pp. 4 & 10.

28   Brady op. cit., pp. 191, 203 & 205.

29   Carlson, op. cit., pp. 9 & 131.

30   Brady, op. cit., pp. 112 & 229-30.

31   Jonathan Maskit, 'On Universalism and Cultural Historicism in Environmental Aesthetics', in Martin Drenthen & Jozef Keulartz (eds), *Environmental Aesthetics* (New York, 2014), 41-58, pp. 56 & 58.

32   Arnold Berleant, 'Reconsidering Scenic Beauty', *Environmental Values*, 19:3 (August 2010), 335-350.

Figure 10.1 *Derwent Water in the English Lake District, a place well known to Ronald Hepburn, the father of modern environmental aesthetics.*

CHAPTER 11

SATISFACTIONS

The philosophers have particular ways of conceptualising the 'aesthetic', sets of rules for deciding which experiences could qualify as 'aesthetic', and many models for how to explain the aesthetic experience. Unhappily, most seem to disagree with their peers in numerous important respects. Meanwhile, from a more hands-on point of view, one notes that aesthetics, although given status by being a branch of philosophy, is just one among several forms of satisfaction to be derived from landscape. Some philosophers do rightly warn: 'the significance of the garden cannot be restricted to the domain of the aesthetic.'[1]

The gentle exercise of one's senses can give a quiet sense of temporarily passing out of this world into one of tranquility and well-being. The warm and comfortable feeling accompanying an appreciation of beauty can be recognised as emotional. The sublime is rather different – still emotional but more the sort of surprised feeling when realizing that you have been challenged, or have expanded your awareness or understanding. The outdoors can give opportunities for recreation in which the challenge of the exercise itself gives rewards, though it may be carried out in beautiful surroundings; and there are several further forms of appreciation.

This Chapter therefore looks at a wider topic than environmental aesthetics – some of these satisfactions – and then ends by suggesting some features of a practical approach to the recognition of and planning for them.

Sensual pleasure

I had guests to stay and went for a walk with them over the fields. One particular patch is a wet area where common spotted orchids* were to be seen just above the ragged robin* and meadowsweet*. It was a warm day, and on climbing the bank above this scene we sat down on the ancient grassland which gave a soft and springy landing. Before long we lay back and closed our eyes, opening ourselves to the warmth of the sun. It was a vacant pleasure to think of nothing except the thought that we were doing nothing. A dog could be heard barking at some distance,

---

* UK common names: common spotted orchid (*Dactylorhiza fuchsii*); ragged robin (*Lychnis flos-cuculi*); meadowsweet (*Filipendula ulmaria*).

and a few insects buzzed past, but above all it was comfortable being gently irradiated. We lay there without speaking for maybe five or ten minutes until the grass started to turn prickly and we felt guilty at doing nothing. Time to press on!

Formalism

David Cooper reminds us of Merleau-Ponty's observation that a first impression yields the 'atmosphere' or 'style' of a place, a quality that recedes once we pay closer attention to what is being experienced.[2] Ronald Hepburn advised that landscape appreciation should recognise both 'a sensuous component and a thought-component', the one immediate, the other bringing analogies to mind.[3] Stephen Kaplan hypothesised that 'a rapid, unconscious type of cognition may precede certain affective judgments'.[4] Under 'Beauty' below we will mention the first 'split-second impression' of a view.

Why some configurations of walls, paths, trees and views are instantly beautiful is a never-ending quest in art and photography. It is much easier to analyse what makes a good view than to explain why it does. Most attempts, though, agree that the key is composition, and not the content. Books explaining the principles of composition for 'history painting' (the most respected form of art) were found from the seventeenth century, and the forms in the landscape that

Figure 11.1 *William Gilpin's etching of Goodriche Castle, Herefordshire, above the River Wye: it is deliberately crude, as he was discussing composition, not content.*

Figure 11.2 *Wimpole Hall, Cambridgeshire: a Brown landscape of rolling grassland down to water and rising again to loose woodland and a folly.*

would make satisfactory pictures were carefully analysed in the late eighteenth century by William Gilpin and the Picturesque theorists in England (fig. 11.1). This picturesque way of seeing has not expired, but lives on as 'significant form', as described by the twentieth-century art critic, Clive Bell, and more generally as 'formalism' by observers of the phenomenon such as Jerome Stolnitz.[5]

A painting or a photograph, analysed dispassionately, displays merely an assemblage of lines, shapes, colours, tones and textures. These elements will have been organised or composed according to a number of principles such as balance, proportion, contrast, emphasis, movement, pattern, rhythm, unity, variety and so forth to suggest forms, masses and spaces. A strong but simple composition of shapes (irrespective of what they actually are), underlying colours, and contrasts between light and dark, will strike the eye, draw the viewer into the painting and direct attention to the principal feature. For whatever psychological reason, this will cause the formalist to experience what Gilpin called 'beauty' and Bell called 'aesthetic emotion'.

Considering views in the real three-dimensional world, and still concentrating on formalism, rather than content or idea, the

Formalism

Figure 11.3 *A beautiful formal garden – the Victorian parterre at Trentham revived in the 2000s with planting by Tom Stuart-Smith.*

compositional elements and the composition can likewise be analysed, the difference being that they don't *suggest* forms, masses and spaces – they *are* them. The psychological impression of formal beauty is the consequence of composition, whether serendipitous or intended. This is as true for views of Capability Brown parks when open parkland spreads between ancient clumps on knolls and loses itself in swells and hills topped by woods in the distance (fig. 11.2), and architectural gardens of steps and walls, rectangular flower beds, topiary and urns, fountain and the blue distance over a parapet, as it is for fine art (fig. 11.3).

The elements and the principles of composition in modern landscape design are taught as structure, line, proportion, solids, space, texture, colour and unity, all confirming that the formalism continues to have a powerful role in landscape aesthetics. In this field, the effects of time need to be contemplated as well. Another obvious difference from, say, painting is that the visitor to a garden moves around it. This is a factor in the appreciation of sculpture too, which suggests that movement does not alter the nature of the appreciation though it does unfold multiple potential viewpoints. In practice, gardens will have a limited number worth attention, in part because past designers have often organised gardens that way.

One might be forgiven for thinking, from the rapid impression of formalist qualities, that they are instantaneous. The 'direct reality' model of perception superficially fits the experience of those who have sensed them. On the other hand, cognitive scientists research cognitive processing speed, and would argue that perception may be rapid but it is not immediate.

One psychologist, Robert Zajonc, suggested that 'affect', the experience of feeling or emotion, can give rise to an instinctual reaction taking place before cognitive processes take hold. He postulated that this reaction is primary for human beings and other higher animals. His 'affective primacy hypothesis' obviously runs close to formalism in aesthetics. However, one needs to be cautious because this science is certainly not accepted throughout his profession.

So whilst the perception of formal beauty may be an emotional response, and whilst it is certainly rapid, we are not a great deal wiser than Clive Bell, who thought it happens through 'unknown and mysterious laws'. Of course formal beauty is just the first wave of the impressions that come to mind — the others concern content and meaning giving beauty of a maturer kind — but it has been observed that without a strong and felicitous composition a picture or a landscape view will never capture the viewer's appreciative attention.

Beauty

For this author, at any rate, the appreciation of beauty begins with the split-second initial impression, with the scene caught as if it were a 3-D snapshot. Other senses come into play — the sun, the cold, the wind, the smell of the air — when the scene before you becomes more cinematic as you move. It can be almost instantaneously identified as a place visited before. Remarkably, you do not have to see it as before: the viewpoint could be different, the seasonal dress of the landscape is altered, or you are looking at a postcard of a place you know, or you are regarding an actual scene which you have previously noticed in a brochure or on the Internet — never mind, the place is the same one. Rarely is it so unrecognisable that it cannot be identified if indeed it is that place, though the puzzling may take time. If it is not, you are left with a fresh memory.

There are pleasures in these encounters, for the fresh impact on first sight can be memorable because it is emotional, so that it may become lodged in memory, and whenever the place is mentioned that impression is recalled. This may not be just the visual scene; the circumstances may be memorable with it, including, say, that you were cold and it was raining, or coming across the scene suddenly when rounding a corner, or who you were with at the time.

If this place is familiar, or even just vaguely remembered, it is like an old friend. You can enjoy the gentle variations as the breeze disturbs the branches, and patches of sunlight come and go. You smile gently, nod your head in satisfaction, and then seek out different viewpoints where you can repeat this simple but pleasurable act of reacquaintance.

If you have not been there before, you at least know that you like that sort of landscape, and may find that it compares well, or exceeds, your other good examples. In that case you will probably want to spend more time examining it, picking out the outstanding features, and taking photographs to show its best aspects. It thereby becomes familiar, part of your stock of favoured places.

You might seek some clarifications, for example how has the place changed, and is it giving as strong an impression as last time? There may be recollection of its presently unseen features and uses, so where must they be in the view? You may find a desire to approach, or to recall what others have said about it, and you may say something about it yourself.

Why do you like these landscapes? They do not have to be scenes of great grandeur — they could be marshes or glades in a forest. Landscapes evoke a powerful emotional response because they are physical manifestations of cherished ideas. We take pleasure in recognising familiar places, and are excited by new ones, because they reaffirm our view of how parts of the world ought to be. Such notions are dearly held, and are based ultimately on congenial ideas and their signs. It is this that gives pleasurable emotions in consequence. Beauty in this sense is not received from the object itself, but is everything to do with the pleasing sensations they provoke in the mind. Dewey quoted Santayana much: 'value lies in meaning, not in substance; *in the ideal which things approach*, not in the energy which they embody'.[6]

Figure 11.4 *'Walhalla bei Donaustauf'*; Valhalla, near Regensburg, Bavaria, in a print of c.1840.

The sublime

Having written about eighteenth-century aesthetics in *Georgian Gardens: The Reign of Nature* (1983), and experienced for myself the strange but fascinating pleasures of the sublime, supposedly induced by unknowability, vastness, horror and terror, I was intrigued to note a recent proposal for its rehabilitation in modern environmental aesthetics.

This section commences with a moment – not quite life-changing, but which has stuck in memory – which I would class as 'sublime'. A German friend asked whether I wanted to go and see Valhalla. I thought this was pretty odd, for in Norse mythology, I was thinking, Valhalla was a vast hall in Asgard, where Odin received those who had died in combat, and which was in the plot of Richard Wagner's *Das Rheingold*. But I agreed, and on the way a large white temple atop some hills flanking the Danube was pointed out (fig. 11.4). The footpath from the car park had steps and handrails, and it was a long haul up the hill. It was late in the day and I doubted whether we would get there before dusk. There were no visitors apart from our small group and the journey somehow felt illicit, as if we really ought not to be there.

We arrived at the rear of the temple and I began to appreciate the truly massive scale of the building. When walking down the side to the front I could see enough of the view – impressive, but not totally exceptional – and the vast flights of steps falling dangerously one below another down the hillside in the direction of the river. Here my host explained that Valhalla is a hall of fame for distinguished people in the German-speaking world. It was conceived in 1807 by Crown Prince Ludwig of Bavaria, a medieval enthusiast and a strong nationalist. Inside were plaques and busts of German heroes covering 2,000 years of history, and these were still being added to, but nowadays very selectively and non-contentiously.

It was a strange sensation to be in the near presence of these few hundred souls, while standing alone (at least I was unaware of the others) on these steps, and floating above the fading valley. The idea behind the place was so unexpected, and its manifestation so overwhelming, that I could not help wondering. I began to consider the fragmentation of the German-speaking countries, and their achievements, and to think myself into feeling the pride of a German nationalist. I knew what it was to feel the bond with one's own people, one's own cultural heritage. If I had been German, I would have felt very connected at that moment.

And then, coming off my cloud, the warning that German nationalism gave to all nationalisms in the first half of the twentieth century intruded. I wondered whether modern Germans are proud of the place, or embarrassed, or simply regard it as curious historical monument. I hoped they would be proud, to feel the same way as I do as an Englishman about being English, though not necessarily with the aid of a Valhalla. Was this monument, a testimony of thinking nearly two centuries ago, actually an impediment? Of course I did not wish to offend any sensitivities, but I had a better grasp of the questions. Then it was time to return down the path in the dark.

Looking back, I felt that the moment was certainly emotional, though not of the primarily pleasurable kind from beauty, but from the agreeableness and depth of my sudden speculations, heightened by their somewhat surreal setting. Several of the theories on the sublime emphasise the emotion of terror induced by immensity or danger, but in this case, despite the precipitousness of the steps, I was not terrified, or cowed by the immensity of the place. Instead it was pleasurable and memorable by virtue of the unexpected discovery of some of my own feelings and sympathies. Immensity and terror were stage props, but not the opera's plot.

A proportion of us is susceptible to experiences of this nature, though they are difficult to describe or analyse. The heightened consciousness and loss of self noted as 'aesthetic experience' and 'flow activity' in Chapter 4 seem connected. The sublime response likewise has much in common with, and indeed may be what one means as, the ecstatic state when consciousness of an object is so overpowering that the subject dissolves or merges into it.

Such intense elation may be given to only a few of us, but one friend says that he has experienced the heightened state during a service in a Greek Orthodox church, on an occasion when he was picked out by a shaft of evening sunlight. On other occasions when playing in a band the music seemed to have a life of its own, when he was lifted to becoming almost an observer, though of course he was one of those making it. That sounds like what I recognise as 'flow activity'.

Looking at explanations from history, Edmund Burke in 1757 classed the sublime as an emotion, generated by 'whatever is fitted in any sort to excite the ideas of pain and danger … Whatever is in any sort terrible',[7] giving a long list including vastness, obscurity, horror and terror. Many older theories emphasized the qualities of the view itself. On the other hand, Kant argued that the true seat of the sublime is in the mind.

It may be set off by an apprehension of limitlessness (fig. 11.5), so that the human is humbled and powerless, but sublimity 'is not contained in anything in nature, but only in the mind'.[8] Many subsequent authors have pointed to the sense of wonder, and feelings of awe. These can be triggered by an expansion of one's awareness or understanding through conceptual breakthroughs, or by a realisation of the vastness of space and time.

Literature (the art form in question when the sublime was first described by Longinus in Roman times) can provoke such striking thoughts and mental images that the reader is transported. One hears of people encountering paintings in an unusually vivid way, becoming fully immersed in the subject matter and even suffering from extreme emotion, dizziness and hallucinations. Was not Stolnitz referring to experiences of this kind (maybe not so extreme) when he described the 'aesthetic experience' (see Chapter 4 – 'An aesthetic experience')?

In landscape terms one hears of the uplifting feeling of being able to forget the self to become a speck of consciousness in the vastness

Figure 11.5 *A sublime experience: the famous 'Wanderer above the Sea of Fog' (1818) by Caspar David Friedrich.*

of the universe. Philosophers usually write *about* sublimity, and seldom *of* it, but a passage from the British writer, Sara Maitland, reproduced in a chapter by John Wylie on phenomenology provides a vivid description:

> I sat on a rock ... It was so wild and so empty and so free. Quite suddenly and unexpectedly, I slipped a gear, or something like that. There was not me and the landscape, but a kind of oneness: a connection as though my skin had been blown off ... I felt absolutely connected to everything. It was very brief, but it was a total moment.[9]

Sublime experiences cannot be conjured up at will: no one can say 'I am going to have a sublime experience today'. They catch you unawares, and happen only infrequently. If I went to Walhalla again, I would not have at all the same experience. I would greet it as an old friend, but there would be little discovery, and I would not be able to recapture the sublime experience.

Most of the aesthetic theory concerning the sublime in the eighteenth century was in terms of nature. This may have been because many great unknowns, unfathomable mysteries, and the immensity of the universe's dimensions and distances were being glimpsed against the backdrop of experiences in nature. The scope for contemplating nature in a metaphysical way has lessened slightly with modern knowledge in physics and other sciences, whilst inexpensive travel has opened formerly mysterious places to the tourist. Yet ecstasy, or the sublime, in nature has not been reduced to irrelevance, and meanwhile it continues undiminished through literature and the arts.

A topic like the sublime, though, with its indefinite causes and boundaries, and mystical tinge, tends to be skirted around by recent philosophers. Berleant regarded it as being covered adequately by his engagement theory, while Carlson disposed of the sublime in three pages. Against this, Brady has written a whole book on the subject, seeking 'something we can call a contemporary experience of the sublime', which she termed 'the environmental sublime'. In her non-cognitive view, the sublime is reserved exclusively to encounters with nature. Natural objects 'had a causal role' in the 'sublime response', and are not merely triggers for a cognitive process. Literature and music may have 'metaphysical depth' and profundity, but the arts cannot evoke an authentic sublime response.

In Brady's scheme, natural objects in a place of potential sublimity would 'engage the mental powers', and the mixed emotions 'of being overwhelmed and anxious, combined with excitement and pleasure', would evoke feelings of sublimity. Brady's approach, in identifying the primary cause of sublimity as being in the object itself rather than the mind, cannot be reconciled to the account given above. One point of convergence, though, concerns the imagination being 'expanded and invigorated as it tries to cope with greatness', and is a recognisable theme amongst writers on the subject.[10]

Despite the opinion of Brady, this author sees the sublime as an uncommon experience, but may be stimulated by the unfamiliar or extraordinary when it has the power to confound one's expectations or preconceptions, or stretch one's experience, and the mind is released. The sublime may reveal itself elsewhere than in nature, for example in poetry and literature. Those who have undergone this experience find it to be unplanned, personal, transitory and unlike the everyday.

Designed landscapes

This author was once the Inspector at English Heritage responsible for the *Register of Parks and Gardens of Special Historic Interest*, and devised the criteria for grading parks and gardens, adapted from those for the List of Historic Buildings. Several criteria were more-or-less factual, being related to the date of the design (a proxy for rarity), condition, influence on the development of taste, associations with significant historical events or persons and being a representative example of the type of design. Those were fairly easy to assess, given enough research.

However, there were also criteria on design quality. Hence the *Register* would include, for example: 'The best parks and gardens laid out between 1820 and 1880 which are in good or fair condition and of aesthetic merit'. It was a pleasant job, but not so easy when any of my judgements might be tested at public inquiry. The adjective 'best' was altered to the less demanding 'of importance' some years after I left.

Several appreciations recurred on visits. Some were to derelict gardens, overgrown and confused (fig. 11.6). I always did some preparation, even if it was just obtaining a photocopy of an old Ordnance Survey map (the old ones gave so much more information – you can

Figure 11.6 *Osmaston, Derbyshire, quarry garden: a long-abandoned fernery but the features discernible.*

almost 'read' the landscape from the map). However, there have often been unplanned events in derelict gardens, such as agricultural or forestry routes opened across former lawns, now invaded by trees. Disorientation follows as views will have been blocked and features like hedges may have gone. Waterworks may be dry. The inspector becomes a detective inspector. Imagination and interpretation are necessary. There are the surprises of finding features not shown on maps and the odd specimen tree, and the pathos of collapsed greenhouses and grottos. Walking over and over, identifying past features, tracing their continuation and corners through the brambles and undergrowth, and testing one's theories of what an historian might expect, slowly brings order out of chaos. Such an experience cannot be called aesthetic, but there is a considerable satisfaction in making sense out of such corrupted designs with minimal materials.

The first impressions of a well-kept garden were completely different (fig. 11.7). One, indeed, is the evident signs of care – the grand and precisely-clipped hedge, the grass mown to a carpet, the paths smooth and clean, the delightful and colourful denizens of the herbaceous border swelling up and billowing out, the garden's far reaches where one is not sure whether the gardener or his plants are in control. The gardener's craft presents these and many other things to view, and

Figure 11.7 *Eaton Hall, Cheshire: immaculately kept garden, as befits a ducal residence.*

Figure 11.8 *Westwell Manor, Oxfordshire, spiral garden; an agreeable scene is appreciated almost instantaneously.*

the garden becomes a stage for the small events that are the life of the garden. The exquisite whiffs from the winter daphne in February, the orange azalea perfuming the air around in the late afternoon, the birdsong in May in the evening and the bumble bees in the lavender in June. The skill and labour is appreciated for its enabling of these. I have often mused over whether the definition of gardening might be selection from the complexity and roughness of nature to a state in which we humans can most comfortably enjoy it.

The most obviously aesthetic satisfaction, the visual, impresses the visitor seemingly instantaneously. One glance tells you that a view between topiary and under archways is intriguing (fig. 11.8), that the cedar tree is majestic, that the ripple and reflections in the water are enlivening, that the peony is wonderful in form and colour. Yet these attributes are fickle; they can be extinguished in a trice when the sun goes behind a cloud, so no longer illuminates the limestone walls; the flowers on the amelanchier tree are blown away in a few minutes by a wet wind; the wind gets up, turning the water into a choppy sea. Photographers will stand in one place for a considerable time until the sun reappears in order to capture a perfect moment, something to remember.

Designed landscapes may invoke, test and intensify pre-formed thoughts of a philosophical nature and thus be a considerable aid to developing a practical ethic of landscape care and treatment. In this sense gardens could be classed as 'art'.[11] By composing and detailing in accord with their own feelings landscape designers silently embody the ideological and emotional messages of their time in their work. It is important for them not to be obsessed with the meaning of their own work, as argued in Chapter 4, 'The Sociology of Criticism'. They should preferably work with principles (e.g. sustainability) but that is part of the context, rather than the meaning, the distinction being discussed below. It is up to clients to write the brief and 'consumers' – visitors, critics and historians – to picture designs in the right light, notice style and to point out the wider meanings. Whatever the wider motives of a designer, visitors cannot be presumed to appreciate a garden in the way that a designer intended. Often the pleasanter viewpoints in older gardens have come about accidentally, for example.

Turning to assessments of aesthetic value, having recourse to one's own experience is of only limited use, as too many forms of appreciation are at work for the mind to disaggregate them clearly. Once one starts to think about it, the experience is lost in reflection and theory. Ronald Hepburn, an aesthete as well as an aesthetician, asked:

> What is it to appreciate a landscape aesthetically? As several recent writers have claimed, it may be an experience within which many layers can be distinguished. The purely sensory component – colours, shapes, sounds, tactile sensations, smells – seldom if ever exists on its own, for we know that the area of blue to be the blue of the sky, that broken disc to be a reflection, in nearly still water, of the moon, that object by the dried-up lake to be the skull of a sheep or goat. We conceptualise, we recognise, we add context, background, seek out formal relationships – reflectively.[12]

Subjective assessments concern style, fitness, meaning, and other qualitative assessments. They are accompanied by appreciation of achievement, for which a sense of the physical and political context, levels of difficulty, and myriad constraints with which a designer has had to grapple, is needed. The process must, of course, be cognitive. Assessment and reassessment take time: it may take several encounters before the most profound experience is gained. Many visitors share the observation that quite different experiences can be obtained from separate visits some years apart to the same place. Over an extended timescale, the reputations of designers may fluctuate between different generations.[13]

The viewer's experience and skill is also worth emphasising. As Hepburn implied, if the person attempting a judgement has no training or experience, the full significance will elude him, and nothing can be learned. Stolnitz emphasised 'relevant preparation' and gave considerable space to the question of what thoughts and knowledge would be pertinent to aesthetic appreciation.

He said nothing about gardens, but he did not neglect nature. He considered that: 'no assertion that art is aesthetically superior to nature, or vice-versa, is true universally and in all respects ... Satisfaction can be found in both'. With that thought in mind, we might presume that his discussion of the relevance of knowledge to the appreciation of art objects would apply also to designed landscapes. In brief, he set three conditions: it must not weaken or destroy aesthetic attention to the object; it must concern the meaning of the object; and it must enhance the quality and significance of the immediate emotional response.[14]

Following his line of thought, the following would be relevant in gardens: the physical site (topography, water, geology and soil); the owner's wishes; the designer's contribution; the garden's layout and organisation; associations with events that shaped the garden; and (because the visitor explores) a knowledge of what is beyond the immediate view and where things lead. Irrelevant matters would include: the cost of making it, the names of the owner and designer, their biographies, plant names, technical terms, associations that concern extraneous events, imaginative flights of fancy, and beliefs and prejudices about style and personalities.

Many such thoughts may be irrelevant to an *aesthetic* appreciation, but the visitor may still consider them relevant to an *historical* and *cultural* appreciation of the garden's significance. There may have been difficult demands imposed on a garden's design by the client's wishes to achieve a minimal budget, his liking for tennis, and the wish to allow the cars to reach right up to the house. Physical constraints might include climate, slope and property boundaries. The designer may have had to comply with ethical and legal considerations. The historian will muse on the garden's story, date and place in garden history, and on possible comparators. He will bring with him his knowledge of garden history and of the language of historical styles. The range of contextual information that may assist in gauging the achievement that the garden represents may thus be wide.

Armed with all this information, the historian and critic can start to interpret the scene before them. This has two aspects: first the quality of the design, then the meaning, with both leading to an overall assessment of significance. The quality of the design is not the same as the initial impact of a beautiful scene which is an emotional response from its formalist qualities. Quality is reached by careful reflection and stems from appreciation.

The question arises: against what measure can the quality of a garden's composition and content be judged? Some absolute standard is difficult to imagine, but it can be compared to its contemporaries, and can be judged within that context. This does require a switch into another form of expression, in this case the vocabulary of style.[15] Stylistic analysis is an acknowledged skill among art historians, and the principles are equally valid in gardens. Garden designers experimented with forms that expressed the theoretical aims of the fashion at the time. Certain characteristics came to be associated with those ideas, and designers made them more recognisable and distinct (fig. 11.9). In this way style was born. The forms being characteristic, the knowledgeable eye can attribute a design to its period, design tradition and perhaps an individual designer. A garden can be read in

Figure 11.9 *Style: William Sawrey Gilpin explains how to turn this scene with Brownian clumps into one in the Picturesque style by altering the shape and variety of the plantations to give a more natural effect.*

this way even if nothing concrete is known about its history. This skill requires only what can be seen, and the contextual knowledge of the garden history and style of the period.

One is looking for a satisfying match between place, the maker's intentions and execution in the context just elucidated. So how typical or unusual is the garden? Was it a run-of-the mill creation, or was it able to exploit the topography and its water in a creative or innovative way? Could you say the design has masterstrokes? Was the design an intelligent match to the potential of the place? Is there a rightness or fitness about them, so that if you were living at the time the result would seem obvious or inevitable? Does the design sit well and create a powerful sense of place? Does the design express the underlying ideas of the time with clarity? Or are there incongruities of scale, or choices in layout that could have been improved to good effect? Such questioning shapes arguments on the quality of the design.

Appreciating the difficulties that the designer faced in order to achieve the slickness, economy or ingenuity of the solution leads to a judgement of the cleverness of the layout. This satisfaction can be derived from all areas of human endeavour, from elegant chess solutions to designing bridges. This more intellectual form of satisfaction does neither employ the picturesque eye, nor the historian's capability in analysing form and style, but calls upon several other mental capacities (knowledge, imagination, judgement) in order to understand significance and meaning.

This section considers the narrow topic of appreciating historic gardens and commenced with the question of how to identify the 'best' parks and gardens 'of aesthetic merit' within their period, and we are now in a position to offer some thoughts. By way of preface, the experience subjectively remains whole and undivided, and an explanation has to be theoretical rather than empirical. The theory has allowed the whole experience to be broken down into forms of appreciation. First, the picturesque or formalist response is the immediate reaction upon seeing the garden. This is an emotional, fleeting, response that takes place before the intellect recognizes the context of the garden's creation. When this does take place the significance of the garden can deepen the aesthetic response as the mind starts to work out meanings and messages, as expanded upon below. Hence judging the aesthetic and historical significance of historic gardens, at least, can be assisted by several rational arguments, and is more than just a matter of whether the assessor likes the place.

The meaning of gardens

Having been the focus of eighteenth-century discussions of beauty, landscapes and gardens escaped the attention of aestheticians for much of the twentieth century. Those philosophers who bemoaned this towards the end of the century gave several reasons, but the common theme was a perception that 'people no longer "make statements" in the medium of gardening, so that in effect the art of the garden is "dead", the corpse of a once live tradition'.[16]

Nevertheless, gardens retain the potential to make statements. Instead of reading gardens just in their own right, a knowledge of the history and design intent adds another level of meaning. Historians and critics know that designs speak of the culture from which they sprang. The practice of composition points to the temper of the period, and, seen as signs and metaphors, the details may signify the more important underlying imperatives, opportunities, ideals and values. The ultimate object of all design is to translate values into fabric. Indeed, in favourable circumstances, landscape design can transcend the constraints of the brief in ways that architects can only dream about, and can express values more directly and with less equivocation or compromise.

Some gardens are designed to convey messages to those who view or walk through them. One philosopher has commented that: 'gardens play an important symbolic role, serving as a metaphor for the ideal human life and for relations between human beings ... and the divine order'. This way of expressing the point may suggest that the garden or wilderness is the active agent, though. Landscapes do not pop up to represent ideas in the head; it is the mind that seeks actual form in order to illustrate ideas already there and selects or creates a landscape to express them.

Decoding the design by seeing how the idea is expressed, and enlarging upon its significance in one's mind, encourages the observer to thought and experiment. Viewing a garden can prompt various trains of thought – personal as well as cultural associations come into play here. It can contribute to insights into the nature and role of humanity in relation to nature. It may uplift the viewer's notions of identity. There have been successful examples of memorials (fig. 11.10) which serve to stir painful memories, leading to the release of emotion,[17] or at least to contemplation.[18]

In order for gardens, especially, to be promoted to the front ranks of aesthetics again a new sense of the importance of meanings

Figure 11.10 *Landscape of emotion: Vietnam Veterans Memorial in Washington DC, a metaphorical scar on the American psyche.*

needed to be recovered. 'Aesthetic attitude theory' was directed at individuals and their aesthetic encounters. Whilst Stolnitz said little about the outcomes, it will be remembered that Beardsley envisaged 'active discovery' in the making of connections and imaginative engagement. Art refers to important moral acts from history, personal values, a schema for beauty, or some other cherished idea. The meaning is expressed by content, signs, text, or some other device that can carry that meaning. Sometimes the meaning will be clear to the observer, sometimes it needs to be interpreted. Some will strike the observer forcibly and change their world (see Chapter 4 – 'Aesthetic experiences').

Gardens are no different from this general description of art in revealing to appreciators their deeply-held ideas. They may thus be retrieved as 'art' through the revelation of older embodied meanings and the introduction of new ones. The pleasure of discovering and savouring meaning is not to be sought in the composition and features of gardens themselves but in the 'active discovery' they occasion. The visitor should be privately attuned to their statements, echoes, resonances, reminders and barely-perceptible whispers.

Jerome Stolnitz and afterwards Mara Miller have pointed out that the sister art in this respect is often literature:

> The literary evidence suggests that gardens also play an important symbolic role, serving as a metaphor for the ideal human life and for relations between human beings, the state or community, and divinity or the divine order. Chief amongst these, of course, have been the Garden of Eden and Paradise of the Bible and the Qu'ran, the Song of Songs, the Persian *Gulistan* or Rose Garden of Sa'di, and *The Secret Garden of the Kabbalah*.[19]

John Dixon Hunt expanded greatly, and with overwhelming scholarship, on this theme in *Greater Perfections* (1998). The argument continued with 'representations', the 'presentation over again in garden terms of a whole range of other cultural and natural elements and occurrences'. This was not confined to simple copying, as the emphasis would be on provoking the imagination and thereby the idea.[20]

David Cooper, conscious of Zen traditions as well as Western ones, went further in proposing a key to the appreciation of gardens, mostly of the 'homely' sort. It was a sensibility towards 'experiencing things "just as they are", a sense that "nothing has been hidden" from one ... sense of intimacy with them ...', one that promotes care, hope, humility, and above all, serenity. The garden could then be seen as

> ... an epiphany – a symbol, in the Romantic sense – of the relation between the source of the world and ourselves. It is ... peculiarly 'appropriate' to this relation, which is why, over the centuries, paintings of or poems about gardens have exploited the symbolism of the garden and themselves served as vehicles for evoking the sensibility of which I have spoken, and it is the reason, more importantly, why I am also suggesting that in this epiphany the meaning of The Garden, its deep significance for people, is located.[21]

Both these authors tend to see gardens through the eyes of the visitor, interpreting the garden elements encountered as signs towards internal ideas. While these interpretations may have been intended, or they may be fortuitous, the designer will have sought to incorporate messages in order to express or illustrate his own ideas. If gardens are an expression of ideas, can they be seen as both material and conceptual art?

Cooper's 'relation between the source of the world and ourselves' can be expanded upon, for in contemplating gardens we can look backwards and forwards at the same time. Cultural landscapes and productive gardens have meaning in that they show us how humans and nature *have been* and *are* co-existent, or co-dependant. The freedom from necessity and functionality in pleasure gardens and public spaces allows an exploration and demonstration of how the human *could* or *should* relate to nature, in several ways. It thus leaves space for imagination and the epiphanies that generate the meanings of great gardens, and that is why they can be great art.

Assessing aesthetic value

This chapter has concerned 'satisfactions', a deliberately broad term that encompasses everyone's preferences in landscape design, urbanism and countryside planning. It is a more pragmatic way to approach the emotional and intellectual pleasures of landscape and garden than confining them to just the aesthetic as understood through philosophy. One philosopher of everyday aesthetics has rued this past emphasis upon the 'aesthetic attitude':

> One problem is the impoverishment of our aesthetic life. By imposing from the outset a certain artistic criterion on a landscape to assess its aesthetic worth, we are closing our mind to other kinds of aesthetic values which may not fit the criteria.[22]

Landscape aesthetics may be expanding its purview. Emily Brady has written about the sublime. Others like Allen Carlson write about the pleasures of the wilderness and nature, and yet others about those from gardens.[23] There are admirers of snowscapes, marshes and urban plots. It is gradually becoming recognised that there are many diverse forms of sensory and mental satisfaction for the human when engaging with the landscape.

Many possible satisfactions exist, some said to be objective, some subjective. Some are said to be 'affective', giving emotional pleasure, some are clearly cognitive, giving intellectual satisfaction. The less comprehensible forms of satisfaction are, ironically, those given most attention by philosophers. That is because they are portrayed as instantaneous, a 'visceral' response, part of our animal matter, and not open to rational discussion. Beauty and sublimity are the chief pleasures here. Edmund Burke saw that beauty 'no creature of our reason, since it strikes us without any reference to use', and that it was akin to the equally inexplicable 'passions' of terror, pain, pleasure and love.[24] In the twentieth century philosophers attempted to isolate the impact of 'significant form' from the swirl of other responses in order to receive the unmediated instantaneous impact of formalistic beauty. However, no theoretical argumentation has quite solved the conundrum of employing subjective appreciation of some quality in order to define it objectively.

When reading the literature since the eighteenth century, one finds shelf upon shelf of aesthetic theories, with literally scores on offer. Most treat beauty in the landscape and garden as a single or maybe twin pleasure, and only a few venture beyond a theory of how it affects the human to one of why it does. Twentieth century offers on 'why?' include those from Brenda Colvin and Aldo Leopold who thought that beauty was the perception of harmony, and this became influential amongst advocates for nature. Jay Appleton proposed an evolutionary basis for landscape preferences, though support for this dwindled over time. As the proposed causes of beauty come and go, one has to conclude that a single and final explanation remains just beyond our finger-tips.

Attempts at tracing one's own subjective responses can be tried, but have their limits in disassociating the layers within them. At that point one realises that they are merging and mingling with preconceptions of how one ought to respond, in other words one's own theory of how and why pleasure is felt. And theories differ between cultures, some not understanding beauty or enjoying satisfactions in the same terms as Western ones with its particular cultural baggage, and vice-versa.[25] Hence it cannot be assumed that the 'picturesque eye' or 'aesthetic attitude' is an experience recognised across all cultures. Furthermore significant differences in 'perceptual lenses' even within a society that one might have assumed was relatively unified culturally are apparent.[26]

If aesthetic appreciation is a mental event or process, surely psychology could be some help in explaining it? Psychological theories class beauty as a form of pleasure, seeing it as a mental state that humans and other animals experience as positive, enjoyable, and worth seeking. Pleasure includes more specific mental states such as happiness, entertainment, enjoyment, euphoria, and ecstasy. Some neuroscientists have attempted to shape a new discipline, 'neuroesthetics', in order to explain and understand the aesthetic experiences at the neurological level. They suggest that the orbito-frontal cortex, right at the front of brain, is where pain/pleasure, and reward/punishment, feelings are processed. This may be where the emotional appraisal of landscape takes place.

There is the alternative ecocentric approach which has, as an article of faith, that the human mind is one and the same with nature. Whatever is in nature will automatically be perceived. Unfortunately, no fully developed aesthetic theory has emerged from 'direct reality' or deep ecology.

Assessing aesthetic value

Nevertheless, the desire to connect the aesthetic appreciation of landscapes to biological diversity persists and can be seen in a review of the extensive literature, going back as far as Jay Appleton, carried out in 2018 and published by the Royal Society. The authors define aesthetics 'by the characteristics of the observed object, that is from the perspective of the "transmitter" ', though they acknowledge 'the link between a transmitter approach (a focus on the intrinsic characteristics of objects) and a receiver approach (a focus on objects as perceived by the observer)'. They had hopes that factors such as diversity and richness might be common factors, but 'most of the approaches developed so far lack operational definitions and metrics to link the aesthetic perception to biological features of natural landscapes'. Frustrated, they argued that it was these studies that were defective, and that 'to become operational, landscape aesthetics needs to produce metrics that can be used in the framework of biodiversity sciences': a 'paradigm shift' needed to occur.[27]

Cherished ecological notions are as hard to abandon as any other. Another example is the concept of 'natural beauty' which limps on well past the time that it made any real sense. Its distinction from the cultural understanding of landscape beauty arises from the use of language and does not represent actual conceptual differences. No cases can be cited when 'the beauty of nature' is not a cultural construct.[28] Superlative natural phenomena are of course deemed to be so by formalistic standards rather than natural scientific ones.

The aesthetic appeal of gardens, in which art and nature operate on each other, is tackled by some philosophers, but the ecocentrists have avoided the matter. Meanwhile their cause is powerful and many modern writers have, as they see it, sought ways to avoid being trammelled by the rules of the 'aesthetic attitude'. Brady commented that:

> Interest has shifted away from this issue, and has been replaced by a study of the nature of aesthetic properties. The current state of affairs, then, is one where an interest in the environment, natural or otherwise, is gaining ground in aesthetics, while interest in aesthetic experience has largely receded from view.[29]

Most writers, falling over backwards to show respect for the biosphere, commonly judge nature 'in its own terms', that is attribute aesthetic value to the content of the view rather than the observer's mind. But it is a topsy-turvy world when the inanimate defines the terms of its own appreciation.

The guardians of our landscapes have not in general been well served by the theorists, but, in this author's view, certain tenets now seem clear. First, there is the question of perception – how we see and assess the world around. The weight of argument in the chapters above directs us toward the cognitive model. Second, there is no escape from satisfactions of all forms being inherently subjective. No non-cognitive or ecocentric theory has been found to re-cast them as objective.

Form, content or the nature of engagement have been put forward in the attempt to define the 'normal' response. Yet the cause of beauty is deeper than those matters – it concerns the idea (remember Geoffrey Jellicoe in Chapter 1). For example, wilderness areas resonate with some deep yearnings among the sophisticated elite. The 'English garden' from William Kent onwards, and the park landscapes of Capability Brown, are widely admired as beautiful, but they were not simply exercises in form. They stem from ideologies of the 'rural' or 'after nature's own manner' and the neo-classical respectively, and forms were found to express the ideas.[30] So it is with all landscape appreciation. An individual already has the idea of an admirable landscape in the mind, and knows it is admirable because it has been adopted as expressing that individual's personal ideology; this is his taste. Seeing another landscape that does that as well or better causes fresh admiration.

Any method of landscape assessment should thus acknowledge the subjectivity of individual judgements. Arguments can of course be put forward that have been carefully considered, tested by others and that command wide respect. These can be supplemented by qualitative research that identifies the aggregated views of residents, farmers and other 'stakeholders' in order to ascertain the nature, number and depth of preferences and tastes. Subjectivity may make the process of assessment complex and long-winded, but it is the only defensible way to proceed. In retrospect, the Countryside Commission was on the right track in the 1980s.

The authors of the ICOMOS-IFLA *Assessment Guide* (2018) had, as practitioners, arrived at very similar conclusions and argued for a phenomenological or 'experiential' approach. A checklist of 'experiential evocations' (awe, wonder, reverence, delight, tranquillity, elation, anxiety, and other forms of response) was provided in order to guide assessors in determining aesthetic properties. There was also a list of relevant cognitive meanings (perception of beauty, sense of spirituality, immersed in solitude, discernment of lushness, and so forth), and one of landscape attributes (landforms, water, scale, colours, smells, presence of animals, agricultural patterns, etc). Assessors used these lists as an aid to fieldwork (fig. 11.11), and these were collated with the views of local experts such as environmental specialists or landscape planners, and community members. Secondary sources that recorded aesthetic value such as art, literature and poetry, provided supporting

Figure 11.11 *Jim Jim Falls in the wet season, Kakadu National Park, Northern Territory, Australia: important for its cave paintings, rock carvings and ecosystems, it is inscribed on the World Heritage List for its superlative natural beauty.*

information. Assessments were also compared to those of similar areas. Finally, a mainly qualitative report was produced by the experts which included suggestions for delineating those areas that met a threshold of whatever form of significance was being investigated.[31]

The usual criticism of subjective methods is that individual assessments will be too chaotic and yet numerous to be handled and analysed in an effective way. The field study described in the ICOMOS-IFLA guide suggested otherwise. In the long term, assessment has come full circle back to the admittedly rather cruder methods of decades ago. Whether the thought that fifty years of theorising has merely returned us to the more pragmatic methods of former days is satisfactory or frustrating will depend on your point of view.

NOTES AND REFERENCES

1. David Cooper, *A Philosophy of Gardens* (Oxford, 2006), p. 4.

2. Ibid., p. 49.

3. Ronald W. Hepburn, 'Trivial and Serious in Aesthetic Appreciation of Nature', in Salim Kemal & Ivan Gaskell (eds), *Landscape, Natural Beauty and the Arts* (Cambridge, 1993), pp. 65-80; p. 66.

4. Stephen Kaplan, 'Aesthetics, Affect, and Cognition: Environmental Preference from an Evolutionary Perspective', *Environment and Behaviour*, 19/1 (1987), 3-32, 3-4, 17 & 26.

5. Jerome Stolnitz, *Aesthetics and the Philosophy of Art Criticism: a Critical Introduction* (Boston MA, 1960), pp. 134-157.

6. John Dewey, *Art as Experience* (New York, 1934), p. 304.

7. Edmund Burke, *On the Sublime and Beautiful* (London, 1757), p. 13.

8. Immanuel Kant, *Critique of Pure Judgement*, trans. Werner S. Pluhar (London, 1987), pp. 28, 264.

9. John Wylie, 'Landscape and phenomenology', in Howard *et al.*, (eds), *The Routledge Companion to Landscape Studies*, 1st edn (Abingdon, Oxon, 2000), pp 54-65; p. 55.

10. Emily Brady, *The Sublime in Modern Philosophy* (Cambridge, 2013), p. 187.

11. Mara Miller, *The Garden as an Art* (Albany NY, 1993), discusses at length the conditions for gardens to be considered as 'art' and 'great art'.

12. Ronald Hepburn, 'Landscape and the Metaphysical Imagination', *Environmental Values* 5:3 (1996), 191.

13. Capability Brown's reputation, for example, has fluctuated wildly. During his lifetime it was enormous, but was to be derided by the next generation, i.e. by Richard Payne Knight and Uvedale Price, on the grounds that his work was not sufficiently picturesque. Further damage to his reputation was wrought in the late nineteenth century by architects, for example Reginald Blomfield. It was only after Dorothy Stroud wrote her book on Brown in the 1950s that his reputation came to be re-established, and by the 1990s he was again recognised as the towering figure of the period 1750-1780, and his landscapes are being keenly conserved.

14 Stolnitz, op. cit., pp. 52-3.

15 Anne Whiston Spirn, *The Language of Landscape* (New Haven CT, 1988) is a very full modern exploration of the language of landscape elements, mainly in the urban context; she found that this language enabled meanings and significance to be better expressed.

16 Cooper, op. cit, p. 9.

17 The wall with the names of all the American servicemen lost in the Vietnam War in the Mall in Washington DC powerfully evokes feelings of loss and the futility of conflict, at least in the breast of anyone who was conscious of the issues at the time.

18 The Kennedy Memorial at Runnymede, though failing to work at the unconscious level as intended by the Jellicoes, the designers, nevertheless possesses the quality of stimulating reflection; it is a pity that the significance of the site and the symbolism of the design is not spelt out for visitors.

19 Miller, op. cit., p. 25.

20 John Dixon Hunt, *Greater Perfections: the Practice of Garden Theory* (Philadelphia PA, 2000), pp. 76 & 84.

21 Cooper, op. cit., p. 150.

22 Yuriko Saito, 'Cultural construction of national landscapes and its consequences: Cases of Japan and the United States', in Sven Arntzen & Emily Brady (eds), *Humans in the Land, the Ethics and Aesthetics of the Cultural Landscape* (Oslo, 2008), pp. 232, 234.

23 Stephanie Ross, *What Gardens Mean* (Chicago IL, 1998), p. 3.

24 Burke, op. cit., p. 95.

25 Juliet Ramsay (ed), *The Aesthetic Value of Landscapes: Background and Assessment Guide*, ICOMOS-IFLA ISCCL Technical Paper Number 2, 2016.

26 Peter Howard, 'Perceptual Lenses', in Howard *et al.*, op. cit., pp. 43-53.

27 Anne-Sophie Tribot, Julie Deter and Nicolas Mouquet, 'Integrating the Aesthetic Value of Landscapes and Biological Diversity', *Proceedings of the Royal Society B: Biological Sciences* 285 (2018, https://doi.org/10.1098/rspb.2018.0971), 2, 3, 4, 7 & 8.

28 Nora Mitchell, *Study on the application of Criterion VII: Considering Superlative Natural Phenomena and Exceptional Natural Beauty within the World Heritage Convention*, IUCN World Heritage Study № 10 (Gland, Switzerland, 2013), pp. 49-51 & 54.

29 Emily Brady, *Aesthetics of the Natural Environment* (Edinburgh, 2003), p. 7.

30 David Jacques, 'William Kent's 'Notion of Gardening': the Context, the Practice and the Posthumous Claims', *Garden History*, 44:1 (Summer 2016), 24-50: 28-38; John Dixon Hunt, 'Brown and Neo-classicism', *Garden History*, 44: Suppl. 1 (Autumn 2016), 18-27;19-21.

31 Ramsay, op. cit., pp. 32-42.

Figure 11.12 *A fiery sunset in the fall at Glacier National Park, Montana. Is there a distinct category of 'natural beauty', or is the liking of scenes such as this one better explained by a taste for superlatively mountainous scenery together with a strong composition and colour content?*

BIBLIOGRAPHY

Addison, Christopher, *Report of the National Park Committee* (the Addison Report) (London: HMSO: 1931).

Allaby, Michael, *Guide to Gaia* (London: Optima, 1989).

American Humanist Association, *The Humanist Manifesto* (Salt Lake City: AHA, 1933).

Appleton, Jay, 'Landscape Evaluation: the Theoretical Vacuum', *Transactions of the Institute of British Geographers,* 66 (1975).

Appleton, Jay, *The Experience of Landscape* (Chichester: Wiley, 1975).

Appleton, Jay, *The Symbolism of Habitat* (Seattle: University of Washington Press, 1990).

Appleyard, Brian, *Brave New Worlds* (London: Harper Collins, 1999).

Barkow, Jerome H., Lena Cosmides & John Tooby, *The Adapted Mind* (New York: Oxford University Press, 1992).

Beardsley, Monroe C., *The Aesthetic Point of View* (Ithaca, NY: Cornell University Press, 1982).

Bell, Clive, *Art* (London: Chatto & Windus, 1914).

Berger, John, *Ways of Seeing* (London: BBC/Pelican, 1972).

Berleant, Arnold, 'The Experience and Criticism of Art', *Sarah Lawrence Journal* (Winter 1967).

Berleant, Arnold, *The Aesthetics of Environment* (Philadelphia: Temple University Press, 1992).

Berleant, Arnold, 'Reconsidering Scenic Beauty', *Environmental Values*, 19.3 (August 2010).

Bews, John William, *Human Ecology* (Oxford: Oxford University Press, 1935).

Birnbaum, Charles A., *Guidelines for the Treatment of Cultural Landscapes* (Washington DC: National Park Service, 1996).

Blomfield, Reginald, *The Formal Garden in England* (London: MacMillan and Co., 1892, 3rd edn 1901).

'Blueprint for Survival' issue, *The Ecologist* 2 : 1 (January 1972).

Boden, Margaret, *The Creative Mind* (London: Weidenfeld & Nicolson, 1990).

Bookchin, Murray, 'Social Ecology versus Deep Ecology: a Challenge for the Ecology Movement', *Green Perspectives: Newsletter of the Green Progress Project.* 4-5, (Summer 1987).

Botkin, Daniel B., *Discordant Harmonies: a New Ecology for the Twenty-first Century* (Oxford: Oxford University Press, 1990).

Bourassa, Stephen C., *The Aesthetics of Landscape* (London: Belhaven Press, 1991).

Brady, Emily, *Aesthetics of the Natural Environment* (Edinburgh: University of Edinburgh Press; Tuscaloosa AL: University of Alabama Press, 2003).

Brady, Emily, *The Sublime in Modern Philosophy: Aesthetics, Ethics, and Nature* (Cambridge: Cambridge University Press, 2013).

Brereton, Christopher, *The Repair of Historic Buildings: Advice on Principles and Methods* (London: English Heritage, 1991).

Brotherton, Ian, 'Prospect-Refuge Theory: Is it Hazardous?' *Landscape Research,* 4:3 (Autumn, 1979).

Brown, Jane, *The Everywhere Landscape* (London: Wildwood House, 1982).

Burgess, Jacqueline, *et al*, 'People, Parks and the Urban Green: a Study of Popular Meanings and Values for Open Spaces in the City', *Urban Studies,* 25 (1988).

Burke, Edmund, *On the Sublime and Beautiful* (London: J. Dodsley, 1757).

Canter, David V., 'Action and Place: an Existential Dialectic', in Canter, David, Martin Krampen & David Stea (eds), *Ethnoscapes*, Vol.1: *Environmental Perspectives* (Aldershot, Hampshire (abbrev. Hants): Gower, 1988).

Carlson, Allen, 'Appreciation and the Natural Environment', *Journal of Aesthetics and Art Criticism,* 37 (Spring 1979).

Carlson, Allen, *Aesthetics and the Environment: the Appreciation of Nature, Art and Architecture* (Abingdon, Oxfordshire (abbrev. Oxon): Routledge, 2000).

Carroll, Noël, 'On Being Moved by Nature between Religion and Natural History', in Kemal, Salim & Ivan Gaskell (eds), *Landscape, Natural Beauty and the Arts* (Cambridge: Cambridge University Press, 1993).

Charney, Marvin, 'A Garden for the Canadian Center for Architecture', in Richards, Larry (ed), *Canadian Center for Architecture: Building and Gardens* (Montreal: CCA, 1989).

Clamp, P.E., 'Evaluation of the Impact of Roads on the Visual Amenity of Rural Areas' (Report by Ralph Hopkinson, Newton Watson & Partners). *Department of the Environment Research Report 7* (London: HMSO, 1976).

Clark, H.F. ('Frank'), 'Eighteenth Century Elysiums: The Rôle of "Association" in the Landscape Movement', *Journal of the Warburg and Courtauld Institutes*, VI (1943).

Clark, H.F., *The English Landscape Garden* (London: Pleiades, 1948).

Clark, H.F., 'The Sense of Beauty in the 18th, 19th and 20th Centuries', *Journal of the Institute of Landscape Architects* (March 1957).

Clark, H.F., 'The Restoration and Reclamation of Gardens', *Occasional Paper,* No. 1 (London: Garden History Society, 1969).

Clark, Kenneth, *Landscape into Art* (London: John Murray, 1949).

Clifford, Sue & Angela King, *Holding Your Ground* (London: Temple-Smith, 1985).

Clifford, Sue & Angela King, *Local Disticntiveness: Place, Particularity and Identity* (London: Common Ground, 1993).

Clingerman, Forrest, Brian Treanor, Martin Drenthen and David Utsler (eds), *Interpreting Nature: The Emerging Field of Environmental Hermeneutics* (New York: Fordham University Press, 2014).

Cobham Resource Consultants, *Landscape Assessment Guidance.* CCP423 (Northampton: Countryside Commission, 1993).

Collens, Geoffrey, 'The Profession', in Harvey, Sheila & Stephen Rettig (eds), *Fifty Years of Landscape Design* (Reigate, Surrey: Landscape Design Trust, 1985).

Colvin, Brenda, 'Some Differences in English and French Garden Design', *Garden & Landscape* (Autumn 1937).

Colvin, Brenda, *Land and Landscape*, 1st ed. (London: John Murray, 1948).

Colvin, Brenda, *Wonder in a World* (Burford, Oxon: privately printed, 1977).

Compton, Susan, *Henry Moore* (London: Weidenfeld & Nicolson, 1988).

Cooper, David E., *A Philosophy of Gardens* (Oxford: Oxford University Press, 2006).

Corner, James, 'The Obscene (American) Landscape', in Spens, Michael (ed), *Landscape Transformed* (London: Academy Editions, 1996).

Cosgrove, Denis E, *Social Formation and Symbolic Landscape* (Madison WI: University of Wisconsin Press; London: Croom Helm, 1984).

Cosgrove, Denis & Stephen Daniels (eds), *The Iconography of Landscape: Essays on the Symbolic Representation, Design and Use of Past Environments* (Cambridge: Cambridge University Press, 1988).

Costonis, John J., *Icons and Aliens: Law, Aesthetics, and Environmental Change* (Urbana IL: University of Illinois Press, 1989).

Countryside Commission, *New Agricultural Landscapes*, CCP 76 (Cheltenham, Gloucestershire (abbrev. Glos): CC, 1974).

Countryside Commission, *Assessment and Conservation of Landscape Character: the Warwickshire Landscapes Project Approach.* CCP332 (Cheltenham, Glos: CC, 1991).

Countryside Commission, *Conservation Issues in Strategic Plans*, CCP 420 (Cheltenham, Glos: CC, 1993).

Countryside Commission, English Heritage & English Nature, *Conservation Issues in Local Plans*, CCP485 (London: English Heritage, Countryside Commission, English Nature, 1996).

Cronon, William, *Uncommon Ground: Toward Reinventing Nature* (New York: Norton, 1995).

Cronon, William (ed), *Uncommon Ground: Rethinking the Human Place in Nature* (New York: Norton, 1996).

Cronon, William, 'In Search of Nature', Introduction to Cronon, William (ed) *Uncommon Ground ...* (New York: Norton, 1996).

Crowe, Sylvia, *Tomorrow's Landscape* (London: Architectural Press, 1956).

Crowe, Sylvia, *Landscape of Power* (London: Architectural Press, 1958).

Crowe, Sylvia, *Garden Design*, 1st ed. (London: Country Life, 1958).

Csikszentmihályi, Mihályi & Rick E. Robinson, *The Art of Seeing: an Interpretation of the Aesthetic Encounter* (Malibu CA: Getty, 1990).

Dawkins, Richard, *The Blind Watchmaker* (London: Longman, 1986).

Devall, Bill & George Sessions, *Deep Ecology* (Layton, UT: Peregrine-Smith, 1985).

Dewey, John, *Art as Experience* (New York, 1934, reprinted by Berkley Publishing, 2005).

Dower, John, *National Parks in England and Wales* (London: HMSO, 1945).

Drabble, Margaret, *A Writer's Britain: Landscape in Literature* (London: Thames & Hudson, 1979).

Dubos, René, *So Human an Animal* (New York: Scribner, 1968; London: Sphere, 1973).

Dunington-Grubb, Howard, 'Modernismus Arrives in the Garden – to Stay? *Landscape Architecture* 32 (July 1942).

Dunnett, Nigel, 'Harnessing Anarchy', *Landscape Design*, 245 (November 1995), 25-29.

Dunnett, Nigel & James Hitchmough, *Dynamic Landscape: Design, Ecology and Management of Naturalistic Urban Planting* (London: Taylor & Francis, 2004).

Dutton, Geoffrey, 'A Marginal Garden', *Journal of the Royal Horticultural Society*, 3, Part 2 (February 1988).

Dutton, Geoffrey, *Harvesting the Edge: Some Personal Explorations from a Marginal Garden* (Perth: Menard, 1995).

Eckbo, Garrett, *Landscape for Living* (New York: Architectural Record with Duell, Sloan, & Pearce, 1950).

Eden, William Arthur, 'The English Tradition in the Countryside', *Architectural Review* 77 (1935).

Fairbrother, Nan, *New Lives; New Landscapes* (London: Architectural Press, 1970).

Fairclough, Graham, Ingrid Sarlöv & Carys Swanwick, *Routledge Handbook of Landscape Character Assessment* (Abingdon, Oxon: Routledge, 2018).

Findlay, Catherine, 'Bio-power'. *Landscape Design* (December 1996).

Fines, K.D., 'Landscape Evaluation: a Research Project in East Sussex', *Regional Studies* 2 (1968).

Forman, Richard T.T. & Michael Godron, *Landscape Ecology* (New York: Wiley, 1986).

Foster, John (ed), *Protected Landscapes: Summary Proceedings of an International Symposium, 5-10 October 1987* (Manchester: Countryside Commission & IUCN, 1988).

Fraser Darling, Frank, *Wilderness and Plenty*. BBC Reith Lecture (London: BBC, 1969).

Friend, J.K. & W.N. Jessop, *Local Government and Strategic Choice* (London: Tavistock, 1969).

Fuller, Peter, 'The Geography of Mother Nature', in Cosgrove, Denis & Stephen Daniels (eds), *The Iconography of Landscape* (Cambridge: Cambridge University Press, 1988).

Getzels, Jacob W. & Mihályi Csikszentmihályi, *The Creative Vision – a Longitudinal Study of Problem Finding in Art* (New York: Wiley, 1976).

Gibson, James Jerome, *The Ecological Approach to Visual Perception* (Boston: Houghton Mifflin, 1979).

Gilbert, Oliver, *The Ecology of Urban Habitats* (London: Springer, 1989).

Gilpin, William, *Observations on the River Wye, and Several Parts of South Wales, made... 1770* (London: R. Blamire, 1782).

Gilpin, William Sawrey, *Practical Hints upon Landscape Gardening* (London: T. Cadell, 1832).

Glasson, John, *An Introduction to Regional Planning* (London: Hutchinson, 1974).

Gregory, Richard Langton, *Eye and Brain: the Psychology of Seeing*. 3rd ed. (Princeton NJ, Princeton University Press, 1977).

Greswell, Lucinda, 'A Muffled Modernism', *Landscape Design* (September 1990).

Grime, John Philip, *Plant Strategies in Vegetation Processes* (Chichester: Wiley, 1979).

Hansen, Richard & Friedrich Stahl, *Perennials and their Garden Habitats*, 4th edn., trans. Richard Ward (Cambridge, Cambridge University Press: Portland OR, Timber Press, 1993).

Harman, Richard, *Countryside Character* (London: Blandford, 1946).

Hegel, Georg, *The Phenomenology of Mind: Science of the Experience* of *Consciousness,* trans. J.B. Bailey. New edn. (New York: Dover, 2004).

Helliwell, Denis Rodney, *An Evaluation Method for Amenity Trees* (London: Tree Council, 1974).

Henderson, Lawrence Joseph, *The Fitness of the Environment* (New York: Macmillan, 1913).

Hepburn, Ronald W., 'Contemporary Aesthetics and the Neglect of Natural Beauty', in Bernard Williams & Alan Montefiore (eds), *British Analytical Philosophy* (London: Routledge & Kegan Paul, 1966).

Hepburn, Ronald W., 'Trivial and Serious in Appreciation of Nature', in Kemal, Salim & Ivan Gaskell, (eds), *Landscape, Natural Beauty and the Arts* (Cambridge: Cambridge University Press, 1993).

Hepburn, Ronald W., 'Landscape and the Metaphysical Imagination', *Environmental Values*, 5 : 3 (1996).

Hepworth, Barbara, *A Pictorial Autobiography*, rev. ed. (London: Moonraker, 1978).

Hinde, Robert A. & Joan Stevenson-Hinde, *Instinct and Intelligence*. Carolina Biology Reader 63. (Burlington NC: Carolina Biological Supply Co., 1987).

Historic England, *Register of Parks and Gardens of Special Historic Interest*. Now incorporated into *Heritage List for England* (https://historicengland.org.uk/listing/the-list).

Hitchmough, James, 'Natural Neighbours', *Landscape Design*, 229 (April 1994).

Hobhouse, Sir Arthur, *Report of the National Parks Committee* (the Hobhouse Report) (London: HMSO, 1947).

Holland, Alan & Kate Rawles, *Values in Conservation', ECOS* 14 : 1 (1993).

Hopkins, John, 'Critics Forum', *Landscape Design* (February 1994).

Hopkinson, R.G., 'The Quantitative Assessment of Visual Intrusion', *Journal of the Royal Town Planning Institute* (1971).

Hoskins, William G. *The Making of the English Landscape* (London: Hodder & Stoughton, 1955).

Hough, Michael, *Out of Place: Restoring Identity to the Regional Landscape* (New Haven CT: Yale University Press, 1990).

Howard, Peter, Ian H. Thompson & Emma Waterton (eds), *The Routledge Companion to Landscape Studies*, 1st edn. (Abingdon, Oxon: Routledge, 2000).

Howard, Peter, 'Perceptual Lenses', in Howard *et al* (eds), *The Routledge Companion to Landscape Studies*, 1st edn. (Abingdon, Oxon: Routledge, 2000).

Howard of Penarth, Lord, 'Lessons from Other Countries', in Williams-Ellis, Clough (ed), *Britain and the Beast* (London: Dent, 1937).

Hudnut, Joseph, 'The Modern Garden', in Tunnard, Christopher, *Gardens in the Modern Landscape*, 2nd edn. (London: Architectural Press, 1948).

Humphrey, Nicholas, *A History of the Mind* (London: Vintage, 1992).

Hunt, John Dixon, *Greater Perfections: the Practice of Garden Theory* (Philadelphia: University of Pennsylvania Press, 2000).

Hunt, John Dixon, 'Brown and Neo-classicism', *Garden History,* 44: suppl. 1 (Autumn, 2016).

Huxley, Julian, 'The Future of Man – Evolutionary Aspects', in Wolstenholme, Gordon (ed), *Man and His Future* (Boston MA: Little, Brown, 1963).

ICOMOS, *Venice Charter* (1964, digital: https://www.icomos.org/charters/venice_e.pdf)

ICOMOS, *Nara Document on Authenticity* (Digital edn: ICOMOS, 1994) https://www.icomos.org/charters/nara-e.pdf

ICOMOS Australia, *The Australia ICOMOS Guidelines for the Conservation of Places of Cultural Significance* (Burra Charter) (Australia ICOMOS, 1979).

ICOMOS–IFLA International Scientific Committee on Cultural Landscapes, *Guidelines for the Conservation of Cultural Landscapes*. (Devised at Czerniejewo, Poland) (unpublished: ICOMOS, April 1994).

ICOMOS Landscapes Working Group, *Newsletter* (Digital edns: Jacques, David L. (ed), issues 1-5 (June 1991 – January 1993); O'Donnell, Patricia (ed), North American issue (September 1993); Taylor, Ken & Val Kirby (eds), Australasian Issue (March 1994)).

Ingold, Timothy, 'The Temporality of Landscape', *World Archaeology* 25/2 (1993).

Jacques, David. L., 'Landscape Appraisal: The Case for a Subjective Theory', *Journal of Environmental Management*, 10 (1980).

Jacques, David L., *Georgian Gardens: the Reign of Nature* (London: Batsford, 1983).

Jacques, David L., *Strategic Guidance for Heritage Land in London*, CCD28 (Cheltenham, Gloucestershire: Countryside Commission, 1988).

Jacques, David L., 'The Great Reconstruction Debate: the Moment in Time', *CRM Bulletin* 13 : 4 (1990).

Jacques, David L. 'Knowledge is a Value', *Landscape Research* 17 : 2 (Summer 1992).

Jacques, David L., 'The Welcome Complexity of Cherished Landscape', *Paysage et Amenagement* 21, Special Issue (October 1992).

Jacques, David L., 'Landscape Interpretation in the United Kingdom: an Historical Perspective and Outlook', *CRM Bulletin* 17 : 7 (1994).

Jacques, David L., The Rise of Cultural Landscapes', *International Journal of Heritage Studies* 1 : 2 (Winter 1994).

Jacques, David L., 'The Treatment of Historic Parks and Gardens', *Journal of Architectural Conservation*, 1 : 2 (July 1995).

Jacques, David L., 'William Kent's Notion of Gardening: the Context, the Practice and the Posthumous Claims', *Garden History*, 44 : 1 (Summer 2016).

Jacques, David L. & Jan Woudstra, *Landscape Modernism Renounced: the Career of Christopher Tunnard (1910-1979)* (Abingdon, Oxon: Routledge, 2009).

Jellicoe, Geoffrey, 'Consider Your Forebears', *Journal of the Institute of Landscape Architects* (November 1954).

Jellicoe, Geoffrey, *The Guelph Lectures on Landscape Design* (Guelph ON: University of Guelph, 1983).

Jellicoe, Geoffrey, 'Journey into the Future', in *Landscape 89, the Environmental Review* (Reigate, Surrey: Landscape Design Trust, 1989).

Jellicoe, Geoffrey & Susan, *The Landscape of Civilisation* (London: Thames & Hudson, 1989).

Jencks, Charles, *The Architecture of the Jumping Universe: a Polemic – How Complexity Science is Changing Architecture and Culture* (London: Academy Editions, 1995).

Jensen, Jens, *Siftings* (1939; new edn., Baltimore, Maryland: Johns Hopkins University Press, 1960).

Joad, Cyril Edwin Mitchinson, 'The People's Claim', in Williams-Ellis, Clough (ed), *Britain and the Beast* (London: Dent, 1937).

Jung, Carl, *Man and his Symbols* (London: Aldus, 1964).

Kant, Immanuel, *Critique of Judgement* (1790), trans. Werner S. Pluhar (Indianapolis, IN: Hackett Publishing, 1987).

Kaplan, Rachel & Stephen, *The Experience of Nature: A Psychological Perspective* (New York: Cambridge University Press, 1989).

Kaplan, Stephen, ' Aesthetics, Affect, and Cognition: Environmental Preference from an Evolutionary Perspective', *Environment and Behaviour*, 19 : 1 (1987).

Kaplan, Stephen, 'Perception and Landscape: Conceptions and Misconceptions', in Nasar, Jack (ed), *Environmental Aesthetics: Theory, Research and Application* (Cambridge: Cambridge University Press, 1988).

Kaplan, Stephen & Rachel (eds), *Humanscape: Environments for People* (North Scituate MA: Duxbury Press, 1978).

Karmiloff-Smith, Annette, *Beyond Modularity: a Developmental Perspective on Cognitive Science* (Cambridge MA, MIT Press, 1992).

Kemal, Salim & Ivan Gaskell (eds), *Landscape, Natural Beauty and the Arts* (Cambridge: Cambridge University Press, 1993).

Kingsbury, Noel, *The New Perennial Garden* (London: Frances Lincoln, 1996).

Knight, Richard Payne, *The Landscape* (London: G. Nichol, 1794).

Land Use Consultants, *A Planning Classification of Scottish Landscape Resources,* Countryside Commission for Scotland Occasional Paper 1 (Redgorton, Perth: CCS, 1971).

Landscape Research Group, *A Review of Recent Practice and Research in Landscape Assessment.* CCD25 (Cheltenham, Glos: Countryside Commission, 1988).

Law, Ernest, *Shakespeare's Garden, Stratford-upon-Avon* (Oxford: Basil Blackwell, 1922).

Leopold, Aldo, *A Sand County Almanac, and Sketches Here and There* (New York: Oxford University Press, 1949).

Levett, Roger, 'Feedback Loops – Part 2', *Landscape Design* (November 1991).

Lewis, Peirce, 'American Landscape Tastes', in Treib, Marc (ed), *Modern Landscape Architecture: a Critical Review* (Cambridge MA,: MIT Press, 1993).

Light, Andrew & Rolston Holmes (eds), *Environmental Ethics: an Anthology* (Oxford: Wiley-Blackwell, 2002).

Light, Andrew (ed), 'Environmental Philosophy as Social Philosophy', in *Social Philosophy Today 19* (Charlottesville VA: University of Virginia Press, 2018).

Linton, David L., 'The Assessment of Scenery as a Natural Resource', *Scottish Geographical Magazine*, 84 : 3 (December 1968).

Long, Richard, *Walking in Circles* (London: Thames & Hudson, 1991).

Lovelock, James & Sidney Epton, 'The Quest for Gaia', *New Scientist*, vol. 65 (6 February 1975); the ideas were later developed into Kit Pedlar, *The Quest for Gaia* (London: Souvenir Press, 1979) and many further titles.

Lowenthal, David, 'The American Scene', *Geographical Review*, 58 (1968).

Lowenthal, David, 'Finding Valued Landscape', *Progress in Human Geography*, 2 : 3 (1978).

Lowenthal, David, *The Past is a Foreign Country* (Cambridge: Cambridge University Press, 1985).

Lowenthal, David & Hugh C. Prince, 'English Landscape Tastes', *Geographical Review*, 55 (April 1965).

Lyall, Sutherland (ed), *Designing the New Landscape* (London: Thames & Hudson, 1991).

Lynch, Tony, 'Deep Ecology as an Aesthetic Movement', *Environmental Values* 5 : 2 (May 1996).

Lyotard, Jean-François, *The Post-Modern Condition: a Report on Knowledge*, trans. Geoffrey Bennington, Brian Massumi (Fr edn, Paris: Eds Minuit, 1979; Eng edn, Manchester University Press UK/Minneapolis MN: University of Minnesota Press, 1984).

Mandelbrot, Benoit, 'Fractals – a Geometry of Nature', in Hall, Nina (ed), *The New Scientist Guide to Chaos* (London: Penguin, 1992).

Maskit, Jonathan, 'On Universalism and Cultural Historicism in Environmental Aesthetics', in Martin Drenthen & Jozef Keulartz (eds), *Environmental Aesthetics: Crossing divides and Breaking Ground* (New York: Fordham University Press, 2014).

McGibbin, Bill, *The End of Nature* (New York: Doubleday/Anchor Books, 1989).

McHarg, Ian, *Design with Nature,* 1st edn. (Garden City NY: Doubleday, 1969).

Meadows, Dennis L. et al., *The Limits to Growth* (New York: Universe Books, 1972).

Meinig, Donald.W. (ed), *The Interpretation of Ordinary Landscapes* (New York: Oxford University Press, 1979).

Meredith, Jo, *Landscape Assessment: a Countryside Commission Approach.* CCD18 (Cheltenham, Glos: CC, 1987).

Merleau-Ponty, Maurice, *The Phenomenology of Perception*, trans. Colin Smith (London: Routledge & Kegan Paul, 1962).

Meynell, Hugo A., *The Nature of Aesthetic Value* (London: Macmillan, 1986).

Miller, Mara, *The Garden as an Art* (Albany NY: State University of New York Press, 1993).

Mitchell, Nora, *Study on the Application of Criterion VII: Considering Superlative Natural Phenomena and Exceptional Natural Beauty within the World Heritage Convention*, World Heritage Study 10 (Gland, Switzerland: IUCN, 2013).

Mithen, Steven, *The Prehistory of the Mind* (New York: Thames & Hudson, 1996).

Montefiore, Alan, 'Facts, Values and Ideology', in Williams, Bernard & Alan Montefiore (eds), *British Analytical Philosophy* (London: Routledge & Kegan Paul, 1966).

Naess, Arne, 'The Shallow and the Deep, Long-Range Ecology Movement: a summary', *Inquiry* 16:1 (1973).

Nasar, Jack (ed), *Environmental Aesthetics: Theory, Research and Applications* (Cambridge: Cambridge University Press, 1988).

Odum, Eugene & Howard, *The Principles of Ecology* (Philadelphia: W.B. Saunders, 1953).

Orians, Gordon H., 'An Ecological and Evolutionary Approach to Landscape Aesthetics', in Penning-Rowsell, Edmund C. & David Lowenthal (eds), *Landscape Meanings and Values* (London: Allen & Unwin, 1986).

Osborne, Brian S., 'The Iconography of Nationhood in Canadian Art', in Cosgrove, Denis & Stephen Daniels (eds), *The Iconography of Landscape* (Cambridge: Cambridge University Press, 1988).

Oudolf, Piet & Noel Kingsbury, *Planting: a New Perspective* (Portland OR: Timber Press, 2013).

Penning-Rowsell, E. C., G.H. Gullett, G.H. Searle & S.A. Witham, 'Public Evaluation of Landscape Quality', *Planning Research Group Report 13* (Hendon: Middlesex Polytechnic, 1977).

Penning-Rowsell, Edmund C. & David Lowenthal (eds), *Landscape Meanings and Values* (London: Allen & Unwin, 1986).

Pepper, David, John W. Perkins & Martyn J. Youngs, *The Roots of Modern Environmentalism* (London: Croom Helm, 1984).

Pevsner, Nikolaus, *Pioneers of the Modern Movement* (London: Faber, 1936; reissued as *Pioneers of Modernism,* Faber, 1949).

Pevsner, Nikolaus, 'The Genesis of the Picturesque', *Architectural Review*, 96 (November 1944).

Pevsner, Nikolaus, *The Englishness of English Art*. BBC Reith Lecture. (London: Architectural Press, 1955).

Pevsner, Nikolaus, 'Conclusions', in *The Picturesque Garden and its Influence Outside the British Isles*, Proceedings of Colloquium II (Washington DC: Dumbarton Oaks, 1974).

Pole, David, *Aesthetics, Form and Emotion* (London: Duckworth, 1983).

Popper, Karl R., *The Logic of Scientific Discovery* (1959; 6th impression, London: Hutchinson, 1972).

Popper, Karl R., *The Poverty of Historicism* (London: Routledge & Kegan Paul, 1957, revised 1961).

Price, Uvedale, 'A Letter to H. Repton, Esq.', in *Essays on the Picturesque*, III (London/Hereford: J.Robson/D.Walker, 1795).

Pringle, Trevor, ' The Privation of History: Landseer, Victoria and the Highland Myth', in Cosgrove, Denis & Steven Daniels (eds), *The Iconography of Landscape* (Cambridge: Cambridge University Press, 1988).

Purcell, A. Terry , 'Landscape Perception, Preference and Schema Discrepancy', *Environment and Planning,* 14 (1987).

Rackham, Oliver, *The History of the Countryside* (London: Dent, 1986).

Ramsay, Juliet (ed), *The Aesthetic Value of Landscapes: Background and Assessment Guide* (ICOMOS/IFLA ISCCL Technical Paper 2, 2016 – published digitally).

Relph, Edward, *Place and Placenessness* (London: Pion, 1976).

Richards, Ellen H., *Sanitation in Daily Life* (Boston: Whitcomb & Barrows, 1907).

Riegl, Aloïs, 'The Modern Cult of Monuments: Its Character and Its Origin', trans. Kurt W. Forster & Diane Ghirado, *Oppositions*, 25 (Fall 1982).

Robinson, D.G., I.C. Laurie, J.F. Wager & A.L. Traill, *Landscape Evaluation* (Report for the Countryside Commission) (University of Manchester, 1976).

Rose, James C., 'Articulate Form in Landscape Design', *Pencil Points* (February 1939).

Ross, Stephanie, *What Gardens Mean* (Chicago IL.: University of Chicago Press, 1998).

Routley, Richard, 'Is there a Need for a New, an Environmental Ethic?' in *Proceedings of the 15th World Congress of Philosophy* 1 (Sofia: Sophia Press, 1973).

Ruff, Allan R., *Holland and the Ecological Landscape* (Stockport, Cheshire: privately published in UK; University of Delft Press, 1979).

Ruskin, John, *The Seven Lamps of Architecture*, 4th edn. (Orpington, Kent: George Allen, 1883).

Ruskin, John, *Modern Painters,* part III. 2nd American edn. (New York: Wiley, 1849).

Rycroft, Simon, 'Mapping, Modernity and the New Landscape', in Spens, Michael (ed), *Landscape Transformed* (London: Academy Editions, 1996).

Saarinen, Eliel, *Search for Form: A Fundamental Approach to Art* (New York: Reinhold, 1948).

Santayana, George, *The Sense of Beauty: Being the Outlines of Aesthetic Theory* (New York: Scribner, 1896).

Saito, Yuriko, ' Cultural Construction of National Landscapes: Cases of Japan and the United States', in Arntzen, Sven & Emily Brady (eds), *Humans in the Land: the Ethics and Aesthetics of the Cultural Landscape* (Oslo: Unipub - University of Oslo Press, 2009).

Sauer, Carl O., 'The Morphology of Landscape', *University of California Publications in Geography* 2:2 (1925), 19-53.

Schauman, Sally, 'Countryside Landscape Visual Assessment', in Smardon, Richard C., James F. Palmer & John P. Felleman (eds), *Foundations for Visual Project Analysis* (New York: Wiley, 1986)

Schoenaich, Brita von, 'The End of the Border?' *Landscape Design*, 229 (April 1994).

Scott, Sir Leslie Frederick, *Report of the Committee on Land Utilisation in Rural Areas* (the Scott Report) (London: HMSO, 1942).

Scruton, Roger, *The Aesthetics of Architecture* (London: Methuen, 1979).

Searle, John, *Mind, Language and Society* (London: Weidenfield & Nicolson, 1999).

Semple, Ellen Churchill, *Influences on Geographic Environment* (New York: Henry Holt, 1911).

Shafer, Elwood L., John F. Hamilton & Elizabeth A. Schmidt, 'Natural Landscape Preferences: a Predictive Model', *Journal of Leisure Research* 1 : 1 (Winter 1969).

Sharp, Thomas, *Town and Countryside* (Oxford: Oxford University Press, 1932).

Sharp, Thomas, *English Panorama* (London: Dent, 1936).

Sharp, Thomas, *Town Planning* (London: Penguin, 1940).

Shepheard, Peter, *Modern Gardens* (London: Architectural Press, 1953).

Smuts, Jan Christiaan, *Holism and Evolution* (London: Macmillan, 1926).

Snow, Marc, *Modern American Gardens – Designed by James Rose* (New York: Reinhold, 1967).

Spens, Michael (ed), *Landscape Transformed* (London: Academy Editions, 1996).

Spirn, Ann Whiston, *The Language of Landscape* (New Haven CT: Yale University Press, 1988).

Stapledon, Reginald George, 'Economics and the National Park', in Williams-Ellis, Clough (ed), *Britain and the Beast* (London: Dent, 1937).

Stapledon, Reginald George, *The Land Now and To-morrow* (London: Faber, 1935).

Stolnitz, Jerome, *Aesthetics and the Philosophy of Art Criticism: a Critical Introduction* (Boston MA.: Houghton Mifflin, 1960).

Tansley, Arthur G., 'The Use and Abuse of Vegetational Concepts and Terms', *Ecology* 16 (1935), 284-307.

Taylor, Christopher, *The Archaeology of Gardens* (Princes Risborough, Buckinghamshire (abbrev. Bucks): Shire, 1983).

Thacker, Christopher, '"O Tinian! O Juan-Fernandez!": Rousseau's "Elysée" and Anson's Desert Islands', *Garden History*, V/2 (Summer 1977).

Thompson, Ian H., *Ecology, Community and Delight* (London: Spon, 2000).

Thompson, Ian H., 'Landscape and Environmental Ethics', in Howard, Peter *et al.* (eds), *The Routledge Companion to Environmental Studies*, 1st edn. (Abingdon, Oxon: Routledge, 2000).

Thurley, Simon (ed), *The King's Privy Garden at Hampton Court Palace 1689-1995* (London: Apollo, 1995).

Thwaites, Kevin, 'In Search of the Designer's New Mind', *Landscape Design* (September 1996).

Tilley, Christopher, *A Phenomenology of Landscape: Places, Paths and Monuments* (London: Berg/Bloomsbury, 1994).

Treib, Marc (ed), *Modern Landscape Architecture: a Critical Review* (Cambridge MA: MIT Press, 1993).

Treib, Marc, 'Must Landscapes Mean? Approaches to Significance in Recent Landscape Architecture', *Landscape Journal*, 14 (1995).

Tribot, Anne-Sophie, Julie Deter and Nicolas Mouquet, 'Integrating the Aesthetic Value of Landscapes and Biological Diversity', *Proceedings of the Royal Society B: Biological Sciences* 285 (2018, https://doi.org/10.1098/rspb.2018.0971).

Tschumi, Bernard, 'Parc de la Villette, Paris', in Papadakis, Andreas *et al* (eds), *Deconstruction: Omnibus Volume* (London: Academy Editions, 1989).

Tuan Yi-Fu, *Topophilia: a Study of Environmental Perception, Attitudes and Values* (New York: Columbia University Press, 1974).

Tuan Yi-Fu, 'Humanistic Geography', *Annals of the Association of American Geographers*, 66 (1976).

Tunnard, Christopher, *Gardens in the Modern Landscape,* 1st ed. (London: Architectural Press, 1938; 2nd edn., 1948).

UNESCO, *World Heritage Convention* (1972, updated digital version https://whc.unesco.org/en/convention/).

UNESCO, *Report of the 23rd Session of the World Heritage Committee at Marrakesh, Morocco, December 1999* (digital, UNESCO, 2000: https://whc.unesco.org/archive/1999/whc-99-conf209-17e.pdf).

Uzzell, David L., 'Environmental Perspectives on Landscape', *Landscape Research*, 16 : 1 (Spring 1991).

Walpole, Horace, [letter], in Adam Fitz-Adam (pseud.) (ed), *The World*, 6 (London: 8 February 1753).

Walpole, Horace, 'On Modern Gardening', in *Anecdotes of Painting in England* (Strawberry Hill, London: 1782).

Watkin, David, *Morality and Architecture* (Oxford: Clarendon Press, 1977).

Watkin, David, *The Rise of Architectural History* (London: Architectural Press, 1980).

Williams, Bernard & Alan Montefiore (eds), *British Analytical Philosophy* (London: Routledge & Kegan Paul, 1966).

Williams, Raymond, *The Country and the City* (London: Chatto & Windus, 1973).

Williams-Ellis, Clough (ed), *Britain and the Beast* (London: Dent, 1937).

Wilson, Edward. O., *Sociobiology: The New Synthesis* (Cambridge, MA: Harvard University Press, 1975).

Wittkower, Rudolf, *Architectural Principles in the Age of Humanism* (London: Warburg Institute, University of London, 1949).

Wittkower, Rudolf, 'English Palladianism, the Landscape Garden, China and the Enlightenment', *L'Arte* (1969).

Wylie, John, 'Landscape and Phenomenology', in Howard, Peter *et al* (eds), *The Routledge Companion to Landscape Studies,* 1st edn. (Abingdon, Oxon: Routledge, 2000).

LIST OF ABBREVIATED CAPTIONS

Figure numbers:

Part A *Lights of the Forest*	2
1.1 *Jean Canneel-Claes's ultra-functionalist design for his own house and garden.*	3
1.2 *Contrast between mature trees and architecture; Holthanger at Wentworth.*	4
1.3 *The Kelmarsh Hall fan rose garden as developed by Nancy Lancaster.*	6
1.4 *Swimming pool, Donnell residence at Sonoma by Thomas Church & Laurence Halprin.*	9
1.5 *Bosquet at Schönbrunn Palace, Vienna.*	10
1.6 *'St Ives – Oval and Steeple' (1951) by Ben Nicholson.*	11
1.7 *Master Plan for Harlow New Town devised by Frederick Gibberd in 1947.*	12
1.8 *Plan of a garden under and around a house in São Paulo by Burle Marx.*	13
1.9 *Claud Phillimore's plan of Chiswick House grounds 1951.*	15
1.10 *Landscape garden recycled; modernist house and garden drawn by Gordon Cullen.*	16
1.11 *Scene in Barbara Hepworth's garden in St Ives.*	20
1.12 *'New shapes are evolving'; artist's impression of Dounreay nuclear power stations.*	21
1.13 *A garden plan by Laurence Halprin in California.*	23
1.14 *'Two-Piece Reclining Figure: Points' by Henry Moore, 1969.*	25
1.15 *An example of the work of Paul Nash, 'Landscape of the Megaliths' (c.1937).*	25
1.16 *Kennedy Memorial, Runnymede, Surrey, 1964 showing Jellicoe's sketched plan.*	28
1.17 *Paul Cézanne's painting, 'Mont Ste Victoire', 1904-6 – 'like a ritual act of worship'.*	29
2.1 *Rural tradition of planning on rational principles: Heighington, Co. Durham.*	34
2.2 *Garden City aesthetic: Port Sunlight by T. Raffles Davison, 1916.*	35
2.3 *Drawings by Robert Austin included with W.A. Eden's articles in the AR.*	36
2.4 *Cathedral Rocks, Yosemite Valley, painting by Albert Bierstadt, c.1872.*	37
2.5 *Protected from further development for their scenic quality; Lake District. 1905 print.*	38
2.6 *Picturesque beauty: English country village: Water Street, Castle Combe, Wiltshire.*	39
2.7 *John Ruskin's drawing of the Aiguille de Blaitière, in the Mont Blanc massif, in 1856.*	40
2.8 *The wonders of nature: Banff National Park, Canada.*	41
2.9 *John Dower's recommendations for the English and Welsh national parks.*	42
2.10 *Diagram, A Strategy for the South East (1967), British Economic Planning Council.*	43
2.11 *The Tree Council's method for valuing trees from 1974 by Rodney Helliwell.*	44
2.12 *'Suitably sensitised professionals pondering paradise': drawing, UCL, Geog Dept.*	47

2.13 *Component analysis: the analogy to painting by numbers.* 48

2.14 *An equation for predicting visual quality scores of places unseen ...* 50

3.1 *Jan Christiaan Smuts, the person who coined the term 'holism', in 1919.* 54

3.2 *John Dewey, a towering figure in North American philosophy in the early 20th century.* 55

3.3 *The Group of Seven strove to clarify Canadian identity through their painting ...* 57.

3.4 *Preservation of Swedish scenery and objects of nature: Hällingsåfallet in Jämtland.* 59

3.5 *Distinctiveness deriving from landform, climate, soil and use; Colvin's examples.* 61

3.6 *An archetypal Italian garden, drawn by Cecil Stewart; effect of climate upon design.* 62

3.7 *Sylvia Crowe's analysis of Vaux-le-Vicomte.* 63

3.8 *Crowe's rendering of Burle Marx's garden in São Paulo.* 64

3.9 *Villa Savoye, Poissy, by Le Corbusier.* 67

3.10 *Colvin: a 'complete debasement of landscape'; Peacehaven in Sussex.* 68

3.11 *Fairbrother: fitness for purpose in a new agricultural landscape.* 69

3.12 *Fairbrother: a grain silo was as 'at home in the landscape as the church it resembles'* 72

3.13 *The urban- edge problem solved rationally and creatively.* 73

3.14 *Evolution from a primitive state to an advanced one: hostile environments ...* 75

3.15 *Better land-use planning through understanding natural and social systems.* 77

3.16 *Sieve-map layers: constraints being overlain to give the path of minimum damage.* 78

3.17 *Man the hunter; the stage of human evolution when 'prospect-refuge' developed.* 82

3.18 *The apotheosis of prospect symbolism in painting, 'Mount Lefroy' (1930)...* 83

3.19 *Dual symbolism of prospect and refuge: the 'Fisherman's Terrace', Budapest.* 84

3.20 *'River landscape with Apollo and the Cumaean Sibyl' (c.1665) by Salvator Rosa.* 84

4.1 *Culpepper garden at Leeds Castle, replanted by Russell Page in the 1980s.* 89

4.2 *A graph of projected population in Britain, 1955 onwards.* 91

4.3 *The A40 Westway near the White City, London.* 92

4.4 *The traditional use of public parks; Rowntree Park, York.* 93

4.5 *Design as one tool of environmental policy; converting disused mineral lines.* 94

4.6 *Environmental controls seek to limit logging to sustainable forests; Madagascar.* 95

4.7 *Fractals in the vegetable world; a Romanesco broccoli.* 98

4.8 *A ceramic serpent by Beverley Pepper in the Parc de l'Estacio del Nord, Barcelona.* 99

4.9 *Homo habilis had social skills plus a technical intelligence through tool-making.* 102

4.10 *Ancient animal wall painting in the Chauvet cave at Vallon-Pont-d'Arc, France.* 103

4.11 *Willendorf Venus, a statuette of c. 27,000 BC, Naturhistorische Museum, Vienna.* 106

4.12 *Shaking preconceptions: one of Igor Miteraj's giant masks.* 108

4.13 *Gardens as a state of mind: the enclosed yard derives from the desire to protect ...*	111
4.14 *Style revealing mentality; Tudor style at New College, Oxford.*	112
4.15 *Seek the zeitgeist; garden plan by Percy Cane.*	113
4.16 *View of watering place at Tenian – Anson – inspiration Rousseau's 'Julie's Garden'.*	114
4.17 *Style: stepping-stone path characteristic of modernist landscapes.*	118
4.18 *Cartoon of Charles Darwin by Leslie Starke.*	122
5.1 *The King's Knot, Stirling Castle; interpretation of aerial photographs informed history.*	125
5.2 *Ridge and furrow landscape at Dumbleton, Gloucestershire.*	126
5.3 *Rural poverty in Leinster in the 1840s by Robert Thomas Landells.*	128
5.4 *Honghe Hani rice terraces, Yunnan Province, China.*	135
5.5 *Machu Picchu, Peru; a 15th century Inca citadel.*	136
5.6 *Spiritual values attached to a mountain monastery: Monserrat, Catalonia, Spain.*	137
5.7 *Etching of 'King John signing Magna Carta by John Leech.*	138
5.8 *The Club of Rome's predictions in 1972.*	139
5.9 *The Phyllis Cormack, later renamed Greenpeace sailing to Alaska.*	140
5.10 *Arne Naess, prophet of Deep Ecology.*	143
5.11 *James Gibson's optic arrays.*	146
5.12 *Kennedylaan at Heerenveen, The Netherlands.*	154
5.13 *Hafod House by John Warwick Smith; a landscape of harmony, 18th century.*	156
6.1 *Hemel Hempstead water garden designed by Geoffrey Jellicoe.*	163
6.2 *Granite setts representing pilgrims; Kennedy Memorial at Runnymede, Surrey.*	164
6.3 *Primitive Man hunting animals. Museum of Vietnamese History*	166
6.4 *Deer park with weak prospect-and-refuge symbolism.*	167
6.5 *Supposed triune structure of the human brain.*	169
6.6 *Ameliorative landscape acceptable in reducing the impact of a road.*	171
6.7 *Torre Abbey Sands, Torquay, Devon; preferred by the public.*	176
6.8 *Shell poster of Rye Marshes by Paul Nash.*	177
6.9 *Common Ground's cider table, representation of the community orchards project.*	178
6.10 *Celebrating local identity, sculpture by Peter Randall-Page.*	179
6.11 *Pain at the loss of place; objectors to the removal of a splendid monkey-puzzle tree.*	182
6.12 *Mapping landscape character; Arden in Warwickshire.*	188
6.13 *Landscape character zones in the South Downs, Sussex & Hampshire*	189
6.14 *Landscape near Swansea by James Ward c. 1805.*	190
7.1 *Period garden at New Place, Stratford-upon-Avon*	195
7.2 *Asynchrony: Real Jardin Botanico, Madrid.*	196

7.3 *Falsification of the evidence: Jardin de Diane de Poitiers at Chenonceau.* 197
7.4 *The crime of deception: Packwood House, Warwickshire.* 198
7.5 *Edzell Castle Garden, Angus: 'restored' in the 1930s to what it might have been.* 199
7.6 *Destructive reconstruction at Kirby Hall, Northamptonshire: George Chettle's scheme.* 200
7.7 *Drottningholm Palace, Sweden, Chinese Pavilion, in new 1950s setting* 201
7.8 *Wilanów Palace garden outside Warsaw., restored because the form mattered.* 201
7.9 *Restoration in spirit, Chiswick House grounds, West London.* 202
7.10 *Kratochvile in Netolice, Czech Republic, a modern analogy of the original concept.* 203
7.11 *Hohenzollern Castle, Baden-Würtemberg, rebuilt between 1846 and 1867.* 204
7.12 *Notre-Dame Cathedral, Paris, under restoration by Viollet-le-Duc from 1844.* 205
7.13 *Interpreters at the John Dickinson Plantation, near Dover, Delaware,* 207
7.14 *Abbotsford House Visitor Centre, Scotland – new work in an historic context.* 208
7.15 *David Garrick as Gloucester in Shakespeare's Richard III.* 209
7.16 *Mrs Beeton's supper table for 16 persons – ephemeral* 210
7.17 *Ephemerality – Finnish ice sculpture at the 2009 festival in China.* 211
7.18 Kloster Kamp terraced garden, Kamp-Lintfort, North Rhine-Westphalia, 2004. 214
7.19 Westbury Court, Glos, restored pavilion and canal, 1967-72. 215
7.20 Hampton Court, Middlesex, Privy Garden, restored 1994-5 – acme of accuracy. 216
7.21 *Excavations at Hampton Court Privy Garden, 1994.* 217
7.22 *Emmetts, Kent, devastation after the great storm of 1987.* 220
7.23 *Weston Park, Staffordshire, looking south.* 221
7.24 *Château of Fontainebleau, World Heritage site, France..* 224
7.25 *Studley Royal, Yorkshire, temple and water garden, World Heritage site.* 225
7.26 *Monticello, Virginia, World Heritage site.* 226
7.27 *Avebury, Wiltshire,ditch and standing stones, World Heritage site.* 227
7.28 *'Hunting Buffalo' by Alfred Jacob Miller. 1858.* 228
7.29 *Print of the English Lake District, Cumbria, natural and cultural Landscape.* 229
7.30 *Value depending on cultural association, Tonga Ria, sacred Maori site.* 232
7.31 *Jabal Umm Fruth rock bridge, Wadi Rum protected area, Jordan.* 235
7.32 *The Wadi ul Rum landscape, Jordan.* 236
7.33 *Wasdale Head, English Lake District, initially refused World Heritage status.* 240

8.1 *Stoke-on-Trent garden festival grounds, 1986; temporary post-modernism.* 242
8.2 *Post-modern Victorian gate piers, Crystal Palace, south London.* 242
8.3 *Rosemary Verey's interlacing knot garden, Barnsley House, Gloucestershire.* 243
8.4 *Gasworks Park, Seattle, designed by Richard Haag, 1970s.* 244
8.5 *Central Forest Park, Stoke-on-Trent, at the planting stage, 1970s.* 245
8.6 *Duisberg Nord ex-steelworks Landscape Park by Peter Latz and team, 1991.* 246
8.7 *Canadian Center for Architecture, Montreal: relating new work to its historic context.* 247

338 *List of abbreviated captions*

8.8　Little Sparta, Scotland: attempting to express
spiritual ideas through association.　248
8.9　Deconstruction misapplied as a philosophy of design; Parc de la Villette, Paris.　249
8.10　Snail & snake mounds, Portrack House,
Dumfries, Garden of Cosmic Speculation.　250
8.11　Jac. P. Thijssepark in Amstelveen, The Netherlands, created in 1949.　252
8.12　Professor Geoffrey Dutton in his garden in Perthshire.　253
8.13　Philip Fry discusses his garden at Kemptville, Ontario.　254
8.14　Garden at Slifka Beach House, Sagaponack NY, by Oehme and Van Sweden.　257
8.15　The Eden Project in Cornwall – prairie planting by James Hitchmough.　258
8.16　Land Art: Richard Long's 'A Line in Ireland'.　260
8.17　One of David Nash'd wooden sculptures in Kew Gardens.　261
8.18　An example of Andy Goldsworthy's walling.　262

9.1　Claude Monet's painting of the Gare St Lazare, Paris, 1877　269
9.2　Clifton Nurseries shop in Covent Garden, London, designed by Terry Farrell.　272
9.3　The Lasket, Herefordshire, created in the 1970s by Roy Strong and his wife Julia.　273

10.1　Derwent Water in the English Lake District, well known to Ronald Hepburn　294

11.1　William Gilpin's etching of Goodriche Castle, Herefordshire.　296
11.2　Wimpole Hall, Cambridgeshire; a Brown landscape.　297
11.3　The Victorian parterre at Trentham revived in the 2000s.　298
11.4　Valhalla, near Regensburg, Bavaria, in a print of c. 1840.　301
11.5　The famous 'Wanderer above the Sea of Fog' (1818) by Caspar David Friedrich.　304
11.6　A long-abandoned fernery at Osmaston, Derbyshire, quarry garden.　306
11.7　Eaton Hall, Cheshire, immaculately kept garden as befits a ducal residence.　307
11.8　Westwell Manor, Oxfordshire, spiral garden; an agreeable scene …　308
11.9　Style: William Sawrey Gilpin explains
how turn the scene into a Picturesque one.　311
11.10　Landscape of emotion: Vietnam Veterans Memorial in Washington DC.　314
11.11　Jim Jim Falls in the wet season, Kakadu National Park, Australia.　320
11.12　Fiery sunset in Glacier National Park, Montana.　323
End page　Reine in the Lofoten Archipelago, Norway.　352

CREDITS FOR FIGURES

Very many thanks are due to the communal spirit of the commons.wikimedia.org project. A financial contribution has been made in acknowledgement of the use of these Creative Commons images:

Telmomeana, cover; Hertzi Pinki, 1.5; Rufus 46, 1.14; Smithsonian American Art Museum, Bequest of Marvin J. and Shirley F. Sonosky, 2.4; United States Library of Congress, 2.5, 3.1, 3.2; The Victorian Web, 2.7; Art Gallery of Ontario, Canada, 3.3; Sjoge~commonswiki, 3.4; Trustees of the Wallace Collection, London, 3.20; The National Archives, UK, 4.3; Erik Patel, 4.6; Jon Sullivan, 4.7; Nairobi National Museum/ ninara, 4.9; Matthias Kabel, 4.11; Chosovi, 4.12; Daniel Csörföly, 4.13; Panoramio, 5.1, 8.3; Geograph/ Adrian Phillips, 5.2; Jialiang Gao, 5.4; Diego Delso, 5.5; Mikipons, 5.6; Andres Musta, 5.10; National Library of Wales, 5.13; HappyMidnight, 6.3; PAFCA, 6.5; Geograph/ Nigel Cox, 6.6; TuckDB postcards, 6.7; Lenta, 6.8; Yale Center for British Art, New Haven, CT, 6.14; Jule955, 7.4; Jonathan Oldenbuck, 7.5; Arild Vågen, 7.7; Diana Dufková, 7.10; A. Kniesel, 7.11; State Library of Victoria, Australia, 7.12; Topher carr, 7.14; The Holburne Museum, Bath, UK, 7.15; Rincewind42, 7.17; Hans Peter Schaefer, 7.18; Nemanja Stijak, 7.24; Sbuckley, 7.26; Blake Patterson, 7.27; Walters Art Museum, Baltimore, USA, 7.28; Michal Klajban, 7.30; David Bjorgen, 7.31; Bernard Gagnon, 7.32; Geograph/ Malc McDonald, 8.2; Visitor7, 8.4; yellow book ltd, 8.8; Reza1615, 8.9; J.K. Gillon, 8.10; Jon, 8.15; Vicky25, 8.17; Mcginnly, 8.18; Harvard Art Museum/ Fogg Museum, Cambridge MA, 9.1; Max Pixel, 10.1; Kunstanstalt des Bibliographisches Instituts in Hildburghausen Germany, 11.4; Kunsthalle Hamburg, Germany, 11.5.

The author has provided the following images: 1.3, 1.11, 2.6, 3.10, 3.12, 4.4, 4.8, 4.14, 4.15, 4.16, 5.12, 6.2, 7.2, 7.3, 7.8, 7.9, 7.19, 7.25, 8.1, 8.6, 8.7, 8.12, 8.13, 9.3, 11.6, 11.7, 11.8, 11.10. The following are published under the terms of the UK Open Government Licence: 2.9, 2.10, 6.12, 6.13. The following are out of copyright: 3.10, 4.14, 4.15, 4.16, 5.3, 5.7, 6.4, 7.1, 7.6, 7.16, 7.29, 11.1, 11.9.

Other images have or appear to have the following copyright holders:

Tuntwaffle, title page; Nels Dzyre, foreword; Architectural Press, 1.1, 1.4, 1.8, 1.10, 2.2, 2.3, 4.17; Packard Publishing, 1.13, 3.7, 3.8; Country Life Picture Library, 1.2; Tate Images, 1.6; Harlow New Town Library, 1.7; Georgian Group, 1.9; United Kingdom Atomic Energy Authority, 1.12; Albright-Knox Art Gallery, Buffalo, N.Y., Contemporary Art Fund 1948, 1.15; Estate of Sir Geoffrey Jellicoe, 1.16; Wikiart/ Stiftung Sammlung E. G. Bührle, Zurich, 1.17; Oxford University Press, 2.1; Travel with Kally K., 2.8; Tree Council, 2.11; Prof. Ron Cooke, 2.12; Institute of British Geographers, 2.13; University of Manchester, 2.14; John Murray Press, 3.5, 3.6; Jan Woudstra, 3.9, 8.11; Aerofilms Ltd, 3.11, 3.13; Northrop Grumman, 3.14; Wallace Roberts & Todd, LLC, 3.15, 3.16; Look and Learn History Picture Library, 3.17; Wikiart/ McMichael Canadian Art Collection, Kleinburg, Ontario, 3.18; Keith Scurr, executors of, 3.19; Thousand Wonders/ NZGandG, 4.1; www.ukisfull.co.uk , 4.2; Richard Flenley, 4.5, 8.5; the late Leslie Starke, 4.18; Dennis Meadows, 5.8; Rex Weyler/ Greenpeace, 5.9; Houghton Mifflin, 5.11; Museum of English Rural Life/ The Landscape Institute, 6.1; Common Ground, 6.9, 6.10; Jonathan Denby and his *Slow Life* blog, 6.11; Delaware Division of Historical and Cultural Affairs, 7.13; The Historic Royal Palaces Trust, 7.20, 7.21; National Trust Images, 7.22; Weston Park Trust, 7.23; Travel Trip Journey, 7.33; The Cultural Landscape Foundation/ Sara Cedar Miller, 8.14; Richard Long/ Artimage, 8.16; The Conway Library, The Courtauld Institute of Art, 9.2; Steffie Shields, 11.2; Joe Wainwright, 11.3; Director of National Parks, Parks Australia, 11.11; Reddit/ Nate Luebbe, 11.12; Tomáš Havel, end page.

Grateful thanks are extended to those who have granted permission to reproduce. All reasonable effort has been made to trace and request permission from other copyright holders, and apologies are offered with respect to the cases where this has not proved feasible.

INDEX

A

Abbotsford House (Scottish Borders) fig. 7.14

Adami, Valerio (1935-) 249

Addison, Joseph (1672-1719) 172

Addison, Christopher, Viscount Addison (1869-1951) his committee 39

aerial photography 125, fig. 5.1

aesthetics 280, 281, 286, 295, of nature 17, 40-2, 132, 147, 153-4, 174, 228, 231, 234, 292, 305, 318, figs 2.8 & 7.31, of the countryside 1, 33, 39-41, 71, 171, 184, 285, 287, of geometry 19, of harmony 35, 53, 61-3, 65-6, 79, 317, from the unconscious 26-7, 161-4, as truth 153, as symbol of the good 268, as satisfying taste 127, of information processing 173, from fitness 62, 171, 268, as evolved preference 150, 317, as sublimated gratification 81, 166-7, in neuroscience 317, *see also* 'environmental aesthetics', 'formalism', 'functionalism' and 'ideas represented by landscape'

aesthetic attitude theory 284, 287, 318, criteria for 281, 290, disinterestedness 284-7, 290, sympathetic attention 280, 284, relevance 280, 288-9, preparation 285, 288, critiques of 146, 316

aesthetic experience 55, 79-80, 107, 150, 174, 280, 284, 287, 289, 'an experience' 107-8, 303, flow activity 107-8, 121, 303, arousal model 147, via triune brain 169,

Aiguille de Blaitière, Mont Blanc (France) fig. 2.7

Alhambra, The (Spain) 112

Alison, Archibald (1757–1839) 16

Alliance for Historic Landscape Preservation 230

Amchitka (Alaska) 140

Anson, George, Baron Anson (1697-1762) 113, fig. 4.16

Anstey Cove, Torquay (Devon) 176, fig. 6.7

anthropocentrism, *see* 'values'

antidote theory, *see* 'nature'

Appleton, Jay (1919-2015) 79-84, 165-6

Architecture 96, style in 14, 117, 204, theories in 1, *Architectural Review* 17, 35-6

Aristotle (384 BC - 322 BC) 152

arousal model, *see* 'aesthetics'

art 8, 105, shaking preconceptions 107, fig. 4.12, fine art 286-7, abstract art 19, 22, 145, 280, gardens as great/ high art 8-11, 213, 309, 313-6, sisterhood of 10, 64, 315

assessment, assessors, *see* under landscape

association, principle of, 6, 16

associative landscapes 136, 231, 234, figs 5.6 & 7.30

attributes, *see* qualities

Austin, Robert (1895-1973) fig. 2.3

B

Banff National Park (Alberta) fig. 2.8

Bauer, Walter (1877-1960) 202, fig. 7.7

Beardsley, Monroe C. (1915-1985) 284, 314

beauty, *see* 'aesthetics'

Beaux-Arts 14, 18

Beeton, Isabella Mary (1836-1865) 210, fig. 7.16

behaviourism, animal 80, human 100-1, 103-4, 175

Bell, Clive (1881-1964) 19, 147, 280, 297, 299

Berger, John (1926-2017) 127

Berleant, Arnold (1932-) 146, 175, 280, 283, 285, 287, 290, 292, 305

Betjeman, John (1906-1984) 10

Bews, John William (1884-1938) 53-5, 65, 74

biophilia 155

Blenheim Palace (Oxfordshire) 225

Blomfield, Sir Reginald (1856-1942) 198

Bookchin, Murray (1921-2006) 150, 152

Botkin, Daniel (1938-) 230

Bourassa, Steven Corey (1957-), 168-9

Brady, Emily (1969-) 284, 287, 289, 290, 305, 316, environmental sublime 305

Brown, Lancelot ('Capability') (1716-1783) 83, 117, 213, 298, fig. 11.2

Index **341**

Brundtland, Gro Harlem (1939-) 141
Buda Castle (Hungary) fig. 3.19
Bunyan, John (1628-1688) 27
Burke, Edmund (1730-1797) 172, 303, 316
Burlington, 3rd Earl of (1694-1753) 15, 17, 115
Burra Charter, *see* ICOMOS Australia

C

Canadian Center for Architecture, Montreal (Quebec) 246-7, fig. 8.7
Cane, Percy (1881–1976) 89, fig. 4.15
Canneel-Claes, Jean (1909–1989) 3, fig 1.1 & 4.17
Carlson, Allen (1949-) 132, 174, 283, 285, 288, 290-1, 305, 316
Carmichael, Franklin (1890-1945) fig. 3.3
Carroll, Noël (1947-) 147
Carson, Rachel (1907-1964) 142
Castle Combe (Wiltshire) figs 2.6 & 2.13
Cézanne, Paul (1839-1906) 10, fig. 1.17
Chaco Culture (New Mexico) 326
Chambord, Château de (France) 325
chaos 74, 98, 250
Charles, Prince of Wales (1948-) 272
Charnes Estate farm buildings (Staffordshire) fig. 3.12
Charney, Melvin (1935-2012) 246-7, fig. 8.7
Chenonceau, Château de (France) 197-8, fig. 7.3
cherished ideas, *see* idealised images
Chettle, George (1886-1957) 199, 237, fig. 7.6
Chiswick House (Middlesex) 15, 17, 19, 115, 202, fig. 1.9
Church, Thomas (1902-1978) 13, 114, fig. 1.4
Ciołek, Gerard (1909-1966) 202, fig. 7.8
Clark, H.F. ('Frank') (1902–1971) 14-7, 18, 115, 202
Clark, Sir Kenneth (1903-1983) 10, 26, 127
Cleere, Henry (1926-2018) 278
Clifton Nurseries shop, Covent Garden (London) 271-2, fig. 9.2
climate and soil 6, 60-4, 69-70, 83, 124, fig 3.5 & 3.8
Club of Rome 139, 141, fig. 5.8
cognition, *see* 'perception'

Colvin, Brenda (1897–1981) 7, 28, 32, 41, 55, 60, 79, biological balance 61, 66-7
Common Ground 179, figs 6.9 & 6.10
complexity 74-5, 96-7, 99, 250
component analysis 1, 46-8, 169-70, 174, fig. 2.13
composition, principles of, 10, 22, 297-9, fig. 1.13
consciousness 104-5, 162, 274
conservation principles 88, 132, 141, 203-6, 209, 212-3, 218-21, 233, 263-4
contextualism, *see* 'garden design'
convictions 96-7, 137
Cooper, David (1942-) 287, 296, 315-6
Cosgrove, Denis (1948-2008) 128-9, 273
cosmogenic world view 99
cosmology 105, 274
cosmos, the, 19, 21, 27-8, 45, 161, fig. 1.12
country planning, *see* 'landscape planning'
countryside, English, 33-39, 127-8, figs 2.3, 2.6 & 5.3, access to 33, 40, 42, 59, agricultural revolution in 68-73
Countryside Commission (superseded 2006) 69, 178, 186, 189, 221-2, 229, 232, 319, Countryside Stewardship Scheme 190
creativity 7, 13-4, 21-2, 24, 105, 115, 153
criticism 115-8, 207
Cronon, William (1954-) 151, 174, 235
Crowe, Dame Sylvia (1901-1997) 21, 62-3, 165, fig. 3.7
Crystal Palace (Kent) 11, 241, fig. 8.2
Cullen, Gordon (1914-1994) fig. 1.10
cultural geography 124-7, 275, 'new' cultural geography 127-9, 150-1, 273, 278, reading the landscape 125, palimpsests 125, fig. 5.2
cultural history 123, 292
cultural landscapes 124, 134-7, 148, rice terraces 135, 228, 231, fig. 5.4, cultivation terraces fig. 5.6, vineyards 135, 231, recognition of 223-31, 234, conservation of 222, 232-3
cultural turn, the, 271

D

Daniels, Stephen (1950-) 129-30

Darvil, Timothy (fl. 1980s-2010s) 278
Darwin, Charles (1809-1882) 110, fig. 4.18
Davison, Thomas Raffles (1853-1937) fig. 2.2
Dawkins, Richard (1941-) 99
deconstruction 249
derelict land 95, 131, 243, fig. 4.5, its reclamation 244-5
descriptive aesthetics, *see* 'phenomenology'
designations 184, 186-7, 222
designed landscapes 135, 195-203, 264, criteria for assessment 306-12, conservation of 212-24
Dewey, John (1859-1952) 55-6, 79-80, 107, 146, 150, 165, 175, 183, 285, 300, fig. 3.2
Diane de Poitiers (1499-1566) 197-8
direct realism, *see* 'ecological psychology'
disinterestedness, *see* 'aesthetic attitude theory'
Donnel Residence, Sonoma (California) fig. 1.4
Dounreay nuclear power station (Caithness) fig. 1.12
Dower, John (1900-1947) 42, fig. 2.9
Drabble, Margaret (1939-) 181
dreams 23-4, 26
Drottningholm (Sweden) 202, fig. 7.7
dualism, or polarities 90, 96, 142, 290, 271
Dubos, René (1901-1982) 153
Duisberg Nord Landscape Park (Nordrhein-Westfalen) 245-6, fig. 8.6
Dumbleton (Gloucestershire) fig. 5.2
Dunnett, Nigel (1962-) 258-9
Dutton, Geoffrey (1924-2010) 252-4, fig. 8.12
E
East Sussex study 46
Eaton Hall (Cheshire) fig. 11.7
Eckbo, Garrett (1910-2000) 5, 13
ecocentrism 88, 124, 129-30, 142-4, 148-51, 273, 283, 285, 290, ecosophy 75, 144, critiques of 130, 150-1
ecological psychology 144, 147, 167, 283, 286, affordances 145, 173, 283, 286, invariants 145, 149

ecology 52, 65, 95, 317, deep ecology 142-4, 148-50, 152, 156, 273, shallow ecology 144, historical ecology 130
ecosystems 51, 65, 148
Eden, William Arthur (fl. 1930s-1970s) 19, 31, 35-7, 126
Edzell Castle (Angus) 199, fig. 7.5
engagement, *see* 'environmental aesthetics'
English Heritage 206, 219-23, 306
English landscape garden, *see* 'garden design'
English Nature 222
environmental aesthetics Chapter 10, 292, levels of engagement 287, engagement model 147, 151, 281, 283-7, natural environmental model 283, 288 290, integrated aesthetics 287, 289, post-modern 291
environmental determinism 1, 51-53, 58-9, 124, 150
environmental ethics 124, 130, 144, normative 138, from personal values 138, connection to aesthetics 267
environmental hermeneutics 269
environmental history 151, 174, 235
environmental psychology 79, 175
environmentalism 76, 124, 129, 139, 142, 149, 272-1, 280
ephemerality 195, 209-12, 219, desirability of recording 212, 219
eugenics, *see* 'environmental determinism'
European Landscape Convention [foreword]
everyday landscape 8, 125, 175, 181-3, 259-60, 276, 285
evolutionary psychology 101-2, 104, evolved faculties 101, 104-5, 165, joined-up thinking 103, 105, 162
existentialism 276
experts 47, 92-3, 170, 184-5, 187, 223, 319, fig. 2.12, skills and judgement 45, 108, 116, 185-6, 284, 289, 291, 310
expressionism 6, 22-6

F

faculties, mental, *see* 'evolutionary psychology'
Fairclough, Graham (fl. 1980s-2010s) 278
Fairbrother, Nan (1913-1971) 71-3
Farrell, Terry (1938-) 271
Feray, Jean (1914-1999) 213
Fines, Kenneth Donald (1923-2008) 46-7
Finlay, Ian Hamilton (1925-2006) 248, fig. 8.8
fitness 74
Flenley, Richard (fl. 1970s-2010s) 245
Florence Charter, *see* ICOMOS
Fontainebleau, Château de (France) 213, 225, fig. 7.24
formalism, in art 19, 296-8, in landscape assessment, 46-8, 170, 287, 296-9, neo-Platonism 1, 6, 19, 21, 46, significant form 1, 19, 21, 280, 316
Foucault, Michel (1926-1984) 127, 129
Fowler, Peter (1938-) 278
fractal geometry 98
free will 104-5, 276, 281
Friedrich, Caspar David (1774-1840) fig. 11.5
Freud, Sigmund (1856-1939) 22,
Fry, Philip (fl. 1990s-2010s) 254-5, fig. 8.13
Fuller, Peter (1947-1990) 153, 155
functionalism 1, 3-8, 70-1, 73, aesthetic reward through, 1, 5, 17, 35, 69-70, 170, fig.6.6

G

Gaia hypothesis, 74-5, 152
Goldsworthy, Andy (1956-) 262-3, fig. 8.18
garden city, the, 18, 33, fig. 2.2
garden design 5, 7-8, 21-2, 28, 35, 83, 110, fig. 1.3, Islamic 62, 111, fig. 4.13, Italian 14, 63, fig. 3.6, Baroque 14, the landscape garden 10, 15, 16, 17, 18, 61-2, 114, high Victorian 11, Arts and Crafts 3, 5, 200, Colonial style 89, modernist 6, 13-4, 117, fig. 4.17, in California 13, in Brazil 13, 64, new formal 6, 89, 242-3, 272, post-modern 88, 241-3, contextualism in 243-7, philosophy into 248-50, quality of, 306, 311-2

garden history 17, 112, 123, 125, 130, 310
gardening 94, 278, 308, 313
Gare Saint-Lazare, Paris (France) fig. 9.1
Garrick, David (1717-1779) 209, fig. 7.15
Gas Works Park, Seattle (Washington State) 243-4, fig. 8.4
genes 51, 103-4, 105
genius 8-9, 26, 96
gestalt psychology 145, 149, 152
Gibberd, Sir Frederick (1908-1984) fig. 1.7
Gibson, James Jerome (1904-1979) 145, 167, 283, fig. 5.11
Gilpin, William (1724-1804) 297, fig. 11.1
Gilpin, William Sawrey (1762-1843) fig. 11.9
Goldsworthy, Andy (1956-) 262-3, fig. 8.18
Goodchild, Peter (1947-) [foreword]
Great Storm, The (1987) 219, fig. 7.22
Greenpeace 140, fig. 5.9
Gregory, Richard (1923-2010) 100, 283,
Grime, Philip (fl. 1960s-2010s) 256-7
Gropius, Walter (1883-1969) 5
Group of Seven 56, 83, figs 3.3 & 3.18

H

Haag, Richard (1923-2018) 244, fig. 8.4
habitat theory 79-81, 167
Hafod Uchtryd (Ceredigion) fig. 5.13
Hällingsåfallet (Sweden) fig. 3.4
Halprin, Lawrence (1916-2009) fig. 1.4, fig 1.13
Hampton Court (Greater London) 216-8, figs 7.20 & 7.21
Hansen, Richard (1912-2001) 256-7
Harbin International Ice and Snow Sculpture Festival (China) fig. 7.17
Harlow New Town (Essex) 11, fig. 1.7
harmony, in the universe 19, 21, 26, in the environment 22, 66, with nature 55, 58, 65, 155, 229-30, debunking of 230
Harris, Lawren (1885-1970) fig. 3.18
Head-Smashed-In Buffalo Jump (Alberta) 225, fig. 7.28

Hegel, Georg Wilhelm Friedrich (1770-1831) 110, 275

Heidegger, Martin (1889-1976) 276,

Heighington (County Durham) fig. 2.1

Helliwell, D. Rodney (1940-2018) fig. 2.11

Hemel Hempstead Water Gardens (Hertfordshire) 164, fig. 6.1

Henderson, Laurence Joseph (1878-1942) 74

Hepburn, Ronald (1927-2008) 174, 280-2, 296, 309

Hepworth, Barbara (1903-1975) 20, fig. 1.11

Hermelin, Baron Sven (1900-1984) 114

Het Loo (Netherlands) 216-8,

high art, *see* 'art'

Hill, Oliver (1887-1968) 3, fig. 1.2

historicism 90, 110-1

history, use of 108-115, 223, 264

Hitchmough, James (1956-) 256-9, fig. 8.15

Hobhouse, Arthur (1886-1965), his committee 42

Hohenzollern Castle (Baden-Württemberg) fig. 7.11

holism 2, 52-5, 65, 144-6, 152, 282-3, 274, 277-8, 287, 290

Holthanger, Wentworth Estate (Surrey) fig. 1.2

Homo erectus 101, 102

Homo habilis 101, fig. 4.9

Homo sapiens 102-3, 110

Hoskins, William George (1908-1992) 126

Hudnut, Joseph (1886-1968) 7, 14

human ecology, 1-2, 6, 21, 51-5, 65, 73, 76, 79-80, 138, 155, 165

humanised landscapes 33-7, 39, 171

Hunt, John Dixon (1936-) 315

hunting, *see* 'instincts'

Husserl, Edmund (1859-1938) 275

Huxley, Sir Julian (1887-1975) 73

I

ICOMOS 227-8, 234, 236, Venice Charter 205, 213, 218, 233, Florence Charter 10, 213-5, Nara Document 206

ICOMOS Australia, *Burra Charter* 233-4

ICOMOS-IFLA International Scientific Committee on Historic Gardens and Sites (on Cultural Landscapes from 1999) (ISCCL), 213, *Assessment Guide* 319-20

ICOMOS Landscapes Working Group 230, 239, Czerniejewo guidelines 208, 232-3, 239

iconography 105, 129, 131, 163, fig. 4.11

idealism 274, 276

ideas represented by landscape 11, 15-7, 169-72, 202, cultural meanings 128-30, 151, idealised images 127, 130, 172-4, 299-300, 313, cherished ideas 123, 151 184, 300, 319, active discovery 285, 314, re-presentations 315, *see also* 'landscape tastes'

identity, national 130, 180, based on the land 56-9, local 176, 178

imagination 172, 174, 280-1, 284, 305, 315-6

integrated aesthetics, *see* 'environmental aesthetics'

Ingold, Timothy (1948-) 277

International Council for Monuments and Sites, *see* ICOMOS

International Federation of Landscape Architects (IFLA) 10, 213

International Union for the Conservation of Nature, *see* IUCN

Institute of Landscape Architects (ILA) (later Landscape Institute) 10, 89

instincts 165-7, 169, 299, for hunting 2, 81, 165, fig. 6.3

integrated approach, *see* 'values'

integrated aesthetics, see 'environmental aesthetics'

interpretation 206-8, fig. 7.13

Ironbridge Gorge (Shropshire) 225

Italian Charter of Restoration 214

IUCN 227-8, 234-6, 234, 236, protected landscapes 225-7, 229-30

J

Jackson, John Brinkerhof (1909-1996) 125-7, 275

Jac. P. Thijssepark, Amstelveen (Netherlands) 252, fig. 8.11

Jellicoe, Sir Geoffrey (1900-1996) 10-1, 26, 161-4, 213, figs 1.6, 6.1 & 6.2

Jencks, Charles (1939-) 99, 250, figs. 4.8 & 8.10

Jensen, Jens (1860-1951) 26, 57, 60, 155, 251

Joad, Cyril Edwin Mitchinson (1891-1953), 59, 60

Johnes, Thomas (1748-1816) 155

joined-up thinking, *see* evolutionary psychology

Jung, Carl (1875-1961), 1, 22-4, 161-3,

K

Kakadu, Jim Jim Falls (Northern Territory, Australia) fig. 11.11

Kant, Immanuel (1724-1804) 8, 268, 303

Kaplan, Stephen & Rachel (fl.1970s-2010s) 79, 172, 283, 296

Keen, Mary (1940-), [foreword]

Kelmarsh Hall (Northants) fig. 1.3

Kennedy Memorial, Runnymede (Surrey), 27, 164, fig. 1.16

Kennedylaan, Heerenveen (Netherlands) 154, fig. 5.12

Kent, William (1685-1748) 115,

King's Knot (Stirling) fig. 5.1

Kingsbury, Noel (1957-) 257, 259

Kirby Hall (Northamptonshire) 199, fig. 7.6

Klee, Paul (1879-1940) 26

Kloster Kamp, Kamp-Lintfort (Nordrhein-Westfalen) fig. 7.18

Kratochvile, Netolice (Czech Republic) 202-3, fig. 7.10

Kuča, Otakar (1927-2018) 202

L

Lake District (Cumbria) 227-9, 236, 239, figs. 2.5, 7.33, 10.1

Lamarckism 51

Lancaster, Nancy (1897-1994) fig. 1.3

land art 259-63

Land Use Consultants 245, figs 4.5 & 8.5

landscape appreciation 2, 267, 280, 285, 288, 309-10, 317, perceptual lenses 317

landscape architecture, *see* 'landscape design'

landscape assessment 42-3, 280, 292, 316-20, assessors 45, 116, 184, 290-1, judgement 185, 289-90, consensus 116, 169, 292, cultural influences on 283-4, 286, 289, 292, landscape evaluation 45-6, 78, 170, 184, 287, objective methods 33, 44-5, 88, 184-5, 291, practical objectivity model 290-1, subjective methods 1, 184-5, 309, landscape beauty/ quality Chapter 2, 67, 78, 131, 172, 184-90, 280, 297, 299-300

landscape, definition of 148, change inherent in 208, 223, management of 224, 232-4, 264, ethics of care 65-8, 233, 309

landscape character 60, 68, 184, 186-90, figs 6.12 & 6.13

landscape design 1, 3-4, 95, 141, 243, style in 60-1, 64, 115, 117-8, 311-2, fig. 11.9, forms in 5, 13-7, unity in 61-2, 64, functionalism in 1, appealing to the unconscious 26-8, 162-3, post-industrial fig. 4.5, theory in , among the fine arts 1, 6, 10, *see* also 'garden design'

landscape evaluation, *see* 'landscape assessment'

landscape planning 37, 55, 68-73, 76-78, 131, 170, 280

landscape protection 38-42, 186, 189

landscape professions 1, 89, 95, 180

landscape tastes 126-7, 173, 184-5, 190, 319, consensus in 185, surveys of 129, 184-5, 319

landscape theory 1-2, 88, 142, 267

landscape value, *see* 'landscape assessment'

Landseer, Edwin (1802-1873) 155

Landells, Robert Thomas (1838-1877) fig. 5.3

Lasket, The (Herefordshire) fig. 9.3

lateral thinking 96

Latz, Peter (1939-) 245, fig. 8.6

laws and regulations 95, 139, 141-2, 223, figs 4.6 & 5.7

Le Corbusier (Charles-Édouard Jeanneret) (1887-1965) 66

Le Nôtre, André (1613-1700) 14, 63

Le Roy, Louis Guillaume (1924-2012) 93-4, 113, 154

Leeds bypass (Yorkshire) fig. 3.13
Leeds Castle (Kent) fig. 4.1
Leinster (Ireland) fig. 5.3
Leopold, Aldo (1887-1948), his land ethic, 66, 79, 144, 230
Levens Hall (Cumbria) 198-9
Lewis, Peirce (1927-2018) 127, 177
lieux de mémoire 180
Light, Andrew (1968-) 268
Linton, David Leslie (1906-1971) 44-5
Little Sparta (Scotland) 248, fig. 8.8
Locke, John (1632-1704) 286,
Long, Bernard (1947-1990s) fig. 3.17
Long, Richard (1945-) 259-60, 266, fig. 8.16
Lorenz, Konrad (1903-1989) 81, 165
Loudon, John Claudius (1783-1843) 131
Lovelock, James (1919-) 74, 98, 152
Lowenthal, David (1923-2018) 126-7, 130, 176, 184,
Ludwig, Crown Prince of Bavaria, King Ludwig I 1825-1848 (1786-1868), 302
Lyotard, Jean-François (1924-1998) 271
M
Machu Picchu (Peru) 135, fig. 5.5
Magna Carta 139, fig. 5.7
Maitland, Sara (1950-) 304
management plans 221-2, 233
Marxism 110, 127, 129-30, 152, 277
Marx, Roberto Burle (1909-1994) 13, 17, 114, figs 1.8 & 3.8
Maskit, Jonathan (fl. 1990s-2010s) 292
McGrath, Raymond (1903-1977) 3
McHarg, Ian (1920-2001) 74, 76-8, 98, 165
McKibben, William Ernest (1960-) 151
Meinig, Donald (1924-) 127
meanings 123, 127-9, 132, 175, 184, 234, 268, 277, 309, 319, of gardens 312-6, fig. 11.10
Merleau-Ponty, Maurice (1908-1961) 276-7, 296
metanarratives 148, 271-4
metaphysics 1-2, 75, 152-6, 165-7, 174

Miller, Mara (fl. 1980s-2010s) 315
mind, the, 60, 172, 278, blank slate state 60, social science model 60, 106, in ecological psychology 145, in cognition 100-1, representations 149, 173-4
misoneism 24
Miteraj, Igor (1944-2014) fig. 4.12
modern movement, or modernism 3-5, 7, 18, 89-91, 111, 200, 263, 267
Mondrian, Piet (1872-1844) 26
Monet, Claude (1840-1926) fig. C.1
Monserrat (Catalonia) 136, fig. 5.6
Montefiore, Alan (1926-) 281
Mont Saint-Victoire (France) fig. 1.17
Monticello (Virginia) 225, fig. 7.26
monuments 10, 131, 200, 205, 213-4, 223
Moody Gardens, Galveston (Texas) 27
Moore, Henry (1898-1986) 11, 24-6, 146, fig. 1.14
morality 2, 104, 137-42, 152
morphology 171
Morris, Desmond (1928-) 165
Morris, William (1834-1896) 111,
mountains 40, 45, 70, 82, 123, 153, 168, 180, 222, figs 2.7 & 2.8
Mount Lefroy (Alberta) fig. 3.18
Muir, John (1838-1914) 141
Munich Alten Pinakothek (Bavaria) fig. 1.14
N
Naess, Arne (1912-2009) 142, 273, fig. 5.10
Nash, David (1945-) 261-2, fig. 8.17
Nash, Paul (1889-1946) 11, 24-6, figs 1.15, 6.8
national character 51, 56-7
National Parks, British, 1, 33, 38-42
National Parks, North America, 33, 38, 206
National Trust 38, 40
natural beauty, *see* 'aesthetics'
natural environmental model, *see* 'environmental aesthetics'
natural selection, law of, 51, 74

nature, benefits of 58, as antidote to cities 58, 70, into garden design 113, oneness or unity with 58, 62, 66, inspiration from 153, a cultural construct 151, conservation of 59, 65, 95, 123,

negentropy 74

neo-Platonism, *see* 'formalism'

New College (Oxford) fig. 4.14

new work, in historic context 234, 263-4, fig. 7.14

Nicholson, Ben (1894-1982) 11, fig. 1.6

Nora, Pierre (1931-) 180

Notre-Dame de Paris (France) fig. 7.12

nuclear weapons 29, 140, 248

O

objective relativism 289

objectivism 45, 170, 288-92, 305, 318

Odum, Eugene (1913-2002) & Howard (1924-2002) 65

Oehme & van Sweden practice 256, fig. 8.14

Office/ Ministry of Works (superseded 1970) 19, 199, 207

Orians, Gordon (1932-) 150, 168

Osmaston Park (Derbyshire) fig. 11.6

Oudollf, Piet 259

ozone layer 142

P

Packwood Hall (Warwickshire) 198-9, fig. 7.4

Page, Russell (1906-1985) 6, 89, fig. 4.1

Palladianism 18-9,

Paradise 47

Parc de la Villette, Paris (France) 249, fig. 8.9

Peacehaven (Sussex) fig. 3.10

Pechère, René (1908-2002) 11, 30, 213

Pepper, Beverley (1922-) fig. 4.8

Pepper, David (1945-) 129

perception 280, cognitive 100-1, 123, 145-6, 162, 173-4, 282-3, 284, 309, 319, in formalism 45-6, 299, in holism 55, in ecological psychology 145, 149, in phenomenology 276-7, first impressions 277, 296, 299-300, 312, sequential 145, 147, 299

Petite-Pierre, La (France) 225-31

Pevsner, Sir Nikolaus (1902-1983) 4-6, 14, 17, 18, 111, 114-5

phenomenology 146, 283, 274-8, 285, descriptive aesthetics 286, 319

Phillimore, Claud (1911-1994) fig. 1.9

Phyllis Cormack, the, 140, fig. 5.9

philosophy of aesthetics 280, of environmentalism, of ethics

Picturesque, the, 15, 18, 45, 287, 297, 312, fig. 11.9

place 130, 174-80, 233-4, 275, insiders 178, action/place 175

planting design, naturalistic 251-9

pluralism 92, 178, 223, 289

Pole, David (1923-1977) 107

Pollock, Jackson (1912-1956) 146

Pope, Alexander (1688-1744) 115-6

Popper, Karl (1902-1994) 97, 274, 277

Porritt, Sir Jonathan (1950-), 75

Port Sunlight (Cheshire) fig. 2.2

Portrack House 'Garden of Cosmic Speculation' (Dumfries and Galloway), 250, fig. 8.10

post-modernism 88, Chapter 4, 241, 271-2

post-structuralism 108, 130, 148, 235, 271, 291

Poussin, Nicolas (1594-1665) 10

practical knowledge, *see* 'convictions'

preferences 45, 79, 88, Chapter 6, 172-4, 176-7, 184-5, 281, 289, 291-2, effect of familiarity upon 174, 176, seen as problematic 45-6, 170, 172, 185

preparation, *see* 'aesthetic attitude theory'

Price, Sir Uvedale (1747-1829) 18, 172, 182-3

primitivism 24, 146

Prince, Hugh (1927-2013) 126-7

prolepsis 111, 121

prospect-refuge theory 81-3, 165-8, figs 3.17, 3.19, 3.20, 6.4

public parks 93-4, 119, 181, 219, 221

Pugin, Augustus (1812-1852) 204
Purcell, Terry (fl. 1980s-2010s) 173
Q
qualities of landscapes 45, 131, 133, 186, 223, 280, 287, 319
quantitative revolution 43-4, 127, 275, fig. 2.11
R
Rackham, Oliver (1939-2015) 130
Randall-Page, Peter (1954-) fig. 6.10
rational comprehensive planning 43, 93, 97, 131, fig. 2.10
Real Jardín Botánico, Madrid (Spain) fig. 7.2
regional planning 43, fig. 2.10
rehabilitation 218
relevance, see 'aesthetic attitude theory'
religious faith or beliefs 28-9, 53, 96-7, 104, 152
Relph, Edward (1944-) 178
Repton, Humphry (1752-1818) 130, 131
restoration of designed landscapes Chapter 7, restoration-in-spirit 15 196, 203, period-style gardens 195, reconstruction 196, 200, 204-6, 214-8, conjectural repair 206, accurate repair 204-5, 216, 224, archaeology in 216-8, fig. 7.21, maintenance 224, asynchrony 197, 199, authenticity in 205-6, fig. 7.2
rice terraces, see cultural landscapes
Riegl, Aloïs (1858-1905) 206
rights 139, intrinsic to all life 144, 149, 156
Robinson, William (1838-1935) 11
Romanticism 15, 17, 18
Roper, Lanning (1912-1983) 6, 89
Rose, James (1913-1991) 8-9
Roguet, Félix (fl. 1870s) 197, fig. 7.3
Rosa, Salvator (1615-1673) fig. 3.20
Rousseau, Jean-Jacques (1712-1778) 113, 153, 155
Routley, Richard (1935-1996) 144
Rowntree Park (York) fig. 4.4
Ruff, Allan R. (1940-) 154
Runnymede (Surrey) 27, 164, figs. 1.18 & 6.2

Ruskin, John (1819-1900) 40, 129, 153, 204-5, fig. 2.7
Rutherford Laboratory, Harwell (Oxfordshire) 164
S
St Ives (Cornwall), fig. 1.6, fig. 1.11
São Paulo, garden by Burle Marx (Brazil) figs 1.8 & 3.8
Santayana, George (1863-1952) 282, 300
satisfactions from landscape 174-5, 267, Chapter 11, sensual 295-6
Sauer, Carl Ortwin (1889-1975) 124, 128, 135, 152, 275
scenic beauty/ quality, see 'landscape assessment'
scenery, see 'countryside' and 'mountains'
schemata, see 'the mind, representations'
science 75, 281, 283, 274-5, 288-90
Schönbrunn Palace, Vienna (Austria) fig. 1.5
Scott, Sir Gilbert (1811-1878) 204
Scruton, Sir Roger (1944-) 268
Scurr, Keith (1940-2018) fig. 3.19
Semple, Ellen Churchill (1863-1932) 52-3
Sessions, George (d.2015) 152
sharawadji 18
Sharp, Thomas (1901-1978) 33-5, 126, figs 2.1 & 2.2
Shell Guides & posters 176, fig. 6.7
Shepheard, Sir Peter (1913-2002) 5, 8
signs, see 'symbols from culture'
significance, see 'value imbued in landscape'
significant form, see 'formalism'
Slifka Beach House (New York) fig. 8.14
Smuts, Jan (1870-1950) 53-5, 85, fig. 3.1
Society for the Protection of Ancient Buildings (SPAB) 205-6
sociobiology 104
sociology 51, 54, 271
South Downs (Sussex & Hampshire) fig. 6.13
Spencer, Herbert (1820-1903) 51
Spinoza, Baruch (1632-1677) 296
Stamp, Sir Dudley (1898-1966) 33, 35

Stapledon, Sir Reginald George (1882-1960) 58-9, 65, 79
stewardship, 1, 65, 76-8, 144, 264
Stewart, Cecil (1911-1964) fig, 3.6
Stoke-on-Trent (Staffordshire) reclamation work 244-4, fig. 8.5, garden festival 241, fig. 8.1,
Stolnitz, Jerome (1925-) 284, 287, 288-9, 297, 303, 310, 315
Stonehenge, Avebury and associated sites (Wiltshire) 225, fig. 7.25
Strong, Sir Roy (1935-) 272, fig. 9.2
Stroud, Dorothy (1910-1997) 117
Studley Royal (Yorkshire) 225, fig. 7.25
style, *see* 'landscape design'
subconscious, the, *see* 'unconscious'
subjectivism, *see* 'ways of seeing'
sublime, the, 1, 301-5,
    fine art and 303
 literature and 303, 315
Sundon Hills (Bedfordshire) fig. 3.11
surrealism 24
sustainability 141-2, 144
Swift, Jonathan (1667-1745) 155
symbols, in unconscious 24-7, 81, 162-3, fig. 1.15, from culture, signs, 16, 128, 163-4, 168, 313, 315
systems theory 65, 145

T

Tandy, Clifford (d.1979) 245,
Tansley, Sir Arthur George (1871-1955) 65
terroirs 232
Thijsse, Jacobus ('Jac.') Pieter (1865-1945) 154
Thompson, Ian H. (1955-) 267-8,
Tilley, Christopher (1955-) 278
Tinian (Northern Mariana Islands) 113, fig. 4.16
Tonga-riro (New Zealand) 231, fig. 7.30
town planning 7, 51, 71
Treib, Marc (1943-) [foreword]
Trentham Hall (Staffordshire) fig. 11.3

Trevelyan, George Macaulay (1876-1962) 67
triune brain theory 169, fig 6.5
Tschumi, Bernard (1944-) 249, fig. 8.9
Tuan Yi-Fu (1930-) 127, 275
Tunnard, Christopher (1910-1979) 3, 5, 7, 16, 18, 35, 114, 132

U

ugliness 60, 65, 70, 170, 268, fig. 9.1
Uluru (Northern Territory, Australia) 231
uncertainty 96
unconscious, collective, 1, 24, 27, 29, 79-81, 138, 161-3
unconscious, the, 21-9, 58, 96
UNESCO 134, 227-9, 231, 238, World Heritage Convention 223-4, 229-31, 234-6, World Heritage List 124, 224-5
US Forest Service 66, 79, 172
US Soil Conservation Service 179, 185
US Standards for the Treatment of Historic Properties 218-9
unity, *see* 'landscape design' or 'nature'
universal truths/laws 18 22, 24-6, 29, 45, 90, 148, 161, 281, 223, 250, 271, sensed through nature 153
universalists, the, 292
universe, the, *see* 'cosmos, the'

V

Valhalla (Bavaria) 301-2, fig. 11.4
values, anthropocentric 142, 148, 151, 286
values, ecocentric 142, 149, 236, biodiversity 142, 223, 229, 318
value, nature conservation 65, 76-8, 123, 131, 189, 222, 251
values, human or cultural 88, 109, 123-4, 130-1, 148-50, 173, 234, 268, 274, 281, linked multiple 123, 130, 136, 222, 232, from knowledge 130-4, value judgements 131, 134, 281-2
values, imbued in fabric 45, 123, 131, 206, 223, determining priorities 134, integration of 189, 222, 236, 264

values, personal, 132, 134, 137-8, 140-1, 144, 151
Vaux-le-Vicomte (France) fig. 3.7
Venice Charter, *see* ICOMOS,
Vera, André (1881-1971) & Paul (1882-1957) 114
Verey, Rosemary (1918-2001) 241, 272, fig. 8.3
Versailles, Château de (France) 225
Vietnam Veterans Memorial (Washington D.C.) fig. 11.10
Villa Savoye, Poissy (France) 66, fig. 3.9
Viollet-le-Duc, Eugène (1814-1879) 204, fig. 7.12
visual intrusion 47-8
visual quality, *see* 'landscape quality'
von Keyserling, Hermann (1880-1946) 275

W

Wadi Rum (Jordan) 234, figs 7.31 & 7.32
Wagner, Richard (1813-1883) 301
Walpole, Horace (1717-1797), 4th Earl of Orford, 209-10
Warwickshire Landscape Project fig. 6.12
Watkin, David (1941-2018), 121, 122 (refs)
ways of seeing 125, 127, 129, 278, 289-92, 300
Westbury Court (Gloucestershire) 216, fig. 7.19

Westmacott, Richard (1941-) fig. 4.5
Westway (A40) (London) fig. 4.3
Westwell Manor (Oxfordshire) fig. 11.8
Wilanów Palace, Warsaw (Poland) 200, fig. 7.8
wilderness 33, 124, 144, 151, 268
Willendorf Venus fig. 4.11
William III, Prince of Orange, King of England from 1688 (1640-1702) 217
Williams, Raymond (1921-1988) 127-8
Wilson, Edward Osborne (1929-) 155
Wimpole Hall (Cambridgeshire) fig. 11.2
Wittkower, Rudolph (1901-1971) 17, 18-9
Woburn Abbey (Bedfordshire) 94
Wolseley Park (Staffordshire) 241, 265
Wordsworth, William (1770-1850), 227, 228
World Heritage, *see* UNESCO
Wylie, John (fl. 1990s-2010s) 275, 304

X Y Z

Yosemite (California) 38, fig. 2.4
Zajonc, Robert (1923-2008) 299
zeitgeist, the, 1-2, 3, 8, 14-5, 26, 111-5, 121
Zen Buddhism 97, 315

Reine, seen from the summit of Reinebringen (altitude 448 metres), in the Lofoten Archipelago, Norway. This photograph was one of the winners of the Fine Art Photography Award, 2014. The photographer, Tomáš Havel, observed: 'Standing there, feeling the wind in your face and enjoying such a beautiful view of Lofoten giants ... this photograph depicts just how small humans are in comparison to the nature that surrounds us and shows one of the most beautiful scenery of our planet. We spent the whole night watching this midnight sun show high above the mountains.' Obviously a special moment! Note the customary gesture of nature appreciation on the peak to the right.